The Fathers Know Best

JIMMY AKIN

The Fathers Know Best

*Your Essential Guide to the
Teachings of the Early Church*

SAN DIEGO
2010

NIHIL OBSTAT: I have concluded that the materials presented in this work are free of doctrinal or moral errors.

Bernadeane M. Carr, STL
5 October, 2010

IMPRIMATUR: In accord with 1983 CIC §3, permission to publish this work is hereby granted.
+ *Robert H. Brom,* Bishop of San Diego
5 October, 2010

With the exception of quotes from the Church Fathers, all Scripture selections are taken from the Catholic Edition of the *Revised Standard Version of the Bible,* copyright 1965, 1966 by the Division of Christian Education of the National Council of the Churches of Christ in the United States of America. Used by permission. All rights reserved. If any copyrighted materials have been inadvertently used in this work without proper credit being given in one manner or another, please notify the publisher in writing so that future printings of this work may be corrected accordingly.

Published by Catholic Answers, Inc.
2020 Gillespie Way
El Cajon, California 92020
(888) 291-8000 (orders)
(619) 387-0042 (fax)
www.catholic.com (web)

Cover design by Devin Schadt
Typesetting by Loyola Book Composition

Printed in the United States of America
ISBN 978-1933919-34-8

Contents

Foreword

For the first forty years of my life, it never crossed my mind that I needed anything else but the Bible to know what I needed to believe to be a faithful Christian. When I was in seminary and preparing to become a Protestant pastor I studied the history of Christianity, but with a certain slant that skirted any acknowledgment of the historical importance of the Catholic Church. For me, as well as most of my fellow seminarians, the important history essentially ended with the closure of the New Testament and picked up again with the sixteenth century Protestant reformation.

I certainly knew of some significant Christian figures and events from those "lost" fifteen hundred years, but for me and the congregations I pastored, all that was important was the Bible—which had been "saved" from the clutches of the "Whore of Babylon" through the courage of the Reformers. The few references I had read from the writings of the early Christian writers (I don't remember referring to them as early Church "Fathers") were selectively chosen to demonstrate that the early Church was more like Protestantism than Catholicism.

Then, by God's grace, my eyes were opened to the problems of Protestantism. Without question, it was my discovery of the witness of the early Church Fathers that most opened my heart and mind toward the Catholic faith. Fortunately, God provided helpers to assist me in finding and working my way through the few available collections of the Fathers, most of which were out of print and some badly skewed by anti-Catholic translators. Through their witness, the Catholicism of the early Church became so obvious that my family and I knew that if we were to follow the truth then we had no option but to become Catholic.

After his Resurrection, Jesus gave his Apostles what has traditionally been called the Great Commission: "Go therefore and

9

make disciples of all nations, baptizing them in the name of the Father and of the Son and of the Holy Spirit, teaching them to observe all that I have commanded you" (Mt 28:19–20). What they taught was the Gospel. This Gospel, however, included far more than the minimalist outline of Christ's saving sacrifice on the Cross preached by so many modern Christian evangelists. It also included far more than what can be gleaned from the New Testament Gospels and Epistles, which themselves allude to this wider apostolic teaching.

In Second Thessalonians 2:15, Saint Paul exhorted his Christian brethren to "stand firm and hold to the traditions which you were taught by us, either by word of mouth or by letter." To the Corinthian Christians, he wrote, "maintain the traditions even as I have delivered them to you" (1 Cor 11:2). Saint Paul's preferred means of passing along the "full" Gospel was not in letter form, but in person by word of mouth. He would only write if he couldn't be there in person, as we find in his comment to his "true child in the faith," Timothy: "I hope to come to you soon, but I am writing these instructions to you so that, if I am delayed, you may know how one ought to behave in the household of God, which is the Church of the living God, the pillar and bulwark of the truth" (1 Tm 3:14–15).

The full Gospel—the Apostolic Tradition or deposit of faith —included all aspects of "how one ought to behave in . . . the Church," which included, therefore, church order, structure, discipline, and liturgy, as well as the growing theological questions. And this deposit of faith was to be passed on just as it had been received: "What you have heard from me before many witnesses entrust to faithful men who will be able to teach others also" (2 Tm 2:2).

This passage has many implications, but it particularly highlights that the new theology of *sola scriptura* that arose fifteen hundred years later in the cauldron of the Protestant Reformation truncated the fullness of the Gospel by limiting it to the written Word. *Sola scriptura* certainly does not describe how Christian truth was transmitted or defined in the early days of the Church, and it is the discovery of this fact—as well as so many other fallacies associated with the doctrine of *sola scriptura*—that has opened the hearts of so many Protestants to consider the fullness and beauty of the Catholic faith.

A large majority of Christians today believe that all one needs to know about the early Church can be gleaned from the book of Acts, and that beyond that, the essence of early Church structure, liturgy, and praxis is somehow a prototype of what they experience in their modern-day Protestant churches. But if the inspired words of the New Testament do not contain all that the Apostles taught the early Christians, then how does one discover the rest of what these early Christians believed? The answer to this—at least for hundreds of modern Protestant ministers who have surprisingly found their way home to the Catholic Church—is in the writings of the early Church Fathers.

During the first centuries of the Church, there were hundreds of other writings besides those which the Church later determined were to be included in the inspired canon of Sacred Scripture (see chapter 22). Some of these writers were converts and disciples of the Apostles, thereby receiving the Apostolic Tradition directly, like a racer's baton passed from Jesus to his Apostles to them. Others were the converts and disciples of these earlier converts, and on and on, fulfilling Saint Paul's instructions to Timothy. The bishops of the Church declared that these writings were not to be included in the Canon, yet they recognized the value and authenticity of these faithful Christian writers by declaring them Fathers of the Church. In their writings, we hear how the teachings of Jesus and his Apostles spread through evangelization to shape lives, cultures—even civilizations.

How, though, can we access such a large corpus of writings, especially when they were written in languages that most of us today have not had the patience to learn? For this, we are particularly blessed by this release of Jimmy Akin's superbly compiled synopsis of the writings of the early Church Fathers. There are other collections, which have helped many discover the beauty and importance of what these early writers reveal about the expanding and persecuted early Church. But Akin's finely selected and categorized collection provides a far more accessible introduction into the full Catholicity of the early Christians. As a convert himself and a well-honed apologist, Jimmy knows the topics that are most crucial for those wanting and needing to know what the early Church believed—especially in those doctrinal areas where Catholics and non-Catholics bump heads.

—Marcus Grodi
President and founder of the
Coming Home Network International

PART ONE

I. Introduction

1. About This Book

This is a handbook designed to help you learn about the role of the Church Fathers, the world in which they lived, who they were, and what they taught on various subjects. It is divided into two main parts. Part One provides background on the Fathers, and Part Two provides excerpts from their writings, arranged by topic.

Because it is a handbook, you do not have to read it from beginning to end. If you wish, you can go directly to those subjects that most interest you, then refer to other sections for more information. For example, you might turn immediately to the "Infant Baptism" chapter in Part Two, see what the Fathers had to say about it, and then turn to the "Know Your Fathers" chapter in Part One to read the brief biographies of the Fathers who were quoted on infant baptism. Next, you might want to see where they lived and turn to "The World of the Fathers," which offers maps showing their locations.

Whatever path you choose to take through this book, it will offer a wealth of information.

Part Two is based on a series of columns that originally appeared in *This Rock* magazine, published by Catholic Answers. Other employees of Catholic Answers oversaw the column before my time, but for twelve years—from the June 1993 issue to the column's end in the December 2005 issue—I compiled and edited it by collecting quotations from the early Church Fathers on a variety of topics and writing introductions to them.

Like this book, the column was called "The Fathers Know Best"—a whimsical title based on *Father Knows Best*, the radio and television comedy starring Robert Young.

"The Fathers Know Best" was popular, and a series of tracts were produced based on it. The new book format allows a richer and more comprehensive look at the Fathers and their world, as well as the addition of more background material in Part One.

A Work of Apologetics

This is a work of Catholic apologetics, meaning that it seeks to provide evidence for the Catholic faith. This is the rationale for the selection of topics in Part Two. They are subjects about which Catholic teaching has been controversial. By reading what the Fathers had to say about them, you will see that Catholic teaching on these subjects is not something new, but goes back to the earliest ages of the Church.

This does not mean that the earliest writers expressed this teaching as clearly or precisely as it would be expressed in later ages. Nor does it mean that the views that are quoted were the only ones circulating among early Christians. But the lines of continuity between the teachings found in their centuries and in ours is a witness to the antiquity of the Catholic faith, which comes to us from Christ and the apostles.

So that you can see the development of the line of teaching on each topic from the earliest centuries to later ones, the quotations from the Fathers are presented in chronological order within each chapter.

Be aware that the earliest quotation provided for each subject does not represent when that particular teaching or practice first occurred. So much has been lost from the early centuries that this can almost never be the case. In fact, only a tiny fraction of the literature of the ancient world has survived—Christian literature included—making it virtually certain that, whatever the earliest quotation offered for a particular topic, it does not represent its first appearance in history.

A good example is St. Ignatius of Antioch's use of the term *Catholic*. His letters contain the first surviving uses of the term as applied to the Church, but the casual way he uses it, without any explanation, makes it clear that he expects his readers to know it already. This means that the term must have been in use even earlier than his letters, likely decades earlier since he treats it as an accepted term.

Most of the time, lines of teaching are traced that affirm or deny a particular viewpoint, but not always. There are today subjects on which Catholics can have a range of different opinions, subjects on which there is no single acceptable Catholic teaching. For example, there is the question of how the six days of creation found in Genesis 1 are to be interpreted. Are they literal, twenty-four-hour days or something else? The Church does not have a definitive interpretation and Catholics can have different opinions (though it should be noted that the *Catechism of the Catholic Church* sees them as symbolic; CCC 337). In chapters on this sort of topic, Fathers offering a variety of opinions on the same subject are quoted to show that then, as now, there was a legitimate diversity of opinion.

The Sources Used

Most of the quotations are from the writings of the Church Fathers themselves—the various homilies, letters, treatises, and other works they penned.

In some cases, though, they are from individuals who technically aren't Fathers, but rather "ecclesiastical writers" (see "About the Fathers" for an explanation of the distinction). A few such individuals were schismatics or held views that would be deemed heretical in later ages. This does not stop them from being important witnesses to what Christians believed in the ages in which they lived, even if they themselves were not correct on every point.

Also quoted are ancient creeds, ancient burial inscriptions, the writings of regional and ecumenical councils, and certain writings that, though we don't know who authored them, are still informative ancient Christian documents. There are even quotations from some of the first Christian novels, because works of fiction can shed light on what the Christian community of the day believed, just as modern Christian novels do.

A Word About Dating

Dates for each of the sources used are provided. This is easier to do for writings from the later centuries, for which more information survives. We often know the exact year of birth and death of the later Fathers. For earlier Fathers, it can only be established that they were born or died "around" a certain year. In some cases, it is known that they died in or around a year, but it is not known when they were born. In other cases, no knowledge exists of births or deaths, only that they wrote around a certain time.

The problem of dating is especially difficult when it comes to anonymously written documents, which almost invariably are undated. Scholars must look to clues within the documents themselves to try to determine when they were written. Often "sometime in the third century" or "late second century" is the most that is known.

This is not unusual; all historians of this period struggle with this problem.

A complicating factor applies to the very earliest documents. Often writings are dated relative to each other. For example, "This document quotes the Gospel of John, which means it must have been written after the Gospel of John." But that only raises the question, "When was the Gospel of John written?"

Almost two hundred years ago, a group of scholars in Europe began to challenge the authenticity of the New Testament documents and, using a highly skeptical methodology, assigned very late dates to them, asserting that many were not written until a century or more after the events in question. This extreme viewpoint has been progressively rolled back by the work of other scholars, who have shown that the New Testament documents were written earlier, in line with the traditional view. Still, the process is incomplete, and many modern scholars hold relatively late dates for many New Testament documents, though they are all placed in the first century.

Some scholars, however, have gone further. A notable example was John A. T. Robinson, a twentieth-century Anglican scholar who wrote a book entitled *Redating the New Testament*, in which he argued that the entire New Testament was likely written before A.D. 70, when the Jewish temple was destroyed.

I must say that I find this view convincing. Books like Hebrews and Revelation speak of the temple as if it were still functioning (Heb 10:11; Rv 11:1), no book of the New Testament records the destruction of the temple as an accomplished fact (though the authors would have loved to list this as a fulfilled prophecy on Jesus' part), and the book of Acts was probably written around A.D. 62, because that is where the story suddenly stops, with Paul under house arrest in Rome, awaiting his trial before the emperor.

If the New Testament books were written earlier than thought, it would pull the dates of other documents earlier as well. These include works like the *Didache*, Hermas of Rome's *The Shepherd*, Pope St. Clement's *Letter to the Corinthians*, and the so-called *Letter of Barnabas*. More will be said on this later in the book, but it appears that these works also were written earlier than commonly supposed.

One last note on dating. In Part Two of the book a single date is assigned to each document rather than a range of possible dates for purposes of concision.

About the Quotations

The vast majority of the quotations contained in this book are taken from the thirty-eight-volume set of ante-Nicene, Nicene, and post-Nicene Fathers published by T. & T. Clark between 1867 and 1900. This is an extensive, public domain translation that can be found at a number of locations online. Readers thus can easily look up the quotations to read them in their original contexts.

Unfortunately, the set was not exhaustive (in fact, it deliberately excluded certain works deemed to be too Catholic by its Protestant editors), so it is supplemented here with a modest number of "fair use" quotations from other translations (see "Translations Used" for a full listing). For ease of reading and consistency of style, all quotations have been conformed to modern usage.[1] These modifications have been done in good faith to make the work more accessible to a twenty-first century audience, but the quotations can be read online in all the archaic glory of the source translations to confirm that they have been represented accurately.

If readers go beyond this book and learn more about the Fathers (and I hope they do!), they will find that there are inconsistencies in how the Fathers and their writings are referred to. For example, the individual that some works refer to as "Clement of Rome" is the same person other works refer to as "Pope Clement" or "Pope St. Clement I." Similarly, the second century Church Father St. Irenaeus of Lyons will be said to be the bishop of Lugdunum, of Lyons, and of Lyon—because the same place has had different names in different ages.

The works of the Fathers are also cited in different ways. Sometimes their names are given in long form, in short form, left untranslated, and even abbreviated (e.g., St. Irenaeus's work *Against Heresies* may also be listed as *On the Detection and Overthrow of the So-Called Gnosis*, *Adversus haereses*, or *Adv. haer.*). This can create a bewildering array of references for the non-specialist. As an aid to the reader, an appendix entitled Documents Used is included that lists the individual documents quoted in this book, along with some of their alternate names.

Different translations also subdivide the works of the Fathers differently, using different internal numbering schemes. In general, this book uses the numbering system found in the transla-

---

[1] For example, "today" instead of "to-day," "connection" instead of "connexion," "your" instead of "thy" and "thine," Arabic rather than Roman numerals, contemporary capitalization, replacing obsolete terms and awkward constructions.

tion from which the particular quotation was drawn (usually the thirty-eight-volume set, though see Translations Used for more detail). Sometimes alternate numbering is provided in brackets. For example, Firmilian of Caesarea's letters are quoted and the citation *Letters* 74[75]:17 is given. This means that the quotation is taken from letter number 74, though in some translations it is listed as letter 75. The 17 after the colon tells you that it is section 17 of the letter.

Sometimes a document name is followed by a bare number, such as 12. In this case the work is a short one and section 12 of it is quoted. In some citations there are as many as three numbers separated by colons. For example, 3:42:7 would be a reference to book 3, chapter 42, section 7 of the work. Numbers will always run from the larger units that make up a work to the smaller ones.

The quotations may appear in more than one chapter, in cases where they may illustrate more than one point (e.g., a quotation may illustrate both the fact that Peter was in Rome and that he was the Rock on which the Church is built).

Acknowledgments

I would like to thank all those who had any part in the production of this work, either when it was a column in *This Rock* or in preparing it for tract or book form. In particular I would like to thank Karl Keating, Mark Brumley, Patrick Madrid, Terrye Newkirk, Cherie Peacock, Jennifer Phelps, Tim Ryland, Mark Wheeler, and especially Jon Sorensen.

2. About the Fathers

Tradition!

Tradition is important to every person and every group of people. It is part of our very identity. It represents our education, our culture, everything that has been handed on to us by the previous generation. Tradition is—literally—what is handed on. The term comes from the Latin word *tradere*, "to hand on." Not all traditions are important. Some are frivolous or even harmful (see Mk 7:8 and Col 2:8 on traditions that are merely "of men"). But some are very important indeed.

For Christians, the faith that has been handed on to us from Christ and the apostles is of unparalleled importance. In Catholic circles, this passing down of the faith is referred to as "sacred Tradition" or "apostolic Tradition" (with a capital "T" to distinguish it from other, lesser, "lower-case" traditions, including those merely "of men").

At first the apostles handed on the faith orally—through their preaching—but with time some of them and their associates wrote the documents that form the New Testament, which together with the Old Testament comprise sacred Scripture. Since Scripture has been handed down to us from the apostles, it can be seen as the written part of Sacred Tradition.

Whether or not an item of Tradition was written down in Scripture, it was still important and binding for believers. A number of places in the New Testament exhort the reader to maintain Sacred Tradition (e.g., 1 Cor 11:2; 2 Thes 3:6), and in 2 Thessalonians 2:15, St. Paul bluntly tells his readers to "stand firm and hold to the traditions which you were taught by us, either by word of mouth or by letter." So whether Christian Tradition was received orally or in writing, it was authoritative.

Another noteworthy passage is 2 Timothy 2:2, in which the apostle instructs his protégé, "what you have heard from me before many witnesses entrust to faithful men who will be able to teach others also." Bearing in mind that this letter is Paul's swan song, written just before he died (2 Tm 4:6–8), Paul is exhorting the transmission of Sacred Tradition across generations of Christian leaders—from his generation, to Timothy's generation, to the ones that will follow.

It was through the Church Fathers that this transmission would be accomplished.

The Fathers of the Church

Certain individuals in the early Christian centuries are referred to as Church Fathers or "the Fathers of the Church." The origin of this analogy is found in the New Testament, which depicts the apostles as the fathers both of individual converts[2] and as the fathers of particular churches.[3]

Since the apostles spiritually provided for, taught, and disciplined those under their care, it was natural to apply the analogy of fatherhood to them (though of course this has its limits and must not be confused with the unique Fatherhood of God; see Mt 23:9). After the time of the apostles, others also spiritually provided for, taught, and disciplined the Christian community, and it was natural to apply the analogy of fatherhood to them as well. This was the case especially with bishops, who were regarded as the spiritual fathers of the communities that they served.

In time, the concept came to be applied in a general way to those who shaped the faith and practice of the Church in its earliest centuries. They became "Fathers" not only for their own age but for all ages that would follow.

Some of these—the ones who heard the preaching of the apostles themselves or lived very shortly after the time of the apostles —came to be called the "Apostolic Fathers" or "Sub-Apostolic Fathers." Together with the Fathers of later ages, they were important witnesses to the apostolic Tradition.

Though pronounced somewhat differently in Greek and Latin, the word for "father" in both languages is *pater*. A number of terms have been derived from this word, and on account of it we refer to the early Christian centuries as the *patristic* age (the age "of the fathers") and to the study of the Fathers as *patrology*.

---

[2] 1 Cor 4:17; Phil 2:22; 1 Tm 1:2, 18; 2 Tm 1:2; 2:1; Ti 1:4; Phlm 10; 1 Pt 5:13.

[3] 1 Cor 4:14; 2 Cor 12:14; Gal 4:19; 1 Jn 2:1; 3 Jn 4.

Who Is a Father?

As the concept developed, to qualify as a Church Father an individual eventually had to meet four basic criteria. He had to possess antiquity, orthodoxy, holiness, and approval by the Church. Those who lacked one or more of these qualities were not referred to as "Fathers" but as "ecclesiactical (Church) writers."

The first test—antiquity—referred to the age in which the individual lived. This criterion is fairly straightforward. The age of the Fathers covered the period from the first century, when Jesus and the apostles lived, through to the age of St. Isidore of Seville in the west (he died in 636) and St. John of Damascus in the east (he died around 749). Those who worked in this period are potential Church Fathers, though the end of this age is debated and the line can be drawn at different points. (The age of the Fathers is commonly reckoned to have ended earlier in the West, with the death of Isidore of Seville in 636.)

The second test—orthodoxy, or correct teaching—is more subtle. It is complicated by the fact that what is considered orthodox in one age may be considered heterodox or even heretical in a later one.

Jesus promised that after his time he would send another Advocate—the Paraclete, the Holy Spirit—who would lead Christians into "all truth" (Jn 16:13). The record of Church history shows that this process unfolded over time, with the Church gaining a fuller, more precise understanding of the apostolic Tradition as the centuries progressed. This means that the men of one age cannot be held to the standards of a later age.

For example, one cannot expect the Fathers who wrote before the ecumenical councils of Nicaea I (A.D. 325) and Constantinople I (A.D. 381) to express their faith in the Trinity in the same refined, precise way as the Fathers who lived after these councils. The terminology needed to do so simply had not yet been worked out in their day. This is also why figures such as St. John Cassian can be both a saint and the apparent originator of Semi-Pelagianism—a view that in his day was not infallibly defined as heretical but which later would be.

The third test—holiness of life—is still harder to determine. Holiness can be expressed in more than one way, such as by gentleness toward one's opponents (owing to love for the persons involved) as well as by harshness toward them (owing to love for the truths that they are denying). Both those who displayed their holiness by being kind and those who displayed it by being harsh came to be regarded as Church Fathers. If a person has been given the title "Saint," it is an indicator that he left a reputation for holiness. This is what the Latin term for "saint"—*sanctus*—means: "holy." On the other hand, the absence of the title "Saint" does not mean that he was unholy.

The fourth and final criterion—approval by the Church—is also tricky. Certainly if an individual came to be regarded as a saint, it indicates Church approval. It must be remembered, though, that in the patristic age the pope was not yet involved in declaring individuals from far-flung parts of the Christian world to be saints. Papal canonization would not begin until around the year 1000. Still, before this time, the popular acclaim of an individual as a saint would seem to constitute Church approval.

Despite these four criteria, there is still some ambiguity and arbitrariness regarding who counts as a Father. Origen of Alexandria's reputation as a theologian was so tarnished by later controversies that he would seem to be disqualified on grounds of unorthodoxy (along with those who shared his views, such as St. John Chrysostom), yet he is sometimes reckoned a Father. Similarly, Tertullian died outside of communion with the Church and would seem to lack the sanctity needed, yet he is sometimes considered as a Father. Normally one would think these two would not be classified as Fathers but as "ecclesiastical writers"—the category to which an individual of this period belongs if he does not meet the criteria for being a Father. For example, in a single homily (May 23, 2010) Benedict XVI made a passing reference to Origen as a Father, but he refrained from using this term in his audiences on Origen (April 25 and May 2, 2007).

Oral or Written?

In addition to the ambiguity regarding who is a Father, there are also some misconceptions about them. One concerns the way they bear witness to Tradition. We often speak in a way that contrasts Scripture and Tradition by saying that the former is written while the latter is oral.

It is certainly true that sacred Scripture is written down,[4] and it is true that oral preaching has a role in how Tradition is passed down, but there is more to it than that. It is true that the Church Fathers preached the faith to their own generation, but we do not have audio recordings of their sermons. We know what their teachings were, but this has not come to us through a two-thousand-year process of one person orally teaching only what he had orally received.

We know the teachings of the Church Fathers because their sermons were written down. They also wrote letters, theological treatises, liturgical books, and various other writings. It is through these means—written ones—that knowledge of the Fathers has been transmitted to us.

That's because we are a literate culture that uses writing rather than a storytelling tradition to pass down knowledge over long periods of time. Our scholars don't have to memorize long cycles of unwritten stories. We write them down. And so the writings of the Church Fathers are the main way their teachings have been preserved.

Although oral teaching has a role in passing on Tradition, particularly in communicating it to each new generation, writing also plays a substantial role, which leads to a second possible misconception.

---

[4] That's what the term "scripture" means—"that which is written"—from the Latin word *scribere*, "to write."

The Uniqueness of Scripture

Despite the fact that the writings of the Church Fathers are written and are an important witness to apostolic Tradition, they cannot be treated the same way sacred Scripture is treated. The books of the Old and the New Testaments are unique in that they are fully inspired by the Holy Spirit. This gives them certain properties that all other writings lack.

According to the *Catechism of the Catholic Church*:

> [The] Church, relying on the faith of the apostolic age, accepts as sacred and canonical the books of the Old and the New Testaments, whole and entire, with all their parts, on the grounds that, written under the inspiration of the Holy Spirit, they have God as their author, and have been handed on as such to the Church herself.
>
> God inspired the human authors of the sacred books. To compose the sacred books, God chose certain men who, all the while he employed them in this task, made full use of their own faculties and powers so that, though he acted in them and by them, it was as true authors that they consigned to writing whatever he wanted written, and no more.
>
> The inspired books teach the truth. Since therefore all that the inspired authors or sacred writers affirm should be regarded as affirmed by the Holy Spirit, we must acknowledge that the books of Scripture firmly, faithfully, and without error teach that truth which God, for the sake of our salvation, wished to see confided to the Sacred Scriptures [CCC 105–107].

Since no other writings are inspired, the writings of the Church Fathers do not have God as their author in this way. There is no guarantee that the Fathers expressed everything and only those things that God wanted expressed, that everything in their writings is something that the Holy Spirit would assert, or that they teach the truth without error.

While the Holy Spirit certainly worked in the lives of the Fathers, per Jesus' promise, and while the Holy Spirit preserved the Christian faith in the Church as a whole, he did not intervene in a way that would protect each Father, or each Father's writings, from all error. The Fathers could and did make mistakes. Some entertained ideas or expressed themselves in ways that would later be ruled incompatible with the faith. They also disagreed with each other—sometimes vehemently—and not just on matters of expression or emphasis but on substance.

Consequently, one cannot simply prooftext using the writings of the Fathers or treat what one Father says as if it definitively settles a matter all by itself.

This is one reason we need the magisterium of the Church to settle disputed cases regarding what authentically belongs to Scripture and what authentically belongs to Tradition.

There is another aspect of the relationship between Scripture and the writings of the Fathers that is often misunderstood.

Means vs. Content

Sometimes people think of extra-scriptural Tradition as if its purpose is to teach us things not mentioned in Scripture. If that were the case, then there would be precious little, if any, Tradition, because the Church Fathers are not concerned with conveying "secret teachings" of Jesus not found in the Bible.

There are a few (a very few) sayings that some early sources outside of the Gospels attribute to Jesus. These are known as the *agrapha* (Greek, "unwritten ones"), and it is possible that some of them genuinely go back to Jesus,[5] but they are not what the Fathers are principally concerned with.

What does occupy the Fathers is the explanation and defense of the same faith that is presented in the Scriptures, which was "once for all delivered to the saints" (Jude 3). Their role is principally to explain and elaborate things that are mentioned in Scripture.

A classic example of this is the mode of baptism. Much ink has been spilled in recent centuries regarding the proper way to admin-

---

[5] The only one that does for certain is found in Acts 20:35, where St. Paul quotes Jesus as having said, "It is more blessed to give than to receive"—but this is still in Scripture rather than the writings of the Fathers.

ister baptism. Should individuals be immersed in water? Should water be poured on them? Sprinkled on them? What is the correct way? Is there even a single correct way? Can different but equally correct ways be used?

There has been controversy on this point because the Bible simply doesn't tell us what the mode of baptism is. There was no need for it to do so. The writings of the New Testament were directed at people who were already converted, who had already been baptized. They knew what mode or modes the Church used to baptize people.

Because the Bible doesn't tell us, people have been left combing Scripture for hints—possible shades of meaning in Greek terms, the physical situation of various accounts of baptism in the Gospels and Acts, the images connected with baptism in different New Testament passages. But from Scripture alone it is very unclear, and it would be nice if we had a direct statement about how the first generation of Christians baptized.

In fact, we do. But not in the New Testament. Instead, it is found in a document called the *Didache*, which was probably written in the mid-first century—during the time of the apostles themselves—though it is not part of the New Testament. According to the *Didache*, one should baptized in "living" (i.e., running) water. If that is not possible, one should baptize in standing water. If possible in cold water, otherwise warm. If that is not possible, one should pour water over the head three times, invoking the Father, the Son, and the Holy Spirit (see chapter 39, where we will quote this passage).

But even the *Didache* does not completely settle the mode of baptism. It talks about baptizing in running or standing water, but does that mean immersing the person in the water or—as is often depicted in early Christian art—having the person stand in the water while water is poured over his head, as in the third option mentioned? The text does not settle the matter, but it does show that there were at least some variations in how baptism was done in the first century and that pouring was one of them.

The *Didache* and other early writings primarily shed light on things mentioned in Scripture rather than providing new, extra-scriptural teachings because there are very few parts of the Christian faith, if any, that are entirely unmentioned in Scripture. Virtually everything is reflected, or presupposed, or implied, or mentioned in passing. There are a few things that may not be (e.g., the Assumption of Mary), but even these are debatable cases that may be reflected in Scripture (e.g., Rv 12:1). The Church Fathers thus pass on the same faith that Scripture teaches, but by different means. They express fundamentally the same content, but in a different way, and with a different level of detail.

The Fathers and the Magisterium

Thus far we have talked about the relationship of the Fathers and Scripture, but we should touch also on their relationship to the magisterium of the Church. The magisterium is the Church's teaching authority (from the Latin root *magister*, "teacher"). It is exercised by the pope and the bishops teaching in union with him.

Since many of the Church Fathers were bishops—and even popes—there obviously is an overlap between them and the magisterium. Some of them were part of the magisterium in their day. This means that these Fathers had the potential to teach not just as individual theologians but with the greater authority conveyed by their office and even with the supreme teaching authority of the Church.

At times they did just that. Though the doctrine of the Church's infallibility had not yet been worked out in detail, the patristic age saw the Church exercising its teaching authority in a definitive, and thus infallible, way.

This happened particularly at the ecumenical councils that were held in the period. These councils definitively taught that certain teachings were incompatible with the Catholic faith, and their definitive teachings enjoyed the protection of the Holy Spirit, who Christ promised would guide the Church into all truth.

The Holy Spirit's guidance does not ensure that every individual remains in truth, but it does ensure that the Church will be maintained in truth, so that it can serve as "the pillar and bulwark of the truth" in this world (1 Tm 3:15). This would not happen if the magisterium of the Church could definitively bind the faithful to believe what is false, and so the Church understands that the Holy Spirit will prevent the magisterium from definitively teaching things that are false. It doesn't exercise its definitive teaching authority often, but when it does, the faithful can be sure of its accuracy.

This gift of infallibility can be exercised both by the pope and by the bishops of the Church teaching in union with him. That happens in a special way when the bishops are gathered together in an ecumenical council.

It should be borne in mind that although popes and ecumenical councils can teach infallibly, that doesn't mean that they always teach infallibly. Much of what they say is not infallible, and they do not intend it to be. Thus the quotations from various popes in this book should not be assumed to be infallible. Neither should the canons of the ecumenical councils quoted. Some statements, such as the *Nicene Creed*, which was produced by the First Council of Nicaea and the First Council of Constantinople, are infallible. But the question of what papal and conciliar statements are infallible is beyond the scope of this book. It seeks to illustrate the teaching of the Church Fathers in a general way rather than making a detailed study of the early actions of the magisterium.

The Fathers as a group, not just the ones who were part of the magisterium, carry a special authority. As witnesses to sacred Tradition, their testimony is valuable, and the more united and emphatic they are in their testimony, the more weighty it is—to the point that when they have moral unanimity on a subject, it may be considered certain.

This seems to be the case, for example, regarding the interpretation of John 3, where Jesus speaks of being "born again" or "born of water and the Spirit." Though some in recent centuries have tried to interpret this as a reference to something other than baptism (e.g., by saying that Jesus' reference to "water" means "the word of God" or "amniotic fluid"), this was not the case in the age of the Fathers. After an extensive search, I have been unable to find any patristic source that denied that this passage referred to baptism (see chapter 37). This kind of complete unanimity among the Fathers may be somewhat uncommon, but it definitely occurs.

II. The World of the Fathers

3. The World at a Glance

In this section we look at the world in which the Church Fathers lived with the help of a series of maps showing where they dwelled.

The first map shows the entire Roman world with some notable cities marked. Subsequent maps focus on particular regions within this world and offer additional detail, including modern country borders, so you can see what nations ancient cities existed in.

Accompanying each map is a narrative timeline describing the beginnings of Christianity in the area down to the end of the age of the Church Fathers. This is not an exhaustive history but focuses on the people and events touched on in this book.

Some places have an added specifier, such as Antioch "in Syria" and Antioch "in Pisidia." This is because some cities in the ancient world had the same names and they were specified by region to let you know which was meant—just as we have Hollywood, California, and Hollywood, Florida. To avoid a visual jumble, we haven't reproduced ancient regional boundaries and names, but we have kept the specifiers when two cities have the same name.

4. "My Witnesses in Jerusalem"

You shall receive power when the Holy Spirit has come upon you; and you shall be my witnesses in Jerusalem and in all Judea and Samaria and to the end of the earth [Acts 1:8].

This verse is often said to reflect the outline of the book of Acts. After the Holy Spirit was poured out on the apostles on the day of Pentecost, they were empowered to preach the gospel —first at Jerusalem, then in the surrounding parts of Judea and Samaria, and finally across the whole Roman world.

The expansion was accompanied by challenges and struggles.

One of the first was the persecution that arose after the martyr-dom of St. Stephen (Acts 7), which drove much of the Christian community away from Jerusalem and into surrounding areas. There were also theological conflicts. Some early Christians insisted that one had to be circumcised and become a Jew to be saved. At the Holy Spirit's prompting (Gal 2:1), this led to the first Church council at Jerusalem (Acts 15), which set the pattern for how Christians would often solve doctrinal disputes in the future.

Among the problems the region faced were a series of wars. The first broke out in A.D. 66, when the Jewish community revolted against Roman rule. In July of A.D. 70 the temple in Jerusalem was destroyed, fulfilling Jesus' prophecy (Mt 24). Another rebellion broke out in 115 and a third and final one in 132, after which the Romans banished Jews from Jerusalem and rebuilt it as the Roman city Aelia Capitolina.

Around 105, one of the major second-century apologists, St. Justin Martyr, was born in Flavia Neapolis (now Nablus in the West Bank). He left his homeland and eventually settled in Rome, where he was martyred around 165. While in Rome he met a Syrian named Tatian, who after Justin's death returned to the east and founded the heretical sect known as the Aquarii.

Another group of heretics who were prominent in this part of the world in the 100s were the Ebionites, who held that Jesus was only a human Messiah and who insisted on keeping the Jewish Law.

In the mid-200s Mani of Seleucia-Ctesiphon began to prophesy and founded the Gnostic sect Manicheanism.

Around 263 Eusebius of Caesarea was born. Before his death in 340 he would become a bishop and play a notable role in the Arian controversy. He would also befriend the emperor Constantine I, but he is best known as the father of Church history, about which he wrote several books.

A contemporary of Eusebius was Aphrahat, who headed the monastery of Mar Mattai (St. Matthew). He was born around

270 and died some time after 345. He wrote many treatises and is referred to as the "Persian Sage."

St. Cyril of Jerusalem was born around 315 and died around 386. He is known for the lectures he gave to catechumens. They make interesting reading, since he talked to his audience about the very holy places in Jerusalem where the events of the Gospels happened.

St. Jerome, though born in a distant land, took up residence in Bethlehem in the 380s. There he completed his work on the Vulgate and conducted many other literary endeavors. He died in Bethlehem around 419.

Sozomen was a Church historian who wrote at Constantinople in the mid 400s, but he was born in Bethelia in what is now the Gaza Strip.

A little-known priest named Timothy of Jerusalem gave an important homily on the death and Assumption of Mary. Unfortunately, scholars differ on when he lived; it could have been any time between 300 and 700.

As the age of the Church Fathers began in this part of the world, it could be said to end here. The patristic age is commonly reckoned to end with the life of St. John of Damascus, who was born around 676 and died around 749.

5. *The Second Holy Land*

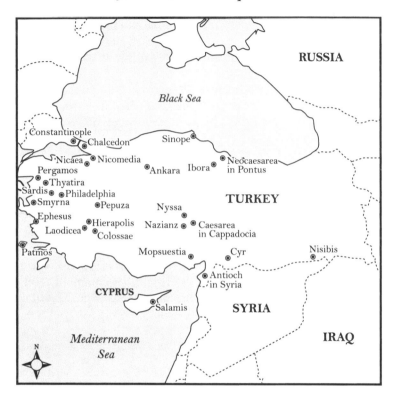

In the age of the Fathers, the Christian community was so active in what is now Turkey that it has sometimes been called the "second holy land."

The Christian faith took root early here. Some of the Christians who fled Jerusalem following the martyrdom of St. Stephen came as far as Antioch in Syria (now part of Turkey; the ancient borders of Syria were different), where they preached the faith to their fellow Jews (Acts 11:19).

In fact, it was in Antioch that the followers of Jesus were first called "Christians" (Acts 11:26)—an indication of how important this region was to early Christian history.

St. Paul's epistles to the Galatians, Ephesians, and Colossians were all written to churches in what is now Turkey, and all seven of the "seven churches of Asia" to whom St. John sent the book of Revelation were located in the Roman province of Asia Minor in western Turkey.

The second century here was very active. Around 110 St. Ignatius, bishop of Antioch in Syria, was taken to Rome and martyred. His fellow bishop, St. Polycarp of Smyrna, was martyred a few decades later, in 155. Not all bishops met this fate, though. St. Abercius of Hierapolis seems to have died peacefully around 190. Before doing so, he composed a beautiful epitaph for his tomb, in which he asked for the prayers of those who read it.

Another second-century bishop of Hierapolis, St. Papias, collected oral testimonies from those who had heard the apostles and on that basis wrote an *Explanation of the Sayings of the Lord* around 130.

Several of the great apologists of the second century dwelled in this region, including St. Melito, bishop of Sardis, who wrote a defense of Christianity to the Emperor Marcus Aurelius, and St. Theophilus, bishop of Antioch, who wrote the treatise *To Autolycus*.

Christians in this age had to contend with heresies. Already in the time of St. Ignatius of Antioch, Docetism was present, and both Marcionism and Montanism originated here in the mid-100s.

Around 160 a priest of Iconium reportedly wrote one of the first Christian novels, *The Acts of Paul and Thecla*.

In the 200s St. Gregory Thaumaturgus (i.e., "the Wonder-Worker") was bishop of Neocaesarea in Pontus. His colleague Firmilian was bishop of Caesarea in Cappadocia.

Around 250 a Christian named Pionius was martyred at Smyrna. It is because of him that we still have the second-century account of *The Martyrdom of Polycarp*, which he rediscovered after being guided by a vision.

The 300s saw an enormous amount of activity in this area.

This was partly because in 313 co-emperors Constantine I and Licinius issued the Edict of Milan, which proclaimed toleration for Christians and ended the age of persecutions. Also, in 330, Constantine, by then sole emperor, made the newly built city of Constantinople the capital of the empire. The toleration of Christianity and the presence of the first Christian emperor ensured that the region would be a focal point in history.

The end of the age of persecutions meant questions concerning how to deal with Christians who had faltered during the persecutions but now wanted to return to the Church. A regional council was held in Ankara in 314 that dealt with this subject.

Constantine also hired Lactantius, a North African who had come to Nicomedia to teach rhetoric, to tutor one of his sons.

The Arian crisis broke out, and in 325 Constantine convoked what would be the first ecumenical council, Nicaea. Though Arianism was condemned at this council, the crisis intensified and went on for many decades.

As a result of the theological conflict, certain Fathers rose to prominence. Especially noteworthy are the "three Cappadocian" Fathers—St. Basil of Caesarea in Cappadocia, St. Gregory of Nazianz, and St. Gregory of Nyssa—each of whom played an important role battling Arianism.

As the conflict continued, related heresies such as Semi-Arianism, Apollinarism, and Pneumatomachianism arose. This led in 381 to the second ecumenical council, Constantinople I, which defined the divinity of the Holy Spirit and completed work on the *Niceno-Constantinopolitan ("Nicene") Creed*.

A regional council held at Laodicea in 360 issued canons dealing with a variety of subjects.

Among the notable writers in this century are St. Evagrius of Pontus, a native of Ibora, and St. Ephraim of Nisibis, who wrote such beautiful hymns that he is often called "the harp of the Spirit."

Things did not slow down in the 400s. The first decade of this century saw the deaths of two saintly antagonists—St. Epiphanius, bishop of Salamis on the island of Cyprus, and the gifted preacher

St. John Chrysostom, who had been patriarch of Constantinople, though he died in exile.

This century also saw two ecumenical councils. The first was held in 431 at Ephesus and dealt with the perceived heresy of Nestorius, patriarch of Constantinople. The reaction against Nestorianism spawned a counter-heresy known as Monophysitism, a form of which was popularized by one of Nestorius' own priests, Eutyches, who gave rise to Eutychianism. The rival heresy was dealt with at the Council of Chalcedon in 451.

Additional controversial figures of the period included Theodore of Mopsuestia (who was suspected of Nestorianism after his death around 428) and Theodoret of Cyr. Both of these bishops, together with Ibas, bishop of Edessa, were the subjects of the "Three Chapters" controversy that occupied the Second Council of Constantinople in 553, though all had been dead for nearly a century by the time it met.

Another variant of Monophysitism—Monothelitism, which held that Christ had only one will—arose and was condemned at the Third Council of Constantinople, which was held in 680 and 681.

Finally, the heresy of Iconoclasm broke out in the 700s and was repudiated at the Council of Nicaea II in 787.

It is noteworthy that all seven of the ecumenical councils accepted by both East and West occurred in Turkey and that both the first and the last of these took place in Nicaea.

Though this region was once the "second holy land" for Christianity, it was eventually conquered by Muslim forces, and today the Christians who remain there are a small, oppressed minority.

6. Greece and Rome

Christianity came early to this part of the world. St. Luke mentions that Jews and converts to Judaism from as far away as Rome were present on the day of Pentecost in Jerusalem (Acts 2:10–11). Presumably some embraced the preaching of the apostles and took their new faith home with them.

St. Paul's epistles to the Romans, Corinthians, Philippians, and Thessalonians were written to churches in this region. The Gospel of Luke and the book of Acts seem to have been written at Rome between 60 and 62, when Paul was under house arrest there. The second epistle of St. Peter also was written at Rome shortly after this.

Both Peter and Paul were put to death during the persecution of the Emperor Nero, probably in 64, after he blamed Christians for the great fire of Rome.

Nero himself was declared a public enemy by the Roman senate and was forced to commit suicide in 68, leading to the disastrous "year of four emperors" in 69, when amid a convulsive series of civil wars Galba, Otho, Vitellius, and finally Vespasian held the imperial office in quick succession. The last of these was a general who returned to Rome from Israel, where he had been fighting to put down the Jewish rebellion that had begun in 66. To finish the job, he left his son, the future Emperor Titus, who destroyed the Jewish temple in July of 70.

It is likely that St. Clement of Rome (who may or may not have been pope by this time) wrote his *Letter to the Corinthians* in early 70, before the destruction of the temple. After his letter arrived, it became associated with an anonymous homily that was written around 80 and mistakenly attributed to him, which resulted in it being called *Second Clement*. Another writer of this time was Hermas of Rome, who wrote a famous work called *The Shepherd* based on a reported private revelation.

In the early 100s what would later become known as the *Apostles' Creed* began to take form as the baptismal creed used in Rome.

The 100s also witnessed a number of notable apologists writing in Greece, such as Athenagoras and St. Aristides, both of Athens.

St. Justin Martyr came to Rome and was martyred there around 165. One of his students, Tatian the Syrian, returned to the east and started the heretical sect known as the Aquarii.

Important works from the late 100s include a letter from St. Dionysius, bishop of Corinth, to Pope St. Soter of Rome and a partial account of the canon of scripture known as the Muratorian Fragment, which was later discovered at Milan.

Around 210 a priest of Rome named Caius wrote a critique of Montanism, and in the 220s another priest of Rome, Sabellius, began the heresy that bears his name. The same decade a Roman

layman named Municius Felix wrote what may be the first surviving Christian treatise in the Latin language, marking the beginning of the shift from Greek to Latin in the Christian West.
The mid-200s were notable for the appearance of two Roman
priests who became antipopes. The first was St. Hippolytus of
Rome, who reconciled with the Church before his death in 235,
which is why he is accounted a saint. The second was Novatian of
Rome, who before his death in 258 started a schism that endured
for some time.

In the 260s, Pope St. Dionysius held a regional council that
condemned the errors of Sabellius.

The late 200s and early 300s saw a great deal of activity in this
region, and not all of it in Italy. The great scripture scholar St.
Victorinus of Pettau wrote in this period, before he perished in
303. St. Methodius of Philippi, an opponent of Origenism, was
martyred in 311, shortly before the Edict of Milan was issued in
313, and the age of persecutions ended.

The Arian crisis was dealt with not only at the first ecumenical
council at Nicaea in 325, but also at other councils, including the
Council of Sardica around 343. Pope St. Julius I had hoped that
this would be an ecumenical council, but it did not gain enough
participation from the East.

After the second ecumenical council, at Constantinople in 381,
Pope St. Damasus I held a regional council at Rome in 382,
which affirmed the primacy of Rome and also dealt with the
canon of Scripture. His successor, Pope St. Siricius I, also held
a regional council in Rome, which condemned the errors of the
monk Jovinian.

A major figure though much of this century was St. Ambrose
of Milan, who converted St. Augustine. Born around 338 and
dying in 397, Ambrose is a Doctor of the Church, which means
he belongs to a special group of writers who have received papal
recognition for their contribution to Christian theology. Ambrose
was one of the first four individuals to be designated a Doctor of
the Church. This happened in 1298, long after his death.

Another Doctor of the Church born in this region was St. Jerome.

He was born around 347 in Dalmatia, which was located mostly in the modern state of Croatia, though partly in Bosnia-Herzegovina.

A less welcome figure of this period was Pelagius, who came to Rome from the British Isles and around 400 began the heresy that bears his name. His teachings were condemned by Pope St. Innocent I (reigned 401–417) and Pope St. Celestine I (422–432), who also commissioned St. Patrick's mission to Ireland.

Though not in Rome, another important figure of this time was St. Peter Chrysologus. He was born in the Forum Cornelii and became bishop of Ravenna. He is a Doctor of the Church.

One of the most important popes in Church history was St. Leo I, one of a handful to bear the title "the Great." He reigned from 440 to 461 and sent an important document to the fourth ecumenical council, at Chalcedon in 451, where the fathers of the council proclaimed "Peter has spoken through Leo!"

A pope of similar stature was Pope St. Gregory I, who also bears the title "the Great." He reigned from 590 to 604 and guided the Church at a crucial period of transition into the Middle Ages.

Finally, Pope St. Agatho reigned briefly from 678 to 681 and helped prepare the way for the Third Council of Constantinople (680–681), which condemned the heresy of Monothelitism.

7. The Far West

It is unclear how quickly Christianity reached this part of the world, though St. Paul mentions in Romans 15:24–28 that he planned to go to Spain after he visited Rome. Pope St. Clement in his *Letter to the Corinthians* seems to indicate that he did so before returning to Rome to be martyred under Nero.

One of the most important second-century Fathers was St. Irenaeus, who was born in Turkey around 140 but became the second bishop of Lyons. He died in 202.

Paul's visit to Spain is fictionalized in one of the first Christian novels, the *Acts of Xanthippe and Polyxena*, which dates to the 200s. Another interesting piece of literature was written around 285 in France, where an anonymous author used the writings of Tertullian of Carthage to produce the *Poem Against the Marcionites*.

During the Arian crisis of the 300s, St. Hilary of Poitiers—sometimes called "the Athanasius of the West"—strongly opposed the Arians. He lived from around 315 to around 367 and became a bishop even though he was married.

Around 375 an individual named Pectorius died at Autun and left a well-known inscription on his tomb similar to that of St. Abercius of Herapolis.

Another notable individual of this century was St. Pacian of Barcelona—another married bishop—who died around 385.

In the early 400s a monk from France named Leporius was expelled from his monastery for his heterodox beliefs, which seemed to involve a form of Nestorianism, though this heresy had not yet arisen under that name. Fortunately, he found his way to North Africa and was corrected by St. Augustine, who helped him return to France with a letter of recommendation.

While St. Augustine was battling the followers of Pelagius in this period, some sought a middle course between the two positions. After 428, St. John Cassian and his fellow monks at Marseilles began to teach Semi-Pelagian ideas. So did St. Vincent of Lerins. These ideas had not been defined as heretical in their day, which is why these men are still reckoned as saints. But not every monk in France was enamored of Semi-Pelagianism. One who rejected it was St. Prosper of Aquitaine, who corresponded with St. Augustine and later went to Rome.

The major evangelization of Ireland took place in this century, when St. Patrick (died around 460) and St. Sechnall (died around 447) conducted their missions.

A final noteworthy individual from this period was St. Gregory, bishop of Tours. He was born in 538 and died in 594, and is most famous for having written ten books on the history of the Franks.

Several regional councils were held in this area, including the Council of Elvira, which met in Spain around the year 300, and two councils held in Orange in modern France. The first was in 441 and the second, more famous council, was in 529. It was presided over by St. Caesarius of Arles (died 542), condemning Pelagianism and affirming certain points of St. Augustine's teaching.

8. North Africa

While we don't think of North Africa as a Christian place today, it was very much so before the Muslim conquests of the 600s.

Christianity came early to Ethiopia, for Philip the evangelist converted the Ethiopian eunuch in Acts 8. Later in the first century, St. Mark became the bishop of Alexandria, Egypt—a city that already had a large Jewish population and that had been the place where the Septuagint Greek version of the Old Testament had been translated.

Alexandria continued to be an important Christian center throughout this period. In the later 100s, St. Clement of Alexandria served as the head of the famous catechetical school of that city. One of his pupils, Origen, succeeded him as head of the school in the early 200s.

Another very famous figure of this day was Tertullian of Carthage, a layman and lawyer who was born around 157 and died around 245. He wrote vigorously in defense of Christian orthodoxy for a time but eventually slid into the Montanist sect, so he is not a saint.

Carthage was also an important Christian center, and not just because of Tertullian. St. Cyprian of Carthage served as its influential bishop, until he died in 258, and a series of regional councils were held there.

Because North Africa was under Roman control at this time, it was subject to the persecutions the Roman emperors launched against the Church. A particularly noteworthy account of the persecution of Septimus Severus was produced in 203 at Carthage. This document, *The Martyrdom of Perpetua and Felicity*, is composed of text written by Perpetua herself, as well as others who were present.

St. Peter, bishop of Alexandria and a former head of its catechetical school, was martyred around 311, just before the Edict of Milan was promulgated in 313, and religious toleration was provided for Christians. In North Africa a rigorist view was often taken on the question of how to deal with Christians who had lapsed during the persecutions, resulting in a schism headed by Donatus of Carthage.

An outright heresy erupted during the tenure of St. Alexander, bishop of Alexandria. In the early 300s one of his priests, Arius, denied the divinity of Christ and touched off the Arian controversy. It swiftly grew in strength, and to resolve it the emperor convoked the first ecumenical council in Nicaea, in 325. St. Alexander attended, as did his deacon, St. Athanasius, who became his successor as bishop in 326.

Two of St. Athanasius's friends were St. Serapion, bishop of

Thmuis (died around 350), who wrote a sacramentary, and St. Anthony of Egypt (died around 356), the father of desert monasticism. St. Athanasius wrote a famous *Life of St. Anthony*, which helped spread his style of monasticism. Another contemporary of St. Athanasius was Didymus the Blind, who had been blind from childhood but who nevertheless became a famous scholar, and the final head of the catechetical school of Alexandria, before he died around 398. His students included St. Jerome and Rufinus of Aquileia.

After St. Athanasius, the most famous bishop of Alexandria is probably St. Cyril of Alexandria, an exceedingly cruel man who nevertheless is a saint and Doctor of the Church. He served as papal legate to the third ecumenical council, in Ephesus in 431, and died in 444.

These figures lived in and around Alexandria and Carthage, but there were many other Christian centers in North Africa.

About 330 a curious figure named Arnobius of Sicca died. He had at first been a pagan and an anti-Christian apologist, but he converted to the faith. His local bishop was suspicious of him, and to prove how sincere he was, Arnobius wrote a seven-volume work against paganism. The work shows how enthusiastic he was about his new faith—and how little he understood it at that stage. Still, he was sincere. He had also been the teacher of Lactantius, who left North Africa and eventually tutored one of the sons of Constantine I.

Another North African figure of the fourth century was St. Optatis, bishop of Milevis, who battled the Donatist schism and died around 385.

By far the most famous North African was St. Augustine, bishop of Hippo Regius. Born in 354 to a pagan father and a Christian mother, his life's journey took him to Italy, where he was converted by St. Ambrose of Milan. He returned to North Africa and became a bishop, and the most prolific writer of the patristic age. He died in 430.

Among St. Augustine's battles was a conflict with the heresy Pelagianism and, later, with Semi-Pelagianism. The great North

African Doctor of the Church held very strict views on grace and predestination (contra Pelagius), and not everyone in his day (or ours) agreed with them. One who did, though, was St. Fulgence, bishop of Ruspe, who was one of his great defenders. He died in 527, about a century after St. Augustine and about century before the Muslim invasion of North Africa began.

There were a variety of regional councils held in this region during the age of the Church Fathers. In 393, St. Augustine presided over a council in his own see of Hippo. Many councils were held at Carthage. There were at least ten, the earliest of which took place in the mid-200s. Some were presided over by Cyprian and reflected his view that baptisms performed by heretics were invalid, so people converting from heretical sects had to be re-baptized. Not everyone in North Africa agreed with this, including the anonymous author of the *Treatise on Re-Baptism*, which supported the correct view that the validity of baptism does not depend on the right belief of the one administering it.

One council, held at Carthage in 419, surveyed the results of previous North African councils and put them together as a body of canon law known as the *African Code*.

III. *Ad Fontes!*—"To the Sources!"

The cry *"Ad fontes!"* (Latin, "To the sources!") has been used in a variety of contexts in the Renaissance, in the Reformation, and by Catholic figures such as Erasmus of Rotterdam. The idea is that we should reexamine the sources of our culture and our faith so that we may be more firmly grounded in them. During the Second Vatican Council the same idea was expressed by the term *ressourcement*, which indicated a return to or reexamination of sources, including the writings of the Church Fathers.

In this section we will look briefly at the individual Church Fathers and other ecclesiastical writers of the patristic age, at the regional and ecumenical councils that were held then, at various writings that were in circulation, and at the heretics and schismatics that the Church Fathers had to deal with.

9. Know Your Fathers

This chapter provides short biographies of the various Church Fathers and ecclesiastical writers who are quoted in this work.

ST. ABERCIUS OF HIERAPOLIS

Born around 118; died around 190. Bishop of Hierapolis (modern Pamukkale, Turkey). Known for composing his own epitaph before his death and having it inscribed on stone.

POPE ST. AGATHO

Reigned from 678 to 681. Already very elderly (reportedly over 100) when he became pope, he had a short but active reign in which he held councils in the West to prepare the way for the sixth ecumenical council—Constantinople III—to which he sent legates and a letter. The council condemned Monothelitism and healed the schism over this heresy, although Agatho did not live to see the results of the council.

ST. ALEXANDER OF ALEXANDRIA

Died 326. Patriarch of Alexandria, Egypt and mentor of St. Athanasius. Combated the Arians and participated in the Council of Nicaea I.

ST. AMBROSE OF MILAN

Born around 338; died 397. Bishop of Milan, Italy. One of the four original Doctors of the Church. Originally a government official, he became bishop in a most extraordinary way. While he was trying to keep the peace between opposing groups of Catholics and Arians who were vehemently disputing who should be the new bishop of Milan, the two groups began chanting that Ambrose should be the new bishop, though he was not yet baptized. (The Arians felt that although Ambrose was Catholic in belief he would be a kinder bishop than they otherwise would likely get.) He resisted strongly but eventually gave in and was baptized and ordained bishop. Later, he assisted in the conversion of St. Augustine, to whom he gave the famous advice now paraphrased as "When in Rome, do as the Romans do."

ST. ANTHONY OF EGYPT

Born around 250 at Herakleopolis Magna; died 356. A layman who lived in a variety of places in Egypt. Though hailed as "the Father of Monasticism," he was not the first monk, but he was one of the first (if not the first) ascetics known to retire to the desert. A biography of him by St. Athanasius of Alexandria helped spread his style of monasticism.

ST. APHRAHAT THE PERSIAN SAGE

Born around 270; died after 345. Writer of treatises. Little is known about his life, but his writings survive. Invariably called the "Persian Sage," he was an ascetic and possibly a bishop. One late source says he was head of the monastery at Mar Mattai (St. Matthew), near present-day Mosul, Iraq.

ST. ARISTIDES OF ATHENS

Wrote around 140. One of the early Greek apologists. Said to be a Christian philosopher in Athens, Greece.

ARNOBIUS OF SICCA

Died around 330. An early Christian apologist, he was born pagan and was at first an anti-Christian apologist. He converted to Christianity, and to prove his sincerity to the local bishop he wrote a seven-volume work against paganism. The work shows him to be very enthusiastic about his new faith, though his grasp of Christian doctrine was still shaky. Lived in Sicca (modern El Kef, Tunisia). Lactantius was one of his students.

ST. ATHANASIUS OF ALEXANDRIA

Born around 295; died 373. A Doctor of the Church. As a deacon he accompanied St. Alexander of Alexandria to the Council of Nicaea I. He succeeded Alexander as patriarch of Alexandria and was a tireless defender of Trinitarianism and foe of the Arians. His time as bishop was stormy, and he was expelled from his see five times but regained it each time.

ATHENAGORAS OF ATHENS

Died shortly after 180. An early Christian philosopher and apologist. Considered the most eloquent of the early apologists. Little is known of his life.

ST. AUGUSTINE OF HIPPO

Born 354; died 430. One of the four original Doctors of the Church. Of Berber descent, he was born to a pagan father (Patricius) and Christian mother (St. Monica), in Thagaste (modern Souk Ahras, Algeria). He spent some time as a Manichean before becoming a Christian. He was baptized by St. Ambrose of Milan.

Before becoming Christian, St. Augustine fathered a son (Adeodatus) by a concubine. After baptism, he became bishop of Hippo Regius, Numidia (now Annaba, Algeria). The most prolific of the Church Fathers, and one of the most important theologians in history.

ST. BASIL OF CAESAREA IN CAPPADOCIA

Born around 330; died 379. A Doctor of the Church. He was the bishop of Caesarea in Cappadocia (now Kayseri, Turkey) and a major defender of Trinitarian theology when the Arian crisis was at its worst. He had a fiery temper. Together with his younger brother, St. Gregory of Nyssa, and his friend, St. Gregory of Nazianz, he is one of the three Cappadocian Fathers. Also known as St. Basil the Great.

ST. CAESARIUS OF ARLES

Born around 469; died 542. He was bishop of Arles in what is now France. The most influential French bishop of his day, he presided at the Second Council of Orange, which condemned Semi-Pelagianism.

CAIUS OF ROME

Wrote around 210. A priest of the diocese of Rome during the reign of Pope Zephyrinus (198–217). His work, *A Disputation with Proclus* (a critique of Montanism), survives in fragmentary form in Eusebius's writings. Also known as Gaius (a variant of the same name).

POPE ST. CELESTINE I

Reigned from 422 to 432. Opposed various heretical and schismatic groups of his day. Sent legates to the Council of Ephesus. One of his last official acts was commissioning St. Patrick's mission to Ireland.

POPE ST. CLEMENT I

Probably wrote in early 70. Various ancient sources place him as the first, second, or third successor of St. Peter. (Most commonly, he is held to be the third, after Linus and Cletus.) He was the author of a single surviving *Letter to the Corinthians*, which is often dated around 95, but this is too late a date.

William Jurgens points to internal evidence that places it no later than 80 or so (the date he favors) and possibly up to ten years earlier. John A. T. Robinson shows internal evidence that places it in the first part of the year 70. Specifically, Clement refers to sacrifices still being offered at the temple in Jerusalem, which was destroyed in July of 70. Clement also refers to the repeated crises that have prevented him from writing to the Corinthians until now, which is a likely reference to the violent "year of four emperors" in 69, a time of civil war that followed the forced suicide of Nero in 68. In it Galba, Otho, and Vitellius were successively acclaimed emperor and then killed or forced to commit suicide before Vespasian finally took office.

The epistle may or may not have been written before Clement was pope. He was, in any event, a major figure of the period, as demonstrated by the fact that a number of later works were attributed to him or written about him. Also referred to as "Clement of Rome."

ST. CLEMENT OF ALEXANDRIA

Born around 150; died around 214. A layman who, though famed for his connection with Alexandria, was not an Egyptian but was probably born in Athens. After becoming Christian and traveling in search of Christian wisdom, he settled in Alexandria, where he served as the head of that city's catechetical school. After a few years, he was forced to flee and, around a decade later, died in what is now Turkey. One of his students was Origen.

CONSTANTINE I

Born around 272; died 337. The first Christian emperor—an office he shared with Licinius from 306 until 324, when he became sole emperor. His conversion was prompted by a private revelation in which he was told to conquer in the sign of the cross. He moved the capital of the empire to Byzantium, which was rebuilt as Constantinople (now Istanbul, Turkey). In 313 he and his co-emperor issued the Edict of Milan, which proclaimed religious toleration. He did not, however, make Christianity the official religion of the Roman Empire. In 325 he convoked the Council of Nicaea I to deal with the Arian crisis. Though the council endorsed Trinitarianism, it did not stop the controversy. Constantine was eventually baptized by the Arian bishop of Nicomedia, the city in which he lay dying. Sometimes called "Constantine the Great."

ST. CYPRIAN OF CARTHAGE

Born around 205; died 258. He was bishop of Carthage (now a suburb of Tunis, Tunisia). He presided at the Council of Carthage of 256. He got along well with Pope St. Cornelius I but had a falling out with Pope St. Stephen I over whether baptisms performed by heretics were valid (Cyprian wrongly held that they were not). For a time he had to shepherd his flock while in hiding due to persecution. Eventually he was martyred by beheading.

ST. CYRIL OF ALEXANDRIA

Died 444. A Doctor of the Church. Patriarch of Alexandria, Egypt, Cyril was a harsh man who dealt cruelly with his enemies, including Jews, Novatians, St. John Chrysostom, and Nestorius. A mob of his followers brutally murdered the female pagan philosopher Hypatia, though there is no evidence that they did so at his direction. Despite his flaws, he was an important theologian and papal legate to the Council of Ephesus.

ST. CYRIL OF JERUSALEM

Born around 315; died 386. A Doctor of the Church. Bishop of Jerusalem. He lived during the Arian crisis and was expelled from his see three times, regaining it each time. Known for his lectures to catechumens.

POPE ST. DAMASUS I

Reigned from 366 to 384. He changed the liturgical language of Rome from Greek to Latin, commissioned St. Jerome's Latin translation of Scripture, presided over the regional Council of Rome of 382, composed many epigrams, and issued several surviving letters.

DIDYMUS THE BLIND

Born around 313; died around 398. A layman who was blind from childhood, he became a major theologian and author. He was the last head of the catechetical school of Alexandria, Egypt. His students included St. Jerome and Rufinus of Aquileia. He was known for his kindness, and for the fact that he shared a few of Origen's heterodox opinions. Most of his writings are lost.

POPE ST. DIONYSIUS

Reigned from 260 to 268. He held a regional council in Rome that defended the orthodox view of God against Modalists and Subordinationists. He also ransomed Christians in Turkey who had been enslaved by barbarian tribes.

ST. DIONYSIUS OF CORINTH

Wrote around 170. Bishop of Corinth, Greece. He is known for having written a letter to Pope St. Soter. This letter survives in fragmentary form in the writings of Eusebius of Caesarea.

ST. EPHRAIM THE SYRIAN

Born around 306; died 373. A Doctor of the Church. He was a deacon of the Church of Nisibis in Mesopotamia (now Nusaybin, Turkey). Often called "the lyre (or harp) of the Holy Spirit," he wrote many hymns in Syriac (a form of Aramaic).

ST. EPIPHANIUS OF SALAMIS

Born around 315; died 403. Though born in Palestine, he became bishop of Salamis on the island of Cyprus. He had an angry disposition, and his targets included St. John Chrysostom and John of Jerusalem. His writings, nevertheless, contain valuable information that would have otherwise been lost to history. He performed the forcible ordination of St. Jerome's brother, Paulinian, to the priesthood (see St. Jerome).

EUSEBIUS OF CAESAREA IN PALESTINE

Born around 263; died 340. Bishop of Caesarea in Palestine (now Caesarea Maritima, Israel). He tried to steer a middle course between Arianism and Trinitarianism, though he did eventually subscribe to the creed produced at the Council of Nicaea I, which he attended. He was close to Constantine I, whose life he wrote. Known as the father of Church history for his major work *Ecclesiastical History*.

EVAGRIUS OF PONTUS

Born 345; died 399. A deacon and an ascetic, he was a native of Ibora in Pontus (now Turhal, Turkey). He held some heterodox views of Origen. His writings are mostly lost.

FIRMILIAN OF CAESAREA IN CAPPADOCIA

Died around 268. Bishop of Caesarea in Cappadocia (now Kayseri, Turkey). A friend of Origen and St. Gregory Thaumaturgus, as well as a supporter of St. Cyprian of Carthage in the conflict over heretical baptisms.

ST. FULGENCE OF RUSPE

Born 467; died 527. Bishop of Ruspe (now the ruin Thelepte, near Feriana, Tunisia). His thought on grace and predestination is very similar to St. Augustine's, though he lived later.

POPE ST. GREGORY I

Reigned from 590 to 604. One of the four original Doctors of the Church. Though born to a wealthy family, he sold his possessions and established monasteries, one of which he dwelled in. He practiced asceticism to the point that he damaged his health. Reluctantly, he was drawn from the monastery into the service of the pope. Eventually, he was elected pope himself, though for a time he sought to avoid the office. He guided the Church during a crucial period of transition between antiquity and the Middle Ages. Commonly referred to as "Gregory the Great."

ST. GREGORY OF NAZIANZ

Born around 330; died around 389. A Doctor of the Church. Though he is styled as being "of Nazianz," he actually was born in the nearby town of Azianz. His father, also named Gregory, became bishop of Nazianz, and the younger Gregory was eventually made a priest of his father's diocese. Later he was made bishop of the tiny community of Sasima, though he never assumed his office there. Instead, he served for a time as patriarch of Constantinople and also bishop at Nazianz. A reluctant bishop, he eventually retired to his family's home in Azianz. He was a close friend of St. Basil of Caesarea, despite the latter's fiery temper. Together with St. Gregory of Nyssa, these three are known as the great Cappadocian Fathers since they all lived in Cappadocia in what is now central Turkey. He participated in the First Council of Constantinople.

ST. GREGORY OF NYSSA

Born about 335; died after 394. The younger brother of Basil of Caesarea. He decided against becoming a churchman and married, but later was persuaded to return to an ecclesiastical career. Against his wishes, he was consecrated bishop of Nyssa (now a ruin just north of Harmandali, Turkey) by his brother. He participated in the First Council of Constantinople. A great defender of Trinitarianism and a versatile author. Together with his brother and St. Gregory of Nazianz, he is one of the three great Cappadocian Fathers.

ST. GREGORY OF TOURS

Born 538; died 594. Bishop of Tours in what is now France. He was highly respected in his day and is best known for writing ten books chronicling the history of the Franks.

ST. GREGORY THAUMATURGUS

Born around 213; died around 273. He was converted to the faith by Origen and later consecrated the first bishop of Neocaesarea in Pontus (now Niksar, Turkey). His appellation *Thaumaturgus* means "wonder-worker" or "miracle-worker" and is based on the many miracles he is reported to have performed. Also called "St. Gregory the Wonder-Worker" and "St. Gregory the Miracle-Worker."

ST. HEGESIPPUS

Wrote around 180. Possibly based in Palestine. His memoirs of his travels exist only in fragmentary form today (mostly in Eusebius), but are an important source of information about early Christianity.

HERMAS OF ROME

Wrote around 80 in Rome. He was an early Christian known for his work *The Shepherd*, which was based on his purported visions. The book was considered canonical by some early writers but ultimately was not included in Scripture. His work is often held to have been written later, around 145, but this is based on a misstatement in the Muratorian Fragment that Hermas was the brother of Pope St. Pius I. John A. T. Robinson argues persuasively that he wrote during or before the reign of Pope St. Clement I, who is mentioned in *The Shepherd* as being alive at the time. Origen reports that he is the same Hermas mentioned in Romans 16:14.

ST. HILARY OF POITIERS

Born around 315; died around 367. A Doctor of the Church. He converted from paganism and, though he was married, he was also elected bishop of Poitiers in what is now France. A strong opponent of the Arians, he is sometimes referred to as "the Athanasius of the West." Like St. Athanasius of Alexandria, he was for a time exiled, but he regained his see.

ST. HIPPOLYTUS OF ROME

Died in 235. The first known anti-pope and the only anti-pope who is a saint. He was a priest of the diocese of Rome who came into conflict with his bishop, Pope St. Zephyrinus. When the latter died and Pope St. Callistus I was elected in his place, St. Hippolytus broke communion and his followers elected him as a rival pope, making him the first anti-pope. In 235 he and the current pope, St. Pontianus, were exiled to the island of Sardinia, where they were reconciled with each other and beheaded. His ultimate reconciliation and martyrdom are why St. Hippolytus is considered a saint. He was a prolific writer, but most of his works are lost.

ST. IGNATIUS OF ANTIOCH

Died around 110. He was the third bishop of Antioch (near the current city of Antakya, Turkey). He heard the apostle John. In the reign of the Emperor Trajan, he was taken to Rome and martyred. On the way he wrote six letters to various churches and one to St. Polycarp of Smyrna. These letters are an invaluable resource concerning early Christianity. They also exist in a long form that includes interpolations of the fourth century, and there is an abridgement of them in Syriac. The original, short version is quoted in Part Two except for a single quotation of the long version in chapter 18 (as noted there).

POPE ST. INNOCENT I

Reigned from 401 to 417. In civil affairs, he was unable to prevent Rome from being sacked by the Goths, but in theological affairs he was a vigorous defender of papal primacy.

ST. IRENAEUS OF LYONS

Born around 140; died around 202. Originally from modern Turkey, where he heard St. Polycarp of Smyrna, he ended up becoming the second bishop of Lyons (now Lyon; then called

Lugdunum), in what is now France. He intervened in a dispute between Pope St. Victor I and Bishop Polycrates of Ephesus on the date on which Easter should be celebrated. He also wrote against Gnosticism in his masterwork, *Against Heresies.*

ST. JEROME

Born around 347; died around 419. One of the four original Doctors of the Church. Originally from Dalmatia (located mostly in modern Croatia), he was educated in Rome and traveled extensively. He attended the Council of Rome in 382 and became the secretary of Pope Damasus, who instigated Jerome's most famous work—the translation of the Bible in Latin known as the Vulgate. This gradually replaced previous Latin translations of Scripture. After the death of Damasus he moved to Bethlehem, where he continued his translation work. Jerome made many enemies as a result of his explosive temper and his ability to hold grudges even after the death of his opponents. At one point Jerome needed additional priestly help with the monasteries he ran, and to supply the need St. Epiphanius of Salamis ordained Jerome's own brother —a monk named Paulinian—forcibly and against his will. (At this point Jerome was at odds with his own bishop, John of Jerusalem —a split which Epiphanius fostered.) To keep Paulinian from objecting, he was first gagged and then ordained a deacon. A Mass was held, with Paulinian serving the deacon's part. Then he was grabbed, tied up and gagged again, and ordained a priest.

ST. JOHN CASSIAN

Born around 360; died around 435. His place of birth is uncertain, though he spent time in Bethlehem, Egypt, and Rome before settling in Marseilles in what is now France. There he founded a monastery for men and one for women. Though he is considered a saint, he is not on the Church's universal calendar. He also was the apparent founder of Semi-Pelagianism, though he took little part in the controversy over this position since he died shortly after it broke out.

ST. JOHN CHRYSOSTOM

Born around 359; died 407. A Doctor of the Church. Originally from Antioch in Syria (now Antakya, Turkey), he eventually and reluctantly became the patriarch of Constantinople. An extraordinary preacher, he was nicknamed *Chrusostomos* (Greek for "golden-mouthed"). A reformer at Constantinople, he was in conflict both with other churchmen and with the royal court, which twice had him exiled. Though the first time he was quickly brought back (the next day, in fact), the second time he died en route to his place of exile. One of his most famous works, and one that helped earn him his nickname, was a series of sermons he preached on "the incident of the statues." When he was a newly ordained priest, a mob of tax protestors went on a rampage in Antioch and, in addition to vandalizing the city and the local prefect's palace, they tore down the statues of the Emperor Theodosius and the late Empress Flacilla and dragged them through the streets. When the riot was over and reality set in, the city was terrified of what would happen next. A series of executions began, and the rumor went round that Theodosius was so enraged that he was contemplating the total destruction of the city, which many began to flee. The local bishop, Flavian, went to appeal directly to the emperor, and while he was gone John preached a famous series of sermons to comfort the population, offer them hope, and prepare them for the afterlife, should Flavian's mission fail. All ended well when Flavian returned and announced that Theodosius had wept upon hearing his appeal on behalf of the city and that he had decided to spare it. It is suspected that John may have written the eloquent speech Flavian delivered to the emperor.

ST. JOHN OF DAMASCUS

Born around 676; died around 749. A Doctor of the Church. John was born into an Arab Christian family in Damascus, in the modern state of Syria. Hence he is often called St. John Damascene. Like his father and grandfather, John served for a time as an official of the Muslim caliph. Eventually he left this post and became a monk and priest in the monastery of Mar Saba, near Jerusalem. During the Iconoclastic controversy, John argued vigorously against the Iconoclasts. He is also noted for his writing on the Assumption of Mary. The date of his death is considered the end of the period of the Church Fathers.

POPE ST. JULIUS I

Reigned from 337 to 352. He held a regional council in Rome and wrote in defense of St. Athanasius of Alexandria. He was a firm opponent of the Arians and a defender of the primacy of Rome. He urged the calling of the Council of Sardica of 343 to deal with the Arian crisis. It was hoped that this would be an ecumenical council, but many Eastern bishops, including Arian bishops, refused to participate.

ST. JUSTIN MARTYR

Born around 105; died around 165. Justin was born at Flavia Neapolis (now Nablus in the West Bank), and he adhered to several philosophies before becoming a Christian. Traveling to Rome, he founded a school. One of his students was Tatian the Syrian. The most important apologist of his day, and patron of apologists. Eventually he and several companions were martyred, so he is commonly called "St. Justin Martyr."

LACTANTIUS

Born around 250; died shortly after 317. A student of Arnobius. Of pagan parentage, Lactantius was born in North Africa (most likely in modern Algeria or Tunisia). He was invited by the Emperor Diocletian to become a teacher of Latin rhetoric in Nicomedia (now Izmit, Turkey). After Lactantius became a Christian and Diocletian began to persecute Christians, he had to leave his post. Surviving a subsequent period of poverty, he was recalled to service by Constantine the Great, who asked him to tutor one of his sons.

POPE ST. LEO I

Reigned from 440 to 461. A Doctor of the Church. Faced many difficulties in his reign, including invasions by barbarian tribes (he successfully negotiated with Attila the Hun to avoid the sacking of Rome) and conflict with various heretics and schismatics, especially Nestorians and Monophysites. He annulled the results of a council at Ephesus in 449, which he dubbed the "Robber Council." At a distance, he played an important role in the Council of Chalcedon in 451. More of his writings survive than for any previous pope. Commonly referred to as "Leo the Great."

LEPORIUS

Wrote around 426. A French monk who was expelled from his monastery because of his unorthodox beliefs. He apparently held that Christ was two separate persons, one human and one divine, though the Nestorian controversy had not yet arisen. He may also have held Pelagian ideas. After his expulsion, he found his way to North Africa, where St. Augustine helped him regain orthodox beliefs. Subsequently, St. Augustine and one of the Councils of Carthage helped him develop an accurate profession of faith, which was sent back to the French bishops along with a letter of recommendation.

ST. MELITO OF SARDIS

Died around 177. The bishop of Sardis (now Sart, Turkey). Little is known of his life. He was a prolific author, but most of his works are lost or survive only in quotations in other authors. One noted work was an *Apology for Christianity*, written to the Emperor Marcus Aurelius.

ST. METHODIUS OF PHILIPPI

Died around 311. The bishop of Philippi (modern Filippoi in Greece) and a strong opponent of Origen's teachings. He was martyred shortly before Constantine I established toleration for Christians. Most of his writings are lost.

MINUCIUS FELIX

Wrote around 226. A Roman layman and lawyer, he wrote a dialogue titled *Octavius* that is one of the oldest (if not the oldest) surviving Christian treatises in Latin.

NOVATIAN OF ROME

Died in 258. A prominent priest in Rome, he became an antipope following the election of Pope St. Cornelius. He then led a schismatic movement, the Novatians, which had rigorist tendencies but did not have substantively different theology. This movement survived for some centuries. Because he died a schismatic, Novatian is not considered a Church Father but an ecclesiastical writer.

ST. OPTATUS OF MILEVIS

Born around 320; died around 385. Bishop of Milevis (now Mila, Algeria). He wrote against the Donatists.

ORIGEN OF ALEXANDRIA

Born around 185; died around 253. One of the greatest scholars and biblical exegetes of Christian history. After St. Clement of Alexandria, he ran the catechetical school of that city. He was extremely influential in his own day and afterwards and played a foundational role in the practice of *lectio divina*. After controversy arose about him being allowed to preach as a layman, he was ordained a priest by two bishops in Palestine. This enraged his own bishop in Alexandria, who held councils deposing and excommunicating him. He moved to Caesarea in Palestine (now Caesarea Maritima, Israel), where he continued his catechetical work. It is reported that he castrated himself so that he could tutor women without suspicion of impropriety, but this is doubtful and may be a rumor spread by his critics. He had a lifelong desire to be a martyr. His father was a martyr, and his mother once hid Origen's clothes to keep him from leaving the house and turning himself in to the authorities as a Christian. Though not martyred, late in life he was imprisoned and tortured in the persecution of the Emperor Decius. He never fully recovered and died at Tyre in modern Lebanon. After his death, some of his ideas were the occasion of great controversies. These included his belief in the pre-existence of souls and his belief that all spirits would eventually be reconciled with God. Because of the controversies, Origen is not reckoned as a saint.

ST. PACIAN OF BARCELONA

Died around 385. Bishop of Barcelona in what is now Spain. St. Jerome dedicated his *Illustrious Men* to Pacian's son and lists Pacian among the illustrious men.

ST. PAPIAS OF HIERAPOLIS

Wrote around 130. Bishop of Hierapolis (now Pamukkale, Turkey) and friend of St. Polycarp of Smyrna. He conducted extensive interviews with those who had directly heard the apostles' preaching. As a result he wrote an *Explanation of the Sayings of the Lord*. Though only fragments of it survive, it contains valuable information about the early Church.

ST. PATRICK

Born around 387; died around 460 (or 493, according to some sources). His Latin name was Patricius. Born to Roman parents in the west of Great Britain, Patrick was captured by pirates and taken to Ireland, where he was sold as a slave. Following a private revelation, he escaped and, following another private revelation, he returned to Ireland as a missionary bishop. His mission was authorized by Pope St. Celestine I. He is buried at Downpatrick, County Down, Ireland.

PECTORIUS OF AUTUN

Died around 375. Pectorius was a Christian living in modern Autun, France. His grave featured an inscription similar in wording and importance to that of St. Abercius of Hierapolis.

ST. PETER CHRYSOLOGUS

Born around 405; died around 450. A Doctor of the Church. Originally from Forum Cornelii (now Imola, Italy), he became the archbishop of Ravenna (also in modern Italy). His nickname "Chrysologus" means "golden-worded" and refers to his preaching, though it may not have been used during his lifetime.

ST. PETER OF ALEXANDRIA

Died around 311. Bishop of Alexandria and former head of that city's catechetical school. He was opposed to the teachings of Origen and was martyred in the persecution started by the Emperor Diocletian.

ST. PIONIUS OF SMYRNA

Died around 250. A Christian martyred during the persecution of Emperor Decius at Smyrna (now Izmir, Turkey). Guided by a private revelation, he found an age-worn edition of *The Martyrdom of Polycarp* and had it copied.

ST. POLYCARP OF SMYRNA

Born around 68; died around 155. Bishop of Smyrna (now Izmir, Turkey). He was a hearer of the apostle John. One of St. Ignatius of Antioch's letters is addressed to him, and he himself wrote to the Philippians. An account of his martyrdom—*The Martyrdom of Polycarp*—is an important work of hagiography.

ST. PROSPER OF AQUITAINE

Died after 455. A layman and monk from the Aquitaine region of what is now France, Prosper was an opponent of the Semi-Pelagianism that had broken out in the area. He wrote St. Augustine, though he did not know him personally. Later he served at Rome under Pope St. Leo I.

PSEUDO–IGNATIUS

Probably wrote in the 300s. A number of letters were historically ascribed to St. Ignatius of Antioch, though they were actually written by someone after his time. This person, referred to as Pseudo-Ignatius, may have been the same person who in the fourth century produced the longer versions of Ignatius's authentic letters. There also may have been more than one person who composed the Pseudo-Ignatian letters. Despite the fact that they are not genuinely from Ignatius, they serve as witnesses to beliefs and practices in the age of the Fathers.

PSEUDO–JOHN

Wrote around 550. An unknown author writing in the persona of St. John the Evangelist. He composed an account of the Assumption of Mary.

PSEUDO–JUSTIN

Probably wrote in the 200s under the name of St. Justin Martyr. Composed the *Hortatory Address to the Greeks* arguing for Christianity over paganism. Noted for his superior literary style.

PSEUDO–MELITO

Wrote around 475. An unknown author writing in the persona of Melito of Sardis. He composed an account of the Assumption of Mary.

ST. SECHNALL OF IRELAND

Died around 447. His Latin name was Secundinus. Bishop and missionary to Ireland, he founded a church in what is now Dunshauglin, County Meath, Ireland. A contemporary of St. Patrick and the composer of a famous hymn in praise of the latter.

ST. SERAPION OF THMUIS

Wrote around 350. Bishop of Thmuis (now Tell el-Timai, Egypt) and friend of St. Athanasius of Alexandria. He was the author of a sacramentary or book of prayers used in the celebration of the sacraments.

POPE ST. SIRICIUS I

Reigned from 384 to 399. The successor of Pope St. Damasus, Siricius was an active pope who issued decrees on a variety of matters. He was a friend of St. Ambrose and held a council in Rome that condemned the monk Jovinian, who (ironically) was an opponent of asceticism.

SOZOMEN OF CONSTANTINOPLE

Wrote around 444. A layman born in Bethelia (near modern Gaza City in the Gaza Strip). He later traveled for his education and settled in Constantinople, where he practiced law and wrote two books covering the history of the Church down to his own day.

TATIAN THE SYRIAN

Wrote around 170. Originally a pagan, Tatian was a native of Syria who became a Christian. He went to Rome and was a student of St. Justin Martyr. Temperamentally, Tatian was an extremist. In 172 he went back to the Middle East and founded a heretical sect known as the Aquarii (Greek, "Water-ites") because they refused all use of wine, even in the celebration of the Eucharist, insisting on water. They also forbade marriage. Nevertheless, Tatian produced an important harmony of the four Gospels known as the *Diatesseron* (from the Greek for "through four") and an *Address to the Greeks* in which he attacked Greek religion and culture.

TERTULLIAN OF CARTHAGE

Born around 157; died around 245. He was a native of Carthage (now a suburb of Tunis, Tunisia) and a layman, though there are some reports that he became a priest. He was the first major Christian author to write in Latin, and his works contain much valuable information on this period in Christian history. Unfortunately, Tertullian gradually became more and more rigorist, drifting from the Catholic Church and ultimately becoming a Montanist. Some of his followers remained until the fourth century, when they were converted by St. Augustine.

THEODORE OF MOPSUESTIA

Born around 350; died around 428. He was born at Antioch in Syria (modern Antakya, Turkey) but became bishop of Mopsuestia in Cilicia (now Yakapinar, Turkey). He was a friend of St. John Chrysostom. After his death, he fell under suspicion of Nestorianism (though he lived before the Nestorian controversy). The Second Council of Constantinople condemned his person and writings as part of the "Three Chapters" controversy. This tarnished his reputation, and thus he is not a saint. Modern scholars tend to doubt that he was guilty of Nestorianism.

THEODORET OF CYR

Born around 393; died around 466. A native of Antioch in Syria (modern Antakya, Turkey), he was reluctantly ordained bishop of Cyr (also called Cyrus and Cyrrhus), which today is a ruin a little north of Kilis, Turkey, near the Syrian border. He played an important role in the Nestorian and Monophysite controversies. He was deposed by the "Robber Council" or "Council of Thieves" held in Ephesus in 449, but Pope St. Leo I declared its results null. Theodoret participated in the Council of Chalcedon, but the Second Council of Constantinople condemned certain of his writings as part of the "Three Chapters" controversy.

ST. THEOPHILUS OF ANTIOCH

Died around 188. He was an adult convert to Christianity who became the seventh bishop of Antioch (modern Antakya, Turkey).

His only surviving work is an apologetic treatise entitled *To Auto-lycus.*

TIMOTHY OF JERUSALEM

Wrote sometime between 300 and 700. A priest of Jerusalem who gave a homily referring to the death and Assumption of Mary. His dates are disputed. Martin Jugie assigns him to the fourth or fifth century, while Bernard Capelle argues for the sixth or seventh centuries.

ST. VICTORINUS OF PETTAU

Died around 303. The bishop of Pettau (now Ptuj, Slovenia). He wrote commentaries on Scripture, as well as works against heresies. Today his writing survives only in fragments.

ST. VINCENT OF LERINS

Died around 445. He was a priest and monk at the monastery on the island of Lerins (modern Ile Saint-Honorat, off the French Riviera). Despite the fact that he appears to have had Semi-Pelagian views (common for the time in his area), he is held in considerable esteem today and is noted for his statement that Christian doctrine is to be interpreted in accord with Christian Tradition, which is what has been believed "everywhere, always, by everyone" among faithful Christians.

10. Know Your Councils

This section provides short descriptions of the various councils and synods that are quoted in this work.[1]

Most councils are "regional." These gather bishops from a particular region and produce results binding on only that region.

---

[1] In the ancient world, the terms "council" (Latin, *concilium*) and "synod" (Greek, *sunodos*) were used interchangeably. Later they took on slightly different meanings. To prevent confusion they are all referred to in this book as "councils." Other works will refer to some of these same events as synods.

Some councils are "ecumenical." These seek to gather a large number of bishops from a broader range of the Christian world. With the consent of the pope, their results are binding for the whole Church.

ANKARA

A regional council held shortly after Easter in 314 in what is now Ankara, Turkey (then capital of the Roman province of Galatia, now capital of Turkey). It dealt with how to handle the cases of Christians who had committed various sins during the recent persecution of the Church, which had just ended. It also dealt with various other sins and the penances to be assigned to them. Also known as the Council of Ancyra.

CARTHAGE OF 256

Presided over by St. Cyprian in Carthage (now a suburb of Tunis, Tunisia). Most famous for dealing with the issue of baptisms performed by heretics.[2]

CARTHAGE OF 397

Presided over by Bishop Aurelius of Carthage. Most famous for dealing with the canon of Scripture.

CARTHAGE OF 401

Presided over by St. Aurelius, bishop of Carthage. Held in two sessions—June and September (sometimes reckoned as separate councils). Quotations in Part Two are from the latter.

CARTHAGE OF 419

Also presided over by St. Aurelius. It approved a collection of legal canons known as the *African Code*.

---

[2] A series of regional councils were held in Carthage. In this work several of them are quoted. Unfortunately, there is no agreed upon way to number these councils (first, second, third, etc.). To avoid confusion they are identified by the years in which they occurred.

CHALCEDON

The fourth ecumenical council. Held in 451 in the city of Chalcedon (now within the city of Istanbul, Turkey). Most famous for defining that Christ has two natures—divine and human—that are united but distinct.

CONSTANTINOPLE I

The second ecumenical council. Held in 381 in the city of Constantinople (now Istanbul). Most famous for defining the divinity of the Holy Spirit and writing the final part of the *Niceno-Constantinopolitan ("Nicene") Creed* that is said at Mass.

CONSTANTINOPLE II

The fifth ecumenical council. Held in 553 in the city of Constantinople. Condemned the "Three Chapters" (i.e., the person and writings of Theodore of Mopsuestia, certain writings of Theodoret of Cyr, and a letter of Ibas of Edessa).

CONSTANTINOPLE III

The sixth ecumenical council. Held from 680 to 681 in the city of Constantinople. Condemned the heresy of Monothelitism.

ELVIRA

A regional council probably held in the year 300, though possibly slightly later, in the city of Elvira (in or near Granada, Spain). Issued a variety of canons.

EPHESUS

The third ecumenical council. Held in 431 in Ephesus (near Selçuk, Turkey). Most famous for defining that Mary may be called *Theotokos* ("God-bearer" or "Mother of God").

HIPPO

A regional council held in 393 in Hippo Regius, the see of St. Augustine (modern Annaba, Algeria). Most famous for dealing with the canon of Scripture. Several additional councils were later held at Hippo, but quotations in Part Two are from the first.

LAODICEA

A regional council held around 360 in Laodicea (in modern Denizli Province, Turkey). Issued a variety of canons.

NICAEA I

The first ecumenical council. Held in 325 in the city of Nicaea (modern Iznik, Turkey). Most famous for defining the divinity of Christ against the Arians and writing the majority of the *Niceno-Constantinopolitan ("Nicene") Creed* that is said at Mass.

NICAEA II

The seventh ecumenical council. Held in 787 in the city of Nicaea (modern Iznik, Turkey). Most famous for opposing the Iconoclast heresy by defining the legitimate use of icons.

ORANGE II

A regional council held in 529 in the city of Orange in modern France. Most famous for dealing with the Pelagian heresy. An earlier council was held in Orange in 441, but quotations in Part Two are from the later one.

ROME

A regional council held in Rome in 382 under Pope St. Damasus I. This council affirmed papal primacy and dealt with the canon of Scripture before the councils of Hippo and Carthage.

SARDICA

A regional council held around 343 in the city of Sardica (now Sophia, Bulgaria). It was called to deal with problems related to the Arian crisis.

11. Know Your Writings

This section offers short descriptions of additional writings quoted in this work. They are either by an unknown author or they do not have a single author, as with the creeds.

ACTS OF PAUL AND THECLA

An example of what appears to be early Christian fiction. Written around 160, *The Acts of Paul and Thecla* provides additional stories of St. Paul, besides those mentioned in the book of Acts. It includes an account of his martyrdom at Rome as well as the only known description of him from antiquity. Though it is difficult to know how much of the book has a historical basis, it describes Paul as "a man small in size, bald-headed, bandy-legged, well-built, with eyebrows meeting, rather long-nosed, full of grace. For sometimes he seemed like a man, and sometimes he had the countenance of an angel." It possibly was written at Iconium (Konya, in modern Turkey). Tertullian reports that its author was a priest who said he wrote it "for the love of Paul," but who nevertheless lost his position over the book.

ACTS OF XANTHIPPE AND POLYXENA

Another example of early Christian fiction. Written around 250, it tells thrilling adventure stories about two sisters in Spain (the title characters) and their conversions to Christ, and is set during the ministry of the apostles, several of whom appear in the stories. Sometimes known as the *Acts of Xanthippe and Polyxena and Rebecca* (the latter being a minor character in the story).

AFRICAN CODE

A collection of legal canons promulgated by various regional councils in North Africa. Dealing primarily with matters of church governance, they were gathered together and reaffirmed by the Council of Carthage of 419.

APOCALYPSE OF PETER

A non-canonical apocalypse written around 135. In it, St. Peter receives a vision of both heaven and hell. Known for its vivid depictions of the punishments for different kinds of sinners. Also known as the Revelation of Peter. Not to be confused with a similarly titled work, the *Gnostic Apocalypse of Peter*.

APOSTOLIC CONSTITUTIONS

Compiled around 400, the *Apostolic Constitutions* contain a large amount of legal and liturgical material. It is presented as coming from the apostles and as having been compiled and distributed by Pope St. Clement I, but this is a fiction. The first six of the eight books of the work are an expanded version of the *Didascalia*, and the seventh book is based on the *Didache*. The overall collection was very influential in Church history.

ASCENSION OF ISAIAH

This work may be a Christian revision of an earlier Jewish work. Written around 90, it tells the story of the martyrdom of the prophet Isaiah. It also contains accounts of prophetic visions of the coming of Jesus (expressly so-named in the text) and the end of the age.

ATHANASIAN CREED

An important creed written around 425. The author is unknown, but it was often attributed to St. Athanasius of Alexandria because it reflects the Trinitarian theology he vigorously defended. It is also sometimes called the Pseudo-Athanasian Creed.

EARLY CHRISTIAN INSCRIPTION

Archaeology has uncovered a significant number of early Christian inscriptions, chiefly on tombs, and they shed light on the belief and practice of early Christians. Several inscriptions written in the early centuries are quoted in Part Two. These are taken from the collection *Christian Inscriptions* by H. P. V. Nunn, which provides a convenient numbering system for them (see Translations Used).

CLEMENTINE HOMILIES

Written around 290. A didactic novel based on the supposed life of Pope St. Clement I, who is the title character. Its intent was to present the reader with theological and apologetic information in the form of homilies by St. Peter, which Clement allegedly witnessed. It appears to be based on an earlier document about the life of Clement, written perhaps around 220, into which the homilies have been inserted. The homilies display ideas like those of the heretical Ebionites. See also: *Clementine Recognitions, Letter of Clement to James.*

CLEMENTINE RECOGNITIONS

Written around 320. A didactic novel very similar to the *Clementine Homilies* that appears to be based on the same earlier document about the life of Clement. The narrative passages of the two often agree word-for-word, though the *Recognitions* tells a somewhat more elaborate story in which Clement's family members are sequentially re-discovered and recognized (hence the title of the work). The homiletic material in the work is more orthodox and expressly endorses the Trinity. It was translated from Greek into Latin by Rufinus of Aquileia between 390 and 410. Together the *Homilies* and *Recognitions* are known as the *Clementines* or *Pseudo-Clementines*. There is a great deal of disagreement about their precise relationship and dating. The dates offered here, like those of many early documents of unknown authors, are educated guesses.

DIDACHE

Written around the year 50, this is an early Christian manual describing morality, liturgy, and certain Church teachings. Written in the age when apostles and prophets were still prominent in the Church and before the three-fold ministry of bishop, priest, and deacon had been fully developed. Its name comes from the fact that it is supposed to represent the teaching (Greek, *didache*, pronounced "DID-ah-KAY" in English) of the twelve apostles, though the text does not claim to be written by them. Despite the valuable window it gives us into first century Christianity, it is not among the canonical scriptures. Also known as *The Teaching of the Twelve Apostles.*

DIDASCALIA

Written around 225 and influenced by the *Didache*, this is a Church manual offering legal and liturgical insights into the era in which it was written. The word *didascalia* is a synonym for *didache*, and so the work is also presented as the teaching of the twelve apostles. Also known as the *Didascalia of the Twelve Apostles.* It was later updated as the *Apostolic Constitutions.*

LETTER OF BARNABAS

One of the earliest Christian documents outside the New Testament. It was likely written around A.D. 75, though some place it in the first half of the second century. It is the earliest surviving document to refer to the destruction of the temple in Jerusalem (A.D. 70) as a past event. It argues for Christianity as the fulfillment of Judaism using an allegorical method. St. Clement of Alexandria and others interpreted it as the work of the apostle Barnabas, the companion of St. Paul, but today this is thought very unlikely. Its author is sometimes called "Pseudo-Barnabas" (i.e., "False Barnabas") as a result. Other have held it to be the work of an otherwise unknown author, Barnabas of Alexandria.

LETTER OF CLEMENT TO JAMES

Written around 290. A fictional letter ostensibly written by Pope St. Clement I to St. James, bishop of Jerusalem, informing him of the death of Peter and his own ordination as the bishop of Rome. It serves as a preface to the *Clementine Homilies.*

MARTYRDOM OF PERPETUA AND FELICITY

Written around 203. A famous account of the sufferings of Ss. Perpetua and Felicity and their companions, who lived at Carthage (now a suburb of Tunis, Tunisia). It is remarkable in that much of the text is taken from Perpetua's own diary, as well as the writings of others who were present.

MARTYRDOM OF POLYCARP

Written around 156, this document tells the story of the arrest and martyrdom of St. Polycarp, bishop of Smyrna. It is the oldest surviving contemporary account of a martyrdom outside of the New Testament.

MURATORIAN FRAGMENT

Written around 178. One of the earliest lists of the books in the biblical canon. It exists in fragmentary form (both the beginning and ending of the document are missing). It is so-named because it was discovered by the historian Fr. Ludovico Antonio Muratori (1672–1750) in the Ambrosian Library in Milan.

ODES OF SOLOMON

Written around 125. A collection of early Christian poems or hymns. Not to be confused with the Psalms of Solomon, a similar work of Jewish origin with which they were sometimes bound.

ON THE END OF THE WORLD

Date uncertain. This lengthy discourse has historically been attributed to St. Hippolytus of Rome, but modern scholarship doubts this, and it is often attributed to an unknown Pseudo-Hippolytus. Not to be confused with the authentic writings of Hippolytus which also deal with the end of the world and the Antichrist. If it is by Hippolytus, contrary to what is commonly thought, it would date to the early 200s. If it is by another hand, perhaps a hundred years later. In the date estimate in Part Two, the difference is split.

POEM AGAINST THE MARCIONITES

Written around 285. An anonymous poem critiquing the Marcionites. It is influenced by the writings of Tertullian of Carthage and was sometimes wrongly attributed to him.

PROTOEVANGELIUM OF JAMES

Written around 150. A narrative describing the events leading up to the birth of Christ and a defense of the perpetual virginity of Mary. The unknown author writes in the persona of James, who is presented in the work as the Lord's stepbrother via Joseph. While non-canonical, it has had a powerful effect on Mariology and Christian art and tradition. "Protoevangelium" means "first gospel"—a reference to its account of events occurring before those of the canonical Gospels. Also called the *Gospel of James*, *Book of James*, and *Infancy Gospel of James*.

RYLANDS PAPYRUS 470

Written about 250 or 300. It contains a Greek version of the Marian prayer/hymn known as the *Sub Tuum Praesidium* (Latin, "Under your protection"). It includes the title *Theotokos* ("God-bearer," "Mother of God"), which would be controversial in the Nestorian conflict of the early 400s. Some claim that the handwriting of the prayer suggests it was copied about 250. Even if the specific papyrus is dated to 300 (or later), the fact that it was an established hymn suggests that it was in use even earlier.

SECOND CLEMENT

Though often described as the second letter of Clement to the Corinthians, this work actually is not a letter, nor is it by Pope St. Clement I. It is a homily, possibly composed at Corinth. Similarities concerning the Church's penitential discipline suggest it may have been written around the same time as *The Shepherd* of Hermas, which is commonly dated about 150. However, following Robinson, I think Hermas of Rome wrote around 80 and suggest a similar date for *Second Clement*. Also known as the *Second Letter of Clement*.

TO DIOGNETUS

Written between 125 and 200. An anonymous work of Christian apologetics directed to a prominent official (Diognetus, though that name may be a pseudonym to mask the recipient's identity). There are many theories regarding who wrote it and who the recipient was.

TREATISE ON RE-BAPTISM

Written around 257. A treatise that appears to be written by an unknown, probably African, bishop during the controversy over whether heretical baptisms were valid. It critiqued the position of St. Cyprian of Carthage and (ironically) was preserved along with copies of his writings.

12. Know Your Heresies

This chapter offers brief descriptions of various heresies and schisms that were active during the period of the Church Fathers.

A heresy, as the term is used in this book, is the refusal to accept a point of doctrine that has been revealed by God and infallibly defined by the Church.

A schism, by contrast, does not deny such doctrines but breaks communion with the Church and operates independently.

Note that because of the way doctrine develops, a person in one age can entertain views later declared heretical without himself being classified as a heretic (i.e., in his own day the view was permitted; it was later doctrinal development that showed it to be incompatible with the Christian faith).

ADOPTIONISM

According to this view, Jesus was simply a man who was adopted as the Son of God—an event typically identified with his baptism. It is a form of Monarchianism and is sometimes termed "dynamic Monarchianism."

APOLLINARISM

Founded by Apollinarius the Younger, bishop of Laodicaea (in modern Denizli Province, Turkey) in the late 300s. It was condemned at the First Council of Constantinople in 381. This view held that Christ had a human body and the human ability to think, feel, experience hunger and pain, etc., but no human mind. Instead, he had only a divine mind. Since this position held that Christ does not have two complete natures but rather a combination of the two, it is a form of Monophysitism. The correct position is that Christ has both a divine mind and a human mind because he has both a complete divine nature and a complete human nature.

AQUARII

Founded by Tatian the Syrian in the late second century. The name means "Water-ites." This sect forbade the use of wine, even in the Eucharist, as well as marriage and the eating of meat.

ARIANISM

Founded by Arius, a priest of Alexandria, Egypt, in the early 300s. Arius held that originally the Son of God did not exist. There was a time in which there was a single divine Person who became the Father when he created the Son out of nothing. The Son was the first of all created beings and thus separate from the Father in being. The heresy was condemned at the first ecumenical council— Nicaea I in 325—but the controversy intensified and lasted much longer.

DOCETISM

This view held that Jesus did not really have a body, that he was a supernatural being who only appeared to have one. The name comes from the Greek word *dokein* ("to appear," "to seem"). The view appears to have existed in the first century, and some passages in the New Testament may be meant to refute it (Lk 24:37–43; Jn 1:14; 1 Jn 1:1; 4:1–3; 2 Jn 7). It was definitely present in the early 100s, when St. Ignatius of Antioch wrote against it, and it continued for some time, in conjunction with Gnosticism.

DONATISM

A schism that formed in North Africa in the early 300s. It takes its name from Donatus, bishop of Casae Nigrae (located south of modern Tebessa, Algeria) and later bishop of Carthage (now a suburb of Tunis, Tunisia). The schism concerned the proper treatment of those who had compromised the Christian faith during persecution. The Donatists held a rigorist attitude and deemed sacraments celebrated by compromised churchmen to be invalid. The schism lasted for some time and was combated a century later by St. Augustine.

EBIONITISM

A Jewish-Christian sect that originated in the first or second century. Its name is derived from the word *evyon* (Hebrew, "poor"). Its members held that the Mosaic Law was obligatory and that Jesus was not divine, not born of a Virgin, and did not die an atoning death. He was a purely human Messiah. This group rejected most of the New Testament (especially the writings of Paul) and used a mutilated form of Matthew's Gospel titled *The Gospel of the Hebrews*. Some Ebionites also held Gnostic ideas.

EUTYCHIANISM

See Monophysitism.

GNOSTICISM

A group of heretical movements that were influential mostly in the second and third centuries, though they lasted until later and traces of them existed even earlier. Their name comes from the Greek word *gnosis* ("knowledge"), and their adherents claimed to have a special knowledge of the divine, different than that possessed by orthodox Christians.

What that knowledge consisted of is somewhat difficult to say, as Gnostic groups held widely differing ideas. Some common themes in Gnostic circles were the ideas that the true God is remote and that the world was made by a lesser being known as the Demiurge (Greek, *demiourgos*, "artisan"), who fashioned an imperfect, pain-filled world.

The Demiurge was sometimes (not always) identified with the God of the Old Testament.

Often matter was said to be evil or a hindrance to the soul, with contradictory conclusions drawn by different Gnostic groups (e.g., that the body should be disciplined with asceticism or that the body doesn't matter so one can engage in any kind of licentious acts).

Gnostics wrote their own scriptures, with detailed, imaginative descriptions of how the cosmos came to be and how it works. These include works such as the so-called Gospels of Mary, Philip, and Judas Iscariot.

Despite these common elements, Gnosticism was broad and loosely knit, and it is not possible to list a single, simple set of beliefs that defined it.

ICONOCLASM

This view is opposed to the devotional use of images. Its name is derived from the Greek term *eikonoklasmos* ("image breaking"). Sometimes icons in churches were literally broken in Iconoclastic fervor. During the age of the Fathers, a period of Iconoclasm was initiated by the Emperor Leo III around 730. The controversy lasted some decades, and the Iconoclast position was condemned at the seventh ecumenical council, Nicaea II, in 787.

MACEDONIANISM

See Pneumatomachianism.

MANICHEANISM

Founded by the supposed prophet Mani, who was born in or near Seleucia-Ctesiphon (now a ruin called Al-Mada'in in Iraq). In the mid-200s, he founded a sect that claimed to be the fulfillment of a prophetic tradition including Buddha, Zoroaster, and Jesus. He taught an elaborate dualistic and Gnostic system of how the cosmos came to be, fusing elements of different religions. For a time, St. Augustine was a member of this sect before becoming a Christian.

MARCIONISM

Founded by Marcion of Sinope (now Sinop, Turkey). The son of the bishop of Sinope, Marcion had a falling out with his father and afterward traveled to Rome, where he set up his own sect in the mid-100s. He taught ideas common in Gnostic circles, though also quite different from many Gnostic teachings. He desired to strip Christianity of everything Jewish and produced his own set of scriptures by using only a mutilated version of Luke's Gospel and Paul's epistles, from which everything positive about Judaism and the Old Testament had been removed. He accepted the idea that the world was created by a Demiurge, a subordinate god identified with the God of the Old Testament, but who was distinct from the supreme, good God who he held to be the Father of Jesus Christ.

MODALISM

This view holds that the Father, Son, and Holy Spirit are not three Persons but three modes that a single divine Person exists in or experiences. These are often compared to how a single person can be a son, a husband, and a father, or how water can exist in liquid, solid, and gaseous states. It is often called Sabellianism because it was popularized by Sabellius, a priest in Rome who was excommunicated by Pope St. Callistus I in 220. This heresy is also called "modal Monarchianism" and "Patripassianism"—the latter because it implied that the Father suffered in the Passion of Jesus since the two are one Person.

MONARCHIANISM

This view holds that there is only one Person in the Godhead (the Father), who is the sole ruler of all creation. (The Greek term *monarchos* means "one source.") It can be understood different ways, resulting in different heresies—in particular, Modalism and Adoptionism. Not to be confused with the orthodox statement that the Father is the sole origin or *arche* of the Son and the Spirit, who proceed from him outside of time (see chapter 19, on the *Filioque* controversy).

MONOPHYSITISM

This view is the opposite of Nestorianism. Whereas the latter holds that Christ is two Persons, one human and one divine, this view holds that Christ is a single Person who has a single divine-human nature. Hence its name (Greek, *mono-* + *phusis*, "single nature").

There were different forms of Monophysitism. One form, such as that held by Apollinarius (see Apollinarism) held that Jesus' nature was a hybrid, with the divine mind taking the place of a human mind. Another form, named Eutychianism after Eutyches, a priest of Constantinople, held that the divine and human had fused in Christ the way a drop of liquid (representing the human) can be dissolved in the sea (representing the divine).

St. Cyril of Alexandria was sometimes thought to be a Monophysite, but this is based on a misreading of his writings.

Monophysitism was rejected by the fourth ecumenical council, the Council of Chalcedon, in 451, though "Monophysite" churches have survived down through history.

In recent decades there have been a number of joint statements between the Catholic Church and various Eastern churches that have historically been considered Monophysite. These statements have stressed that, regardless of past problems, the churches now profess the same understanding of Christ, even if they express themselves differently.

MONOTHELITISM

This is the view that Christ has a single will (Greek, *mono-* + *thelema*), which is divine. It was proposed in the 600s as a compromise position between Monophysitism and the orthodox understanding of Christ as formulated by the Council of Chalcedon. Monothelitism is mistaken because, if Christ has a complete divine nature and a complete human nature then he must have two wills, one divine and one human, even if these two wills are never in opposition to each other. Monothelitism was rejected at the sixth ecumenical council—Constantinople III, which met in 680 and 681.

MONTANISM

A schism founded in the mid-100s by Montanus of Pepuza (in what is now Usak Province, Turkey), who claimed to be a prophet. He issued revelations along with two supposed prophetesses, Maximilla and Priscilla (also called Prisca). The sect was rigorist and focused on ongoing prophecy. Its most famous adherent was Tertullian of Carthage, who became a Montanist after his Catholic period. By the time of St. Augustine, the sect had dwindled, and St. Augustine himself reconciled a congregation of Montanists in his area to the Church.

NESTORIANISM

Named after Nestorius, patriarch of Constantinople. This view holds that Christ was two people—a divine Person and a human person. Since only the latter was in Mary's womb, it would be inappropriate to refer to her as *Theotokos* ("God-bearer" or "Mother of God"). This heresy was condemned at the Council of Ephesus in 431, which asserted the correct position that Christ is one Person who has two natures—a divine nature and a human nature. Since mothers have persons rather than natures in their wombs, the Person of Christ was in her womb and she could be called *Theotokos*.

Ironically, it appears that Nestorius expressed himself badly and was not guilty of the heresy that bears his name. After he was deposed, he dwelled in a monastery in El-Kharga, Egypt, maintaining his orthodoxy. He died in communion with the Church.

In 1994 a common declaration was signed by Pope John Paul II and Mar Dinkha IV of the Assyrian Church of the East—one of the surviving "Nestorian" churches. This declaration stated that, whatever differences there may have been in the past, the two churches now find themselves professing the same understanding of Christ, even if it is articulated differently.

NOVATIANISM

A schism founded in the 250s by Novatian of Rome. It was a rigorist sect that opposed the readmission to communion of those who had lapsed during persecution. It also opposed second marriages.

ORIGENISM

A set of theological views attributed, accurately or inaccurately, to Origen of Alexandria. While not arousing any great controversy during his life, after his death these views became the object of great dispute. They included the idea that the soul, though created by God, exists before it is born in a body and that, ultimately, all—even demons—would be reconciled with God.

PATRIPASSIANISM

See Modalism.

PELAGIANISM

A set of heretical views espoused by Pelagius, a layman and monk who came from somewhere in the British Isles. He arrived in Rome sometime in the late 300s and continued his preaching there into the early 400s. His views included the claims that original sin did not fundamentally taint human nature (that Adam only set a bad example for us to follow), that newborn children are in the same state as Adam before the fall, that free will makes it possible to lead a sinless life without God's grace, and that Jesus merely set a good example for us to follow. St. Augustine strongly contested Pelagianism. It was condemned at the regional council of Orange II in 529.

PNEUMATOMACHIANISM

According to the meaning of their Greek name, the *Pneumatomachi* were "those who fight against the Spirit." This heresy denied the deity of the Holy Spirit. Also called "Macedonianism" after Patriarch Macedonius I of Constantinople (though, ironically, we have no evidence today that he had anything to do with this view). It was condemned by the first ecumenical council of Constantinople in 381, when the current section of the *Nicene Creed* concerning the Holy Spirit was written.

SABELLIANISM

See Modalism.

SEMI-ARIANISM

A failed attempt to find a middle ground between Arianism and Trinitarianism. Arians asserted that the Father, Son, and Spirit are three separate beings, while Trinitarianism holds that they are three Persons in one Being (or "Substance"), meaning that the Son is "of the same substance" (Greek, *homoousios*) with the Father. Semi-Arians tried to say that the Son was "of similar substance" (Greek, *homoiousios*) to the Father. This was verbal sleight of hand that didn't solve anything, but it did give rise to the expression "an iota of difference" (the Greek letter iota being the difference between *homoousios* and *homoiousios*).

SEMI-PELAGIANISM

A heresy founded by St. John Cassian, abbot of the monastery of St. Victor in Marseilles, France. Around 428, he and his fellow monks sought a middle way between Pelagianism and the teachings of St. Augustine. They didn't get the balance right and maintained, wrongly, that the beginning of faith can be achieved by free will without God's grace (though God's grace is necessary for achieving and growing faith itself), that human nature without grace can merit a certain claim on grace, and that final perseverance in the faith can be achieved by the just man in his own strength, without additional grace from God. These views were condemned at the regional council of Orange II in 529.

SUBORDINATIONISM

A group of heresies that hold that the Son and the Holy Spirit are subordinate to the Father in nature and being. This includes

Arianism as well as many strains of Gnosticism and other views that hold the Son and Spirit to be less than the Father in nature and being. Not to be confused with the view that the Son and Spirit are subordinate to the Father in their procession (the Son eternally proceeds from the Father and the Spirit from the Father and the Son) and in their missions (both do the will of the Father). It is their nature and being that are in question.

PART TWO

IV. God

13. The One True God

Though half of the world population today belongs to monotheistic religions—teaching the existence of one God—this was a very unusual position in the first century, when pagan polytheism —belief in multiple gods—was the norm.

Still, the early Christians were firmly monotheistic and were even willing to die as martyrs, recognizing—as Jesus taught in John 17:3—that "this is eternal life, that they know you—the only true God."

Despite this statement and numerous others concerning the existence of one—and only one—God, some quasi-Christian groups reject Jesus' teaching. Mormons, for example, claim that there is an innumerable number of gods and that new gods are being formed all the time. According to some Mormon sources, some gods are older than the Father, and according to all Mormon sources, human beings can eventually become gods.

This contradicts what God himself says in the book of Isaiah: "Is there a God besides me? . . . I know not any" (Is 44:8). "Before me no god was formed, nor shall there be any after me" (Is 43:10).

The following quotations show that the Church Fathers had a clear understanding of monotheism. The proposition that God is one constitutes one of the central tenets in the dogma of the Trinity. In coming chapters we see that the Fathers also taught the other aspects of the Trinity.

POPE ST. CLEMENT I

What do you think, beloved? Didn't Moses know beforehand that this would happen? Undoubtedly he did; but he acted thus, that there might be no sedition in Israel, and that the name of the true and only God might be glorified; to whom be glory forever and ever. Amen [*Letter to the Corinthians* 43:6 (A.D. 70)].

ST. IGNATIUS OF ANTIOCH

For the most divine prophets lived according to Christ Jesus. On this account they were persecuted, being inspired by his grace to fully convince the unbelieving that there is one God, who has manifested himself by Jesus Christ his Son, who is his eternal Word, who does not proceed from silence, and in all things pleased him that sent him [*Letter to the Magnesians* 8 (c. A.D. 110)].

ST. JUSTIN MARTYR

There will be no other God, Trypho, nor was there from eternity any other . . . but he who made this universe. Nor do we think that there is one God for us and another for you, but that he alone is God who led your fathers out of Egypt with a strong hand and a high arm. Nor have we trusted in any other, for there is no other, but him, in whom you also have trusted, the God of Abraham, and of Isaac, and of Jacob [*Dialogue with Trypho* 11 (c. A.D. 155)].

ST. IRENAEUS OF LYONS

The Church, though dispersed throughout the whole world, even to the ends of the earth, has received from the apostles and their disciples this faith: [She believes] in one God, the Father Almighty, maker of heaven, and earth, and the sea, and all things that are in them; and in one Christ Jesus, the Son of God [*Against Heresies* 1:10:1 (c. A.D. 189)].

Nothing was either above him or after him; nor was he influenced by anyone, but of his own free will he created all things, since he is the only God, the only Lord, the only Creator, the only Father, alone containing all things, and himself commanding all things into existence [ibid., 2:1:1].

His will is the substance of all things, then he is discovered to be the one and only God who created all things, who alone is omnipotent, and who is the only Father rounding and forming all things, visible and invisible, those that may be perceived by our senses and those that cannot, heavenly and earthly, "by the word of his power" [Heb 1:3]; and he has fitted and arranged all things by his wisdom, while he contains all things, he himself can be contained by no one: he is the former, he the builder, he the discoverer, he the Creator, he the Lord of all [ibid., 2:30:9].

TERTULLIAN OF CARTHAGE

The object of our worship is the one God, who, by the word of his command, by the reason of his plan, and by the strength of his power has brought forth from nothing this whole construction of elements, bodies, and spirits for the glory of his majesty; which is why the Greeks have bestowed upon the world the name "cosmos" [*Apology* 17 (A.D. 197)].

[T]here is only one God, and he is none other than the Creator of the world, who produced all things out of nothing through his own Word, first of all sent forth [*Prescription Against Heretics* 13 (c. A.D. 200)].

We do indeed believe that there is only one God, but we believe that under this dispensation, or, as we say, "divine economy," there is also a Son of this one and only God, his Word, who proceeded from him and through whom all things were made and without whom nothing was made [*Against Praxeas* 2 (c. A.D. 218)].

ORIGEN OF ALEXANDRIA

The specific points that are clearly handed down through the apostolic preaching are these: First, that there is one God who created and arranged all things, and who, when nothing existed, called all things into existence, and that in the final period this God, just as he had promised through the prophets, sent the Lord Jesus

Christt. . . . Secondly, that Jesus Christ himself, who came, was
born of the Father before all creatures; and after he had ministered
to the Father in the creation of all things. . . . Then, thirdly, the
apostles related that the Holy Spirit was associated in honour and
dignity with the Father and the Son [*Fundamental Doctrines* Preface
4 (C. A.D. 225)].

ST. HIPPOLYTUS OF ROME

The one God, the first and only, both Creator and Lord of all
things, had nothing co-eternal. . . . No, he was one, to himself
alone. And when he so willed, he created those things that before
had no existence other than in his will to make them and in so
far as he had knowledge of what would be, for he also has foreknowledge [*Refutation of All Heresies* 10:28 (C. A.D. 227)].

NOVATIAN OF ROME

We must therefore believe, according to the rule prescribed, in
the Lord, the one true God, and consequently in him whom he
has sent, Jesus Christ, who would not have linked himself to the
Father if he did not wish to be understood to be God also, for he
would have separated himself from him if he did not wish to be
understood to be God [*The Trinity* 16 (c. A.D. 235)].

Thus God the Father, the founder and Creator of all things, who
knows no beginning, invisible, infinite, immortal, eternal, is one
God; to whose greatness, or majesty, or power nothing can be
compared; of whom, when he willed it, the Son, the Word, was
born. . . . [H]e then, since he was begotten of the Father, is always in the Father. And I thus say that I may show him not to
be unborn, but born. But he who is before all time must be said
to have been always in the Father; for no time can be assigned to
him who is before all time [ibid., 31].

PSEUDO-JUSTIN

[God] himself by his own prophets testifies when he says, "I,
God, am the first," and after this, "And beside me there is no

other God" [Is 44:6]. On this account, then, God did not mention any name when he sent Moses to the Hebrews, but by a participle he mystically taught them that he is the one and only God [*Hortatory Address to the Greeks* 21 (c. A.D. 250)].

ST. GREGORY THAUMATURGUS

We therefore acknowledge one true God, the one first cause, and one Son, very God of very God, possessing by nature the Father's divinity—that is to say, being the same in substance with the Father; and one Holy Spirit, who by nature and in truth sanctifies all, and makes divine, as being also of the substance of God. Those who speak either of the Son or of the Holy Spirit as a creature we anathematize [*Sectional Confession of Faith* 15 (c. A.D. 256)].

There is one God. . . . There is a perfect Trinity, in glory and eternity and sovereignty, neither divided nor estranged. Therefore there is nothing either created or in servitude in the Trinity; or anything added on, as if at some former period it was nonexistent, and at some later period it was introduced. And thus neither was the Son ever wanting to the Father, nor the Spirit to the Son; but the same Trinity abides ever without variation and without change [*Declaration of Faith* (c. A.D. 265)].

CLEMENTINE HOMILIES

[T]he Scripture says, "As I live, says the Lord, there is no other God but me. I am the first, I am after this; except me there is no god" [Is 44:6]. And again: "You shall fear the Lord your God, and him only shall you serve" [Dt 6:13; Mt 4:10]. And again: "Hear, O Israel, the Lord your God is one Lord" [Dt 6:4]. And many other passages seal with an oath that God is one, and except him there is no God [*Clementine Homilies* 16:7 (c. A.D. 290)].

CLEMENTINE RECOGNITIONS

[T]hough there are many that are called gods, there is but one true God, according to the testimonies of the Scriptures [*Clementine Recognitions* 3:75 (c. A.D. 320)].

COUNCIL OF NICAEA I

We believe in one God, the Father Almighty, maker of all things visible and invisible [*Nicene Creed* (A.D. 325)].

PSEUDO-IGNATIUS

There is then one God and Father, and not two or three; one who is, and there is no other besides him, the only true [God]. For "the Lord your God," says [the Scripture], "is one Lord" [Dt 6:4]. . . . And there is also one Son, God the Word. . . . And there is also one Paraclete [*Letter to the Philippians* 2 (c. A.D. 350)].

ST. PATRICK

[T]here is no other God, nor has there been before now, nor will there be hereafter, except God the Father unbegotten, without beginning, from whom is all beginning, upholding all things, and his Son Jesus Christ, whom we also confess to have been with the Father always—before the world's beginning. . . . Jesus Christ is the Lord and God in whom we believe . . . and who has poured out the Holy Spirit on us abundantly . . . whom we confess and adore as one God in the Trinity of the sacred name [*Confession of St. Patrick* 4 (c. A.D. 452)].

ST. FULGENCE OF RUSPE

True religion consists in the service of the one true God. That God is one, is truth itself. And just as without that one truth there is no other truth, so also without the one true God there is no other true God. For that one truth is one divinity. And so we cannot say that there are two true gods, just as truth cannot be divided [*Letters* 8:10 (c. A.D. 519)].

GOD HAS NO BODY

14. God Has No Body

Certain groups, notably the Mormons, assert that God the Father has a body. In recent years, this claim has been found among certain American Protestant groups, particularly in the Pentecostal world. Evangelicals such as Finnis Dake, Jimmy Swaggart, Kenneth Copeland, and Benny Hinn have all (at least on occasion) taught this.

People taking this position might point out that man is made in the image of God (Gn 1:26–27) and that there are verses that refer to the strong right arm of God, his all-seeing eyes, and so forth.

This is a misunderstanding that doesn't appreciate the use of metaphor in Scripture. References to God's strong arm, his eyes, and such, are metaphors referring to God's power and knowledge. They are not to be taken literally any more than Scripture's references to God having feathers and wings (e.g., Ps 91:4—"He will cover you with his feathers, and under his wings you will find refuge").

Other verses make the immaterial nature of God clear. In John 4:24 Jesus teaches, "God is spirit, and those who worship him must worship in spirit and truth." Elsewhere he notes, "a spirit has not flesh and bones" (Lk 24:39).

There is a difference between being a spirit and having a spirit. Jesus indicates that the Father is a spirit, not that he merely has one. This implies that he lacks a body and is an entirely spiritual being.

The Church Fathers taught the same, recognizing that God is an unchangeable, immaterial spirit who has an entirely simple ("incomposite") nature—that is, a nature containing no parts. This in itself means that God does not have a body, because all bodies extend through space and thus can be divided into parts. If God cannot be divided into parts then he cannot have a body.

This refers, of course, to God's essence as a spiritual being. It is quite possible for him to take on a human nature, and with it a body, the way the Son did by becoming incarnate. But Christ's human body was not something essential to his divine nature. In his divinity, the Son—like the Father and the Spirit—is entirely immaterial.

TATIAN THE SYRIAN

Our God did not begin to be in time: He alone is without beginning, and he himself is the beginning of all things. God is a Spirit [Jn 4:24], not pervading matter, but the maker of material spirits, and of the forms that are in matter; he is invisible, impalpable, being himself the Father of visible and invisible things [*Address to the Greeks* 4 (c. A.D. 170)].

ATHENAGORAS OF ATHENS

That we are not atheists—as we acknowledge one God, uncreated, eternal, invisible, impassible, incomprehensible, illimitable, who is apprehended only by the understanding and the reason, who is encompassed by light, and beauty, and spirit, and power ineffable, by whom the universe has been created through his *Logos*, and set in order, and is kept in being—I have sufficiently demonstrated [*Plea for the Christians* 10 (c. A.D. 177)].

ST. IRENAEUS OF LYONS

For the Father of all is far from the affections and passions that operate among men. He is a simple being, not compounded together, without diverse members, and completely like and equal to himself, since he is wholly understanding, and wholly spirit, and wholly thought, and wholly intelligence, and wholly reason, and wholly hearing, and wholly seeing, and wholly light, and the whole source of all that is good—just as the religious and pious speak about God [*Against Heresies* 2:13:3 (c. A.D. 189)].

ST. CLEMENT OF ALEXANDRIA

The first substance is everything that subsists by itself, as a stone is called a substance. The second is a substance capable of increase, as a plant grows and decays. The third is animated and sentient substance, as an animal, a horse. The fourth is animate, sentient, rational substance, as man. Therefore each one of us is made of all, having an immaterial soul and a mind, which is the image of God [fragment from *On Providence* (c. A.D. 200)].

Being is in God. God is divine being, eternal and without beginning, unbodied and limitless, and the cause of what exists. Being is what wholly subsists. Nature is the truth of things, or their inner reality. According to others, it is the production of what has come into existence; and according to still others, it is the providence of God that causes the being, and the manner of being, in the things that are produced [ibid.].

What is God? "God," as the Lord says, "is a spirit." Now spirit is properly substance, incorporeal and without limit. What does not consist of a body, or whose existence is not according to breadth, length, and depth, is incorporeal. What has no place, what is wholly in all, and in each entire, and the same in itself, is limitless [ibid.].

No one can correctly express him wholly. Because of his greatness he is ranked as the all, and is the Father of the universe. Nor are there any parts of him. For the One is indivisible; therefore it is also infinite, and without dimensions, and not having a limit. And therefore it is without form and name [*Miscellanies* 5:12 (c. A.D. 207)].

ORIGEN OF ALEXANDRIA

Though our understanding is unable to behold God as he is, it knows the Father of the world from the beauty of his works and the comeliness of his creatures. God, therefore, is not to be thought of as being a body or existing in a body, but as a uncompounded intellectual nature, admitting in himself no addition of any kind [*Fundamental Doctrines* 1:1:6 (c. A.D. 225)].

John, in his Gospel, when asserting that "no one has seen God at any time," declares to all who are capable of understanding that there is no nature to which God is visible: he is not a being who is visible by nature, but escaped or baffled the view of a frailer creature; by the nature of his being it is impossible for him to be seen [ibid. 1:1:8].

First it must be remembered that God is incorporeal. He does not consist of certain parts and distinct members, making up one body. For we read in the Gospel that God is a spirit: invisible, therefore, and an eternal nature, immeasurable and self-sufficient. It is also written that a spirit does not have flesh and bones. Of these the members of a body consist, and of these the substance of God has no need. God, however, who is everywhere and in all things, is all-hearing, all-seeing, all-doing, and all-assisting [*Commentaries on the Psalms* 129(130):3 (c. A.D. 365)].

DIDYMUS THE BLIND

God is simple and of an incomposite and spiritual nature, having neither ears nor organs of speech. A solitary essence and without limit, he is composed of no numbers and parts [*The Holy Spirit* 35 (c. A.D. 371)].

ST. BASIL OF CAESAREA

The operations are various, and the essence simple, but we say that we know our God from his operations, but do not undertake to approach near to his essence [*Letters* 234:1 (A.D. 376)].

ST. AMBROSE OF MILAN

[H]ow can there be any created nature in God? God has an un-compounded nature; nothing can be added to him, and only what is divine is in his nature; filling all things, yet nowhere himself compounded with anything; penetrating all things, yet himself nowhere to be penetrated; present in all his fullness at one and the same moment, in heaven, in earth, in the deepest depth of the sea, to sight invisible, by speech not to be declared, by feeling not to be measured; to be followed by faith, to be adored with devotion; so that whatever title excels in depth of spiritual import, in setting forth glory and honor, in exalting power, this belongs to God [*Faith* 1:16:106 (c. A.D. 379)].

ST. GREGORY OF NYSSA

But there is not, neither shall there be, in the Church of God a teaching such as that which can make One who is single and incomposite not only multiform and patchwork, but also the combination of opposites. The simplicity of the true faith assumes God to be what he is [*Against Eunomius* 1:42 (c. A.D. 382)].

EVAGRIUS OF PONTUS

To those who accuse us of a doctrine of three gods, let it be stated that we confess one God, not in number but in nature. For what is said to be one numerically is not one absolutely, nor is it simple in nature. It is universally confessed, however, that God is simple and not made of parts [*Dogmatic Letter on the Most Blessed Trinity* 8:2 (c. A.D. 383)].

ST. AUGUSTINE OF HIPPO

For in created and changeable things, what is not said according to substance, must, by necessary alternative, be said according to accident. . . . But in God nothing is said to be according to accident, because in him nothing is changeable [*The Trinity* 5:5:6 (c. A.D. 408)].

ST. CYRIL OF ALEXANDRIA

We are not by nature simple; but the divine nature, perfectly simple and incomposite, has in itself the abundance of all perfection and is in need of nothing [*Dialogues on the Trinity* 1 (c. A.D. 421)].

15. The Trinity

The fact that there is only one God is stressed in the Scriptures of the Old Testament (see chapter 22), but when Jesus came he revealed to us more about the life of God, specifically that the one God who exists does so as three divine Persons—the Father, the Son, and the Holy Spirit.

This may be difficult to understand, but that is not surprising. We should not expect God, who is infinitely far above us, to be easy to understand. We should expect there to be mysteries— things we could never deduce and that only he can reveal to us— when it comes to God.

It took the Church some time to hammer out the language to express what Christ had revealed concerning the Father, the Son, and the Spirit. The term "Trinity" came into use in the 100s, and its precise meaning was elaborated in the 300s by the first two ecumenical councils (Nicaea I and Constantinople I, in 325 and 381).

The teaching itself, though, is referenced a number of times in the New Testament. The most famous such passage is Matthew 28:19, in which Jesus tells the apostles: "Go therefore and make disciples of all nations, baptizing them in the name of the Father and of the Son and of the Holy Spirit." This parallelism of the three Persons is not unique to Matthew's Gospel. It appears else-where in the New Testament (e.g., 2 Cor 13:14; Heb 9:14), as well as in the writings of the earliest Christians.

It is taken for granted throughout the New Testament that the Father is God (e.g., Jn 14:1–2).

In the Old Testament, God had identified himself with the name "I Am" (Ex 3:14), and in the New Testament, Jesus applies this name to himself as well. In John 8:58, when questioned about how he has special knowledge of Abraham, Jesus replies, "Truly, truly, I say to you, before Abraham was, I Am." His audience understood exactly who he was claiming to be. "So they took up stones to throw at him; but Jesus hid himself, and went out of the temple" (Jn 8:59).

The Holy Spirit is also identified as God in Acts 5:3-5, in which Peter addresses a man named Ananias who had lied about a donation he was giving. Peter asks why he would "lie to the Holy Spirit and to keep back part of the proceeds of the land? . . . You have not lied to men but to God."

And so, after seeing the Father, the Son, and the Holy Spirit referred to in parallel, it is not surprising to find each one also identified as God.

DIDACHE

[Y]ou baptize this way: Having first said all these things, baptize in the name of the Father, and of the Son, and of the Holy Spirit, in living water. But if you don't have living [i.e. running] water, baptize in other water; and if you cannot baptize in cold, then baptize in warm. But if you have not either, pour water three times on the head in the name of Father and Son and Holy Spirit [*Didache* 7 (c. A.D. 50)].

ST. IGNATIUS OF ANTIOCH

Ignatius, who is also called Theophorus, to the church at Ephesus, in Asia, deservedly most happy, being blessed in the greatness and fullness of God the Father, and predestined before the beginning of time that it should be always for an enduring and unchangeable glory, being united and elected through the true passion by the will of the Father, and Jesus Christ, our God:[1] Abundant happiness through Jesus Christ, and his undefiled grace [*Letter to the Ephesians* 1 (c. A.D. 110)].

For our God, Jesus Christ, was, according to the appointment of God, conceived in the womb of Mary, of the seed of David, but by the Holy Spirit. He was born and baptized, that by his passion he might purify the water [ibid., 18].

---

[1] Note the identification, in this and the following quotation, of Jesus Christ as "our God," recognizing his divinity alongside that of the Father, who is also described as "God" in the second quotation.

ST. JUSTIN MARTYR

Our teacher of these things is Jesus Christ, who also was born for this purpose, and was crucified under Pontius Pilate, procurator of Judaea, in the times of Tiberius Caesar; and that we reasonably worship him, as he is the Son of the true God himself, and holding him in the second place, and the prophetic Spirit in the third, we will prove. For they proclaim our madness to consist in this, that we give to a crucified man a place second to the unchangeable and eternal God, the Creator of all; for they do not discern the mystery herein, to which, as we make it plain to you, we pray you to give heed [*First Apology* 13 (c. A.D. 151)].

ST. THEOPHILUS OF ANTIOCH

It is the attribute of God, of the most high and almighty and of the living God, not only to be everywhere, but also to see and hear all; for he can in no way be contained in a place. . . . The three days before the stars were created are types of the Trinity: God, his Word, and his Wisdom [*To Autolycus* 2:15 (c. A.D. 181)].

ST. IRENAEUS OF LYONS

The Church, though dispersed throughout the whole world, even to the ends of the earth, has received from the apostles and their disciples this faith: [She believes] in one God, the Father Almighty, maker of heaven, and earth, and the sea, and all things that are in them; and in one Christ Jesus, the Son of God, who became incarnate for our salvation; and in the Holy Spirit [*Against Heresies* 1:10:1 (c. A.D. 189)].

TERTULLIAN OF CARTHAGE

We, as we always have done (and more especially since we have been better instructed by the Paraclete, who indeed leads men into all truth), believe that there is only one God, but under the following dispensation, or *oikonomia*, as it is called, that this one and only God has a Son, his Word, who proceeded from himself, by whom all things were made, and without whom nothing was made. We believe he was sent by the Father into the Virgin, and was born of her—being both man and God, the Son of Man and the Son of God, and was called by the name of Jesus Christ; we believe he suffered, died, and was buried, according to the Scriptures, and, after he was raised again by the Father and taken back to heaven, sits at the right hand of the Father, and will come to judge the living and the dead; and that this one God also sent from heaven, according to his own promise, the Holy Spirit, the Paraclete, the sanctifier of the faith of those who believe in the Father, and in the Son, and in the Holy Spirit. This rule of faith has come down to us from the beginning of the gospel, even before any of the older heretics [*Against Praxeas* 2 (c. A.D. 218)].

And at the same time the mystery of the divine economy is safeguarded, for the unity is distributed in a Trinity. Placed in order, the three are the Father, Son, and Spirit. They are three, however, not in condition, but in degree; not in being, but in form; not in power, but in kind; of one being, however, and one condition and one power, because he is one God of whom degrees and forms and kinds are taken into account in the name of the Father, and of the Son, and of the Holy Spirit [ibid.].

Bear always in mind that this is the rule of faith I profess; by it I testify that the Father, and the Son, and the Spirit are inseparable from each other, so you will know in what sense this is said. My assertion is that the Father is one, and the Son one, and the Spirit one, and that they are distinct from each other. This statement is taken in a wrong sense by every uneducated and perversely disposed person, as if it meant a diversity, or implied a separation among the Father, and the Son, and the Spirit [ibid., 9].

Thus the connection of the Father in the Son, and of the Son in the Paraclete, produces three coherent persons, who are yet distinct one from another. These three are one essence, not one person, as it is said, "I and my Father are one" [Jn 10:30], in respect of unity of being, not singularity of number [ibid., 25].

ORIGEN OF ALEXANDRIA

For we do not say, as the heretics suppose, that some part of the substance of God was converted into the Son, or that the Son was procreated by the Father out of things non-existent, or beyond his own substance, so that there once was a time when he did not exist [*Fundamental Doctrines* 4:28 (c. A.D. 225)].

[P]utting away all corporeal conceptions, we say that the Word and wisdom was begotten out of the invisible and incorporeal without any corporeal feeling, as if it were an act of the will proceeding from understanding. Nor, seeing that he is called the Son of (his) love, will it appear absurd if he is also called the Son of (his) will. No, John also indicates that "God is Light," and Paul also declares that the Son is the splendor of everlasting light. As light could not exist without splendor, neither can the Son exist without the Father; for he is called the "express image of his person," and the Word and Wisdom. How, then, can it be asserted that there once was a time when he was not the Son? For that is to say that there was once a time when he was not the Truth, nor the wisdom, nor the life, although in all these he is judged to be the perfect essence of God the Father; for these things cannot be severed from him, or even separated from his essence. And although these qualities are many in understanding, yet in their nature and essence they are one, and in them is the fullness of divinity. This expression we employ—"that there never was a time when he did not exist"—is to be understood with a caveat. For these very words "when" or "never" have a meaning that relates to time, whereas statements regarding Father, Son, and Holy Spirit are to be understood as transcending all time, all ages, and all eternity [ibid.].

ST. HIPPOLYTUS OF ROME

The Logos alone of this God is from God himself; wherefore also the Logos is God, being the substance of God. Now the world was made from nothing; therefore it is not God [*Refutation of All Heresies* 10:29 (c. A.D. 227)].

NOVATIAN OF ROME

For Scripture announces Christ as God, as it announces God himself as man. It has described Jesus Christ as man, as it has described Christ the Lord as God. It does not set him forth as the Son of God only, but also the Son of man; nor only as the Son of man, but it has been accustomed to speak of him as the Son of God. Being of both, he is both, lest if he should be only one, he could not be the other. For as nature has prescribed that he must be believed to be a man who is of man, so nature prescribes that he must be believed to be God who is of God; but if he should not also be God when he is of God, then he should not be man although he is of man. And thus both doctrines would be endangered in one or the other way, by one being convicted to have lost belief in the other. Let them, therefore—who read that Jesus Christ the Son of man is man—read also that this same Jesus is also called God and the Son of God [*The Trinity* 11 (c. A.D. 235)].

POPE ST. DIONYSIUS

Now truly it would be just to take issue with those who destroy the monarchy by dividing and rending it, the most august announcement of the Church of God, into three powers, and distinct substances, and three deities. For I have heard that some who preach and teach the word of God among you are teachers of this opinion, who indeed are diametrically opposed—so to speak—to the opinion of Sabellius. For he blasphemes in saying that the Son himself is the Father, and vice versa; but these in a certain manner announce three gods, in that they divide the holy unity into three different substances, absolutely separated from one another [*Against the Sabellians* 1 (A.D. 262)].

For it is essential that the divine Word should be united to the God of all, and that the Holy Spirit should abide and dwell in God; and thus that the divine Trinity should be gathered into one, as if into a certain head—that is, the omnipotent God of all. . . . It is not a trifling, but a very great impiety, to say that the Lord was in any way made with hands. For if the Son was made, there was a time when he was not; but he always was, if, as he himself declares, he is in the Father. . . . If the Son was made, there was a time when these were not in existence; and thus there was a time when God was without these things, which is utterly absurd [ibid., 1–2].

That admirable and divine unity must not be separated into three divinities, nor must the dignity and eminent greatness of the Lord be diminished by having the name of creation applied to it, but we must believe in God the Father omnipotent, and in Christ Jesus his Son, and in the Holy Spirit. Moreover, that the Word is united to the God of all, because he says, "I and the Father are one" and "I am in the Father, and the Father is in me." Thus the doctrine of the divine Trinity will be maintained in its integrity [ibid., 3].

ST. GREGORY THAUMATURGUS

There is one God. . . . There is a perfect Trinity, in glory and eternity and sovereignty, neither divided nor estranged. Therefore there is nothing either created or in servitude in the Trinity; or anything added on, as if at some former period it was nonexistent, and at some later period it was introduced. And thus neither was the Son ever wanting to the Father, nor the Spirit to the Son; but the same Trinity abides ever without variation and without change [*Declaration of Faith* (c. A.D. 265)].

ST. AUGUSTINE OF HIPPO

All those Catholic expounders of the divine Scriptures, both Old and New, whom I have been able to read, who have written before me about the Trinity, who is God, have purposed to teach, according to the Scriptures, this doctrine, that the Father, and the Son, and the Holy Spirit intimate a divine unity of one and the same substance in an indivisible equality; and therefore that they are not three Gods, but one God: although the Father has begotten the Son, so he who is the Father is not the Son; and the Son is begotten by the Father, so he who is the Son is not the Father;

and the Holy Spirit is neither the Father nor the Son, but rather the Spirit of the Father and of the Son. He is also co-equal with the Father and the Son, and he belongs to the unity of the Trinity [*The Trinity* 1:4:7 (c. A.D. 408)].

ST. SECHNALL OF IRELAND

Hymns, with Revelation and the Psalms of God [Patrick] sings, and expounds them to edify God's people. This law he holds in the Trinity of the sacred name and teaches one being in three persons [*Hymn in Praise of St. Patrick* 22 (c. A.D. 444)].

ST. PATRICK

I bind to myself today the strong power of an invocation of the Trinity—the faith of the Trinity in unity, the Creator of the universe [*Breastplate of St. Patrick* 1 (c. A.D. 447)].

[T]here is no other God, nor has there been before now, nor will there be hereafter, except God the Father unbegotten, without beginning, from whom is all beginning, upholding all things, and his Son Jesus Christ, whom we also confess to have been with the Father always—before the world's beginning. . . . Jesus Christ is the Lord and God in whom we believe . . . and who has poured out the Holy Spirit on us abundantly . . . whom we confess and adore as one God in the Trinity of the sacred name [*Confession of St. Patrick* 4 (c. A.D. 452)].

16. The Three Persons of the Trinity

As the Church meditated on the best way to express the doctrine of the Trinity, there were some errors to be avoided. One of them was expressed in the 200s by a priest named Sabellius. He recognized that there is only one God, but he failed to recognize that the Father, Son, and Holy Spirit are distinct Persons. Instead, he held that God is one Person who has different "offices" or "modes."

This view became known as Sabellianism, Modalism, and Patripassianism. It was called Sabellianism after its founder, Modalism after the three modes or offices that it claimed the one person of the Trinity occupied, and Patripassianism because it implied that the person of the Father (*Pater*) experienced suffering (*passio*) on the cross.

The New Testament, however, reveals that the Father, the Son, and the Spirit are not just modes or offices, but Persons. This is clear, for example, in passages that show Jesus talking to his Father (e.g., Jn 17) or declaring he is going to be with the Father (Jn 14:12, 28; 16:10)—one office of a person cannot go to be with another office of that person—or passages that say the two will send the Holy Spirit while they remain in heaven (Jn 14:16–17, 26; 15:26; 16:13–15; Acts 2:32–33).

Modalism died out in the early Church, but like other misunderstandings of the Trinity, it reappeared periodically. In the early twentieth century, it was revived in the new Pentecostal movement. In that new form, it is often referred to as "Jesus Only" theology since it claims that Jesus is the only person in the Godhead and that the Father, the Son, and the Holy Spirit are merely names, modes, or offices of Jesus. The United Pentecostal Church, as well as numerous smaller Pentecostal groups that call themselves "apostolic churches," teach this view.

In the quotations that follow, the Fathers' rejection of Modalism is shown not only when they condemn it by name, but also by passages in which they speak of one person of the Trinity being with another, being sent from another, or speaking to another.

LETTER OF BARNABAS

And further, my brethren, if the Lord [Jesus] endured to suffer for our soul, he being the Lord of all the world, *to whom God said* at the foundation of the world, "Let us make man after our image, and after our likeness," [Gn 1:26] understand how it was that he endured to suffer at the hand of men [*Letter of Barnabas* 5 (c. A.D. 75), emphasis added].

HERMAS OF ROME

The Son of God is older than all his creation, so that he became the Father's adviser in his creation. Therefore also he is ancient [*The Shepherd* 3:9:12 (c. A.D. 80)].

ST. IGNATIUS OF ANTIOCH

Jesus Christ . . . who was with the Father before the beginning of time, and in the end was revealed. . . . Jesus Christ . . . *who came forth from one Father, and is with and has gone to one.* . . . [T]here is one God, who has manifested himself by Jesus Christ his Son, who is his eternal Word, does not proceed from silence, and in all things pleased him that sent him [*Letter to the Magnesians* 8 (c. A.D. 110), emphasis added].

ST. JUSTIN MARTYR

God speaks in the creation of man with the very same design, in the following words: "Let us make man after our image and likeness." . . . I shall quote again the words narrated by Moses himself, from which we can indisputably learn that [God] conversed with someone distinct from himself and also a rational being. . . . But this offspring who was truly brought forth from the Father, was with the Father before all the creatures, and the Father communed with him [*Dialogue with Trypho* 62 (c. A.D. 155)].

ST. POLYCARP OF SMYRNA

I praise you for all things, I bless you, I glorify you, *along with* the everlasting and heavenly Jesus Christ, your beloved Son, with whom, to you, and the Holy Spirit, be glory both now and to all coming ages. Amen [quoted in *Martyrdom of Polycarp* 14 (c. A.D. 156) emphasis added].

TO DIOGNETUS

[The Father] sent the Word, that he might be manifested to the world. . . . This is he who was from the beginning, who appeared as if new, and was found old. . . . This is he who, being from everlasting, is today called the Son [*To Diognetus* 11 (c. A.D. 160) emphasis added].

ST. IRENAEUS OF LYONS

It was not angels who made us, nor who formed us, neither had angels power to make an image of God, nor anyone else, except the Word of the Lord, nor any power distant from the Father of all things. For God did not stand in need of these [beings] to accomplish what he had determined beforehand should be done, as if he did not possess his own hands. For *with him* were always present the Word and wisdom, the Son and the Spirit, by whom and in whom, freely and spontaneously, he made all things, to whom he speaks, saying, "*Let us* make man after our image and likeness" [Gn 1:26] [*Against Heresies* 4:20:1 (c. A.D. 189) emphasis added].

TERTULLIAN OF CARTHAGE

[S]ome opportunity must be given for reviewing [the statements of heretics], with a view to the instruction and protection of various persons; even if only so that it does not seem that each perversion of the truth is condemned without examination, and simply prejudged; especially in the case of this heresy, which supposes that it possesses the pure truth, in thinking that one cannot believe in only one God in any other way than by saying that the Father, the Son, and the Holy Spirit are the very same Person. As if in this way one were not all, in that all are of one, by unity of substance; while the mystery of the dispensation that distributes the unity into a Trinity is still guarded, placing in their order the three Persons—the Father, the Son, and the Holy Spirit: three, however, not in condition, but in degree; not in substance, but in form; not in power, but in aspect; yet of one substance [*Against Praxeas* 2 (c. A.D. 218)].

Bear always in mind that this is the rule of faith I profess; by it I testify that the Father, and the Son, and the Spirit are inseparable from each other, so you will know in what sense this is said. My assertion is that the Father is one, and the Son one, and the Spirit one, and that they are distinct from each other. This statement is taken in a wrong sense by every uneducated and perversely disposed person, as if it meant a diversity, or implied a separation among the Father, and the Son, and the Spirit [ibid., 9].

ST. HIPPOLYTUS OF ROME

Thus, after the death of Zephyrinus, supposing that he had obtained [the position] he so eagerly pursued, [Pope Callistus] excommunicated Sabellius for not entertaining orthodox opinions [*Refutation of All Heresies* 9:7 (c. A.D. 227)].

NOVATIAN OF ROME

For who does not acknowledge that the person of the Son is second after the Father, when he reads that it was said by the Father, thus to the Son, "Let us make man in our image and our likeness"; and that after this it was said, "And God made man, in the image of God made he him"? Or when he holds in his hands: "The Lord rained upon Sodom and Gomorrah fire and brimstone from the Lord from heaven"? Or when he reads what was said to Christ: "You are my Son, this day have I begotten You. Ask of me, and I will give you the heathens for your inheritance, and the ends of the earth for your possession"? Or when that beloved writer says: "The Lord said unto my Lord, Sit on my right hand, until I shall make your enemies the stool of your feet"? Or when, unfolding the prophecies of Isaiah, he finds this written: "Thus says the Lord to Christ my Lord"? Or when he reads: "I came not down from heaven to do my own will, but the will of him that sent me"? Or: "Because he who sent me is greater than I"? Or when he considers the passage: "I go to my Father, and your Father; to my God, and your God"? Or when he finds it compared with others: "Moreover, in your law it is written that the witness of two is true. I bear witness of myself, and the Father who sent me bears witness of me"? [*The Trinity* 26 (c. A.D. 235)].

And I should have enough to do were I to endeavor to gather together all the passages [of the kind in the previous quotation]

. . . since the divine Scripture, not so much of the Old as also of the New Testament, everywhere shows him to be born of the Father, by whom all things were made, and without whom nothing was made, who always has obeyed and obeys the Father; that he always has power over all things, but as delivered, as granted, as the Father himself permitted to him. And what can be stronger proof that this is not the Father, but the Son, as that the Son is obedient to God the Father, unless, if he be believed to be the Father, Christ may be said to be subjected to another God the Father? [ibid.].

ST. GREGORY THAUMATURGUS

But some treat the Holy Trinity in an awful manner, when they confidently assert that there are not three Persons, and introduce [the idea of] a person devoid of subsistence. We reject Sabellius, who says that the Father and the Son are the same, for he believes that the Father is the one who speaks, and the Son is the Word that abides in the Father, and becomes manifest at the time of the creation, and thereafter reverts to God on the fulfilling of all things. The same affirmation he makes also of the Spirit. We renounce this, because we believe that three Persons—namely, Father, Son, and Holy Spirit—are declared to possess the one Godhead: For the one divinity showing itself according to nature in the Trinity establishes the oneness of its nature [*Sectional Confession of Faith* 7 (c. A.D. 256)].

But if they say, "How can there be three Persons, but one divinity?," we shall make this reply: That there are indeed three Persons, because there is one person of God the Father, and one of the Lord the Son, and one of the Holy Spirit; yet there is only one divinity, because . . . there is one substance in the Trinity [ibid., 14].

POPE ST. DIONYSIUS

Now truly it would be just to take issue with those who destroy the monarchy by dividing and rending it, the most august announcement of the Church of God, into three powers, and distinct substances, and three deities. For I have heard that some who preach and teach the word of God among you are teachers of this opinion, who indeed are diametrically opposed—so to speak— to the opinion of Sabellius. For he blasphemes in saying that the Son himself is the Father, and vice versa; but these in a certain manner announce three gods, in that they divide the holy unity into three different substances, absolutely separated from one another [*Against the Sabellians* 1 (A.D. 262)].

ST. METHODIUS OF PHILIPPI

For the kingdom of the Father, of the Son, and of the Holy Spirit is one, even as their substance is one and their dominion one. Therefore with one and the same adoration we worship the one Deity in three Persons, subsisting without beginning, uncreated, without end, and to which there is no successor. For neither will the Father ever cease to be the Father, nor the Son to be the Son and king, nor the Holy Spirit to be what in substance and personality he is. For nothing of the Trinity will be diminished, either in respect of eternity, communion, or sovereignty [*Oration on the Psalms* 5 (c. A.D. 300)].

ST. ATHANASIUS OF ALEXANDRIA

[The Trinity] is a Trinity not merely in name or figuratively; rather, it is a Trinity in truth and in actual existence. Just as the Father is he that is, so his Word is one that is and is God over all. And neither is the Holy Spirit nonexistent, but he actually exists and has true being. Less than these the Catholic Church does not hold, lest she sink to the level of the Jews of the present time, imitators of Caiaphas, or to the level of Sabellius [*Four Letters to Serapion of Thmuis* 1:28 (c. A.D. 359)].

For they are one, not as one thing divided into two parts, and these nothing but one, nor as one thing twice named, so that the same becomes at one time Father, at another his own Son. For believing this Sabellius was judged a heretic. But they are two, because the Father is Father and is not also Son, and the Son is Son and not also Father; but the nature is one [*Four Discourses Against the Arians* 3:4 (c. A.D. 360)].

COUNCIL OF ROME

We anathematize those also who follow the error of Sabellius in saying that the same one is both Father and Son [Canon 2 (A.D. 382)].

ST. FULGENCE OF RUSPE

See, in short you have it that the Father is one, the Son another, and the Holy Spirit another; in Person, each is other, but in nature they are the same. In this regard Jesus says: "The Father and I, we are one" [Jn 10:30]. He teaches us that *one* refers to their nature, and *we are* to their Persons. In like manner it is said: "There are three who bear witness in heaven, the Father, the Word, and the Spirit; and these three are one" [1 Jn 5:7]. Let Sabellius hear *we are*, let him hear *three*; and let him believe that there are three Persons. Let him not blaspheme in his sacrilegious heart by saying that the Father is the same in himself as the Son is the same in himself and as the Holy Sprit is the same in himself, as if in some way he could beget himself, or proceed from himself. Even in created natures nothing is able to beget itself. Let also Arius hear *one*; and let him not say that the Son is of a different nature, if *one* cannot be said of that, the nature of which is different [*The Trinity* 4:1– 2 (c. A.D. 513)].

17. The Divinity of Christ

Another error regarding the Trinity appeared in the 300s, when a priest named Arius asserted that Jesus was not actually God but was a created being—the first of all created beings. The ensuing controversy led to the first ecumenical council—Nicaea I in 325 —which definitively taught that Christ is God and which wrote the first two parts of the *Nicene Creed*.

In doing so, the council was firmly grounded in Scripture. Christ's divinity is repeatedly attested to in the New Testament. For example, in the Gospel of John we are told that Jesus' opponents sought to kill him because he "called God his Father, making himself equal with God" (5:18). In John 8:58, Jesus applies to himself the Old Testament divine name "I Am." And in John

20:28, Thomas falls at Jesus' feet, hailing him as "My Lord and my God!"—an accolade that Jesus does not rebuke.

Also significant are New Testament passages that apply the title "the First and the Last" to Jesus, which is one of the Old Testament titles of Yahweh: "Thus says the LORD, the King of Israel and his Redeemer, the LORD of hosts: 'I am the first and I am the last; besides me there is no god' " (Is 44:6; see also 41:4; 48:12).

This title is applied to Jesus three times in the book of Revelation: "When I saw him [Christ], I fell at his feet as though dead. But he laid his right hand upon me, saying, 'Fear not, I am the First and the Last' " (Rv 1:17). "And to the angel of the church in Smyrna write: 'The words of the First and the Last, who died and came to life' " (Rv 2:8). "Behold, I am coming soon, bringing my recompense, to repay every one for what he has done. I am the Alpha and the Omega, the First and the Last, the beginning and the end" (Rv 22:12–13).

This last quotation is especially significant since it applies to Jesus the parallel title "the Alpha and the Omega," which Revelation earlier applied to the Lord God: " 'I am the Alpha and the Omega,' says the Lord God, who is and who was and who is to come, the Almighty" (Rv 1:8).

As the following quotations show, the early Church Fathers recognized the divinity of Christ.

ST. IGNATIUS OF ANTIOCH

Ignatius, who is also called Theophorus, to the church at Ephesus, in Asia, deservedly most happy, being blessed in the greatness and fullness of God the Father, and predestined before the beginning of time that it should be always for an enduring and unchangeable glory, being united and elected through the true passion by the will of the Father, and Jesus Christ, our God:[2] Abundant happiness through Jesus Christ, and his undefiled grace [*Letter to the Ephesians*, Greeting (c. A.D. 110)].

---

[2] Note the identification of Jesus Christ as "our God," in each of the quotations by St. Ignatius.

For our God, Jesus Christ, was, according to the appointment of God, conceived in the womb of Mary, of the seed of David, but by the Holy Spirit [ibid., 18].

The Church is beloved and enlightened by the will of him who wills all things that are according to the love of Jesus Christ our God [*Letter to the Romans*, Greeting (c. A.D. 110)].

ST. ARISTIDES OF ATHENS

[Christians] are those who more than all the nations on the earth have found the truth. For they know God, the Creator and fashioner of all things through the only-begotten Son and the Holy Spirit [*Apology* 15 (c. A.D. 140)].

TATIAN THE SYRIAN

We do not act as fools, O Greeks, nor utter idle tales, when we say that God was born in the form of a man [*Address to the Greeks* 21 (c. A.D. 170)].

ST. MELITO OF SARDIS

It is not necessary in dealing with persons of intelligence to reason that the actions of Christ after his baptism are proof that his soul and his body, his human nature, were like ours, real and not phantasmal. The activities of Christ after his baptism, and especially his miracles, gave indication and assurance to the world of the deity hidden in his flesh. Being God and also perfect man, he gave positive proofs of his two natures: of his deity, by the miracles during the three years following after his baptism, and of his humanity, in the thirty years that came before his baptism, during which, by reason of his condition according to the flesh, he concealed the signs of his deity, although he was the true God existing before the ages [fragment in St. Anastasius of Sinai's *The Guide* 13 (c. A.D. 170)].

ST. IRENAEUS OF LYONS

The Church, though dispersed throughout the whole world, even to the ends of the earth, has received from the apostles and their disciples this faith: [She believes] in one God, the Father Almighty, maker of heaven, and earth, and the sea, and all things that are in them; and in one Christ Jesus, the Son of God, who became incarnate for our salvation; and in the Holy Spirit, who proclaimed through the prophets the dispensations of God, and the advents, and the birth from a virgin, and the Passion, and the Resurrection from the dead, and the Ascension into heaven in the flesh of the beloved Christ Jesus, our Lord, and his [future] manifestation from heaven in the glory of the Father "to gather all things in one" [Eph 1:10], and to raise up anew all flesh of the whole human race, in order that to Christ Jesus, our Lord, and God, and Savior, and king, according to the will of the invisible Father, "every knee should bow, of things in heaven, and things in earth, and things under the earth, and that every tongue should confess" [*Against Heresies* 1:10:1 (c. A.D. 189)].

Nevertheless, what cannot be said of anyone else who ever lived, that he is himself God and Lord . . . may be seen by all who have attained to even a small portion of the truth [ibid., 3:19:1–2].

ST. CLEMENT OF ALEXANDRIA

Since the Word was from the beginning, he was and is the divine source of all things; but because he has now assumed the name Christ, consecrated of old, and worthy of power, he has been called by me the New Song. This Word, then, the Christ, the cause of our being at first (for he was in God) and of our well-being, this very Word has now appeared as man, he alone being both God and man—the author of all blessings to us [*Exhortation to the Heathen* 1 (c. A.D. 195)].

For it was not without divine care that so great a work was accomplished in so brief a space by the Lord, who, though despised in terms of his humble appearance, was in reality adored, the expiator of sin, the Savior, the clement, the divine Word, he that is truly the most manifest Deity, he that is made equal to the Lord of the universe; because he was his Son [ibid., 10].

TERTULLIAN OF CARTHAGE

God alone is without sin. The only man who is without sin is Christ; for Christ is also God [*Treatise on the Soul* 41 (c. A.D. 210)].

Thus the nature of the two substances displayed him as man and God—in one respect born, in the other unborn; in one respect fleshly, in the other spiritual; in one sense weak, in the other exceeding strong; in one sense dying, in the other living [*The Flesh of Christ* 5:6–7 (c. A.D. 210)].

That there are two Gods and two Lords is something we will never say; it is not as if the Father and the Son were not God, nor the Spirit God, and each of them God; but formerly two were spoken of as Gods and two as Lords, so that when Christ would come, he might be acknowledged as God and be called Lord, because he is the Son of him who is both God and Lord [*Against Praxeas* 13 (c. A.D. 218)].

ORIGEN OF ALEXANDRIA

He in the last times, divesting himself [of his glory], became a man, and was incarnate although he was God, and while made a man remained the God that he was [*Fundamental Doctrines* Preface 4 (c. A.D. 225)].

ST. HIPPOLYTUS OF ROME

Only the Logos of this God is from God himself; thus the Logos is also God, being the substance of God [*Refutation of All Heresies* 10:29 (c. A.D. 227)].

For Christ is the God above all, and he has arranged to wash away sin from human beings, rendering the old man regenerate [ibid., 10:30].

NOVATIAN OF ROME

If Christ was only man, why did he lay down for us this rule of believing, "And this is life eternal, that they should know you, the only and true God, and Jesus Christ, whom you have sent"? If he did not wish to be understood to be God, why did he add,

"And Jesus Christ, whom you have sent," unless he wished to be received as God? Because if he did not wish to be understood to be God, he would have added, "And the man Jesus Christ, whom you have sent"; but, in fact, he did not, nor did Christ deliver himself to us as Christ only, but associated himself with God, as he wished to be understood by this to be God also, as he is. We must therefore believe, according to the rule prescribed, in the Lord, the one true God, and consequently in him whom he has sent, Jesus Christ, who would not have linked himself to the Father if he had not wished to be understood to be God also: for he would have separated himself from him if he did not wish to be understood to be God [*The Trinity* 16 (c. A.D. 235)].

ST. CYPRIAN OF CARTHAGE

[If a heretic were validly baptized,] he also was made the temple of God. I ask, of what God? If of the Creator, he could not be, because he has not believed in him. If of Christ, he could not become his temple, since he denies that Christ is God. If of the Holy Spirit, since the three are one, how can the Holy Spirit be at peace with him who is the enemy of the Son or of the Father? [*Letters* 72:12 (c. A.D. 255)].

ST. GREGORY THAUMATURGUS

There is one God, the Father of the living Word, who is his subsistent wisdom and power and eternal image: perfect begetter of the perfect begotten, Father of the only-begotten Son. There is one Lord, only of the only, God from God, image and likeness of Deity, efficient Word, wisdom comprehensive of the constitution of all things, and power formative of the whole creation, true Son of true Father, invisible of invisible, and incorruptible of incorruptible, and immortal of immortal and eternal of eternal. And there is one Holy Spirit, having his subsistence from God, and being made manifest by the Son, to men: image of the Son, perfect image of the perfect; life, the cause of the living; holy fount; sanctity, the supplier, or leader, of sanctification; in whom is manifested God the Father, who is above all and in all, and

God the Son, who is through all. There is a perfect Trinity, in glory and eternity and sovereignty, neither divided nor estranged. Therefore there is nothing either created or in servitude in the Trinity; or anything added on, as if at some former period it was nonexistent, and at some later period it was introduced. And thus neither was the Son ever wanting to the Father, nor the Spirit to the Son; but without variation and without change the same Trinity abides ever [*Declaration of Faith* (c. A.D. 265)].

ARNOBIUS OF SICCA

"Is that Christ of yours a god, then?," some raving, wrathful, and excited man will say. "A God," we will reply, "and the God of the inner powers" [*Against the Heathen* 1:42 (c. A.D. 305)].

LACTANTIUS

He became both the Son of God through the Spirit, and the Son of man through the flesh—that is, both God and man [*Divine Institutes* 4:13 (c. A.D. 307)].

We, on the other hand, are [truly] religious, who pray to the one true God. Someone may perhaps ask how, when we say that we worship one God only, we also assert that there are two, God the Father and God the Son—which has driven many into the greatest error . . . [thinking] that we confess that there is another God, and that he is mortal. . . . [But w]hen we speak of God the Father and God the Son, we do not speak of them as different, nor do we separate them, because the Father cannot exist without the Son, nor can the Son be separated from the Father [ibid., 4:29].

COUNCIL OF NICAEA I

We believe . . . in one Lord Jesus Christ, the Son of God, the only-begotten of his Father, of the substance of the Father, God from God, light from light, true God from true God, begotten, not made, being of one substance with the Father. By whom all things were made, both in heaven and in earth [*Nicene Creed* (A.D. 325)].

But those who say, "There was a time when he [the Son] did not exist," and "Before he was born, he did not exist," and "Because he was made from non-existing matter, he is either of another substance or essence," and those who call "God the Son of God changeable and mutable," these the Catholic Church anathematizes [original appendix to the *Nicene Creed* (A.D. 325)].

ST. PATRICK

Jesus Christ is the Lord and God in whom we believe, and whose coming we expect will soon take place, the judge of the living and the dead, who will render to everyone according to his works [*Confession of St. Patrick* 4 (c. A.D. 452)].

18. The Eternal Sonship of Christ

The New Testament repeatedly states that Jesus Christ is the Son of God the Father. This means, among other things, that the Second Person of the Trinity proceeds from the First Person eternally —outside of time.

This is different from the way sons come from fathers inside time, where there is a time when sons do not exist and their fathers give rise to them. Because God is outside of time, there never was a time when the Son did not exist, when the Father was alone and thus not yet a Father.

Both the Father and the Son have always existed in the eternal now, outside of time, but the procession of the Son from the Father means that the former finds his origin (Greek, *archē*, ar-KAY) in the latter. This is why the *Nicene Creed* states that Christ is "the only begotten Son of God, born of the Father before all ages. God from God, light from light, true God from true God, begotten, not made, consubstantial with the Father."

Because of the difficulty our limited minds have in fathoming the divine life of God outside of time, some have rejected this and opted for a view that is easier to understand but that flattens the divine reality.

These individuals hold that Christ was not eternally the Son of God but that he became so only upon the Incarnation. They include certain Protestant authors such as the late J. Oliver Buswell and Walter Martin, and for a time they included John MacArthur, though he later changed his mind and embraced the historic Christian understanding.

This view erases the internal relationships among the Persons of the Trinity. If the Son was not begotten by the Father in eternity then the Father is not eternally Father and the Son is not eternally Son. In this view, they only acquire these roles in relationship to the Incarnation. Further, if the Son does not eternally proceed from the Father, then the Spirit does not eternally proceed from the Father through the Son. Apart from the Incarnation, there would not be the Father, the Son, and the Holy Spirit, but simply three Persons with no eternal relationships among them: Number One, Number Two, and Number Three. Even these numbers would be arbitrary designations (why should one Person be Number One if he does not in some way serve as the origin or *archē* of the other two?).

The Church Fathers had a different view, recognizing that the Bible depicts the Son as the Son prior to the Incarnation. In 1 John 4:9 we read that "the love of God was made manifest among us [in] that God sent his only Son into the world." The Second Person of the Trinity was already the Son when he was sent into the world.

The same truth is taught under a different image in John 1:1, 14 where we read that "in the beginning was the Word, and the Word was with God, and the Word was God. . . . And the Word became flesh and dwelt among us." Here the Word (the Second Person of the Trinity) is pictured as the Word before the world was made. Thus, from all eternity the Word proceeded from God, just as speech proceeds from a speaker or a son proceeds from his father. Under both images, whether as the Word or the Son, the second person is shown eternally proceeding from the First Person.

Of special interest among the following passages are those in which the early Christians wrote of God as Father prior to the

Incarnation. Such passages imply the role of the Second Person as Son before the Incarnation, since, as we have noted, without a Son there is no Father.

ST. IGNATIUS OF ANTIOCH

Jesus Christ . . . was with the Father before the beginning of time, and in the end was revealed [Letter to the Magnesians 6 (c. A.D. 110)].

ST. JUSTIN MARTYR

Jesus Christ is the only proper Son who has been begotten by God, his Word and first-begotten, and power; and, becoming man according to his will, he taught us these things for the conversion and restoration of the human race [First Apology 23 (c. A.D. 151)].

God begot before all creatures a beginning, who was a certain rational power from himself and whom the Holy Spirit calls . . . sometimes the Son . . . sometimes Lord and Word. . . . We see things happen similarly among ourselves, for whenever we utter some word, we beget a word, yet not by any cutting off, which would diminish the word in us when we utter it. We see a similar occurrence when one fire kindles another. It is not diminished by kindling the other, but remains as it was [Dialogue with Trypho 61 (c. A.D. 155)].

ST. IRENAEUS OF LYONS

[The Gnostics] transfer the generation of the word to which men gave utterance to the eternal Word of God, assigning a beginning. . . . And in what respect will the Word of God—yes, God himself, since he is the Word—differ from the word of men, if he follows the same order and process of generation? [Against Heresies 2:13:8 (c. A.D. 189)].

TERTULLIAN OF CARTHAGE

Thus does he make him equal to him: for by proceeding from himself he became his first-begotten Son, begotten before all things

[Col 1:15]; and his only-begotten also, because he alone is begotten of God, in a way peculiar to himself, from the womb of his own heart—even as the Father himself testifies: "My heart," says he, "has issued my most excellent Word" [*Against Praxeas* 7 (c. A.D. 218)].

ST. HIPPOLYTUS OF ROME

Therefore, this sole and universal God, by reflecting, first brought forth the Word—not a word as in speech, but a mental word, the reason for everything. . . . The Word was the cause of the things that came into existence, carrying out in himself the will of him by whom he was begotten. . . . The Logos alone is from God himself; thus the Logos is also God, being the substance of God [*Refutation of All Heresies* 10:29 (c. A.D. 227)].

ORIGEN OF ALEXANDRIA

So also wisdom, since he proceeds from God, is generated from the very substance of God [*Commentary on Hebrews* (c. A.D. 237)].

ST. GREGORY THAUMATURGUS

There is one God, the Father of the living Word, who is his subsistent wisdom and power and eternal image: perfect begetter of the perfect begotten, Father of the only-begotten Son. There is one Lord, only of the only, God from God, image and likeness of Deity, efficient Word, wisdom comprehensive of the constitution of all things, and power formative of the whole creation, true Son of true Father, invisible of invisible, and incorruptible of incorruptible, and immortal of immortal and eternal of eternal. And there is one Holy Spirit, having his subsistence from God, and being made manifest by the Son, to men: image of the Son, perfect image of the perfect; life, the cause of the living; holy fount; sanctity, the supplier, or leader, of sanctification; in whom is manifested God the Father, who is above all and in all, and God the Son, who is through all [*Declaration of Faith* (c. A.D. 265)].

LACTANTIUS

When we speak of God the Father and God the Son, we do not speak of them as different, nor do we separate them, because the Father cannot exist without the Son, nor can the Son be separated from the Father, since the name of Father cannot be given without the Son, nor can the Son be begotten without the Father. Since, therefore, the Father makes the Son, and the Son the Father, they both have one mind, one spirit, one substance; but the former is as it were an overflowing fountain, the latter as a stream flowing forth from it: the former as the sun, the latter as it were a ray extended from the sun [*Divine Institutes* 4:29 (c. A.D. 307)].

COUNCIL OF NICAEA I

We believe . . . in one Lord Jesus Christ, the Son of God, the only-begotten of his Father, of the substance of the Father, God from God, light from light, true God from true God, begotten, not made, being of one substance with the Father. By whom all things were made, both in heaven and in earth [*Nicene Creed* (A.D. 325)].

ST. CYRIL OF JERUSALEM

Believe also in the Son of God, one and only, our Lord Jesus Christ, who was begotten God from God, begotten life of life, begotten light of Light, who is in all things like him who begat him, who received not his being in time, but was before all ages eternally and incomprehensibly begotten of the Father: The wisdom and the power of God, and his righteousness subsisting as a Person, and who sits on the right hand of the Father before all ages [*Catechetical Lectures* 4:7 (c. A.D. 350)].

ST. IGNATIUS OF ANTIOCH

But some most worthless persons are in the habit of carrying about the name [of Jesus Christ] in wicked guile while they practice things unworthy of God, and hold opinions contrary to the doctrine of Christ—to their own destruction, and those who give credit to them—and you must avoid them as you would wild beasts. For "the righteous man who avoids them is saved for ever; but the destruction of the ungodly is sudden, and a subject of rejoicing. For they are dumb dogs, that cannot bark, raving mad, and biting secretly, against whom you must be on your guard, since they labor under an incurable disease. But our physician is the only true God, the unbegotten and unapproachable, the Lord of all, the Father and begetter of the only-begotten Son. We have also as a physician the Lord our God, Jesus the Christ, the only-begotten Son and Word, before time began, but who afterwards became also man, of Mary the Virgin" [*Letter to the Ephesians*, long version, 7 (c. A.D. 350)].

ST. ATHANASIUS OF ALEXANDRIA

When these points are thus proved, their profaneness goes further. "If there never was, when the Son was not," they say, "but he is eternal, and coexists with the Father, you call him no more the Father's Son, but brother." O, senseless and contentious! For if we only said that he was eternally with the Father, and not his Son, their pretended scruple would have some plausibility; but since, when we say he is eternal, we also say he is Son from the Father, how can he that is begotten be considered brother of him who begets? . . . For the Father and the Son were not generated from some preexisting origin, that we may account them brothers, but the Father is the origin of the Son and begat him. . . . While it is proper for men to beget in time, from the imperfection of their nature, God's offspring is eternal, for his nature is ever perfect [*Four Discourses Against the Arians* 1:14 (c. A.D. 360)].

ST. AMBROSE OF MILAN

But the Arians think that they must oppose the fact that he said, "I live by the Father." Certainly (suppose that they conceive the words as referring to his Godhead) the Son lives by the Father, because he is the Son begotten of the Father—by the Father, because he is of one substance with the Father, by the Father, because he is the Word given forth from the heart of the Father, because he came forth from the Father, because he is begotten of the "bowels of the Father," because the Father is the fountain and root of the Son's being [*Faith* 4:10:133 (c. A.D. 379)].

ST. GREGORY OF NAZIANZ

He is called Son because he is identical to the Father in essence; and not only this, but also because he is of him. He is called only-begotten not because he is a unique Son . . . but because he is Son in a unique fashion and not in a corporeal way. He is called Word because he is to the Father what a word is to the mind [*Orations* 30:20 (A.D. 380)].

COUNCIL OF CONSTANTINOPLE I

We believe . . . in one Lord Jesus Christ, the Son of God, the only-begotten of his Father, of the substance of the Father, God from God, light from light, true God from true God, begotten, not made, being of one substance with the Father [*Nicene Creed* (A.D. 381)].

COUNCIL OF ROME

If anyone does not say that the Son was begotten of the Father, that is, of the divine substance of him himself, he is a heretic [Canon 11 (A.D. 382)].

ST. AUGUSTINE OF HIPPO

God gave out his Word, that is, he begot the Son. And you [when you think of a word of human language that you might utter], begettest the word even in your heart according to time; [but] God without time begot the Son by whom he created all times [*Tractates on John* 14:7 (A.D. 416–417)].

ATHANASIAN CREED

The Father is not made nor created nor begotten by anyone. The Son is from the Father alone, not made or created, but begotten. . . . Let him who wishes to be saved think thus concerning the Trinity. But it is necessary for eternal salvation that he faithfully believe also in the Incarnation. . . . He is God begotten of the substance of the Father before time, and he is man born of the substance of his mother in time. . . . This is the Catholic faith; unless everyone believes this faithfully and firmly, he cannot be saved [*Athanasian Creed* (c. A.D. 425)].

ST. PATRICK

Jesus Christ, whom we also confess to have always been with the Father always—before the world's beginning, spiritually and ineffably [he was] begotten of the Father before all beginning [*Confession of St. Patrick* 4 (c. A.D. 452)].

COUNCIL OF CONSTANTINOPLE II

If anyone shall not confess that the Word of God has two nativities, the one from all eternity of the Father, without time and without body; the other in these last days, coming down from heaven and being made flesh of the holy and glorious Mary, Mother of God and always a Virgin, and born of her: Let him be anathema [*Capitula of the Council* 2 [A.D. 553)].

19. Filioque

In the previous chapter we focused on the eternal procession of the Son from the Father, and we saw that this formed a basis for their identities *as* Son and Father. The eternal processions among the persons of the Trinity establish the relationships among the three Persons, including the Holy Spirit.

If the Holy Spirit proceeded from the Father the way that the Son does then he would either be the Son or, perhaps, a second Son. But this is not how Scripture reveals him to us. He is not a Son. Instead he is described as the Spirit "of the Father" (Mt 10:20) and as the Spirit "of the Son" (Gal 4:6). This suggests that both the Father and the Son are involved in the procession of the Spirit.

Passages that speak of the Father and the Son sending the Spirit to believers in this world (Jn 15:26; Acts 2:33) also suggest this. They deal with the external mission of the Holy Spirit, but they also display a set of relationships that reflect the internal—and eternal—relationships among the Persons of the Trinity.

Unfortunately, this has been a source of controversy in Christian history. The Western Church commonly uses a version of the *Nicene Creed* that states that the Holy Spirit proceeds from the Father "and the Son," which in Latin is represented by the word *filioque* (*filius* = "son"; *-que* = "and"). This was not in the original version of the creed, and thus it is not used in Eastern churches.

This is where the controversy arises. Many in the East argue that it was wrong for the West to include this in the creed, either because such an inclusion should have been done in consultation with the East or because they regard it as erroneous. The controversy has been a stumbling block in the relationship between Eastern and Western Christians, but there is hope for overcoming it.

The solution may involve passages from the early Church Fathers, both Latin and Greek, who affirmed that the Spirit proceeds "from the Father *and* the Son" or "from the Father *through* the Son."

These expressions can be seen as equivalent because of the Son's own procession from the Father. Everything the Son has is from the Father. Thus the procession of the Spirit from the Son is something the Son himself received from the Father. The Father remains the sole origin or *archē* of the Persons of the Trinity. Saying that the Spirit proceeds from the Father "and the Son" would thus be equivalent to saying that he proceeds from the Father "through the Son."

The latter affirmation is accepted by some Eastern Orthodox, and led to an attempted reunion of the two churches in 1439 at the Council of Florence: "The Greek prelates believed that every saint, precisely as a saint, was inspired by the Holy Spirit and therefore could not err in faith. If they expressed themselves differently, their meanings must substantially agree. . . . Once the Greeks accepted that the Latin Fathers had really written *filioque* (they could not understand Latin), the issue was settled (May 29). The Greek Fathers necessarily meant the same; the faiths of the two churches were identical; union was not only possible but obligatory (June

3); and on June 8 the Latin *credula* [statements of belief] on the procession [of the Spirit] was accepted by the Greek synod" (*New Catholic Encyclopedia*, 5:972–3). Unfortunately, the union did not take hold. However, such union may still be possible. The *Catechism of the Catholic Church* notes the differences between how Eastern and Western views are expressed and states that "[t]his legitimate complementarity [of expressions], provided it does not become rigid, does not affect the identity of faith in the reality of the same mystery confessed" (CCC 248).[3]

Similarly, today some Eastern Orthodox acknowledge that there need be no separation between the two communions on this issue. Orthodox Bishop Kallistos Ware (formerly Timothy Ware), who previously wrote against the *filioque* doctrine, has stated: "The *filioque* controversy which has separated us for so many centuries is more than a mere technicality, but it is not insoluble. Qualifying the firm position taken when I wrote [my book] *The Orthodox Church* twenty years ago, I now believe, after further study, that the problem is more in the area of semantics and different emphases than in any basic doctrinal differences" (*Diakonia*, quoted from Archbishop Elias Zoghby's *A Voice from the Byzantine East*, 43).

TERTULLIAN OF CARTHAGE

I believe the Spirit to proceed from no other source than from the Father through the Son [*Against Praxeas* 4 (c. A.D. 218)].

ST. GREGORY THAUMATURGUS

And there is one Holy Spirit, having his subsistence from God, and being made manifest by the Son, to men: image of the Son, perfect image of the perfect; life, the cause of the living; holy fount; sanctity, the supplier of sanctification; in whom is mani-

---

[3] For additional information see the document *The Greek and Latin traditions Regarding the Procession of the Holy Spirit* by the Pontifical Council for Promoting Christian Unity, available online.

fested God the Father, who is above all and in all, and God the Son, who is through all [*Declaration of Faith* (c. A.D. 265)].

ST. HILARY OF POITIERS

Concerning the Holy Spirit . . . there is no need to speak, because we are bound to confess him, proceeding, as he does, from Father and Son [*The Trinity* 2:29 (c. A.D. 357)].

But I cannot describe him, whose pleas for me I cannot describe. As in the revelation that your only-begotten was born of you before times eternal, when we cease to struggle with ambiguities of language and difficulties of thought, the one certainty of his birth remains; so I hold fast in my consciousness the truth that your Holy Spirit is from you and through him, although I cannot by my intellect comprehend it [ibid., 12:56].

DIDYMUS THE BLIND

As we have understood discussions . . . about the incorporeal natures, so too it is now to be recognized that the Holy Spirit receives from the Son that which he was of his own nature. . . . So too the Son is said to receive from the Father the very things by which he subsists. For neither has the Son anything else except those things given him by the Father, nor has the Holy Spirit any other substance than that given him by the Son [*The Holy Spirit* 37 (c. A.D. 371)].

ST. EPIPHANIUS OF SALAMIS

The Father always existed and the Son always existed, and the Spirit breathes from the Father and the Son [*Man Well-Anchored* 75 (A.D. 374)].

ST. BASIL OF CAESAREA

One, moreover, is the Holy Spirit, and we speak of him singly, conjoined as he is to the one Father through the one Son, and through himself completing the adorable and blessed Trinity [*The Holy Spirit* 18:45 (A.D. 375)].

Thus the way of the knowledge of God lies from one Spirit through the one Son to the one Father, and conversely the natural goodness and the inherent holiness and the royal dignity extend from the Father through the only-begotten to the Spirit. Thus there is both acknowledgment of the hypostases and the true dogma of the monarchy is not lost [ibid., 18:47].

ST. AMBROSE OF MILAN

That is the fount of the Holy Spirit, for the Spirit is life, as the Lord says: "The words I speak unto you are Spirit and life [Jn 6:64]" [*The Holy Spirit* 1:15:172 (A.D. 381)].

The Holy Spirit, when he proceeds from the Father and the Son, does not separate himself from the Father and does not separate himself from the Son [ibid., 1:11:120].

ST. GREGORY OF NYSSA

For there, with the Father, unoriginated, ungenerated, always Father, the idea of the Son as coming from him yet side by side with him is inseparably joined; and through the Son and yet with him, before any vague and unsubstantial conception comes in between, the Holy Spirit is found at once in closest union [*Against Eunomius* 1:26 (c. A.D. 382)].

ST. AUGUSTINE OF HIPPO

[T]hat which is given has him for a beginning by whom it is given, since it has received from no other source what proceeds from him; it must be admitted that the Father and the Son are a beginning of the Holy Spirit, not two beginnings; but as the Father and Son are one God, and one Creator, and one Lord relative to the creature, so are they one beginning relative to the Holy Spirit. But the Father, the Son, and the Holy Spirit is one beginning relative to the creature, as also one Creator and one God [*The Trinity* 5:14:15 (c. A.D. 408)].

[The one] from whom the Holy Spirit principally proceeds. And therefore I have added the word principally, because we find that the Holy Spirit proceeds from the Son also [ibid., 15:17:29].

Why, then, should we not believe that the Holy Spirit proceeds also from the Son, when he is the Spirit also of the Son? For if the Holy Spirit did not proceed from him, when he showed himself to his disciples after his Resurrection he would not have breathed upon them, saying, "Receive the Holy Spirit" [Jn 20:22]. For what else did he signify by that breathing upon them except that the Holy Spirit proceeds also from him [Tractates on John 99:7 (A.D. 416–417)].

ST. CYRIL OF ALEXANDRIA

Since the Holy Spirit when he is in us effects our being conformed to God, and he actually proceeds from the Father and Son, it is abundantly clear that he is of the divine essence, in it in essence and proceeding from it [Treasury of the Holy Trinity, thesis 34 (c. A.D. 424)].

ATHANASIAN CREED

[T]hat we worship one God in Trinity and Trinity in unity. . . . The Father uncreated, the Son uncreated, and the Holy Spirit uncreated. The Father incomprehensible, the Son incomprehensible, and the Holy Spirit incomprehensible. The Father eternal, the Son eternal, and the Holy Spirit eternal, and yet they are not three eternals but one eternal [Athanasian Creed (c. A.D. 425)].

ST. FULGENCE OF RUSPE

Hold most firmly and never doubt in the least that the same Holy Spirit who is Spirit of the Father and of the Son proceeds from the Father and the Son [The Rule of Faith 54 (A.D. 524)].

ST. JOHN OF DAMASCUS

I say that God is always Father since he has always his Word [the Son] coming from himself and, through his Word, the Spirit issuing from him [*Dialogue Against the Manicheans* 5 (c. A.D. 728)].

Likewise we believe also in one Holy Spirit, the Lord and giver of life . . . God existing and addressed along with Father and Son: uncreated, full, creative, all-ruling, all-effecting, all-powerful, of infinite power, Lord of all creation and not under any Lord; deifying, not deified; filling, not filled; shared in, not sharing in; sanctifying, not sanctified; the intercessor, receiving the supplications of all; in all things like the Father and Son, proceeding from the Father and communicated through the Son [*Exposition of the Orthodox Faith* 1:8 (c. A.D. 746)].

And the Holy Spirit is the power of the Father revealing the hidden mysteries of his divinity, proceeding from the Father through the Son in a manner known to himself, but different from that of generation [ibid., 12].

V. Creation

20. Creation out of Nothing

The Christian faith holds that God created the world *ex nihilo* (Latin, "out of nothing"). Modern science has pointed to the Big Bang as the origin of the world we find around us, and that moment may or may not be the point at which God created everything out of nothing. Whatever light the findings of science may be able to shed on the origin of the cosmos, it remains a truth of the faith that, at some point, however remote in the past, God made the world *ex nihilo*.

Thus the *Catechism of the Catholic Church* states: "We believe that God needs no preexistent thing or any help in order to create, nor is creation any sort of necessary emanation from the divine substance. God creates freely 'out of nothing'" (CCC 296).

Despite the firmness with which this understanding of creation has been held in Christian thought, some have rejected it. Mormons, for example, claim that God at one time lived at or near a star or planet named Kolob, and went on to fashion the world out of a pre-existing substance. In recent years, some in the Pentecostal movement have said similar things. Word-Faith preacher Kenneth Copeland has stated that heaven is another planet and that God created Earth to be a copy of it.

As the following quotations from the Church Fathers reveal, this is very different than what the early Christians believed.

HERMAS OF ROME

And as I prayed, the heavens were opened, and I saw the woman whom I had desired saluting me from the sky, and saying, "Hail, Hermas!" And looking up to her, I said, "Lady, what are you doing here?" And she answered me, "I have been taken up here to accuse you of your sins before the Lord." "Lady," said I, "are you

to be the subject of my accusation?" "No," said she, "but hear
the words which I am going to speak to you. God, who dwells
in the heavens, and made out of nothing the things that exist, and
multiplied and increased them on account of his holy Church, is
angry with you for having sinned against me" [*The Shepherd* 1:1:1
(c. A.D. 80)].

First of all, believe that there is one God who created and finished
all things, and made all things out of nothing. He alone is able to
contain the whole, but he cannot be contained. Therefore have
faith in him, and fear him; and fearing him, exercise self-control.
Keep these commands, and you will cast all wickedness away from
you, and put on the strength of righteousness, and live to God, if
you keep this commandment [ibid., 2:1:1].

ST. ARISTIDES OF ATHENS

Let us proceed then, O king, to the elements themselves, that we
may show in regard to them that they are not gods, but perishable
and mutable, produced out of what did not exist at the command
of the true God, who is indestructible and immutable and invisible; yet he sees all things and, as he wills, modifies and changes
things. What then shall I say concerning the elements? [*Apology*
4 (c. A.D. 140)].

ST. THEOPHILUS OF ANTIOCH

And he is without beginning, because he is unbegotten; and he
is unchangeable, because he is immortal. And he is called God
[*Theos*] because he established [*tetheikenai*] all things with a security that he himself provided; and on account of *théein*, for *théein*
means running, and moving, and being active, and nourishing,
and foreseeing, and governing, and making all things alive. But
he is Lord, because he rules over the universe; Father, because
he is before all things; fashioner and maker, because he is creator and maker of the universe; the highest, because of his being
above all; and Almighty, because he rules and embraces all. For
the heights of heaven, and the depths of the abysses, and the ends
of the earth are in his hand and there is no place where he rests.

For the heavens are his work, the earth is his creation, the sea is his handiwork; man is his formation and his image; sun, moon, and stars are his elements, made for signs, and seasons, and days, and years, that they may serve and be slaves to man; and all things God has made, out of things that were not into things that are, in order that through his works his greatness may be known and understood [*To Autolycus* 1:4 (c. A.D. 181)].

And first, [the prophets of God] taught us with one consent that God made all things out of nothing; for nothing was co-eternal with God: but he being his own place, and wanting nothing, and existing before the ages, willed to make man by whom he might be known; for [man], therefore, he prepared the world. For he that is created is also needy; but he that is uncreated needs nothing [ibid., 2:10].

ST. IRENAEUS OF LYONS

While men cannot make anything out of nothing, but only out of matter already existing, yet God is preeminently superior to men in this point, that he himself called into being the substance of his creation, when previously it had no existence. But the assertion that matter was produced from the *enthymesis* of an *aeon* going astray, and that the *aeon* was far separated from her *enthymesis*, and that, again, her passion and feeling, apart from herself, became matter—is incredible, infatuated, impossible, and untenable [*Against Heresies* 2:10:4 (c. A.D. 189)].

TERTULLIAN OF CARTHAGE

The object of our worship is the one God, who, by the word of his command, by the reason of his plan, and by the strength of his power has brought forth from nothing this whole construction of elements, bodies, and spirits for the glory of his majesty; which is why the Greeks have bestowed upon the world the name "cosmos" [*Apology* 17 (A.D. 197)].

Now, with regard to this rule of faith—that we may from this point acknowledge what we defend—it is what prescribes the belief that there is one God, and that he is none other than the Creator of the world, who produced all things out of nothing through his own Word, first of all sent forth [*Prescription Against Heretics* 13 (c. A.D. 200)].

This rule is required by the nature of the one and only God, who is only one in no other way than as the sole God; and in no other way sole, than as having nothing else [co-existent] with him. So also he will be first, because all things are after him; and all things are after him, because all things are by him; and all things are by him, because they came from nothing: so that reason coincides with the Scripture that says: "Who has known the mind of the Lord? Or who has been his counselor? Or with whom took he counsel? Or who has shown to him the way of wisdom and knowledge? Who has first given to him, and it shall be recompensed to him again?" [Rom 11:33–36] [*Against Hermogenes* 17:1 (c. A.D. 203)].

ST. HIPPOLYTUS OF ROME

On the first day God made what he made out of nothing. But on the other days he did not make out of nothing, but out of what he had made on the first day, by molding it according to his pleasure [fragment from *On Genesis* (A.D. 217)].

ORIGEN OF ALEXANDRIA

The particular points clearly delivered in the teaching of the apostles are as follows: First, that there is one God, who created and arranged all things, and who, when nothing existed, called all things into being—God from the first creation and foundation of the world, the God of all just men, of Adam, Abel, Seth, Enos, Enoch, Noah, Terah, Abraham, Isaac, Jacob, the twelve patriarchs, Moses, and the prophets; and that this God in the last days, as he had announced beforehand through his prophets, sent our Lord Jesus Christ to call to himself in the first place Israel, and in the second place the Gentiles, after the unfaithfulness of the people of Israel. This just and good God, the Father of our Lord Jesus

Christ, gave the law and the prophets, and the Gospels, being also the God of the apostles and of the Old and New Testaments [*Fundamental Doctrines* Preface 4 (c. A.D. 225)].

ST. CYPRIAN OF CARTHAGE

[The mother of the seven Maccabean martyrs said:] "O son, pity me that bore you ten months in the womb, and gave you milk for three years, and nourished you and brought you up to this age; I pray you, O son, look upon the heaven and the earth; and having considered all the things that are in them, understand that out of nothing God made these things and the human race. Therefore, O son, do not fear that executioner; but being made worthy of your brethren, receive death, that in the same mercy I may receive you with your brethren." The mother's praise was great in her exhortation to virtue, but greater in the fear of God and in the truth of faith, that she promised nothing to herself or her son from the honor of the six martyrs, nor believed that the prayer of the brothers would save the one who should deny, but instead persuaded him to share in their suffering, that on the day of judgment he might be found with his brethren [*Exhortation to Martyrdom* 11 (c. A.D. 254)].

ON THE END OF THE WORLD

Then shall the righteous answer, astonished at the mighty and wondrous fact that he, who the hosts of angels cannot look upon openly, addresses them as friends, and they shall cry out to him, "Lord, when saw we you hungry, and fed you? Master, when saw we you thirsty, and gave you drink? You terrible one, when saw we you naked, and clothed you? Immortal, when saw we you a stranger, and took you in? You friend of man, when saw we you sick or in prison, and came to you? You are the ever-living one. You are without beginning, like the Father, and co-eternal with the Spirit. You are he who made all things out of nothing" [*On the End of the World* 43 (c. A.D. 267)].

ST. METHODIUS OF PHILIPPI

[I]n fact out of nothing, man is brought into being, [so] how much rather shall man spring into being again out of a previously existing man? For it is not so difficult to make anything anew after it has once existed and fallen into decay, as to produce out of nothing what has never existed [*Discourse on the Resurrection* 1:14 (c. A.D. 300)].

[A]ll things are placed under you as their cause and author, as he who brought all things into being out of nothing, and gave coherence to what was unstable; as the connecting band and preserver of what has been brought into being; as the framer of things by nature different; as he who, with wise and steady hand, holds the helm of the universe; as the very principle of all good order; as the unbreakable bond of concord and peace [*Oration on Simeon and Anna* 6 (c. A.D. 300)]

LACTANTIUS

[O]ne is foolish to think the one God, who had power to create the universe, is unable to govern what he created. But if he conceives in his mind how immense is that divine work, when before it was nothing, yet that by the power and wisdom of God it was made out of nothing—a work that could only be commenced and accomplished by one—he will understand that what has been established by one is much more easily governed by one [*Divine Institutes* 1:3 (c. A.D. 307)].

Now, having refuted those who entertain false sentiments respecting the world and God, its maker, let us return to the divine workmanship of the world, about which we are informed by the sacred writings of our holy religion. First of all, God made the heaven, and suspended it on high, that it might be his seat, the Creator. Then he founded the earth, and placed it under heaven, as a dwelling-place for man, and the other races of animals. He willed that it should be surrounded and held together by water. But he adorned and filled his own dwelling-place with bright lights; he decked it with the sun, and the shining orb of the moon, and with the glittering signs of the twinkling stars; but he placed on the earth the darkness, which is contrary to these. For in itself the earth contains no light, unless it receives it from the heaven, in which he placed perpetual light, and the gods above, and eternal life; and, on the contrary, he placed on the earth darkness, and the inhabitants of the lower regions, and death. For these things are as far removed from heavenly things, as evil things are from good, and vices from virtues. He also established two parts of the earth opposite to one another, and of a different character—the east and the west; and of these the east is assigned to God, because he himself is the fountain of light, and the enlightener of all things, and because he makes us rise to eternal life. But the west is ascribed to the disturbed and depraved mind, because it conceals the light, because it always brings on darkness, and because it makes men die and perish in their sins. For as light belongs to the east, and the whole course of life depends upon the light, so darkness belongs to the west, and death and destruction are contained in darkness. Then he measured out the other parts—the south and the north, which are closely united with the two former. For what glows with the warmth of the sun is nearest to and closely united with the east; but what is torpid with cold and perpetual ice belongs to the extreme west. For as darkness is opposed to light, so is cold to heat. As, therefore, heat is nearest to light, so is the south to the east; and as cold is nearest to darkness, so is the northern region to the west. And he assigned to each of these parts its own time— namely, the spring to the east, the summer to the southern region, the autumn to the west, and the winter to the north. In these two parts also, the southern and the northern, is contained a figure of life and death, because life consists in heat, death in cold. And as heat arises from fire, so does cold from water. And according to the division of these parts he also made day and night, to complete by alternate succession with each other the courses and perpetual revolutions of time, which we call years. The day, which the first east supplies, must belong to God, as all things do that are of a better character. But the night, which the extreme west brings on, belongs to the rival of God [ibid., 2:10].

ST. ALEXANDER OF ALEXANDRIA

[T]he Word by which the Father formed all things out of nothing was begotten of the true Father himself [*Letters on the Arian Heresy* 1:11 (A.D. 324)].

APOSTOLIC CONSTITUTIONS

[S]o also will he raise all men up by his will, not wanting any assistance. For it is the work of the same power to create the world and to raise the dead. And then he made man, who was not a man before, of different parts, giving to him a soul made out of nothing. But now he will restore the bodies, which have been dissolved, to the souls that are still in being: for the rising again belongs to things laid down, not to things that have no being. So he that made the original bodies out of nothing, and fashioned various forms of them, will also revive and raise up those that are dead [*Apostolic Constitutions* 5:1:7 (c. A.D. 400)].

For you [Father] are eternal knowledge, everlasting sight, unbegotten hearing, untaught wisdom, the first by nature, and the measure of being, and beyond all number; who brought all things into being out of nothing through your only begotten Son, but begot him before all ages by your will, your power, and your goodness, without any instrument, the only begotten Son, God the Word [ibid., 8:2:12].

ST. AUGUSTINE OF HIPPO

O Lord, who are not one thing in one place, and otherwise in another, but the self-same, and the self-same, and the self-same, holy, holy, holy, Lord God Almighty, did in the beginning, which is of you, in your wisdom, which was born of your substance, create something out of nothing. For you created heaven and earth, not out of yourself, for then they would be equal to your only-begotten, and thereby even to you; and in no way would it be right that anything should be equal to you that was not of you. And there was not anything else except you out of which you might create these things, O God, one Trinity, and triune unity; and, therefore, out of nothing you created heaven and earth [*Confessions* 12:7:7 (c. A.D. 400)].

[T]hough God formed man of the dust of the earth, yet the earth itself, and every earthly material, is absolutely created out of nothing; and man's soul, too, God created out of nothing, and joined to the body, when he made man [*City of God* 14:11 (c. A.D. 419)].

21. *Creation in Genesis*

The first chapter of Genesis depicts the creation of the world over a period of six days, each of which consists of an evening followed by a morning (in keeping with the Hebrew reckoning of the day beginning at sunset). If taken literally, this would mean that the world was created in under a week of what seem to be twenty-four-hour days.

This view has been common in Church history, though it is not the only view possible. The Fathers held different opinions on the matter, and their writings show significant variation on how long creation took. Some said only a few days; others argued for a much longer, indefinite period.

Those who took the latter view appealed to the fact "that with the Lord one day is as a thousand years, and a thousand years as one day" (2 Pt 3:8; see also Ps 90:4), that light was created on the first day, but the sun was not created until the fourth day (see Gn 1:3, 16), and that Adam was told he would die the same "day" as he ate of the tree, yet he lived to be 930 years old (Gn 2:17; 5:5).

Catholics are at liberty to believe that creation took a few days or a much longer period, according to how they see the evidence, and subject to any future judgment of the Church (Pius XII's 1950 encyclical *Humani Generis* 36–37).

They need not be hostile to modern cosmology. The *Catechism of the Catholic Church* states that "many scientific studies . . . have splendidly enriched our knowledge of the age and dimensions of the cosmos, the development of life forms, and the appearance of man. These studies invite us to even greater admiration for the greatness of the Creator" (CCC 283). The *Catechism* also states that "Scripture presents the work of the Creator symbolically as a succession of six days of divine 'work,' concluded by the 'rest' of the seventh day" (CCC 337). While these statements are harmonious with the idea that God used a long period of time to produce the world in its current form, they do not preclude an individual from taking a more literal, young earth view.

ST. JUSTIN MARTYR

For as Adam was told that on the day he ate of the tree he would die, we know that he did not complete a thousand years. We have perceived, moreover, that the expression "The day of the Lord is as a thousand years" is connected with this subject [*Dialogue with Trypho* 81 (c. A.D. 155)].

ST. THEOPHILUS OF ANTIOCH

On the fourth day the luminaries were made; because God, who possesses foreknowledge, knew the follies of the vain philosophers, that they were going to say that the things that grow on the earth are produced from the heavenly bodies, so as to exclude God. In order that the truth might be obvious, the plants and seeds were produced prior to the heavenly bodies, for what is posterior cannot produce what is prior [*To Autolycus* 2:15 (c. A.D. 181)].

All the years from the creation of the world [to Theophilus's day] amount to a total of 5,698 years and the odd months and days. . . . [I]f even a chronological error has been committed by us, of, for example, fifty or one hundred, or even two hundred years, yet not of thousands and tens of thousands, as Plato and Apollonius and other mendacious authors have hitherto written. And perhaps our knowledge of the whole number of the years is not quite accurate, because the odd months and days are not set down in the sacred books [ibid., 3:28].

ST. IRENAEUS OF LYONS

And there are some, again, who relegate the death of Adam to the thousandth year; for since "a day of the Lord is as a thousand years" [1 Pt 3:8], he did not overstep the thousand years, but died within them, thus bearing out the sentence of his sin [*Against Heresies* 5:23:2 (c. A.D. 189)].

ST. CLEMENT OF ALEXANDRIA

And how could creation take place in time, seeing time was born along with things that exist? . . . So that we may be taught that the world was originated [in this way], and not suppose that God made it in time, prophecy adds: "This is the book of the generation: also of the things in them, when they were created in the day that God made heaven and earth." For the expression "when they were created" intimates an indefinite and dateless production. But the expression "in the day that God made," that is, in and by which God made "all things," and "without which not even one thing was made," points out the activity exerted by the Son [*Miscellanies* 6:16 (c. A.D. 207)].

ORIGEN OF ALEXANDRIA

For who that has understanding will suppose that the first, and second, and third day, and the evening and the morning, existed without a sun, and moon, and stars? And that the first day was also without a sky? And who is so foolish as to suppose that God, after the manner of a husbandman, planted a paradise in Eden, towards the east, and placed in it a tree of life, visible and palpable, so that one tasting of the fruit by the bodily teeth obtained life? And again, that one was a partaker of good and evil by eating the fruit? And if God is said to walk in the paradise in the evening, and Adam to hide himself under a tree, I do not suppose that anyone doubts that these things figuratively indicate certain mysteries, the history having taken place in appearance, and not literally [*Fundamental Doctrines* 4:16 (c. A.D. 225)].

The text said that "there was evening and there was morning"; it did not say "the first day," but said "one day." It is because before the world existed there was not yet time. But time begins to exist with the following days [*Homilies on Genesis* 1 (c. A.D. 242)].

And since [the pagan Celsus] makes the statements about the "days of creation" ground of accusation, as if he understood them clearly and correctly, some of which elapsed before the creation of light and heaven, the sun and moon and stars, and some after, we shall only make this observation, that Moses must have forgotten that he had said a little before "that in six days the creation of the world had been finished" and that in consequence of his forgetfulness he adds to these words the following: "This is the book of the creation of man in the day when God made the heaven and the earth" [Gn 2:4] [*Against Celsus* 6:51 (c. A.D. 248)].

And with regard to the creation of the light upon the first day . . . and of the [great] lights and stars upon the fourth . . . we have treated it to the best of our ability in our notes upon Genesis, as well as in the foregoing pages, when we found fault with those who, taking the words in their apparent signification, said that the time of six days was occupied in the creation of the world [ibid., 6:60].

For [the pagan Celsus] knows nothing of the day of the Sabbath and rest of God that follows the completion of the world's creation, and that lasts for the duration of the world, and in which all those who have done all their work in their six days will keep the festival with God [ibid., 6:61].

ST. CYPRIAN OF CARTHAGE

As the first seven days in the divine arrangement containing seven thousand years [*Exhortation to Martyrdom* (Treatise 11) 11 (c. A.D. 254)].

ST. VICTORINUS OF PETTAU

God produced that entire mass for the adornment of his majesty in six days; on the seventh he consecrated it . . . with a blessing [*Creation of the World* (c. A.D. 270)].

LACTANTIUS

Therefore let the philosophers, who enumerate thousands of ages from the beginning of the world, know that the six thousandth year is not yet complete. . . . Therefore, since all the works of God were completed in six days, the world must continue in its present state through six ages, that is, six thousand years. For the great day of God is limited by a circle of a thousand years, as the prophet shows who says, "In your sight, O Lord, a thousand years are as one day" [*Divine Institutes* 7:14 (c. A.D. 307)].

ST. BASIL OF CAESAREA

And the evening and the morning were one day. Why does Scripture say one day the first day? Before speaking to us of the second, the third, and the fourth days, would it not have been more natural to call that one the first that began the series? If it therefore says one day, it is from a wish to determine the measure of day and night, and to combine the time they contain. Now twenty-four hours fill up the space of one day [*Six Days of Creation* 2:8 (c. A.D. 367)].

ST. AMBROSE OF MILAN

Scripture established a law that twenty-four hours, including both day and night, should be given the name of day only, as if to say the length of one day is twenty-four hours in extent. . . . [T]he nights in this reckoning are considered to be component parts of the days that are counted. Therefore, just as there is a single revolution of time, so there is but one day. There are many who call even a week one day, because it returns to itself, just as one day does, and one might say seven times revolves back on itself. That is the form of a circle, to begin with itself and to return to itself. Hence, Scripture appeals at times to an age of the world [*Six Days of Creation* 1:10:37 (c. A.D. 394)].

ST. AUGUSTINE OF HIPPO

There is knowledge to be had, after all, about the earth, about the sky, about the other elements of this world, about the movements and revolutions or the magnitude and distances of constellations, about the predictable eclipses of moon and sun, about the cycles of years and seasons, about the nature of animals, fruits, stones, and everything else of this kind. And it frequently happens that even non-Christians have knowledge of this sort that they can substantiate with scientific arguments or experiments. Now it is quite disgraceful and disastrous, something to be on one's guard against at all costs, that they should ever hear Christians spouting what they claim our Christian literature has to say on these topics, and talking such nonsense that they can scarcely contain their laughter when they see them to be *toto caelo*, as the saying goes, wide of the mark. And what is so vexing is not that misguided people should be laughed at, as that our authors should be assumed by outsiders to have held such views and, to the great detriment of those about whose salvation we are concerned, should be written off and consigned to the wastepaper basket as so many ignoramuses. . . . It is in order to take account of this state of things that I have, to the best of my ability, drawn out and presented a great variety of possible meanings to the words of the book of Genesis that have been darkly expressed in order to put us through our paces. I have avoided affirming anything hastily in a way that would rule out any better alternative explanation, leaving everyone free to choose whichever they can grasp most readily in their turn [*Literal Interpretation of Genesis* 1:19–20 (c. A.D. 408)].

But because the trustworthiness of the Scriptures is in question, this, as I have reminded readers more than once, has to be defended from those who do not understand the style of the divine utterances, and who assume when they find anything on these matters in our books, or hear them read out from them, that seems to be contrary to explanations they have worked out, that thus they should not place any confidence in the Scriptures when they warn or tell them about other useful things. It must be stated that our authors knew about the shape of the sky whatever may be the truth of the matter. But the Spirit of God who was speaking through them did not wish to teach people about things that would contribute nothing to their salvation [ibid., 2:9].

So for the sake of argument, let us suppose that these seven days [which we experience in a modern week], which in their stead [in the stead of the days of creation] constitute the week that whirls times and seasons along by its constant recurrence, in which one day is the whole circuit of the sun from sunrise to sunrise— that these seven [modern days] represent those first seven [days of creation] in some fashion, though we must be in no doubt that they are not at all like them, but very, very dissimilar [ibid., 4:27].

One could readily jump to the conclusion, after all, that a day of bodily light was meant, which goes round and round to provide us with the alternations of daytime and nighttime. But then we recall the order in which things were fashioned, and find that all the greenery of the field was created on the third day, before the sun was made on the fourth day, the sun that regulates by its presence this normal day we are used to. So when we hear the word, "When the day was made, God made heaven and earth and all the greenery of the field," we are being admonished to turn our thoughts to that special day we should be striving to track down with our minds, which . . . is certainly not such as the one we are familiar with here [ibid., 5:2].

For in these days [of creation] the morning and evening are counted until, on the sixth day, all things God then made were finished, and on the seventh the rest of God was mysteriously and sublimely signaled. What kind of days these were is extremely difficult or perhaps impossible for us to conceive, and how much more to say! [*City of God* 11:6 (c. A.D. 419)].

We see that our ordinary days have no evening but by the setting [of the sun] and no morning but by the rising of the sun, but the first three days of all were passed without sun, since it is reported to have been made on the fourth day. And first of all, indeed, light was made by the word of God, and God, we read, separated it from the darkness and called the light "day" and the darkness "night"; but what kind of light that was, and by what periodic movement it made evening and morning, is beyond the reach of our senses; neither can we understand how it was and yet must unhesitatingly believe it [ibid., 11:7].

[Pagans] are deceived, too, by those highly mendacious documents that profess to give the history of [man as] many thousands of years, though reckoning by the sacred writings we find that not six thousand years have yet passed [ibid., 12:10].

VI. The Sources of Faith

22. The Canon of Scripture

The canon of Scripture has been the subject of controversy. Although Jesus and the apostles clearly recognized the books of the Old Testament as Scripture, and although some of the apostles and their associates wrote the books of the New Testament, the first generation of Christians did not provide us with a list of which books counted as Scripture and which did not.

As a result, it took some time for the canon to be discerned. At first, there was not even a division between the Old Testament and the New Testament. The books we think of as comprising the New Testament were at first perceived only as new holy books to be added to those that had already been written.

What the existing holy books were could also be unclear, since different groups of Jews honored different traditions regarding which books were sacred. It is clear from the fact that the authors of the New Testament almost always quoted from the Septuagint version of the Old Testament (a Greek translation made in Alexandria) that this version was very important to the first-century Christian community.

This is significant because the Septuagint version contains certain books (1 and 2 Maccabees, Sirach, Wisdom, Baruch, Tobit, and Judith) as well as parts of two other books (Daniel and Esther) that Catholics refer to as "deuterocanonical" (in contrast to the other books of Scripture which are termed "protocanonical"). Protestants do not honor the deuterocanonical books as Scripture and commonly refer to them as the "Apocrypha."

The New Testament nowhere cautions against using these books of the Septuagint, and in fact the authors of the New Testament allude to them (e.g., Heb 11:35 contains a very clear reference to 2 Mc 7). Because of the New Testament's use of the

Septuagint, and its failure to caution against any books of that translation, the early Christian community used this translation, including the deuterocanonical books. Protestant church historian J. N. D. Kelly writes, "It should be observed that the Old Testament thus admitted as authoritative in the Church was somewhat bulkier and more comprehensive. . . . It always included, though with varying degrees of recognition, the so-called apocrypha or deuterocanonical books" (*Early Christian Doctrines*, 53).

Below are patristic quotations regarding each of the deuterocanonical books. Notice how the Fathers quoted these books along with the protocanonical books.

The earliest conciliar lists of the canon, including the deuterocanonical books, are given. (For the sake of brevity some of these are not given in full, but we cite the parts dealing with the deuterocanonicals.)

Note that some of the books of the Bible are known by more than one name. Sirach is also known as Ecclesiasticus, 1 and 2 Chronicles is also known as 1 and 2 Paralipomenon, Ezra and Nehemiah as 1 and 2 Esdras, and 1 and 2 Samuel together with 1 and 2 Kings as 1, 2, 3, and 4 Kings (that is, 1 and 2 Samuel are named 1 and 2 Kings, and 1 and 2 Kings are named 3 and 4 Kings).

It should also be noted that some books were at times grouped together as one book. A famous case is that of Jeremiah, Lamentations, Baruch, and the Letter of Jeremiah, which were often combined in various ways and treated as consisting of as as few as two books.

DIDACHE

Do not be someone who stretches out his hands to receive but withdraws them when it comes to giving [Sir 4:31] [*Didache* 4 (c. A.D. 50)].

POPE ST. CLEMENT I

By the word of his might he established all things, and by his word he can overthrow them. "Who shall say unto him, 'What

have you done?' or, 'Who shall resist the power of his strength?' "
[Wis 12:12] [*Letter to the Corinthians* 27:4-5 (A.D. 70)].

LETTER OF BARNABAS

Since, therefore, [Christ] was about to be manifested and to suffer
in the flesh, his suffering was foreshown. For the prophet speaks
against evil, "Woe to their soul, because they have counseled an
evil counsel against themselves" [Is 3:9], saying, "Let us bind the
righteous man because he is displeasing to us" [Wis 2:12] [*Letter
of Barnabas* 6 (c. A.D. 75)].

ST. POLYCARP OF SMYRNA

Stand fast, therefore, in these things, and follow the example of
the Lord, being firm and unchangeable in the faith, loving the
brotherhood [1 Pt 2:17]. . . . When you can do good, do not defer it, because "alms delivers from death" [Tb 4:10; 12:9]. Be all
of you subject to one another [1 Pt 5:5], having your conduct
blameless among the Gentiles [1 Pt 2:12], and the Lord may not
be blasphemed through you. But woe to him who blasphemes
the name of the Lord [Is 52:5]! [*Letter to the Philippians* 10 (c. A.D.
135)].

ST. IRENAEUS OF LYONS

Those . . . who are believed to be presbyters by many, but serve
their own lusts and do not place the fear of God supreme in their
hearts, and conduct themselves with contempt toward others and
are puffed up with the pride of holding the chief seat [Mt 23:6]
and work evil deeds in secret, saying "No man sees us," shall
be convicted by the Word, who does not judge our outward appearance, or look upon the countenance, but the heart; and they
shall hear those words found in Daniel the prophet: "O you seed
of Canaan and not of Judah, beauty has deceived you and lust
perverted your heart" [Dn 13:56]. You that have grown old in
wicked days, now the sins that you committed before have come
to light, for you have pronounced false judgments and have been

accustomed to condemn the innocent and let the guilty go free, although the Lord says, "You shall not slay the innocent and the righteous" [Dn 13:52, citing Ex 23:7] [*Against Heresies* 4:26:3 (c. A.D. 189); Daniel 13 is not in the Protestant Bible].

Jeremiah the prophet has pointed out that as many believers as God has prepared to multiply those left on the earth should both be under the rule of the saints and minister to this [new] Jerusalem and that [his] kingdom shall be in it, saying, "Look around Jerusalem toward the east and behold the joy that comes to you from God himself. Behold, your sons whom you have sent forth shall come: They shall come in a band from the east to the west. . . . God shall go before you in the light of his splendor, with the mercy and righteousness which proceed from him" [Bar 4:36–5:9] [ibid., 5:35:1; Baruch was often considered part of Jeremiah, as it is here].

ST. HIPPOLYTUS OF ROME

What is narrated [in the story of Susannah] happened at a later time, although it is placed at the front of the book [of Daniel], for it was a custom with the writers to narrate many things in an inverted order in their writings. . . . [W]e ought to give heed, beloved, fearing lest anyone be overtaken in any transgression and risk the loss of his soul, knowing as we do that God is the judge of all and the Word is the eye that nothing done in the world escapes. Therefore, always watchful in heart and pure in life, let us imitate Susannah [fragment from *Commentary on Daniel* (c. A.D. 204); the story of Susannah in Daniel 13 is not in the Protestant Bible].

ST. CYPRIAN OF CARTHAGE

In Genesis [it says], "And God tested Abraham and said to him, 'Take your only son whom you love, Isaac, and go to the high land and offer him there as a burnt offering . . .'" [Gn 22:1–2]. . . . Of this same thing in the Wisdom of Solomon [it says], "Although in the sight of men they suffered torments, their hope is full of immortality . . ." [Wis 3:4]. Of this same thing in the Maccabees [it says], "Was not Abraham found faithful when tested, and it was reckoned to him for righteousness" [1 Mc 2:52; see Jas 2:21–23] [*Testimonies Concerning the Jews*, Book 3 Treatise 12 15 (A.D. 248)].

So Daniel, too, when he was required to worship the idol Bel, which the people and the king then worshipped, in asserting the honor of his God, broke forth with full faith and freedom, saying, "I worship nothing but the Lord my God, who created the heaven and the earth" [Dn 14:5] [*Letters* 55:5 (c. A.D. 253); Daniel 14 is not in the Protestant Bible].

COUNCIL OF ROME

Now indeed we must treat of the divine Scriptures, what the universal Catholic Church accepts and what she ought to shun: Genesis, one book; Exodus, one book; Leviticus, one book; Numbers, one book; Deuteronomy, one book; Joshua [Son of] Nave, one book; Judges, one book; Ruth, one book; Kings, four books [1 and 2 Samuel and 1 and 2 Kings]; Paralipomenon [Chronicles], two books; Psalms, one book; Solomon, three books: Proverbs, one book, Ecclesiastes, one book, Canticle of Canticles [i.e., Song of Songs], one book; likewise Wisdom, one book; Ecclesiasticus [Sirach], one book; Isaiah, one book; Jeremiah, one book, with Ginoth, that is, his Lamentations . . . Job, one book; Tobit, one book; Esdras, two books [i.e., Ezra and Nehemiah]; Esther, one book; Judith, one book; Maccabees, two books [*Decree of Pope Damasus* 2 (A.D. 382)].

COUNCIL OF HIPPO

But the canonical Scriptures are as follows: Genesis, Exodus, Leviticus, Numbers, Deuteronomy, Joshua the Son of Nun, the Judges, Ruth, the Kings, four books, the Chronicles, two books, Job, the Psalter, the five books of Solomon [Proverbs, Ecclesiastes, Song of Songs, Wisdom, Sirach], the Twelve Books of the [Minor] Prophets, Isaiah, Jeremiah, Ezekiel, Daniel, Tobit, Judith, Esther, Ezra, two books [i.e., Ezra and Nehemiah], Maccabees, two books, the Gospels, four books, the Acts of the Apostles, one book, the Letters of Paul, fourteen, the Letters of Peter the apostle, two, the Letters of John the apostle, three, the Letters of James the apostle, one, the Letter of Jude the apostle, one, the Revelation of John, one book [Canon 36 (A.D. 393)].

COUNCIL OF CARTHAGE OF 397

[It has been decided] that nothing except the canonical Scriptures should be read in the Church under the name of the divine Scriptures. But the canonical Scriptures are: Genesis, Exodus, Leviticus, Numbers, Deuteronomy, Joshua, Judges, Ruth, four books of Kings, Paralipomenon, two books, Job, the Psalter of David, five books of Solomon, twelve books of the prophets, Isaiah, Jeremiah, Daniel, Ezekiel, Tobit, Judith, Esther, two books of Esdras, two books of the Maccabees. [Canon 47 (A.D. 397)].

ST. AUGUSTINE OF HIPPO

The whole canon of the scriptures, however, in which we say that consideration is to be applied, is contained in these books: the five of Moses . . . and one book of Joshua [Son of] Nave; one of Judges; one little book that is called Ruth . . . then the four of Kingdoms, and the two of Paralipomenon. . . . [T]here are also others too, of a different order . . . such as Job and Tobit and Esther and Judith and the two books of Maccabees, and the two of Esdras. . . . Then there are the prophets, in which there is one book of the Psalms of David, and three of Solomon. . . . But as to those two books, one of which is entitled Wisdom and the other of which is entitled Ecclesiasticus and which are called "of Solomon" because of a certain similarity to his books, it is held most certainly that they were written by Jesus Sirach. They must, however, be accounted among the prophetic books, because of the authority deservedly accredited to them [*Christian Doctrine* 2:8:13 (A.D. 397)].

APOSTOLIC CONSTITUTIONS

Now women prophesied also. Of old, Miriam the sister of Moses and Aaron [Ex 15:20], and after her Deborah [Jgs 4:4], and after these Huldah [2 Kgs 22:14], and Judith [Jdt 8]—the former under

Josiah, the latter under Darius [*Apostolic Constitutions* 8:1:2 (c. A.D. 400)].

ST. JEROME

What sin have I committed if I follow the judgment of the churches? But he who brings charges against me for relating [in my preface to the book of Daniel] the objections that the Hebrews are wont to raise against the story of Susannah [Dn 13], the Song of the Three Children [Dn 3:29–68], and the story of Bel and the Dragon [Dn 14], which are not found in the Hebrew volume, proves that he is just a foolish sycophant. I was not relating my own personal views, but rather the remarks that they are wont to make against us. If I did not reply to their views in my preface, in the interest of brevity, lest it seem that I was composing not a preface, but a book, I believe I added promptly the remark, for I said, "This is not the time to discuss such matters" [*Apology Against Rufinus* 2:33 (A.D. 401)].

POPE ST. INNOCENT I

A brief addition shows what books really are received in the canon. These are the things of which you desired to be informed verbally: of Moses, five books, that is, of Genesis, of Exodus, of Leviticus, of Numbers, of Deuteronomy, and Joshua, of Judges, one book, of Kings, four books, and also Ruth, of the prophets, sixteen books, of Solomon, five books, the Psalms. Likewise of the histories, Job, one book, of Tobit, one book, Esther, one, Judith, one, of the Maccabees, two, of Esdras, two, Paralipomenon, two books. [Letter *Consulenti Tibi* to St. Exuperius (A.D. 405)].

COUNCIL OF CARTHAGE OF 419

That besides the canonical Scriptures nothing be read in church under the name of divine Scripture. But the canonical Scriptures are as follows: Genesis, Exodus, Leviticus, Numbers, Deuteronomy, Joshua the Son of Nun, the Judges, Ruth, the Kings, four books, the Chronicles, two books, Job, the Psalter, the five books of Solomon [Proverbs, Ecclesiastes, Song of Songs, Wisdom,

Sirach], the Twelve Books of the [Minor] Prophets, Isaiah, Jeremiah, Ezekiel, Daniel, Tobit, Judith, Esther, Ezra, two books [Ezra and Nehemiah], Maccabees, two books, the Gospels, four books, the Acts of the Apostles, one book, the Letters of Paul, fourteen, the Letters of Peter the apostle, two, the Letters of John the apostle, three, the Letters of James the apostle, one, the Letter of Jude the apostle, one, the Revelation of John, one book.

Let this be sent to our brother and fellow bishop, Boniface [Pope St. Boniface I], and to the other bishops of those parts, that they may confirm this canon, for these are the things that we have received from our fathers to be read in church [Canon 24(27), (A.D. 419)].

ST. AUGUSTINE OF HIPPO

We read in the books of the Maccabees [2 Mc 12:43] that sacrifice was offered for the dead. But even if it were found nowhere in the Old Testament writings, the authority of the Catholic Church, which is clear on this point, is of no small weight, where in the prayers of the priest poured forth to the Lord God at his altar, the commendation of the dead has its place [Care to Be Had for the Dead 3 (A.D. 421)].

23. Apostolic Tradition

In chapter 2, we looked at the role of Tradition in the Christian faith. Contrary to the view in the Protestant community, we are not intended to look to "Scripture alone." While we must guard against merely human tradition, the Bible contains multiple references to the respect we must give to apostolic Tradition.

Thus Paul tells the Corinthians, "I commend you because you remember me in everything and maintain the traditions even as I have delivered them to you" (1 Cor 11:2), and he commands the Thessalonians, "So then, brethren, stand firm and hold to the traditions that you were taught by us, either by word of mouth or by letter" (2 Thes 2:15). He even goes so far as to order, "Now we command you, brethren, in the name of our Lord Jesus Christ, that you keep away from any brother who is living in idleness and not in accord with the tradition that you received from us" (2 Thes 3:6).

To ensure that the apostolic Tradition would be passed down after the deaths of the apostles, Paul exhorted Timothy, "[W]hat you have heard from me before many witnesses entrust to faithful men who will be able to teach others also" (2 Tm 2:2). In this passage he refers to the several generations of apostolic succession—his own generation, Timothy's generation, the generation Timothy will teach, and the generation they in turn will teach.

The early Church Fathers, who were links in that chain of succession, recognized the necessity of the traditions that had been handed down from the apostles, as the following quotations show.

ST. PAPIAS OF HIERAPOLIS

And Papias, of whom we are now speaking, confesses that he received the words of the apostles from those who followed them, but says that he was himself a hearer of Aristion and the presbyter John. At least he mentions them frequently by name, and gives their traditions in his writings. . . . [There are] other passages from his works in which he relates some other wonderful events that he claims to have received from Tradition [fragment in Eusebius's *Church History* 3:39:7 (c. A.D. 130)].

TO DIOGNETUS

Then the fear of the Law is chanted, and the grace of the prophets is known, and the faith of the Gospels is established, and the Tradition of the apostles is preserved, and the grace of the Church exults [*To Diognetus* 11 (c. A.D. 160)].

ST. IRENAEUS OF LYONS

As I have already observed, the Church, having received this preaching and this faith, although scattered throughout the whole world, yet, as if occupying but one house, carefully preserves it.

She also believes these points [of doctrine] just as if she had but one soul, and one and the same heart, and she proclaims them, and teaches them, and hands them down, with perfect harmony, as if she possessed only one mouth. For, although the languages of the world are dissimilar, yet the import of the Tradition is one and the same. For the churches that have been planted in Germany do not believe or hand down anything different, nor do those in Spain, nor those in Gaul, nor those in the East, nor those in Egypt, nor those in Libya, nor those that have been established in the central regions of the world. But as the sun, that creature of God, is one and the same throughout the whole world, so also the preaching of the truth shines everywhere, and enlightens all men who are willing to come to a knowledge of the truth. Nor will any one of the rulers in the churches, however eloquent he may be, teach doctrines different from these (for no one is greater than the Master); nor, on the other hand, will he who is deficient in power of expression inflict injury on the Tradition. For the faith being ever one and the same neither does one who is able at great length to discourse about it make any addition to it, nor does one who can say but little, diminish it [*Against Heresies* 1:10:2 (c. A.D. 189)].

Since therefore we have such proofs, it is not necessary to seek the truth from others that is easy to obtain from the Church; since the apostles, like a rich man [depositing his money] in a bank, lodged in her hands most copiously all things pertaining to the truth: so that every man who will can draw from her the water of life [Rv 22:17]. For she is the entrance to life; all others are thieves and robbers. On this account we are bound to avoid them, but to choose the thing pertaining to the Church with the utmost diligence, and to lay hold of the Tradition of the truth. For how stands the case? Suppose there arises a dispute relative to some important question among us, should we not have recourse to the most ancient churches with which the apostles held constant intercourse, and learn from them what is certain and clear regarding the present question? For how should it be if the apostles themselves had not left us writings? Would it not be necessary to follow the course of the Tradition that they handed down to those to whom they committed the churches? [ibid., 3:4:1].

It is within the power of all, in every church, who may wish to see the truth, to contemplate clearly the Tradition of the apostles manifested throughout the whole world; and we are in a position to reckon up those who were instituted bishops in the churches by the apostles, and [to demonstrate] the succession of these men to our own times; those who neither taught nor knew anything these [heretics] rave about. For if the apostles had known hidden mysteries, which they were in the habit of imparting to "the perfect" apart and privately from the rest, they would have delivered them especially to those to whom they were committing the churches. For they were desirous that these men should be very perfect and blameless in all things, men they were leaving behind as their successors, delivering up their own place of government to them; which men, if they discharged their functions honestly, would be a great boon [to the Church], but if they fell away, the direst calamity.

Since, however, it would be very tedious, in such a volume as this, to reckon up the successions of all the churches, we put to confusion all those who, in whatever manner, whether by an evil self-pleasing, by vanity, or by blindness and perverse opinion, assemble in unauthorized meetings, by indicating that Tradition derived from the apostles, of the very great, the very ancient, and universally known Church founded and organized at Rome by the two most glorious apostles, Peter and Paul; also [by pointing out] the faith preached to men, which comes down to our time by means of the successions of the bishops. For it is a matter of necessity that every church agree with this Church, on account of its preeminent authority, that is, the faithful everywhere, because the apostolic Tradition has been preserved continuously by those [faithful men] who exist everywhere [ibid., 3:3:2].

ST. CLEMENT OF ALEXANDRIA

They preserving the Tradition of the blessed doctrine derived directly from the holy apostles, Peter, James, John, and Paul, the sons receiving it from the father (but few were like the fathers), came by God's will to us also to deposit those ancestral and apostolic seeds. And well I know that they will exult; I do not mean delighted with this tribute, but on account of the preservation of the truth, according as they delivered it. For such a sketch as this, will, I think, be agreeable to a soul desirous of preserving the blessed Tradition [*Miscellanies* 1:1 (c. A.D. 207)].

ORIGEN OF ALEXANDRIA

[T]here are many who think they hold the opinions of Christ, and yet some of these think differently from their predecessors, yet, as the teaching of the Church, transmitted in orderly succession from the apostles, and remaining in the churches to the present day, is still preserved, that alone is to be accepted as truth that differs in no respect from ecclesiastical and apostolic Tradition [*Fundamental Doctrines* Preface 2 (c. A.D. 225)].

ST. CYPRIAN OF CARTHAGE

[T]he Church is one, and as she is one, cannot be both within and without. For if she is with Novatian, she was not with Cornelius. But if she was with Cornelius, who succeeded the bishop Fabian by lawful ordination, and whom, beside the honor of the priesthood, the Lord glorified also with martyrdom, Novatian is not in the Church; nor can he be reckoned as a bishop, who, succeeding to no one, and despising the evangelical and apostolic Tradition, sprang from himself. For he who has not been ordained in the Church can neither have nor hold to the Church in any way [*Letters* 75:3 (A.D. 254)].

EUSEBIUS OF CAESAREA

At that time there flourished in the Church Hegesippus, whom we know from what has gone before, and Dionysius, bishop of Corinth, and another bishop, Pinytus of Crete, and besides these, Philip, and Apollinarius, and Melito, and Musanus, and Modestus, and finally, Irenaeus. From them has come down to us in writing the sound and orthodox faith received from apostolic Tradition [*Church History* 4:21:1 (c. A.D. 312)].

ST. ATHANASIUS OF ALEXANDRIA

Again we write, again keeping to the apostolic traditions, we remind each other when we come together for prayer; and keeping the feast in common, with one mouth we truly give thanks to the Lord. Thus giving thanks unto him, and being followers of the saints, "we shall make our praise in the Lord all the day," as the Psalmist says. So, when we rightly keep the feast, we shall be counted worthy of the joy that is in heaven [*Festal Letters* 2:7 (A.D. 330)].

But you are blessed, who by faith are in the Church, dwell upon the foundations of the faith, and have full satisfaction, even the highest degree of faith that remains among you unshaken. For it has come down to you from apostolic Tradition, and frequently accursed envy has wished to unsettle it, but has not been able [ibid., 29].

ST. BASIL OF CAESAREA

Of the beliefs and practices that are preserved in the Church, whether generally accepted or publicly enjoined, some we possess derive from written teaching; others we have received "in a mystery" by the Tradition of the Apostles; and both of these have the same force in relation to true religion. And these no one will gainsay—no one, at all events, who is even moderately versed in the institutions of the Church. For were we to attempt to reject such customs as have no written authority, on the ground that the importance they possess is small, we should unintentionally injure the gospel in its very vitals; or, rather, should make our public definition a mere phrase and nothing more [*The Holy Spirit* 27:66 (A.D. 375)].

ST. EPIPHANIUS OF SALAMIS

It is needful also to make use of Tradition, for not everything can be gotten from sacred Scripture. The holy apostles handed down some things in the Scriptures, other things in Tradition [*Panacea Against All Heresies* 61:6 (c. A.D. 375)].

ST. AUGUSTINE OF HIPPO

[T]he custom, which is opposed to Cyprian, may be supposed to have had its origin in apostolic Tradition, just as there are many things that are observed by the whole Church, and therefore are fairly held to have been enjoined by the apostles, that are not mentioned in their writings [*On Baptism, Against the Donatists* 5:23:31 (A.D. 400)].

But the admonition that [St. Cyprian] gives us, "that we should go back to the fountain, that is, to apostolic Tradition, and thence turn the channel of truth to our times," is most excellent, and should be followed without hesitation [ibid., 5:26:37].

As to those other things that we hold on the authority, not of Scripture, but of Tradition, and that are observed throughout the whole world, it may be understood that they are held as approved and instituted either by the apostles themselves, or by plenary councils, whose authority in the Church is most useful, for example, the annual commemoration, by special solemnities, of the Lord's Passion, Resurrection, and Ascension, and of the descent of the Holy Spirit from heaven, and whatever else is in like manner observed by the whole Church wherever it has been established [*Letters* 54:1:1 (c. A.D. 400)].

ST. JOHN CHRYSOSTOM

"So then, brethren, stand fast, and hold the traditions that you were taught, whether by word, or by letter of ours." From this it is manifest that they did not deliver all things by letter, but many things also unwritten, and in like manner both the one and the other are worthy of credit. Therefore let us think the Tradition of the Church also worthy of credit. It is a Tradition, seek no farther [*Homilies on Second Thessalonians* 4:15 (c. A.D. 402)].

ST. VINCENT OF LERINS

I have often then inquired earnestly and attentively of very many men eminent for sanctity and learning, how and by what sure and universal rule I may be able to distinguish the truth of Catholic faith from the falsehood of heretical pravity; and I have always, and in almost every instance, received an answer to this effect: That whether I or anyone else should wish to detect the frauds and avoid the snares of heretics as they rise, and to continue sound and complete in the Catholic faith, we must, the Lord helping, fortify our own belief in two ways: first, by the authority of the divine law, and then, by the Tradition of the Catholic Church. But here someone perhaps will ask, "Since the canon of Scripture is complete, and sufficient of itself for everything, and more than sufficient, what need is there to join with it the authority of the Church's interpretation?" For this reason—because, owing to the depth of Holy Scripture, all do not accept it in one and the same sense, but one understands its words in one way, another in another; so that it seems to be capable of as many interpretations as there are interpreters. For Novatian expounds it one way, Sabellius another, Donatus another, Arius, Eunomius, Macedonius, another, Photinus, Apollinarius, Priscillian, another, Iovinian, Pelagius, Celestius, another, and lastly, Nestorius, another. Therefore, it is very necessary, on account of so great intricacies of such various error, that the rule for the right understanding of the prophets and apostles should be framed in accordance with the standard of ecclesiastical and Catholic interpretation.

Moreover, in the Catholic Church itself, all possible care must be taken, that we hold that faith which has been believed everywhere, always, by all. For that is truly and in the strictest sense Catholic, which, as the name itself and the reason of the thing declare, comprehends all universally [*Notebooks* 2:4–6 (c. A.D. 434)].

POPE ST. AGATHO

[T]he holy Church of God, the mother of your most Christian power, should be delivered and liberated with all your might (through the help of God) from the errors of such teachers, and the evangelical and apostolic uprightness of the orthodox faith, which has been established upon the firm rock of this Church of blessed Peter, the prince of the apostles, which by his grace and guardianship remains free from all error. The whole number of rulers and priests, of the clergy and of the people, unanimously should confess and preach with us as the true declaration of the apostolic Tradition, in order to please God and to save their own souls [letter read at fourth session of III Constantinople (A.D. 680)].

VII. The Church and the Pope

24. The Catholic Church

The Greek roots of the term *catholic* mean "according to" (*kata-*) "the whole" (*holos*), or more colloquially, "universal." In the early 100s, we find St. Ignatius of Antioch in Syria using the term *catholic* in reference to the Church. This is the first surviving use of the term in this sense, but since Ignatius introduces it without any explanation, it must have been in use earlier, in the latter half of the first century, before the year 100.

The Protestant Church historian J. N. D. Kelly writes: "As regards 'Catholic,' its original meaning was 'universal' or 'general.' . . . In the latter half of the second century at latest, we find it conveying the suggestion that the Catholic is the true Church as distinct from heretical congregations (cf., e.g., Muratorian Fragment). . . . What these early Fathers were envisaging was almost always the empirical, visible society; they had little or no inkling of the distinction which was later to become important between a visible and an invisible Church" (*Early Christian Doctrines*, 190–91).

The term was used in the *Apostles'*, *Nicene*, and *Athanasian* creeds, which came in coming centuries, after the term *catholic* had become a distinctive descriptor for what we call the Catholic Church today. Thus when the *Nicene Creed* refers to the "one, holy, catholic, and apostolic Church," it has in mind a particular communion of Christians that has survived from the first century down to the present day.

Some recent Christians have sought to distinguish between a "small c" use of the term catholic, which embraces a broader group of Christians, and the "large C" use of the term, which refers to members of the Catholic Church as a whole, but the quotations below show the term "Catholic" was used in the patristic age in the "large C" Catholic sense—as the definite name of a visible Church, as well as in a "lower-case" sense of an attribute possessed by this Church.

ST. IGNATIUS OF ANTIOCH

Let no man do anything connected with the Church without the bishop. Let that be deemed a proper Eucharist, which is [administered] either by the bishop, or by one to whom he has entrusted it. Wherever the bishop shall appear, there let the multitude [of the people] also be; even as, wherever Jesus Christ is, there is the Catholic Church [*Letter to the Smyrnaeans* 8 (c. A.D. 110)].

MARTYRDOM OF POLYCARP

This, then, is the account of the blessed Polycarp, who, being the twelfth that was martyred in Smyrna (reckoning those also of Philadelphia), yet occupies a place of his own in the memory of all men, and that he is everywhere spoken of by the heathen themselves. He was not merely an illustrious teacher, but also a preeminent martyr, whose martyrdom all desire to imitate, as it was completely consistent with the gospel of Christ. Having through patience overcome the unjust governor, and thus acquired the crown of immortality, he now, with the apostles and all the righteous [in heaven], rejoicingly glorifies God, even the Father, and blesses our Lord Jesus Christ, the Savior of our souls, the governor of our bodies, and the Shepherd of the Catholic Church throughout the world [*Martyrdom of Polycarp* 19 (c. A.D. 156)].

MURATORIAN FRAGMENT

[Paul also wrote] out of affection and love one to Philemon, one to Titus, and two to Timothy; and these are held sacred in the esteem of the Catholic Church for the regulation of ecclesiastical discipline. There is current also [a letter] to the Laodiceans, [and] another to the Alexandrians, [both] forged in Paul's name to [further] the heresy of Marcion, and several others that cannot be received into the Catholic Church—for it is not fitting that gall be mixed with honey. Moreover, the letter of Jude and two of the above-mentioned (or, bearing the name of) John are counted (or, used) in the Catholic [Church]; and [the book of] Wisdom, written by the friends of Solomon in his honor [Muratorian Fragment (c. A.D. 178)].

TERTULLIAN OF CARTHAGE

Where was [the heretic] Marcion, that shipmaster of Pontus, the zealous student of Stoicism? Where was Valentinus, the disciple of Platonism? For it is evident that those men lived not so long ago—in the reign of Antonius for the most part—and that they at first were believers in the doctrine of the Catholic Church, in the church of Rome under the episcopate of the blessed Eleutherius, until on account of their ever restless curiosity, with which they even infected the brethren, they were more than once expelled [*Prescription Against Heretics* 30 (c. A.D. 200)].

ST. CYPRIAN OF CARTHAGE

They alone have remained without, who, if they had been within, would have had to be cast out. . . . Peter, on whom the Church was to be built, speaks there [Jn 6:67–69], teaching and showing in the name of the Church, that although a rebellious and arrogant multitude of those who will not hear and obey may depart, yet the Church does not depart from Christ; and they are the Church who are a people united to the priest, and the flock that adheres to its pastor. You ought to know that the bishop is in the Church, and the Church in the bishop; and if anyone be not with the bishop, then he is not in the Church, nor those who flatter themselves in vain and creep in, not having peace with God's priests, and think that they communicate secretly with some; while the Church, which is catholic and one, is not cut nor divided, but is indeed connected and bound together by the cement of priests who cohere with one another [*Letters* 68:8 (A.D. 254)].

COUNCIL OF NICAEA I

But those who say: "There was [a time] when he [the Son] was not," and "before he was born, he was not," and "because he was made from non-existing matter, he is either of another substance or essence," and those who call "God the Son of God changeable and mutable," these the Catholic Church anathematizes [original appendix to the *Nicene Creed* (A.D. 325)].

Concerning those who call themselves Cathari [Novatians], that is, "the Clean," if at any time they come to the Catholic Church, it has been decided by the holy and great council that, provided they receive the imposition of hands, they remain among the clergy. However, because they are accepting and following the doctrines of the Catholic and apostolic Church, it is fitting that they acknowledge this in writing before all; that is, that they communicate with the twice married and with those who have lapsed during a persecution [Canon 8 (A.D. 325)].

Concerning the Paulianists who take refuge with the Catholic Church, a decree has been published that they should be fully baptized. If, however, any of these in times past have been in the clerical order, if they have appeared spotless and above reproach, after being baptized let them be ordained by the bishop of the Catholic Church [Canon 19 (A.D. 325)].

ST. CYRIL OF JERUSALEM

[The Church] is called catholic then because it extends over all the world, from one end of the earth to the other; and because it teaches universally and completely the doctrines that ought to come to men's knowledge, concerning things both visible and invisible, heavenly and earthly; and because it brings into subjection to godliness the whole race of mankind, governors and governed, learned and unlearned; and because it universally treats and heals the whole class of sins that are committed by soul or body, and possesses in itself every form of virtue that is named, both in deeds and words, and in every kind of spiritual gift [*Catechetical Lectures* 18:23 (c. A.D. 350)].

And if ever you are sojourning in cities, inquire not simply where the Lord's house is (for the other sects of the profane also attempt to call their own dens houses of the Lord), nor merely where the church is, but where the Catholic Church is. For this is the peculiar name of this holy Church, the mother of us all, the spouse of our Lord Jesus Christ, the only-begotten Son of God [ibid., 18:26].

COUNCIL OF CONSTANTINOPLE I

And [we believe] in the Holy Spirit, the Lord and giver of life, who proceeds from the Father, who with the Father and the Son together is worshipped and glorified, who spoke by the prophets. And [we believe] in one, holy, catholic and apostolic Church. We acknowledge one baptism for the remission of sins, [and] we look for the resurrection of the dead and the life of the world to come. Amen [*Nicene Creed* (A.D. 381)].

Those who embrace orthodoxy and join the number of those who are being saved from the heretics, we receive in the following regular and customary manner: Arians, Macedonians, Sabbatians, Novatians, those who call themselves Cathars and Aristeri, Quartodecimians or Tetradites, Apollinarians—these we receive when they hand in statements and anathematize every heresy that is not of the same mind as the holy, Catholic, and apostolic Church of God [Canon 5].

ST. AUGUSTINE OF HIPPO

We must hold to the Christian religion and to communication in her Church, which is catholic and which is called Catholic not only by her own members but even by all her enemies. For when heretics or the adherents of schisms talk about her, not among themselves but with strangers, willy-nilly they call her nothing else but Catholic. For they will not be understood unless they distinguish her by this name that the whole world employs in her regard [*The True Religion* 7:12 (c. A.D. 390)].

[W]e believe also in the holy Church, [intending thereby] assuredly the Catholic. For both heretics and schismatics style their congregations churches. But heretics, in holding false opinions regarding

God, do injury to the faith itself; while schismatics, on the other hand, in wicked separations break off from brotherly charity, although they may believe just what we believe. As a result neither do the heretics belong to the Catholic Church, which loves God; nor do the schismatics form a part of the same, inasmuch as it loves the neighbor, and consequently readily forgives the neighbor's sins, because it prays that forgiveness may be extended to itself by him who has reconciled us to himself, doing away with all past things, and calling us to a new life [*Faith and the Creed* 10:21 (A.D. 393)].

For in the Catholic Church, not to speak of the purest wisdom, the knowledge of which a few spiritual men attain in this life, so as to know it, in the scantiest measure, indeed, because they are but men, still without any uncertainty (since the rest of the multitude derive their entire security not from acuteness of intellect, but from simplicity of faith)—not to speak of this wisdom, which you do not believe to be in the Catholic Church, there are many other things that most justly keep me in her bosom. The consent of peoples and nations keeps me in the Church; so does her authority, inaugurated by miracles, nourished by hope, enlarged by love, established by age. The succession of priests keeps me, beginning from the very seat of the apostle Peter, to whom the Lord, after his Resurrection, gave it in charge to feed his sheep, down to the present episcopate. And so, lastly, does the name itself of Catholic, which, not without reason, amid so many heresies, the Church has thus retained; so that, though all heretics wish to be called Catholics, yet when a stranger asks where the Catholic Church meets, no heretic will venture to point to his own chapel or house. Such then in number and importance are the precious ties belonging to the Christian name that keep a believer in the Catholic Church, as it is right they should, though from the slowness of our understanding, or the small attainment of our life, the truth may not yet fully disclose itself. But with you, where there are none of these things to attract or keep me, the promise of truth is the only thing that comes into play. Now if the truth is so clearly proved as to leave no possibility of doubt, it must be set before all the things that keep me in the Catholic Church; but if there is only a promise without any fulfillment, no one shall move me from the faith that binds my mind with ties so many and so strong to the Christian religion [*Against the Letter of Mani Called "The Foundation"* 4:5 (A.D. 397)].

If you should find someone who does not yet believe in the gospel, what would you [Mani] answer him when he says, "I do not believe"? Indeed, I would not believe in the gospel myself if the authority of the Catholic Church did not move me to do so [ibid., 5:6].

ST. VINCENT OF LERINS

I have often then inquired earnestly and attentively of very many men eminent for sanctity and learning, how and by what sure and universal rule I may be able to distinguish the truth of Catholic faith from the falsehood of heretical pravity; and I have always, and in almost every instance, received an answer to this effect: That whether I or any one else should wish to detect the frauds and avoid the snares of heretics as they rise, and to continue sound and complete in the Catholic faith, we must, the Lord helping, fortify our own belief in two ways: first, by the authority of the divine law, and then, by the Tradition of the Catholic Church. But here someone perhaps will ask, Since the canon of Scripture is complete, and sufficient of itself for everything, and more than sufficient, what need is there to join with it the authority of the Church's interpretation? For this reason—because, owing to the depth of Holy Scripture, all do not accept it in one and the same sense, but one understands its words in one way, another in another; so that it seems to be capable of as many interpretations as there are interpreters. For Novatian expounds it one way, Sabellius another, Donatus another, Arius, Eunomius, Macedonius, another, Photinus, Apollinarius, Priscillian, another, Iovinian, Pelagius, Celestius, another, and lastly, Nestorius another. Therefore, it is very necessary, on account of so great intricacies of such various error, that the rule for the right understanding of the prophets and apostles should be framed in accordance with the standard of ecclesiastical and Catholic interpretation.

Moreover, in the Catholic Church itself, all possible care must be taken, that we hold that faith which has been believed everywhere, always, by all. For that is truly and in the strictest sense Catholic, which, as the name itself and the reason of the thing declare, comprehends all universally [*Notebooks* 2:4–6 (c. A.D. 434)].

COUNCIL OF CHALCEDON

Since in certain provinces readers and cantors have been allowed to marry, this sacred synod decrees that none of them is permitted to marry a wife of heterodox views. If those thus married have already had children, and if they have already had the children baptized among heretics, they are to bring them into the communion of the Catholic Church [Session 15, Canon 14 (A.D. 451)].

25. Apostolic Succession

Apostolic succession is the line of bishops stretching back to the apostles. It plays several important roles, one of which is guarding the apostolic Tradition, as expressed in St. Paul's instruction to Timothy, "[W]hat you have heard from me before many witnesses entrust to faithful men who will be able to teach others also" (2 Tm 2:2). Here he refers to the first four generations of apostolic succession—his own generation, Timothy's generation, the generation Timothy will teach, and the generation they in turn will teach. Of course, Paul didn't envision the succession ending there but continuing however long the world would last.

The bishops of the Church, many of them in the early days being Church Fathers, are the links in the chain of apostolic succession, and the Fathers regularly appealed to this succession as a test of correct doctrine. This was necessary because heretics could simply put their own interpretations, however bizarre or fanciful, on Scripture. Something in addition to Scripture was needed as a test of doctrine in these cases.

Thus the early Church historian J.N.D. Kelly, a Protestant, writes, "But where in practice was this apostolic testimony or tradition to be found? . . . The most obvious answer was that the apostles had committed it orally to the Church, where it had been handed down from generation to generation. . . . Unlike the alleged secret tradition of the Gnostics, it was entirely public and open, having been entrusted by the apostles to their successors, and by these in turn to those who followed them, and was visible in the Church for all who cared to look for it" (*Early Christian Doctrines*, 37).

He goes on to say: "First, the identity of the oral tradition with the original revelation is guaranteed by the unbroken succession of bishops in the great sees going back lineally to the apostles. Secondly, an additional safeguard is supplied by the Holy Spirit, for the message committed was to the Church, and the Church is the home of the Spirit. Indeed, the Church's bishops are . . . Spirit-endowed men who have been vouchsafed 'an infallible charism of truth' (ibid., citing St. Irenaeus of Lyons, *Against Heresies* 4:26:2).

Thus, on the basis of experience, the Fathers could be "profoundly convinced of the futility of arguing with heretics merely on the basis of Scripture. The skill and success with which they twisted its plain meaning made it impossible to reach any decisive conclusion in that field" (*Early Christian Doctrines*, 41).

POPE ST. CLEMENT I

And thus preaching through countries and cities, they appointed the first fruits [of their labors], having first proved them by the Spirit, to be bishops and deacons of those who should afterwards believe. Nor was this any new thing, since indeed many ages before it was written concerning bishops and deacons. . . . Our apostles also knew, through our Lord Jesus Christ, that there would be strife on account of the office of the episcopate. For this reason, therefore, since they had obtained a perfect foreknowledge of this, they appointed those [ministers] already mentioned, and afterwards gave instructions that when these should fall asleep, other approved men should succeed them in their ministry [*Letter to the Corinthians* 42:4–5; 44:1–2 (A.D. 70)].

ST. HEGESIPPUS

And when I had come to Rome I remained there until Anicetus, whose deacon was Eleutherius. And Anicetus was succeeded by Soter, and he by Eleutherius. In every succession, and in every city, that is held which is preached by the law and the prophets and the Lord [*Memoirs*, cited in Eusebius, *Church History* 4:22:3 (c. A.D. 180)].

ST. IRENAEUS OF LYONS

It is within the power of all, in every church, who may wish to see the truth, to contemplate clearly the Tradition of the apostles manifested throughout the whole world; and we are in a position to reckon up those who were instituted bishops in the churches by the apostles, and [to demonstrate] the succession of these men to our own times; those who neither taught nor knew anything these [heretics] rave about [*Against Heresies* 3:3:1 (c. A.D. 189)].

Since, however, it would be very tedious . . . to reckon up the successions of all the churches, we put to confusion all those who, in whatever manner, whether by an evil self-pleasing, by vanity, or by blindness and perverse opinion, assemble in unauthorized meetings, by indicating that Tradition derived from the apostles, of the very great, the very ancient, and universally known Church founded and organized at Rome by the two most glorious apostles, Peter and Paul; also [by pointing out] the faith preached to men, which comes down to our time by means of the successions of the bishops. For it is a matter of necessity that every church agree with this Church, on account of its preeminent authority, that is, the faithful everywhere, because the apostolic Tradition has been preserved continuously by those [faithful men] who exist everywhere [ibid., 3:3:2].

But Polycarp was not only instructed by apostles, and conversed with many who had seen Christ, but was also, by apostles in Asia, appointed bishop of the Church in Smyrna, whom I also saw in my early youth, for he tarried [on earth] a very long time, and, when a very old man, he gloriously and most nobly suffered mar-

tyrdom, departing this life, having always taught the things he had
learned from the apostles, and that the Church has handed down,
and that alone are true. To these things all the Asiatic churches
testify, as do also those men who have succeeded Polycarp down
to the present time [ibid., 3:3:4].

Since therefore we have such proofs, it is not necessary to seek the
truth from others that is easy to obtain from the Church; since
the apostles, like a rich man [depositing his money] in a bank,
lodged in her hands most copiously all things pertaining to the
truth: so that every man who will can draw from her the water
of life [Rv 22:17]. For she is the entrance to life; all others are
thieves and robbers. On this account we are bound to avoid them,
but to choose the thing pertaining to the Church with the utmost
diligence, and to lay hold of the Tradition of the truth. For how
stands the case? Suppose there arises a dispute relative to some
important question among us, should we not have recourse to
the most ancient churches with which the apostles held constant
intercourse, and learn from them what is certain and clear regarding the present question? [ibid., 3:4:1].

[I]t is incumbent to obey the presbyters who are in the Church
—those who, as I have shown, possess the succession from the
apostles; those who, together with the succession of the episcopate, have received the certain gift of truth, according to the good
pleasure of the Father. But [it is also incumbent] to hold in suspicion others who depart from the primitive succession, and assemble themselves together in any place whatsoever, [looking upon
them] either as heretics of perverse minds, or as schismatics puffed
up and self-pleasing, or as hypocrites, acting thus for the sake of
money and vanity. For all these have fallen from the truth [ibid.,
4:26:2].

True knowledge is [consists in] the doctrine of the apostles, and
the ancient constitution of the Church throughout all the world,
and the distinctive manifestation of the body of Christ according to the successions of the bishops, by which they have handed
down that Church that exists everywhere [ibid., 4:33:8].

TERTULLIAN OF CARTHAGE

[The apostles] then in like manner founded churches in every city, from which all the other churches, one after another, derived the Tradition of the faith, and the seeds of doctrine, and are every-day deriving them, that they may become churches. Indeed, it is only on this account that they will be able to deem themselves apostolic, the offspring of apostolic churches. Everything must necessarily revert to its original for its classification. Therefore the churches, although they are so many and so great, comprise but one primitive Church, (founded) by the apostles, from which they all [spring]. In this way all are primitive, and all are apostolic, while they are all proved to be one, in (unbroken) unity [*Prescription Against Heretics* 20 (c. A.D. 200)].

[W]hat Christ revealed to them [the apostles] can, as I must here prescribe, properly be proved in no other way than by those very churches the apostles founded in person, by declaring the gospel to them directly themselves. . . . If, then, these things are so, it is also manifest that all doctrine that agrees with the apostolic churches—those molds and original sources of the faith—must be reckoned for truth, as undoubtedly containing what the (said) churches received from the apostles, the apostles from Christ, Christ from God. All doctrine must be prejudged as false that savors of incompatibility with the truth of the churches and apostles of Christ and God. It remains, then, to demonstrate whether this doctrine of ours, of which we have now given the rule, has its origin in the Tradition of the apostles, and whether all other doctrines do not ipso facto proceed from falsehood [ibid., 21].

But if there be any (heresies) that are bold enough to plant themselves in the midst of the Apostolic Age, that they may thereby seem to have been handed down by the apostles, because they existed in the time of the apostles, we can say: Let them produce the original records of their churches; let them unfold the roll of their bishops, running down in succession from the beginning, in such a way that [that first bishop of theirs] shall be able to show as his ordainer and predecessor one of the apostles or apostolic men—a man, moreover, who continued steadfast with the apostles. For this is the manner in which the apostolic churches transmit their registers: as the church of Smyrna, which records that Polycarp was placed therein by John; as also the church of Rome, which makes Clement to have been ordained by Peter. In exactly the same way the other churches also exhibit [their several worthies], whom, as having been appointed to their episcopal places by apostles, they regard as transmitters of the apostolic seed. Let the heretics contrive something of the same kind. For after their blasphemy, what is unlawful for them [to attempt]? But should they even try to do so, they will not advance a step. For their very doctrine, after comparison with that of the apostles, will declare, by its own diversity and contrariness, that it had as its author neither an apostle nor an apostolic man; because, as the apostles would never have taught things that were self-contradictory, so the apostolic men would not have taught anything different from the apostles, unless they who received their instruction from the apostles went and preached in a contrary manner. To this test, therefore, will they be submitted for proof by those churches, who, although they don't derive their founder from apostles or apostolic men (as being of much later date, for they are in fact being founded daily), yet, since they agree in the same faith, they are accounted as not less apostolic because they are akin in doctrine. Then let all the heresies, when challenged with these two tests by our apostolic Church, offer proof of how they deem themselves to be apostolic. But in truth they are not, nor are they able to prove themselves to be what they are not. Nor are they admitted to peaceful relations and communion by such churches as are connected with apostles, as they are in no sense themselves apostolic because of their diverse opinions about the mysteries of the faith [ibid., 32].

ST. CYPRIAN OF CARTHAGE

[T]he Church is one, and as she is one, cannot be both within and without. For if she is with Novatian, she was not with

Cornelius. But if she was with Cornelius, who succeeded the bishop Fabian by lawful ordination, and whom, beside the honor of the priesthood, the Lord glorified also with martyrdom, Novatian is not in the Church; nor can he be reckoned as a bishop, who, succeeding to no one, and despising the evangelical and apostolic Tradition, sprang from himself. For he who has not been ordained in the Church can neither have nor hold to the Church in any way [*Letters* 75:3 (A.D. 254)].

ST. JEROME

Far be it from me to censure the successors of the apostles, who with holy words consecrate the body of Christ, and who make us Christians [*Letters* 14:8 (c. A.D. 376)].

ST. AUGUSTINE OF HIPPO

For in the Catholic Church, not to speak of the purest wisdom, the knowledge of which a few spiritual men attain in this life, so as to know it, in the scantiest measure, indeed, because they are but men, still without any uncertainty (since the rest of the multitude derive their entire security not from acuteness of intellect, but from simplicity of faith)—not to speak of this wisdom, which you do not believe to be in the Catholic Church, there are many other things that most justly keep me in her bosom. The consent of peoples and nations keeps me in the Church; so does her authority, inaugurated by miracles, nourished by hope, enlarged by love, established by age. The succession of priests keeps me, beginning from the very seat of the apostle Peter, to whom the Lord, after his Resurrection, gave it in charge to feed his sheep, down to the present episcopate. And so, lastly, does the name itself of Catholic, which, not without reason, amid so many heresies, the Church has thus retained; so that, though all heretics wish to be called Catholics, yet when a stranger asks where the Catholic Church meets, no heretic will venture to point to his own chapel or house. Such then in number and importance are the precious ties belonging to the Christian name that keep a believer in the Catholic Church, as it is right they should, though from the slowness of our understanding, or the small attainment of our life, the truth may not yet fully disclose itself. But with you, where there are none of these things to attract or keep me, the promise of truth is the only thing that comes into play. Now if the truth is so clearly proved as to leave no possibility of doubt, it must be set before all the things that keep me in the Catholic Church; but if there is only a promise without any fulfillment, no one shall move me from the faith that binds my mind with ties so many and so strong to the Christian religion [*Against the Letter of Mani Called "The Foundation"* 4:5 (A.D. 397)].

26. Peter the Rock

Jesus told Peter, "You are Peter, and on this rock I will build my Church, and the gates of hell will not prevail against it" (Mt 16:18).

The literal sense of this passage is that Peter is the rock on which the Church would be built. This does not preclude other metaphors for the foundation of the Church. In fact, the New Testament contains five of them. In addition to this passage, there are others in which its foundation is identified as Christ himself (1 Cor 3:11); as the apostles and New Testament prophets, with Christ as the cornerstone (Eph 2:20); Christ again as the cornerstone, together with ordinary believers as living stones (1 Pt 2:5–6); and finally the twelve apostles as a group (Rv 21:14).

These are all legitimate ways of conceiving the foundation of the Church—and there are still others. But none should be treated as exclusively true or used to deny or diminish the validity of the others.

The Church Fathers picked up on the multiplicity of ways in which the Church's foundation can be viewed, but there was always a healthy recognition that, in one sense, the Church can be seen as uniquely founded on Peter—or Cephas, as he was often called, "Cephas" being a Greek adaptation of the Aramaic word

Kepha, or "rock," which was the name Jesus himself bestowed on the chief of the apostles.

TATIAN THE SYRIAN

Simon Cephas answered and said, "You are the Messiah, the Son of the living God." Jesus answered and said unto him, "Blessed are you, Simon, son of Jonah: flesh and blood has not revealed it unto thee, but my Father which is in heaven. And I say unto thee also, that you are Cephas, and on this rock will I build my Church; and the gates of hades shall not prevail against it" [*Diatesseron* 23 (c. A.D. 170)].

TERTULLIAN OF CARTHAGE

Was anything withheld from the knowledge of Peter, who is called "the rock on which the Church would be built" [Mt 16:18] with the power of "loosing and binding in heaven and on earth? [Mt 16:19]" [*Prescription Against Heretics* 22 (c. A.D. 200)].

[T]he Lord said to Peter, "On this rock I will build my Church, I have given you the keys of the kingdom of heaven [and] whatever you shall have bound or loosed on earth will be bound or loosed in heaven" [Mt 16:18–19]. . . . What kind of man are you, subverting and changing what was the clear intent of the Lord when he himself conferred this upon Peter? Upon *you*, he says, I will build my Church; and I will give to *you* the keys [*Modesty* 21 (c. A.D. 220)].

ORIGEN OF ALEXANDRIA

Look at [Peter], the great foundation of the Church, that most solid of rocks, upon whom Christ built the Church [Mt 16:18]. And what does our Lord say to him? "O you of little faith," he says, "why do you doubt?" [Mt 14:31] [*Homilies on Exodus* 5:4 (c. A.D. 249)].

ST. CYPRIAN OF CARTHAGE

The Lord says to Peter: "I say to you," he says, "that you are Peter, and upon this rock I will build my Church, and the gates of hell will not overcome it. And to you I will give the keys of the kingdom of heaven . . ." [Mt 16:18–19]. On him he builds the Church, and commands him to feed the sheep [Jn 21:17], and although he assigns a like power to all the apostles, yet he founded a single chair [*cathedra*], and he established by his own authority a source and an intrinsic reason for that unity. Indeed, the others were also what Peter was [apostles], but a primacy is given to Peter, by which it is made clear that there is one Church and one chair. . . . If someone does not hold fast to this unity of Peter, can he think that he holds the faith? If he deserts the chair of Peter upon whom the Church was built, can he be confident that he is in the Church? [*Unity of the Catholic Church* 4; first edition (Treatise 1:4) (A.D. 251)].

There is one God, and Christ is one, and there is one Church, and one chair founded upon the rock by the word of the Lord. Another altar cannot be constituted nor a new priesthood be made, except the one altar and the one priesthood. Whosoever gathers elsewhere, scatters [*Letters* 39:5 (A.D. 251)].

Peter, on whom the Church was to be built, speaks there [Jn 6:67–69], teaching and showing in the name of the Church, that although a rebellious and arrogant multitude of those who will not hear and obey may depart, yet the Church does not depart from Christ; and they are the Church who are a people united to the priest, and the flock that adheres to its pastor. You ought to know that the bishop is in the Church, and the Church in the bishop; and if anyone be not with the bishop, then he is not in the Church, nor those who flatter themselves in vain and creep in, not having peace with God's priests, and think that they communicate secretly with some; while the Church, which is Catholic and one, is not cut nor divided, but is indeed connected and bound together by the cement of priests who cohere with one another [*Letters* 68:8 (A.D. 254)].

FIRMILIAN OF CAESAREA

But his error . . . [for he] who does not remain on the foundation of the one Church founded upon the rock by Christ [Mt 16:18], can be learned from this, which Christ said only to Peter:

"Whatever things you shall bind on earth shall be bound also in heaven; and whatever you loose on earth, they shall be loosed in heaven" [Mt 16:19] [quoted in St. Cyprian's *Letters* 74:16 (c. A.D. 255)].

[Pope] Stephen [I] . . . boasts of the place of his episcopate, and contends that he holds the succession from Peter, on whom the foundations of the Church were laid [Mt 16:18]. . . . [Pope] Stephen . . . announces that he holds by succession the throne of Peter [ibid., 74:17 (c. A.D. 255)].

LETTER OF CLEMENT TO JAMES

Be it known to you, my lord, that Simon [Peter], who, for the sake of the true faith, and the sure foundation of his doctrine, was set apart to be the foundation of the Church, and for this end was, by Jesus himself, with his truthful mouth, named Peter [*Letter of Clement to James* 2 (c. A.D. 290)].

CLEMENTINE HOMILIES

[Simon Peter said to Simon Magus in Rome:] "For you now stand in direct opposition to me, who am a firm rock, the foundation of the Church" [Mt 16:18] [*Clementine Homilies* 17:19 (c. A.D. 290)].

ST. OPTATUS OF MILEVIS

You cannot then deny that you do know that upon Peter first in the city of Rome was bestowed the episcopal *cathedra*, on which sat Peter, the head of all the apostles (for which reason he was called Cephas), that, in this one *cathedra*, unity should be preserved by all [*Schism of the Donatists* 2:2 (c. A.D. 367)].

ST. AMBROSE OF MILAN

[Christ] made answer: "You are Peter, and upon this rock will I build my Church. . . ." Could he not, then, strengthen the faith of the man to whom, acting on his own authority, he gave the kingdom, whom he called the rock, thereby declaring him to be the foundation of the Church [Mt 16:18]? [*Faith* 5:57 (c. A.D. 379)].

ST. JEROME

As I follow no leader save Christ, so I communicate with none but your blessedness, that is, with the chair of Peter. For this, I know, is the rock on which the Church is built! [Mt 16:18]. This is the only house where the Paschal Lamb can be rightly eaten [Ex 12:22]. This is the Ark of Noah, and he who is not found in it shall perish when the flood prevails [*Letters* 15:2 (A.D. 376)].

But you say [Mt 16:18], the Church was founded upon Peter: although elsewhere the same is attributed to all the apostles, and they all receive the keys of the kingdom of heaven, and the strength of the Church depends upon them all, yet one among the Twelve is chosen so that when a head has been appointed, there may be no occasion for schism [*Against Jovinianus* 1:26 (c. A.D. 393)].

ST. AUGUSTINE OF HIPPO

For if the lineal succession of bishops is to be taken into account, with how much more certainty and benefit to the Church do we reckon back until we reach Peter himself, to whom, as a figure of the whole Church, the Lord said: "Upon this rock will I build my church, and the gates of hell shall not prevail against it!" [Mt 16:18]. The successor of Peter was Linus, and his successors in unbroken continuity were these: Clement, Anacletus, Evaristus, Alexander, Sixtus, Telesphorus, Iginus, Anicetus, Pius, Soter, Eleutherius, Victor, Zephyrinus, Calixtus, Urbanus, Pontianus, Antherus, Fabianus, Cornelius, Lucius, Stephanus, Xystus, Dionysius, Felix, Eutychianus, Gaius, Marcellinus, Marcellus, Eusebius, Miltiades, Sylvester, Marcus, Julius, Liberius, Damasus, and Siricius, whose successor is the present Bishop Anastasius. In this order of succession no Donatist bishop is found. But, reversing the natural course of things, the Donatists sent to Rome from Africa an ordained bishop, who, putting himself at the head of a few Africans in the great metropolis, gave some notoriety to the name of "mountain men," or Cutzupits, by which they were known [*Letters* 53:1:2 (c. A.D. 400)].

COUNCIL OF EPHESUS

Philip, the presbyter and legate of the Apostolic See [Rome], said: "There is no doubt, and in fact it has been known in all ages, that the holy and most blessed Peter, prince and head of the apostles, pillar of the faith, and foundation of the Catholic Church, received the keys of the kingdom from our Lord Jesus Christ, the Savior and Redeemer of the human race, and that to him was given the power of loosing and binding sins: who down even to today and forever both lives and judges in his successors" [Session 3 (A.D. 431)].

ST. SECHNALL OF IRELAND

Steadfast in the fear of God, and in faith immovable, upon [Patrick] as upon Peter the [Irish] church is built; and he has been given his apostleship by God; against him the gates of hell prevail not [*Hymn in Praise of St. Patrick* 3 (c. A.D. 444)].

POPE ST. LEO I

Our Lord Jesus Christ . . . has placed the principal charge on the blessed Peter, chief of all the apostles. . . . He wished him who had been received into partnership in his undivided unity to be named what he himself was, when he said: "You are Peter, and upon this rock I will build my Church" [Mt 16:18], that the building of the eternal temple might rest on Peter's solid rock, strengthening his Church so surely that neither human rashness could assail it nor the gates of hell prevail against it [*Letters* 10:1 (A.D. 445)].

COUNCIL OF CHALCEDON

[T]he most holy and blessed Leo, archbishop of the great and elder Rome, through us, and through this present most holy synod, together with the thrice blessed and all-glorious Peter the apostle, who is the rock and foundation of the Catholic Church, and the foundation of the orthodox faith, has stripped him [Dioscorus] of the episcopate [Session 3 (A.D. 451)].

27. Peter's Primacy

In the previous chapter, we saw that the early Church Fathers had an awareness of Peter as the rock on which the Church is built. It is a metaphor, but like all metaphors, it has meaning. The fact that Peter was made the foundation of the Church had practical implications. It gave him a special place or primacy among the apostles. As the passages below demonstrate, the early Church Fathers also recognized this.

ST. CLEMENT OF ALEXANDRIA

[T]he blessed Peter, the chosen, the preeminent, the first of the disciples, for whom alone and himself the Savior paid tribute [Mt 17:27], quickly seized and comprehended the saying. And what does he say? "Lo, we have left all and followed you" [*Who Is the Rich Man That Shall Be Saved?* 21 (c. A.D. 200)].

TERTULLIAN OF CARTHAGE

For though you think that heaven is still shut up, remember that the Lord left the keys of it to Peter here, and through him to the Church, which keys everyone will carry with him if he has been questioned and made a confession [of faith] [*Antidote for the Scorpion's Sting* 10 (c. A.D. 211)].

[T]he Lord said to Peter, "On this rock I will build my Church, I have given you the keys of the kingdom of heaven [and] whatever you shall have bound or loosed on earth will be bound or loosed in heaven" [Mt 16:18–19]. . . . What kind of man are you, subverting and changing what was the clear intent of the Lord when he himself conferred this upon Peter? Upon *you*, he says, I will build my Church; and I will give to *you* the keys [*Modesty* 21 (c. A.D. 220)].

ORIGEN OF ALEXANDRIA

[I]f we were to attend carefully to the Gospels, we should also find, in relation to those things that seem to be common to Peter . . . a great difference and a preeminence in the things [Jesus] said to Peter, compared with the second class [of apostles]. For it is no small difference that Peter received the keys not of one heaven but of more, and in order that whatever things he binds on earth may be bound not in one heaven but in them all, as compared with the many who bind on earth and loose on earth, so that these things are bound and loosed not in [all] the heavens, as in the case of Peter, but in only one; for they do not reach so high a stage of power as Peter to bind and loose in all the heavens [*Commentary on Matthew* 13:31 (c. A.D. 249)].

ST. CYPRIAN OF CARTHAGE

The Lord says to Peter: "I say to you," he says, "that you are Peter, and upon this rock I will build my Church, and the gates of hell will not overcome it. And to you I will give the keys of the kingdom of heaven . . ." [Mt 16:18-19]. On him he builds the Church, and commands him to feed the sheep [Jn 21:17], and although he assigns a like power to all the apostles, yet he founded a single chair [*cathedra*], and he established by his own authority a source and an intrinsic reason for that unity. Indeed, the others were also what Peter was [apostles], but a primacy is given to Peter, by which it is made clear that there is one Church and one chair. . . . If someone does not hold fast to this unity of Peter, can he think that he holds the faith? If he deserts the chair of Peter upon whom the Church was built, can he be confident that he is in the Church? [*Unity of the Catholic Church* 4; first edition (Treatise 1:4) (A.D. 251)].

LETTER OF CLEMENT TO JAMES

Be it known to you, my lord, that Simon [Peter], who, for the sake of the true faith, and the sure foundation of his doctrine, was set apart to be the foundation of the Church, and for this end was, by Jesus himself, with his truthful mouth, named Peter, the first fruits of our Lord, the first of the apostles; to whom the Father first revealed the Son; whom the Christ blessed with good reason; the called, and elect [*Letter of Clement to James* 2 (c. A.D. 290)].

ST. CYRIL OF JERUSALEM

The Lord is loving to man, and swift to pardon, but slow to punish. Let no man therefore despair of his own salvation. Peter, the chiefest and foremost of the apostles, denied the Lord three times before a little maid, but he repented and wept bitterly [*Catechetical Lectures* 2:19 (c. A.D. 350)].

[Simon Magus] so deceived the city of Rome that Claudius set up his statue. . . . As the delusion was extending, Peter and Paul, a noble pair, chief rulers of the Church, arrived and set the error right. . . . [T]hey launched the weapon of their prayers against Magus, and struck him down to the earth. And marvelous though it was, yet no marvel. For Peter was there, who carries the keys of heaven [Mt 16:19] [ibid., 6:14–15].

In the power of the same Holy Spirit, Peter also, the chief of the apostles and the bearer of the keys of the kingdom of heaven, healed Aeneas the paralytic in the name of Christ at Lydda, which is now Diospolis [Acts 9:32–34] [ibid., 17:27].

ST. EPHRAIM THE SYRIAN

[Jesus said:] Simon, my follower, I have made you the foundation of the holy Church. I betimes called you Peter, because you will support all its buildings. You are the inspector of those who will build on earth a Church for me. If they should wish to build what is false, you, the foundation, will condemn them. You are the head of the fountain from which my teaching flows; you are the chief of my disciples. Through you I will give drink to all peoples. Yours is that life-giving sweetness that I dispense. I have chosen you to be, as it were, the firstborn in my institution so that, as the heir, you may be executor of my treasures. I have given you the keys of my kingdom. Behold, I have given you authority over all my treasures [*Homilies* 4:1 (c. A.D. 353)].

ST. AMBROSE OF MILAN

[Christ] made answer: "You are Peter, and upon this rock will I build my Church. . . ." Could he not, then, strengthen the faith of the man to whom, acting on his own authority, he gave the kingdom, whom he called the rock, thereby declaring him to be the foundation of the Church [Mt 16:18]? [*Faith* 5:57 (c. A.D. 379)].

ST. JEROME

Simon Peter, the son of John, from the village of Bethsaida in the province of Galilee, brother of Andrew the apostle, and himself chief of the apostles, after having been bishop of the church of Antioch and having preached to the dispersion . . . pushed on to Rome in the second year of Claudius to overthrow Simon Magus, and held the sacerdotal chair there for twenty-five years until the last, the fourteenth, year of Nero. At his hands he received the crown of martyrdom, being nailed to the cross with his head towards the ground and his feet raised on high, asserting that he was unworthy to be crucified in the same manner as his Lord [*Illustrious Men* 1 (A.D. 392)].

But you say [Mt 16:18], the Church was founded upon Peter: although elsewhere the same is attributed to all the apostles, and they all receive the keys of the kingdom of heaven, and the strength of the Church depends upon them all, yet one among the Twelve is chosen so that when a head has been appointed, there may be no occasion for schism [*Against Jovinianus* 1:26 (c. A.D. 393)].

ST. AUGUSTINE OF HIPPO

Among these [apostles] Peter alone almost everywhere deserved to represent the whole Church. Because of that representation of the Church, which only he bore, he deserved to hear "I will give to you the keys of the kingdom of heaven" [*Sermons* 295:2 (c. A.D. 411)].

Who can fail to know that the most blessed Peter was the first of the apostles? [*Tractates on John* 56:1 (A.D. 416–417)].

COUNCIL OF EPHESUS

Philip, presbyter and legate of [Pope Celestine I] said: "We offer our thanks to the holy and venerable synod, that when the writings of our holy and blessed pope had been read to you . . . you joined yourselves to the holy head also by your holy acclamations. For your blessednesses is not ignorant that the head of the whole faith, the head of the apostles, is blessed Peter the apostle" [Session 2 (A.D. 431)].

Philip, the presbyter and legate of the Apostolic See [Rome] said: "There is no doubt, and in fact it has been known in all ages, that the holy and most blessed Peter, prince and head of the apostles, pillar of the faith, and foundation of the Catholic Church, received the keys of the kingdom from our Lord Jesus Christ, the Savior and Redeemer of the human race, and that to him was given the power of loosing and binding sins: who down even to today and forever both lives and judges in his successors" [ibid., session 3].

POPE ST. LEO I

Our Lord Jesus Christ . . . has placed the principal charge on the blessed Peter, chief of all the apostles. . . . He wished him who had been received into partnership in his undivided unity to be named what he himself was, when he said: "You are Peter, and upon this rock I will build my Church" [Mt 16:18], that the building of the eternal temple might rest on Peter's solid rock, strengthening his Church so surely that neither human rashness could assail it nor the gates of hell prevail against it [*Letters* 10:1 (A.D. 445)].

Our Lord Jesus Christ . . . established the worship belonging to the divine [Christian] religion. . . . But the Lord desired that the sacrament of this gift should pertain to all the apostles in such a way that it might be found principally in the most blessed Peter, the highest of all the apostles. And he wanted his gifts to flow into the entire body from Peter himself, as if from the head, in such a way that anyone who had dared to separate himself from the solidarity of Peter would realize that he was himself no longer a sharer in the divine mystery [ibid., 10:1].

And though they have a common dignity, yet they have not uniform rank; because even among the blessed apostles, notwithstanding the similarity of their honorable estate, there was a certain distinction of power, and while the election of them all was equal, yet it was given to one to take the lead of the rest. . . . [So today through the bishops] through whom the care of the universal Church should converge towards Peter's one seat, and nothing anywhere should be separated from its head [ibid., 14:12].

28. Peter in Rome

In previous chapters we have seen that at the beginning of Peter's career as an apostle, Jesus made him the rock on which the Church is built and that this gave him a special primacy. Here we will look at the end of Peter's career, by which time he had traveled to Rome.

This is something that may be referred to in a veiled way in Scripture itself. In his first letter, Peter indicates that he is writing from "Babylon" (1 Pt 5:13), which is often taken to be a code word for Rome. Peter used it, presumably, either as a commentary on the wickedness of the city or to prevent his location from being identified if the letter were intercepted by pagans (which would have been relatively easy since he was writing to a wide array of locations in modern Turkey; see 1 Peter 1:1), or for both of these reasons.

However that may be, the Church Fathers record that Peter did go to Rome, where he and Paul were martyred in the persecution launched by the emperor Nero, which Roman historians indicate took place after the Great Fire of Rome in July of A.D. 64, when Nero tried to fix the blame for the conflagration on the Christian community (Tacitus, *The Annals* 15:44; Suetonius, *The Lives of the Twelve Caesars*, "The Life of Nero," 38).

ST. IGNATIUS OF ANTIOCH

I do not, as Peter and Paul, issue commandments unto you. They were apostles; I am but a condemned man: They were free, while I am, even until now, a servant [*Letter to the Romans* 4 (c. A.D. 110)].

ST. DIONYSIUS OF CORINTH

You [Pope Soter] have thus by such an admonition bound together the planting of Peter and of Paul at Rome and Corinth. For both of them planted and taught us in Corinth. And they taught together in Italy, and suffered martyrdom at the same time [*Letter to Pope Soter* (c. A.D. 170), in Eusebius, *Church History* 2:25:8].

ST. IRENAEUS OF LYONS

Matthew also issued among the Hebrews a written Gospel in their own language, while Peter and Paul were evangelizing in Rome and laying the foundation of the Church [*Against Heresies*, 3:1:1 (c. A.D. 189)].

But since it would be too long to enumerate in such a volume as this the succession of all the churches, we shall confound all those who, in whatever manner, whether through self-satisfaction or vainglory, or through blindness and wicked opinion, assemble other than where it is proper, by pointing out here the succession of the bishops of the greatest and most ancient church known to all, founded and organized at Rome by the two most glorious apostles, Peter and Paul, that church that has the tradition and the faith that comes down to us after having been announced to men by the apostles. With that church [of Rome], because of its superior origin, all the churches must agree, that is, all the faithful in the whole world, and it is in her that the faithful everywhere have maintained the apostolic Tradition [ibid., 3:3:2].

The blessed apostles, then, having founded and built up the Church, committed into the hands of Linus the office of the epis-copate. Of this Linus, Paul makes mention in the Letters to Tim-othy. To him succeeded Anacletus; and after him, in the third place from the apostles, Clement was allotted the bishopric. This man, as he had seen the blessed apostles, and had been conversant with them, might be said to have the preaching of the apostles still echoing [in his ears], and their traditions before his eyes. Nor was he alone [in this], for there were many still remaining who had received instructions from the apostles. In the time of this Clement, no small dissension having occurred among the brethren at Corinth, the Church in Rome despatched a most powerful letter to the Corinthians, exhorting them to peace, renewing their faith, and declaring the Tradition that it had lately received from the apostles, proclaiming the one God, omnipotent, the maker of heaven and earth, the Creator of man, who brought on the deluge, and called Abraham, who led the people from the land of Egypt, spoke with Moses, set forth the law, sent the prophets, and who has prepared fire for the devil and his angels. From this document, whosoever chooses to do so may learn that he, the Father of our Lord Jesus Christ, was preached by the churches, and may also understand the apostolic Tradition of the Church, since this letter is of older date than these men who are now propagating falsehood, and who conjure into existence another god beyond the Creator and the maker of all existing things. To this Clement there succeeded Evaristus. Alexander followed Evaristus; then, sixth from the apostles, Sixtus was appointed; after him, Telesphorus, who was gloriously martyred; then Hyginus; after him, Pius; then after him, Anicetus. Soter having succeeded Anicetus, Eleutherius does now, in the twelfth place from the apostles, hold the inheritance of the episcopate. In this order, and by this succession, the ecclesiastical Tradition from the apostles, and the preaching of the truth, have come down to us. And this is most abundant proof that there is one and the same vivifying faith, which has been preserved in the Church from the apostles until now, and handed down in truth [ibid., 3:3:3].

ST. CLEMENT OF ALEXANDRIA

The Gospel according to Mark had this occasion. As Peter had preached the word publicly at Rome, and declared the gospel by the Spirit, many who were present requested that Mark, who had followed him for a long time and remembered his sayings, should write them out. And having composed the Gospel he gave it to those who had requested it [*Sketches* (c. A.D. 200), in a fragment from Eusebius, *Church History* 6:14:6].

TERTULLIAN OF CARTHAGE

Since, moreover, you are close upon Italy, you have Rome, from which there comes even into our own hands the very authority (of apostles themselves). How happy is its church, on which apostles poured forth all their doctrine along with their blood! Where Peter endures a passion like his Lord's! Where Paul wins his crown in a death like John's! Where the apostle John was first plunged, unhurt, into boiling oil, and thence remitted to his island exile! [*Prescription Against Heretics* 36 (c. A.D. 200)].

For this is the manner in which the apostolic churches transmit their registers: as the church of Smyrna, which records that Polycarp was placed therein by John; as also the church of Rome, which makes Clement to have been ordained in like manner by Peter [ibid., 32].

Let us see what milk the Corinthians drank from Paul; to what rule of faith the Galatians were brought for correction; what the Philippians, the Thessalonians, the Ephesians read by it; what utterance also the Romans give, so very near (to the apostles), to whom Peter and Paul conjointly bequeathed the gospel even sealed with their own blood [*Against Marcion* 4:5 (c. A.D. 209)].

CAIUS OF ROME

It is, therefore, recorded that Paul was beheaded in Rome itself, and that Peter likewise was crucified under Nero. This account of Peter and Paul is substantiated by the fact that their names are preserved in the cemeteries of that place even to the present day. It is confirmed likewise by Caius, a member of the Church, who arose under Zephyrinus, bishop of Rome. He, in a published disputation with Proclus, the leader of the Phrygian heresy, speaks as follows concerning the places where the sacred corpses of the aforesaid apostles are laid: "But I can show the trophies of the apostles. For if you will go to the Vatican or to the Ostian way, you will find the trophies of those who laid the foundations of this church" [*Disputation with Proclus* (c. A.D. 210), in Eusebius, *Church History* 2:25:5–7].

POEM AGAINST THE MARCIONITES

In this chair in which he himself had sat, Peter in mighty Rome commanded Linus, the first elected, to sit down. After him, Cletus too accepted the flock of the fold. As his successor, Anacletus was elected by lot. Clement follows him, well-known to apostolic men. After him Evaristus ruled the flock without crime. Alexander, sixth in succession, commends the fold to Sixtus. After his illustrious times were completed, he passed it on to Telesphorus. He was excellent, a faithful martyr [*Poem Against the Marcionites* 276–84 (c. A.D. 285)].

ST. PETER OF ALEXANDRIA

Thus Peter, the first of the apostles, having been often apprehended, and thrown into prison, and treated with ignominy, was last of all crucified at Rome [*Penance*, canon 9 (A.D. 306)].

EUSEBIUS OF CAESAREA

Victor . . . was the thirteenth bishop of Rome from Peter [*Church History* 5:28:3 (c. A.D. 312)].

LACTANTIUS

And while Nero reigned, the apostle Peter came to Rome, and, through the power of God committed unto him, wrought certain miracles, and, by turning many to the true religion, built up a faithful and steadfast temple unto the Lord. When Nero heard of those things, and observed that not only in Rome, but in every other place, a great multitude revolted daily from the worship of idols, and, condemning their old ways, went over to the new religion, he, an execrable and pernicious tyrant, sprung forward to raze the heavenly temple and destroy the true faith. He it was who first persecuted the servants of God; he crucified Peter, and slew Paul [*Deaths of the Persecutors* 2 (c. A.D. 318)].

ST. CYRIL OF JERUSALEM

And [Simon Magus] so deceived the city of Rome that Claudius set up his statue, and wrote beneath it, in the language of the Romans, "Simoni Deo Sancto," which being interpreted signifies, "To Simon the Holy God." As the delusion was extending, Peter and Paul, a noble pair, chief rulers of the Church, arrived and set the error right; and when the supposed god Simon wished to show himself off, they immediately showed him as a corpse. For Simon promised to rise aloft to heaven, and came riding in a demons' chariot on the air; but the servants of God fell on their knees, and having shown that agreement of which Jesus spoke, that if two of you shall agree concerning anything that they shall ask, it shall be done unto them [Mt 18:19], they launched the weapon of their concord in prayer against Magus, and struck him down to the earth. And marvelous though it was, yet no marvel. For Peter was there, who carries the keys of heaven: and nothing wonderful, for Paul was there, who was caught up to the third heaven, and into paradise, and heard unspeakable words, which it is not lawful far a man to utter [*Catechetical Lectures* 6:14–15 (c. A.D. 350)].

ST. OPTATUS OF MILEVIS

You cannot then deny that you know that upon Peter first in the city of Rome was bestowed the episcopal *cathedra*, on which he sat, the head of all the apostles (for which reason he was called Cephas), that, in this one *cathedra*, unity should be preserved by all [*Schism of the Donatists* 2:2 (c. A.D. 367)].

POPE ST. DAMASUS I

Likewise it is decreed: . . . [W]e have considered that it ought to be announced that although all the Catholic churches spread abroad through the world comprise one bridal chamber of Christ, nevertheless, the holy Roman church has been placed at the forefront not by the conciliar decisions of other churches, but has received the primacy by the evangelic voice of our Lord and Savior, who says: "You are Peter, and upon this rock I will build my Church, and the gates of hell will not prevail against it; and I will give to you the keys of the kingdom of heaven, and whatever you shall have bound on earth will be bound in heaven, and whatever you shall have loosed on earth shall be loosed in heaven" [Mt 16:18–19].

In addition to this, there is also the companionship of the vessel of election, the most blessed apostle Paul, who contended and was crowned with a glorious death along with Peter in the city of Rome in the time of Caesar Nero. . . . They equally consecrated the above-mentioned holy Roman church to Christ the Lord; and by their own presence and by their venerable triumph they set it at the forefront over the others of all the cities of the whole world.

The first see, therefore, is that of Peter the apostle, that of the Roman Church, which has neither stain nor blemish nor anything like it. The second see, however, is that at Alexandria, consecrated in behalf of blessed Peter by Mark, his disciple and an evangelist, who was sent to Egypt by the apostle Peter, where he preached the word of truth and finished his glorious martyrdom. The third honorable see, indeed, is that at Antioch, which belonged to the most blessed apostle Peter, where first he dwelt before he came to Rome and where the name "Christians" was first applied, as to a new people [Decree of Damasus 3 (A.D. 382)].

ST. JEROME

Simon Peter, the son of John, from the village of Bethsaida in the province of Galilee, brother of Andrew the apostle, and himself chief of the apostles, after having been bishop of the church of Antioch and having preached to the dispersion . . . pushed on to Rome in the second year of Claudius to overthrow Simon Magus, and held the sacred chair there for twenty-five years until the last, the fourteenth, year of Nero. At his hands he received the crown of martyrdom, being nailed to the cross with his head towards the ground and his feet raised on high, asserting that he was unworthy to be crucified in the same manner as his Lord [*Illustrious Men* 1 (A.D. 392)].

ST. AUGUSTINE OF HIPPO

If all men throughout the world were such as you most vainly accuse them of being, what has the chair of the Roman Church done to you, in which Peter sat, and in which Anastasius sits today? [*Answer to the Letters of Petilian the Donatist* 2:51:118 (c. A.D. 402)].

29. Peter's Successors

The Fathers recognized Peter as the rock on which Jesus declared he would build his Church; this gave him a special primacy; and he traveled to Rome, where he was martyred. In this chapter we see that the Fathers also recognized that Peter left a successor in Rome. Thus the bishop of Rome—the pope—continued to fulfill Peter's role in subsequent generations of the Church.

ST. IRENAEUS OF LYONS

The blessed apostles, then, having founded and built up the Church, committed into the hands of Linus the office of the episcopate [*Against Heresies* 3:3:3 (c. A.D. 189)].

TERTULLIAN OF CARTHAGE

For this is the manner in which the apostolic churches transmit their registers: as the church of Smyrna, which records that Polycarp was placed therein by John; as also the church of Rome, which makes Clement to have been ordained in like manner by Peter [*Prescription Against Heretics* 32 (c. A.D. 200)].

ST. CYPRIAN OF CARTHAGE

The Lord says to Peter: "I say to you," he says, "that you are Peter, and upon this rock I will build my Church, and the gates of hell will not overcome it. And to you I will give the keys of the kingdom of heaven . . ." [Mt 16:18–19]. On him he builds the Church, and commands him to feed the sheep [Jn 21:17], and although he assigns a like power to all the apostles, yet he founded a single chair [*cathedra*], and he established by his own authority a source and an intrinsic reason for that unity. Indeed, the others were also what Peter was [i.e., apostles], but a primacy is given to Peter, by which it is made clear that there is one Church and one chair. . . . If someone does not hold fast to this unity of Peter, can he think that he holds the faith? [*Unity of the Catholic Church* 4; first edition (Treatise 1:4) (A.D. 251)].

Moreover, they still dare—a false bishop having been appointed for them by heretics—to set sail and to bear letters from schismatic and profane persons to the throne of Peter, and to the chief church [at Rome] whence priestly unity takes its source [*Letters*, 54:14 (A.D. 252)].

EUSEBIUS OF CAESAREA

Victor . . . was the thirteenth bishop of Rome from Peter [*Church History* 5:28:3 (c. A.D. 312)].

Paul testifies that Crescens was sent to Gaul [2 Tm 4:10], but Linus, whom he mentions in the Second Letter to Timothy [2 Tm 4:21] as his companion at Rome, was Peter's successor in the episcopate of the church there, as has already been shown. Clement also, who was appointed third bishop of the church at Rome, was, as Paul testifies, his co-laborer and fellow soldier [Phil 4:3] [ibid., 3:4:9–10].

POPE ST. JULIUS I

[The] judgment [against Athanasius] ought to have been made, not as it was, but according to the ecclesiastical canon. . . . Are you ignorant that the custom has been for word to be written first to us, and then for a just decision to be passed from this place [Rome]? If any suspicion rested upon the bishop there, notice of it ought to have been sent to the church here; but, after neglecting to inform us, and proceeding on their own authority as they pleased, they now desire to obtain our agreement with their decisions, though we never condemned him. Not so have the constitutions of Paul, or the traditions of the Fathers directed; this is another form of procedure, a novel practice . . . . [W]hat I write is for the common good. For what we have received from the blessed apostle Peter is what I signify to you [*Letter on Behalf of Athanasius* (A.D. 341), contained in St. Athanasius, *Apology Against the Arians* 1:2:35].

COUNCIL OF SARDICA

But if in any province a bishop has a matter in dispute against his brother bishop, one of the two shall not call in a bishop from another province as judge. But if judgment has gone against a bishop in any cause, and he thinks he has a good case, in order that the question may be reopened, let us honor the memory of St. Peter the apostle, and let those who tried the case write to Julius, the bishop of Rome, and if he judges that the case should be retried, let it be done, and let him appoint judges; but if he finds that the former decision need not be disturbed, what he has decreed shall be confirmed. Is this the pleasure of all? The synod answered: "It is our pleasure" [Canon 3 (A.D. 342)].

ST. OPTATUS OF MILEVIS

You cannot then deny that you know that upon Peter first in the city of Rome was bestowed the episcopal *cathedra*, on which he sat, the head of all the apostles (for which reason he was called Cephas), that, in this one *cathedra*, unity should be preserved by all, lest the other Apostles might claim—each for himself—separate *cathedras*, so that he who should set up a second Cathedra against the unique *cathedra* would already be a schismatic and a sinner. Well then, on the one *cathedra*, which is the first of the endowments, Peter was the first to sit [*Schism of the Donatists* 2:2 (c. A.D. 367)].

ST. JEROME

Since the East, shattered as it is by the longstanding feuds, subsisting between its peoples, is bit by bit tearing into shreds the seamless vest of the Lord. . . . I think it my duty to consult the chair of Peter, and to turn to a Church [Rome] whose faith has been praised by Paul [Rom 1:8]. I appeal for spiritual food to the Church whence I have received the garb of Christ. . . . Evil children have squandered their patrimony; you alone keep your heritage intact [*Letters* 15:1 (c. A.D. 376)].

As I follow no leader save Christ, so I communicate with none but your blessedness, that is, with the chair of Peter. For this, I know, is the rock on which the Church is built! [Mt 16:18]. This is the house where alone the Paschal Lamb can be rightly eaten [Ex 12:22]. This is the Ark of Noah, and he who is not found in it shall perish when the flood prevails [ibid., 15:2].

The Church is rent into three factions, and each of these is eager to seize me for its own. The influence of the monks is of long standing, and it is directed against me. I meantime keep crying: "He who clings to the chair of Peter is accepted by me." Meletius, Vitalis, and Paulinus all profess to cleave to you, and I could believe the assertion if it were made by one of them only. As it is, either two of them or else all three are guilty of falsehood. Therefore I implore your blessedness, by our Lord's cross and Passion, those necessary glories of our faith, as you hold an apostolic office, to give an apostolic decision. Only tell me by letter with whom I am to communicate in Syria [ibid., 16:2].

[Pope] Stephen . . . was the blessed Peter's twenty-second successor in the see of Rome [*Dialogue Against the Luciferians* 23 (c. A.D. 382)].

ST. AMBROSE OF MILAN

[The Novatian heretics] have not the succession of Peter, who hold not the chair of Peter, which they rend by wicked schism; and this, too, they do, wickedly denying that sins can be forgiven [by the sacrament of confession] even in the Church, whereas it was said to Peter: "I will give unto thee the keys of the kingdom of heaven, and whatsoever thou shalt bind on earth shall be bound also in heaven, and whatsoever thou shall loose on earth shall be loosed also in heaven" [Mt 16:19] [*Penance* 1:7:33 (A.D. 388)].

ST. JEROME

Clement, of whom the apostle Paul writing to the Philippians says, "With Clement and others of my fellow-workers whose names are written in the book of life," the fourth bishop of Rome after Peter, if indeed the second was Linus and the third Anacletus, although most of the Latins think that Clement was second after the apostle [*Illustrious Men* 15 (A.D. 392)].

ST. AUGUSTINE OF HIPPO

For if the lineal succession of bishops is to be taken into account, with how much more certainty and benefit to the Church do we reckon back until we reach Peter himself, to whom, as a figure of the whole Church, the Lord said: "Upon this rock will I build my Church, and the gates of hell shall not prevail against it!" [Mt 16:18]. The successor of Peter was Linus, and his successors in unbroken continuity were these: Clement, Anacletus, Evaristus . . . [*Letters* 53:1:2 (c. A.D. 400)].

If all men throughout the world were such as you most vainly accuse them of being, what has the chair of the Roman Church done to you, in which Peter sat, and in which Anastasius sits to-day? [*Answer to the Letters of Petilian the Donatist* 2:51:118 (c. A.D. 402)].

COUNCIL OF EPHESUS

Philip the presbyter and legate of the Apostolic See said: "There is no doubt, and in fact it has been known in all ages, that the holy and most blessed Peter, prince and head of the apostles, pillar of the faith, and foundation of the Catholic Church, received the keys of the kingdom from our Lord Jesus Christ, the Savior and Redeemer of the human race, and that to him was given the power of loosing and binding sins: who down even to today and forever both lives and judges in his successors. The holy and most blessed pope Celestine, according to due order, is his successor and holds his place, and us he sent to supply his place in this holy synod" [Session 3 (A.D. 431)].

POPE ST. LEO I

Whereupon the blessed Peter, as inspired by God, and about to benefit all nations by his confession, said, "You are the Christ, the Son of the living God." Not undeservedly, therefore, was he pronounced blessed by the Lord, and derived from the original rock that solidity that belonged both to his virtue and to his name [Peter] [*Tome of Leo* (Letters 28:5) (A.D. 449)].

As for the resolution of the bishops, which is contrary to the Nicene decree, in union with your faithful piety, I declare it to be invalid and annul it by the authority of the holy apostle Peter [*Letters* 105:3 (A.D. 452)].

COUNCIL OF CHALCEDON

After the reading of the foregoing letter, the most reverend bishops cried out: This is the faith of the fathers, this is the faith of the apostles. So we all believe, thus the orthodox believe. Anathema to him who does not thus believe. Peter has spoken thus through Leo. So taught the apostles. Piously and truly did Leo teach, so taught Cyril. Everlasting be the memory of Cyril. Leo and Cyril taught the same thing, anathema to him who does not so believe. This is the true faith. Those of us who are orthodox thus believe. This is the faith of the fathers [Session 2 (A.D. 451)].

30. The Authority of the Pope

The Church Fathers understood Peter's successors to share his special authority or primacy.

In a variety of ways, the Fathers attest to the fact that the church of Rome was the central, authoritative church. They rely on Rome for advice, for mediation of disputes, and for guidance on doctrinal issues. They note, as St. Ignatius of Antioch does, that Rome holds "the presidency" among the other churches, and that, as St. Irenaeus of Lyons explains, "because of its superior origin, all the churches must agree" with Rome. They are also clear on the fact that it is communion with Rome and the bishop of Rome that causes one to be in communion with the Catholic Church. This displays a recognition that, as St. Cyprian of Carthage puts it, Rome is "the principal church, in which sacerdotal unity has its source."

Most significant are passages in which the popes themselves, by their statements or actions, reveal an awareness of their unique role, such as when Pope St. Victor I excommunicated the churches of Asia Minor as a group, after which the other bishops sought to change his mind but did not say that he lacked the ability to do this.

POPE ST. CLEMENT I

Owing, dear brethren, to the sudden and successive calamitous events that have happened to us, we feel that we have been somewhat tardy in turning our attention to the points about which you consulted us; and especially to that shameful and detestable sedition, utterly abhorrent to the elect of God, that a few rash and self-confident persons have kindled to such a pitch of frenzy that your venerable and illustrious name, worthy to be universally loved, has suffered grievous injury. . . . It is right and holy, therefore, men and brethren, to obey God rather than to follow those who, through pride and sedition, have become the leaders of a detestable emulation. For we shall incur no slight injury, but rather great danger, if we rashly yield ourselves to the inclinations of men who aim at exciting strife and tumults, to draw us away from what is good . . . we may reach the goal set before us in truth wholly free from blame. Joy and gladness you will afford us, if you become obedient to the words written by us and through the Holy Spirit root out the lawless wrath of your jealousy according to the intercession we have made for peace and unity in this letter [*Letter to the Corinthians* I, 14, 63 (A.D. 70)].

HERMAS OF ROME

You will write two books, and you will send the one to Clemens and the other to Grapte. And Clemens will send his to foreign countries, for permission has been granted to him to do so [*The Shepherd* 1:2:4 (c. A.D. 80)].

ST. IGNATIUS OF ANTIOCH

Ignatius . . . to the Church that has obtained mercy, through the majesty of the most high Father, and Jesus Christ, his only-begotten Son; the Church that is beloved and enlightened by the will of him that wills all things according to the love of Jesus Christ our God, that presides in the place of the Romans, worthy of God, worthy of honor, worthy of the highest happiness, worthy of praise, worthy of obtaining her every desire, worthy of being deemed holy, and that presides over love, and is named from Christ, and from the Father [*Letter to the Romans*, Greeting (c. A.D. 110)].

You have never envied any one; you have taught others. Now I desire that those things may be confirmed [by your conduct], which in your instructions you enjoin [on others] [ibid., 3].

ST. DIONYSIUS OF CORINTH

From the beginning it has been your practice to do good to all the brethren in various ways, and to send contributions to many churches in every city. Thus relieving the want of the needy, and making provision for the brethren in the mines by the gifts you have sent from the beginning, you Romans keep up the hereditary customs of the Romans, which your blessed Bishop Soter has not only maintained, but added to, furnishing an abundance of supplies to the saints, and encouraging the brethren from abroad with blessed words, as a loving father his children [*Letter to Pope Soter* (c. A.D. 170), in Eusebius, *Church History* 4:23:10].

Today we have passed the Lord's holy day, in which we have read your letter. Whenever we read it, we shall be able to draw advice, as also from the earlier letter, which was written to us through Clement [ibid., 4:23:11].

The same witnesses also recommended Irenaeus, who was at that time a presbyter of the parish of Lyons, to the bishop of Rome [Pope St. Eleutherius], saying many favorable things about to him, as the following shows: "We pray, father Eleutherius, that you may rejoice in God in all things and always. We have requested our brother and comrade Irenaeus to carry this letter to you, and we ask you to hold him in esteem, as zealous for the covenant of Christ" [ibid., 5:4:1–2].

ST. IRENAEUS OF LYONS

Since, however, it would be very tedious, in such a volume as this, to reckon up the successions of all the churches, we put to confusion all those who, in whatever manner, whether by an evil self-pleasing, by vanity, or by blindness and perverse opinion, assemble in unauthorized meetings, by indicating that Tradition derived from the apostles, of the very great, the very ancient, and universally known Church founded and organized at Rome by the two most glorious apostles, Peter and Paul; also [by pointing out] the faith preached to men, which comes down to our time by means of the successions of the bishops. For it is a matter of necessity that every church agree with this church, on account of its preeminent authority, that is, the faithful everywhere, in so far as the apostolic Tradition has been preserved continuously by those [faithful men] who exist everywhere [Against Heresies 3:3:2 (c. A.D. 189)].

ST. CYPRIAN OF CARTHAGE

If anyone considers and examines these things, there is no need for a long discussion and arguments. There is easy proof of faith in a short summary of the truth. The Lord says to Peter: "I say to you," he says, "that you are Peter, and upon this rock I will build my Church, and the gates of hell will not overcome it. And to you I will give the keys of the kingdom of heaven . . ." [Mt 16:18–19]. On him he builds the Church, and commands him to feed the sheep [Jn 21:17], and although he assigns a like power to all the apostles, yet he founded a single chair [*cathedra*], and he established by his own authority a source and an intrinsic reason for that unity. Indeed, the others were also what Peter was [i.e., apostles], but a primacy is given to Peter, by which it is made clear that there is one Church and one chair. . . . If someone does not hold fast to this unity of Peter, can he think that he holds the faith? If he deserts the chair of Peter upon whom the Church was built, can he be confident that he is in the Church? [*Unity of the Catholic Church* 4; first edition (Treatise 1:4) (A.D. 251)].

Cyprian to [Pope St.] Cornelius his brother, greeting. You have acted, dearest brother, with diligence and love, in quickly sending us Nicephorus the acolyte, who told us the glorious gladness for the return of the confessors, and most fully instructed us against the new and mischievous devices of Novatian and Novatus for attacking the Church of Christ [*Letters* 48:1 (A.D. 251)].

Cyprian to Antonianus his brother, greeting. . . . You wrote . . . for me to transmit a copy of those same letters to [Pope St.] Cornelius our colleague, so that he might lay aside all anxiety, and know at once that you held communion with him, that is, with the Catholic Church [*Letters* 51:1 (A.D. 252)].

[Pope St.] Cornelius was made bishop by the judgment of God and of Christ, by the testimony of almost all the clergy, by the suffrage of the people who were then present, and by the assembly of ancient priests and good men . . . when the place of Fabian, that is, the place of Peter and the degree of the sacerdotal throne was vacant, which being occupied by the will of God, and established by the consent of all of us, whoever now wishes to become a bishop, must needs be made from without; and he cannot have the ordination of the Church who does not hold the unity of the Church [*Letters* 51:8 (A.D. 252)].

After such things as these, moreover, they still dare—a false bishop having been appointed for them by heretics—to set sail and bear letters from schismatic and profane persons to the throne of Peter, and to the chief Church from which priestly unity takes its source [*Letters* 54:14 (A.D. 252)].

FIRMILIAN OF CAESAREA

[Pope] Stephen [I] . . . boasts of the place of his episcopate, and contends that he holds the succession from Peter, on whom the foundations of the Church were laid [Mt 16:18]. . . . [Pope] Stephen . . . announces that he holds by succession the throne of Peter [quoted in St. Cyprian's *Letters* 74:17 (c. A.D. 255)].

EUSEBIUS OF CAESAREA

A question of no small importance arose at that time. For the parishes of all Asia, held from an older tradition that the fourteenth day of the moon, on which the Jews were commanded to sacrifice the lamb, should be observed as the feast of the Savior's passover. . . . But it was not the custom of the churches in the rest of the world to end it at this time, as they observed the practice that, from apostolic Tradition, has prevailed to the present time, of terminating the fast on the day of the Resurrection of our Savior. Synods and assemblies of bishops were held on this account, and all, with one consent, through mutual correspondence, drew up an ecclesiastical decree that the mystery of the Resurrection of the Lord should be celebrated on the Lord's Day, and that we should observe the close of the paschal fast on this day only. . . . Thereupon Victor, who presided over the church at Rome, immediately attempted to cut off from the common unity the parishes of all Asia, and the churches that agreed with them, as heterodox; and he wrote letters and declared all the brethren there excommunicated. But this did not please all the bishops. And they asked him to consider the things of peace, and of neighborly unity and love. . . . [St. Irenaeus of Lyons] fittingly admonished Victor that he should not cut off whole churches of God that observed the tradition of an ancient custom [*Church History* 5:23:1–5:24:11 (c. A.D. 312)].

Thus Irenaeus, who truly was well named, became a peacemaker in this matter, exhorting and negotiating on behalf of the peace of the churches. And he conferred by letter about this question, not only with Victor, but also with most of the other rulers of the churches [ibid., 5:24:18].

POPE ST. JULIUS I

[The] judgment [against Athanasius] ought to have been made, not as it was, but according to the ecclesiastical canon. . . . Are you ignorant that the custom has been for word to be written first to us, and then for a just decision to be passed from this place [Rome]? If any suspicion rested upon the bishop there, notice of it ought to have been sent to the church here; but, after neglecting to inform us, and proceeding on their own authority as they pleased, they now desire to obtain our agreement with their decisions, though we never condemned him. Not so have the constitutions of Paul, or the traditions of the Fathers directed; this is another form of procedure, a novel practice. . . . [W]hat I write is for the common good. For what we have received from the blessed apostle Peter is what I signify to you [*Letter on Behalf of Athanasius* (A.D. 341), contained in St. Athanasius, *Apology Against the Arians* 1:2:35].

COUNCIL OF SARDICA

It is necessary to add this—that bishops shall not pass from their own province to another province in which there are bishops, unless upon invitation from their brethren, that we seem not to close the door of charity. But if in any province a bishop has a matter in dispute against his brother bishop, one of the two shall not call in a bishop from another province as judge. But if judgment has gone against a bishop in any cause, and he thinks he has a good case, in order that the question may be reopened, let us honor the memory of St. Peter the apostle, and let those who tried the case write to Julius, the bishop of Rome, and if he judges that the case should be retried, let it be done, and let him appoint judges; but if he finds that the former decision need not be disturbed, what he has decreed shall be confirmed. Is this the pleasure of all? The synod answered, It is our pleasure [Canon 3 (A.D. 342)].

If it seems good to you, it is necessary to add to this decision full of sincere charity you have pronounced, that if any bishop be deposed by the sentence of these neighboring bishops, and asserts that he has fresh matter in his defense, a new bishop not be settled in his see unless the bishop of Rome judge and render a decision [Canon 4 (c. A.D. 342)].

ST. OPTATUS OF MILEVIS

You cannot then deny that you know that upon Peter first in the city of Rome was bestowed the episcopal *cathedra*, on which he sat, the head of all the apostles (for which reason he was called Cephas), that, in this one *cathedra*, unity should be preserved by all. Neither do the apostles proceed individually on their own, and anyone who would [presume to] set up another chair in opposition to that single chair would, by that very fact, be a schismatic and a sinner. . . . Recall, then, the origins of your chair, those of you who wish to claim for yourselves the title of holy Church [*Schism of the Donatists* 2:2 (c. A.D. 367)].

ST. JEROME

As I follow no leader save Christ, so I communicate with none but your blessedness, that is, with the chair of Peter. For this, I know, is the rock on which the church is built [Mt 16:18]! This is the only house where the Paschal Lamb can be rightly eaten [Ex 12:22]. This is the Ark of Noah, and he who is not found in it shall perish when the flood prevails [*Letters* 15:2 (A.D. 376)].

The Church is rent into three factions, and each of these is eager to seize me for its own. The influence of the monks is of long standing, and it is directed against me. I meantime keep crying: "He who clings to the chair of Peter is accepted by me." Meletius, Vitalis, and Paulinus all profess to cleave to you, and I could believe the assertion if it were made by one of them. As it is, either two of them or else all three are guilty of falsehood. Therefore I implore your blessedness, by our Lord's cross and Passion, those necessary glories of our faith, as you hold an apostolic office, to give an apostolic decision. Only tell me by letter with whom I am to communicate in Syria (ibid., 16:2).

COUNCIL OF CONSTANTINOPLE I

The bishop of Constantinople however shall have the prerogative of honor after the bishop of Rome, because Constantinople is new Rome [Canon 3 (A.D. 381)].

ST. AUGUSTINE OF HIPPO

[T]here are many other things that most justly keep me in her bosom. The consent of peoples and nations keeps me in the Church; so does her authority, inaugurated by miracles, nourished by hope, enlarged by love, established by age. The succession of priests keeps me, beginning from the very seat of the apostle Peter, to whom the Lord, after his Resurrection, put in charge of feeding his sheep, down to the present episcopate [of Pope Siricius] [*Against the Letter of Mani Called "The Foundation"* 4:5 (A.D. 397)].

[On this matter of the Pelagians] two councils have already been sent to the Apostolic See [the bishop of Rome], and from there replies too have come. The matter is at an end; would that the error too might be at an end! [*Sermons* 131:10 (c. A.D. 411)].

POPE ST. CELESTINE I

We enjoin upon you [my legates to the Council of Ephesus] the necessary task of guarding the authority of the Apostolic See. And if the instructions handed to you have to mention this and if you have to be present in the assembly, if it comes to controversy, it is not yours to join the fight but to judge of the opinions [on my behalf] [*Letters* 17 (A.D. 414)].

POPE ST. INNOCENT I

In seeking the things of God . . . following the examples of ancient tradition . . . you have strengthened . . . the vigor of your religion with true reason, for you have acknowledged that judgment is to be referred to us, and have shown that you know what is owed to the Apostolic See, if all of us desire to follow the apostle himself [Peter], from whom the episcopate itself and the total authority of this name have emerged. Following him, we know how to condemn evils just as well as we know how to approve what is laudable. Or rather, guarding with your priestly office what the Fathers instituted, you did not regard what they had decided by divine, not human, judgments, as something to be trampled on. They did not regard anything as decided, even though it was the concern of distant and remote provinces, until it had come to the notice of this See [Rome], so that what was a just pronouncement might be confirmed by the authority of this See, and then other churches —just as all waters proceed from their source and, through the various regions of the whole world, remain pure liquids from an uncorrupted head. [*Letters* 29:1 (A.D. 417)].

COUNCIL OF EPHESUS

Philip, presbyter and legate of the Apostolic See, said: We offer our thanks to the holy and venerable synod, that when the writings of our holy and blessed pope had been read to you, the holy members, by our [or your] holy voices, you joined yourselves to the holy head by your holy acclamations. For your blessedness is not ignorant that the head of the whole faith, the head of the apostles, is blessed Peter the apostle. And since now our mediocrity, after being tempest-tossed and much vexed, has arrived, we ask that you order that there be laid before us what things were done in this holy council before our arrival; in order that according to the opinion of our blessed pope and of this present holy assembly, we may ratify their determination [Session 2 (A.D. 431)].

POPE ST. LEO I

Our Lord Jesus Christ . . . instituted the observance of the divine religion. . . . But this mysterious function the Lord wished to be the concern of all the apostles, but in such a way that he has placed the principal charge on the blessed Peter, chief of all the apostles, and from him, as from the head, wishes his gifts to flow to all the body: so that anyone who dares to secede from Peter's solid rock may understand that he has no part or lot in the divine mystery. . . . And so we would have you recollect, brethren, as we do, that the Apostolic See, such is the reverence in which it is held, has numerous times been consulted by the priests of your province as well as others, and in the various matters of appeal, as the old usage demanded, it has reversed or confirmed decisions [*Letters* 10:1–2 (A.D. 445)].

As for the resolution of the bishops that is contrary to the Nicene decree, in union with your faithful piety, I declare it to be invalid and annul it by the authority of the holy apostle Peter [ibid., 105:3].

But if in what you believed necessary to be discussed and settled with the brethren, their opinion differs from your own wishes, let all be referred to us. . . . And though [the bishops] have a common dignity, yet they have not uniform rank; because even among the blessed apostles, notwithstanding the similarity of their honorable estate, there was a distinction of power, and while the election of them all was equal, yet it was given to one to take the lead. From this model a distinction has arisen among bishops also, and by an important ordinance it has been provided that everyone should not claim everything for himself, but that there should be in each province one whose opinion has priority among the brethren, and again that those whose appointment is in the greater cities should undertake a fuller responsibility, through whom the care of the universal Church should converge towards Peter's one seat, and nowhere should be separated from its head [ibid., 14:12].

ST. PETER CHRYSOLOGUS

We exhort you in every respect, honorable brother, to heed obediently what has been written by the most blessed pope of the city of Rome, for blessed Peter, who lives and presides in his own see, provides the truth of faith to those who seek it. For we, by reason of our pursuit of peace and faith, cannot try cases on the faith without the consent of the bishop of Rome [*Letters* 25:2 (A.D. 449)].

COUNCIL OF CHALCEDON

Bishop Paschasinus, guardian of the Apostolic See, stood in the midst [of the Council Fathers] and said, "We received directions at the hands of the most blessed and apostolic bishop of the Roman city [Pope St. Leo I], who is the head of all the churches, that say that Dioscorus is not to be allowed to sit in the [present] assembly, but that if he should attempt to take his seat, he is to be cast out. This instruction we must carry out" [Session 1 (A.D. 451)].

After the reading of the foregoing letter [i.e., the Tome of Leo], the most reverend bishops cried out: This is the faith of the fathers, this is the faith of the apostles. So we all believe, thus the orthodox believe. Anathema to him who does not thus believe. Peter has spoken thus through Leo [Session 2 (A.D. 451)].

POPE ST. GREGORY I

Your most sweet holiness [Bishop Eulogius of Alexandria] has spoken much in your letter to me about the chair of St. Peter, prince of the apostles, saying that he himself now sits on it in the persons of his successors. And indeed I acknowledge myself to be unworthy. . . . I gladly accepted all that has been said, in that he has spoken to me about Peter's chair, who occupies Peter's chair. And though special honor to myself in no way delights me . . . who can be ignorant that the holy Church has been made firm in the solidity of the prince of the apostles, who derived his name from the firmness of his mind, so as to be called Peter, from *petra*. And to him it is said by the voice of the truth, "To you I will give the keys of the kingdom of heaven" [Mt 16:19]. And again it is said to him, "And when you are converted, strengthen your brethren" [Lk 22:32]. And once more, "Simon, son of John, do you love me? Feed my sheep" [Jn 21:17] [*Letters* 7:40 (c. A.D. 597)].

VIII. Morality

31. Mortal Sin

The *Catechism of the Catholic Church* states:

> Sins are rightly evaluated according to their gravity. The distinction between mortal and venial sin, already evident in Scripture, became part of the tradition of the Church. It is corroborated by human experience.
>
> Mortal sin destroys charity in the heart of man by a grave violation of God's law; it turns man away from God, who is his ultimate end and his beatitude, by preferring an inferior good to him. Venial sin allows charity to subsist, even though it offends and wounds it (CCC 1854–55).

Since charity is the principle that unites us to God, and since mortal sin destroys charity, mortal sin causes us to lose our salvation unless we repent (CCC 1861).

The fact that Christians can lose their salvation through mortal sin is reflected in dozens of New Testament passages, as well as in the writings of the early Church Fathers.

It was not until John Calvin that anyone would claim that it was impossible for a true Christian to lose his salvation. That was a theological novelty of the sixteenth century, unheard of in the first fifteen hundred years of Church history.

Fortunately, most Christians today acknowledge that it is possible to lose one's salvation. Catholics, Eastern Orthodox, Lutherans, Anglicans, Methodists, and Pentecostals acknowledge the possibility of mortal sin in some form. However, Presbyterians, Baptists, and those who have been influenced by these two movements commonly reject mortal sin.

The reality of mortal sin was particularly recognized in the age of persecutions. It was clear to the early Fathers that "baptism . . .

now saves you" (1 Pt 3:21; see the upcoming chapters on baptism). It was also clear that, during the persecutions, some who were baptized and who had been saved nevertheless denied Christ. Since Christ taught that "whoever denies me before men, I also will deny before my Father who is in heaven" (Mt 10:33), the Church Fathers recognized that it was possible to lose the grace of salvation after baptism.

This was the case even for thinkers with a strict understanding of predestination, such as St. Augustine (see below) and the other high predestinarians (Fulgence, Aquinas, Luther) before Calvin. In their view, being predestined to come to God does not mean being predestined to remain with God.

DIDACHE

Watch for your life's sake. Do not let your lamps be quenched, or your loins be unclothed; but be ready, for you know not the hour in which our Lord comes [Mt 24:42]. But often shall you come together, seeking the things that are befitting to your souls: for the whole time of your faith will not profit you, if you be not made perfect in the last time [*Didache* 16 (c. A.D. 50)].

HERMAS OF ROME

And as many of them . . . as have repented, shall have their dwelling in the tower [i.e., the Church]. And those of them who have been slower in repenting shall dwell within the walls. And as many as do not repent at all, but abide in their deeds, shall utterly perish. . . . But if anyone relapse into strife, he will be cast out of the tower, and will lose his life. Life is the possession of all who keep the commandments of the Lord [*The Shepherd* 3:8:7 (c. A.D. 80)].

ST. IGNATIUS OF ANTIOCH

And pray without ceasing on behalf of other men. For there is in them hope of repentance that they may attain to God. For cannot he that falls arise again, and he that goes astray return? [*Letter to the Ephesians* 10 (c. A.D. 110)].

ST. JUSTIN MARTYR

[E]ternal fire was prepared for him who voluntarily departed from God and for all who, without repentance, persevere in apostasy [fragment in St. Irenaeus of Lyons, *Against Heresies* 5:26:2 (c. A.D. 153)].

ST. IRENAEUS OF LYONS

[T]o Christ Jesus, our Lord, and God, and Savior, and king, according to the will of the invisible Father, "every knee should bow, of things in heaven, and things on earth, and things under the earth, and that every tongue should confess" [Phil 2:10–11] to him, and that he should execute just judgment towards all. . . . [T]he ungodly and unrighteous and wicked and profane among men [shall go] into everlasting fire; but [he] may, in the exercise of his grace, confer immortality on the righteous, and holy, and those who have kept his commandments, and have persevered in his love, some from the beginning [of their Christian course], and others from [the date of] their penance, and may surround them with everlasting glory [*Against Heresies* 1:10:1 (c. A.D. 189)].

TERTULLIAN OF CARTHAGE

Yet most men either shun this work, as a public exposure of themselves, or else defer it from day to day. I presume (they are) more mindful of modesty than salvation; just like men who, having contracted some malady in the more private parts of the body, avoid the probing of physicians, and so perish of their own bashfulness. It is intolerable for modesty to make satisfaction to the offended Lord! To be restored to its forfeited salvation! Truly you are honorable in your modesty; bearing an open forehead for sinning, but an abashed one for deprecating! I give no place to bashfulness when I am a gainer by its loss; when it exhorts the man, "Respect not me; it is better that I perish through you than you through me" [*Repentance* 10 (c. A.D. 203)].

Discipline governs a man, power sets a seal upon him, apart from the fact that power is the Spirit, but the Spirit is God. What did the Spirit teach? That there must be no communicating with the works of darkness. Observe what he says. Who, moreover, was able to forgive sins? This is his prerogative alone: for "who remits sins but God alone?" And, of course, (who but he can remit) mortal sins, such as those committed against himself, and against his temple? [*Modesty* 21 (c. A.D. 220)].

ST. CYPRIAN OF CARTHAGE

Moreover, how much are they both greater in faith and better in their fear, who . . . confess this very thing to God's priests, and make the conscientious avowal. . . . I entreat you, beloved brethren, that each one should confess his own sin, while he who has sinned is still in this world, while his confession may be received, while the satisfaction and remission made by the priests are pleasing to the Lord [*The Lapsed* (Treatise 3) 28–29 (A.D. 251)].

ST. BASIL OF CAESAREA

The clergyman who is deposed for mortal sin shall not be excommunicated [*Letters* 199:31 (A.D. 375)].

ST. PACIAN OF BARCELONA

Stinginess is redeemed by generosity, insult by apology, perversity by honesty, and for whatever else, amends can be made by practice of the opposite. But what can he do who is contemptuous of God? What shall the murderer do? What remedy shall the fornicator find? . . . These are capital sins, brethren, these are mortal. Someone may say: "Are we then about to perish? . . . Are we to die in our sins?" . . . I appeal first to you brethren who refuse penance for your acknowledged crimes; you, I say, who are timid after your impudence, who are bashful after your sins, who are not ashamed to sin but now are ashamed to confess [*Sermon Exhorting to Penance* 4 (c. A.D. 387)].

ST. JEROME

Some offenses are light, some heavy. It is one thing to owe ten thousand talents, another to owe a farthing. We shall have to give account of the idle word no less than of adultery; but it is not the same thing to be put to the blush and to be put upon the rack, to grow red in the face and to ensure lasting torment. . . . You observe that if we entreat for smaller offenses, we obtain pardon: if for greater ones, it is difficult to obtain our request: and that there is a great difference between sins [*Against Jovinianus* 2:30 (c. A.D. 393)].

ST. AUGUSTINE OF HIPPO

[N]othing could have been devised more likely to instruct and benefit the pious reader of sacred Scripture than that, besides describing praiseworthy characters as examples, and blameworthy characters as warnings, it should also narrate cases where good men have gone back and fallen into evil, whether they are restored to the right path or continue irreclaimable; and also where bad men have changed, and have attained to goodness, whether they persevere in it or relapse into evil; in order that the righteous may not be lifted up in the pride of security, nor the wicked hardened in despair of a cure [*Reply to Faustus the Manichean* 22:96 (A.D. 400)].

[A]lthough they were living well, [they] have not persevered therein; because they have of their own will been changed from a good to an evil life, and on that account are worthy of rebuke; and if rebuke should be of no avail, and they persevere in their ruined life until death, they are worthy of divine condemnation forever. Neither shall they excuse themselves, saying—as now they say, "Why are we rebuked?"—so then, "Why are we condemned? Since we returned from good to evil, we did not receive the perseverance by which we would abide in good?" They shall by no means deliver themselves by this excuse from righteous condemnation . . . since it may be said, "O man, in what you have heard and kept, in that you might persevere if you want" [*Rebuke and Grace* 11 (c. A.D. 426)].

Whoever, then, are made to differ from that original condemnation by such bounty of divine grace, there is no doubt but that it is provided that they should hear the gospel, and when they hear they believe, and in the faith that works by love they persevere unto the end; and if, perchance, they deviate from the way, when they are rebuked they are amended and some of them, although they may not be rebuked by men, return into the path they had left; and some who have received grace in any age are withdrawn from the perils of this life by swiftness of death. For he works all these things in them who made them vessels of mercy, who also elected them in his Son before the foundation of the world by the election of grace: "And if by grace, then is it no more of works, otherwise grace is no more grace" [Rom 11:6]. For they were not so called as not to be elected, in respect of which it is said, "For many are called but few are elected" [Mt 20:16]; but because they were called according to the purpose, they are surely also elected by the election of grace, not of any precedent merits of theirs, because to them grace is all merit [ibid., 13].

[O]f two pious men, why to the one should perseverance be given unto the end, and to the other it should not, God's judgments are even more unsearchable. . . . Had not both been called and followed him that called them? And had not both become, from wicked men, justified men, and both been renewed by the washing of regeneration? [*The Gift of Perseverance* 21 (c. A.D. 428)].

ST. CAESARIUS OF ARLES

Although the apostle [Paul] has mentioned many grievous sins, we, nevertheless, lest we seem to promote despair, will state briefly what they are: Sacrilege; murder; adultery; false witness; theft; robbery; pride; envy; avarice; and, if it is of long standing, anger; drunkenness, if it is persistent; and slander are reckoned in their number. If anyone knows that these sins dominate him, if he does not do worthy penance and for a long time, if such time is given him . . . he cannot be purged in that transitory fire of which the apostle spoke [1 Cor 3:11-15], but the eternal flames will torture him without remedy. But since the lesser sins are, of course, known to all, and it would take too long to mention them all, it will be necessary for us only to name some of them. . . . There is no doubt that these and similar deeds belong to the lesser sins that, as I said before, can scarcely be counted, and from which not only all Christian people, but even all the saints could not and cannot always be free. We do not, of course, believe that the soul is killed by these sins, but still they make it ugly by covering it as if with pustules and horrible scabs [*Sermons* 179(104):2 (c. A.D. 522)].

32. Abortion

The Christian faith has always rejected abortion as a grave evil. Writings from the first century onward condemn it as murder.

Some Fathers pointed in particular to this passage from Exodus: "If men who are fighting hit a pregnant woman and she gives birth prematurely [Hebrew: 'so that her child comes out'], but there is no serious injury, the offender must be fined whatever the woman's husband demands and the court allows. But if there is serious injury, you are to take life for life, eye for eye, tooth for tooth, hand for hand, foot for foot" (Ex 21:22–24).

Another passage worth bearing in mind is James 2:26, which says that "the body without the spirit is dead." The soul is the life principle of the body, what makes it alive. Since from the time of conception the child's body is alive (as shown by the fact it is growing), the unborn child must already have its soul.

In 1995 Pope John Paul II declared that the Church's teaching on abortion "is unchanged and unchangeable. Therefore, by the authority which Christ conferred upon Peter and his successors . . . I declare that direct abortion, that is, abortion willed as an end or as a means, always constitutes a grave moral disorder, since it is the deliberate killing of an innocent human being. This doctrine is based upon the natural law and upon the written word of God, is transmitted by the Church's tradition and taught by the ordinary and universal magisterium. No circumstance, no purpose, no law whatsoever can ever make licit an act which is intrinsically illicit, since it is contrary to the law of God which is written in every human heart, knowable by reason itself, and proclaimed by the Church" (*Evangelium Vitae* 62).

The early Church Fathers agreed. Fortunately, abortion, like all sins, is forgivable; and forgiveness is as close as the nearest confessional.

DIDACHE

And the second commandment of the teaching: You shall not commit murder, you shall not commit adultery [Ex 20:13–14], you shall not commit pederasty, you shall not commit fornication, you shall not steal [Ex 20:15], you shall not practice magic, you shall not practice witchcraft, you shall not murder a child by abortion nor kill what is begotten. You shall not covet the things of your neighbor [Ex 20:17], you shall not forswear yourself [Mt 5:34], you shall not bear false witness [Ex 20:16] [*Didache* 2 (c. A.D. 50)].

LETTER OF BARNABAS

The way of light, then, is as follows. If anyone desires to travel to the appointed place, he must be zealous in his works. The knowledge, therefore, that is given to us to walk in this way, is the following. . . . You shall not slay the child by procuring abortion; nor shall you destroy it after it is born [*Letter of Barnabas* 19 (c. A.D. 75)].

APOCALYPSE OF PETER

And near that place I saw another strait place into which the gore and the filth of those who were being punished ran down and became a lake: and there sat women having the gore up to their necks, and over against them sat many children who were born to them out of due time, crying; and there came forth from them sparks of fire that smote the women in the eyes: and these were the accursed who conceived and caused abortion [*The Apocalypse of Peter* 25 (c. A.D. 135)].

ATHENAGORAS OF ATHENS

What man of sound mind, therefore, will affirm, while such is our character, that we are murderers? . . . [W]hen we say that those women who use drugs to bring on abortion commit murder, and will have to give an account to God for the abortion, on what principle should we commit murder? For it does not belong to the same person to regard the very fetus in the womb as a created being, and therefore an object of God's care, and when it has passed into life, to kill it; and not to expose an infant, because those who expose them are chargeable with child murder, and on the other hand, when it has been reared to destroy it [*Plea for the Christians* 35 (c. A.D. 177)].

TERTULLIAN OF CARTHAGE

In our case, murder being forbidden, we may not destroy even the fetus in the womb, while the human being derives blood from other parts of the body for its sustenance. To hinder a birth is merely a speedier mankilling; nor does it matter whether you take away a life that is born, or destroy one that is coming to the birth. That is a man that is going to be one; you have the fruit already in its seed [*Apology* 9 (A.D. 197)].

[A]mong surgeons' tools there is a certain instrument formed with a nicely adjusted flexible frame for opening the uterus and keeping it open; it is further furnished with an annular blade, by means of which the limbs within the womb are dissected with anxious but unfaltering care; its last appendage being a blunted or covered hook, with which the entire fetus is extracted by a violent delivery. There is also a copper needle or spike, by which the actual death is managed in this furtive robbery of life: from its infanticide function, they give it the name of *embruosphaktēs*, the slayer of the infant, which was of course alive. Such apparatus was possessed both by Hippocrates, and Asclepiades, and Erasistratus, and Herophilus, that dissector of adults, and the milder Soranus himself, who all knew well enough that a living being had been conceived, and pitied this most luckless infant state, which had first to be put to death, to escape being tortured alive [*Treatise on the Soul* 25 (c. A.D. 210)].

Now we allow that life begins with conception, because we contend that the soul also begins from conception; life taking its commencement at the same moment and place that the soul does [ibid., 27].

The Law of Moses, indeed, punishes with due penalties the man who shall cause abortion [Ex 21:22–24] [ibid., 37].

MINUCIUS FELIX

There are some women who, by drinking medical preparations, extinguish the source of the future man in their bowels, and thus commit a parricide before they bring forth. And these things assuredly come down from the teaching of your gods. . . . To us it is not lawful either to see or to hear of homicide [*Octavius* 30 (c. A.D. 226)].

ST. HIPPOLYTUS OF ROME

[W]omen, reputed believers, began to resort to drugs to produce sterility, and to gird themselves round, so to expel what was being conceived on account of their not wishing to have a child either by a slave or any paltry fellow, for the sake of their family and excessive wealth. Behold, into how great impiety that lawless one has proceeded, by committing adultery and murder at the same time! [*Refutation of All Heresies* 9:7 (c. A.D. 227)].

LACTANTIUS

For when God forbids us to kill, he not only prohibits us from open violence, which is not even allowed by the public laws, but he warns us against the commission of those things esteemed lawful among men. . . . Therefore let no one imagine that this is allowed, to strangle newborn children, which is the greatest impiety; for God breathes into their souls for life, and not for death. But men, that there may be no crime with which they may not pollute their hands, deprive souls as yet innocent and simple of the light that they themselves have not given.

Can any one, indeed, expect that they would abstain from the blood of others who do not abstain from their own? But these are without any controversy wicked and unjust [*Divine Institutes* 6:20 (c. A.D. 307)].

COUNCIL OF ANKARA

Concerning women who commit fornication, and destroy what they have conceived, or who are employed in making drugs for abortion, a former decree excluded them until the hour of death, and to this some have assented. Nevertheless, being desirous to use somewhat greater leniency, we have ordained that they fulfill ten years [of penance], according to the prescribed degrees [Canon 21 (A.D. 314)].

ST. BASIL OF CAESAREA

The woman who purposely destroys her unborn child is guilty of murder. With us there is no nice enquiry as to its being formed or unformed. In this case it is not only the being about to be born who is vindicated, but the woman in her attack upon herself; because in most cases women who make such attempts die. The destruction of the embryo is an additional crime, a second murder, at all events if it is done with intent. The punishment, however, of these women should not be for life, but for the term of ten years. And let their treatment depend not on mere lapse of time, but on the character of their repentance [*Letters* 188:2 (A.D. 374)].

Women also who administer drugs to cause abortion, as well as those who take poisons to destroy unborn children, are murderesses [ibid., 188:8].

ST. JEROME

I cannot bring myself to speak of the many virgins who fall every day and are lost to the bosom of the Church, their mother. . . . Some go so far as to take potions, that they may ensure barrenness, and thus murder human beings almost before their conception. Some, when they find themselves with child through their sin, use drugs to procure abortion, and when (as often happens) they

die with their offspring, they enter the lower world laden with
the guilt not only of adultery against Christ but also of suicide
and child murder [*Letters* 22:13 (A.D. 384)].

ST. JOHN CHRYSOSTOM

I beseech you, flee fornication. . . . Why sow where the ground
makes it its job to destroy the fruit? Where there are many efforts
at abortion? Where there is murder before the birth? For even
the harlot you do not let continue a mere harlot, but make her
a murderess also. You see how drunkenness leads to whoredom,
whoredom to adultery, adultery to murder, or rather to something
even worse than murder. For I have no name to give it, since it
does not take away the thing born, but prevents its being born.
Why then do you abuse the gift of God, and fight with his laws,
and follow after what is a curse as if it were a blessing, and make
the chamber of procreation a chamber for murder, and arm the
woman that was given for childbearing into slaughter? For with
a view to drawing more money by being agreeable and an object
of longing to her lovers, even this she will do, heaping upon your
head a great pile of fire. For even if the daring deed be hers, yet
the cause of it is yours [*Homilies on Romans* 24 (c. A.D. 391)].

APOSTOLIC CONSTITUTIONS

You shall not use magic. You shall not use witchcraft; for he says,
"You shall not suffer a witch to live." You shall not slay your child
by causing abortion, nor kill what is begotten; for "everything that
is shaped, and has received a soul from God, if it be slain, shall
be avenged, as being unjustly destroyed" [*Apostolic Constitutions*
7:1:3 (c. A.D. 400)].

33. Contraception and Sterilization

Natural law teaches, and the Christian faith has always recognized, that sexual activity belongs in marriage. Sex is how babies are produced, and babies need to be raised by parents who are committed to each other in marriage. Sex outside of marriage is not legitimate. This is how God has designed human reproduction to work.

We must respect his design, and that includes not interfering with the sexual act within marriage. Consequently, the Christian faith has always condemned the use of contraception to thwart the marital act.

The problem with contraception is also reflected in the Bible. Both forms mentioned in Scripture—*coitus interruptus* and sterilization—are rejected (Gn 38:9–10; Dt 23:1).

The Christian rejection of contraception was universal until 1930, when at that year's Lambeth Conference the Anglican church allowed the use of contraception in limited circumstances. Soon the entire Protestant world had collapsed on this issue. Fortunately, in recent years some in the Protestant community have begun to reevaluate this issue.

While we tend to think of contraception as a modern phenomenon, it actually was common in the Greco-Roman world, with a variety of contraceptive practices in use (e.g, sterilization, oral contraceptives, *coitus interruptus*, oral sex).

The Church Fathers opposed all these on principle. They also at times used language suggesting that procreation was the only purpose for sexual behavior. Subsequent doctrinal development has refined this matter, recognizing that it also plays a role in strengthening marriage and promoting the good of the spouses. Yet this "unitive" aspect of the marital act cannot be separated from its procreative aspect.

LETTER OF BARNABAS

Moreover, [Moses] has rightly detested the weasel. For he means, "Thou shalt not be like to those whom we hear of as committing wickedness with the mouth, on account of their uncleanness; nor shall thou be joined to those impure women who commit iniquity with the mouth" [*Letter of Barnabas* 10 (c. A.D. 75)].

ST. CLEMENT OF ALEXANDRIA

Because of its divine institution for the propagation of man, the seed is not to be vainly ejaculated, nor is it to be damaged, nor is it to be wasted [*Instructor of Children* 2:10:91:2 (c. A.D. 197)].

To have coitus other than to procreate children is to do injury to nature [ibid., 2:10:95:3].

ST. HIPPOLYTUS OF ROME

[W]omen, reputed believers, began to resort to drugs to produce sterility, and to gird themselves round, so to expel what was being conceived on account of their not wishing to have a child either by a slave or any paltry fellow, for the sake of their family and excessive wealth. Behold, into how great impiety that lawless one has proceeded, by committing adultery and murder at the same time! [*Refutation of All Heresies* 9:7 (c. A.D. 227)].

LACTANTIUS

But truly parricides complain of the scantiness of their means, and allege that they have not enough for bringing up more children; as though, in truth, their means were in the power of those who possess them, or that God did not daily make the rich poor, and the poor rich. If anyone shall be unable to bring up children on account of poverty, it is better to abstain from marriage than with wicked hands to mar the work of God [*Divine Institutes* 6:20 (c. A.D. 307)].

God gave us eyes not to see and desire pleasure, but to see acts performed for the needs of life; so too, the genital ["generating"] part of the body, as the name itself teaches, has been received by us for no other purpose than the generation of offspring [ibid., 6:23:19].

COUNCIL OF NICAEA I

If anyone in sickness has been subjected by physicians to a surgical operation, or if he has been castrated by barbarians, let him remain among the clergy; but, if anyone in sound health has castrated himself, it behooves that such a one, if [already] enrolled among the clergy, should cease [from his ministry], and henceforth should not be promoted. But, as this is said of those who willfully do the thing and presume to castrate themselves, so if any have been made eunuchs by barbarians, or by their masters, and should otherwise be found worthy, such men the canon admits to the clergy [Canon 1 (A.D. 325)].

ST. JOHN CHRYSOSTOM

[I]n truth all men know that they who are under the power of this disease are wearied even of their father's old age; and what is sweet, and universally desirable, the having children, they esteem grievous and unwelcome. Many with this view have even paid money to be childless, and have maimed their nature, not only by slaying their children after birth, but by not suffering them to be born at all [*Homilies on Matthew* 28:5 (c. A.D. 370)].

Since the man who has mutilated himself, in fact, is subject to a curse, as Paul says, "I would they were even cut off which trouble you." And very reasonably. For such a one is venturing on the deeds of murderers, and giving occasion to those who slander God's creation, and opens the mouths of the Manicheans, and is guilty of the same unlawful acts as those Greeks who mutilate themselves. For to cut off our members is a work of demoniacal agency, and satanic device, that they may bring up a bad report on the work of God, that they may mar this living creature, that imputing all not to the choice but to the nature of our members, the more part of them may sin in security, as being irresponsible; and doubly harm this living creature, both by mutilating the members, and by impeding the free choice on behalf of good deeds [ibid., 62:3].

ST. AUGUSTINE OF HIPPO

This proves that you [Manicheans] approve of having a wife, not for the procreation of children, but for the gratification of passion. In marriage, as the marriage law declares, the man and woman come together for the procreation of children. Therefore, whoever makes the procreation of children a greater sin than copulation forbids marriage and makes the woman not a wife but a mistress, who for some gifts presented to her is joined to the man to gratify his passion [*Morals of the Manicheans* 18:65 (A.D. 388)].

ST. JOHN CHRYSOSTOM

I beseech you, flee fornication. . . . Why sow where the ground makes it its job to destroy the fruit? Where there are many efforts at abortion? Where there is murder before the birth? For even the harlot you do not let continue a mere harlot, but make her a murderess also. You see how drunkenness leads to whoredom, whoredom to adultery, adultery to murder, or rather to something even worse than murder. For I have no name to give it, since it does not take away the thing born, but prevent its being born. Why then do you abuse the gift of God, and fight with his laws, and follow after what is a curse as if it were a blessing, and make the chamber of procreation a chamber for murder, and arm the woman that was given for childbearing into slaughter? For with a view to drawing more money by being agreeable and an object of longing to her lovers, even this she will do, heaping upon your head a great pile of fire. For even if the daring deed be hers, yet the cause of it is yours. Hence too come idolatries, since many, with a view to become acceptable, devise incantations, and libations, and love potions, and countless other plans. Yet still after such great unseemliness, after slaughters, after idolatries, the thing seems to belong to things indifferent, and to many who have wives too. The mingle of mischief is the greater, for sorceries are applied not to the womb that is prostituted, but to the injured wife, and there are plottings without number, and invocations of devils, and necromancies, and daily wars, and truceless fightings, and home-cherished jealousies [*Homilies on Romans* 24 (c. A.D. 391)].

Observe how bitterly [Paul] speaks against their deceivers: . . . "I would that they that unsettle you would even cut themselves off" [Gal 5:12]. . . . On this account he curses them; and his meaning is as follows—for them I have no concern, "A man that is heretical after the first and second admonition refuse" [Ti 3:10]. If they will, let them not only be circumcised, but mutilated. Where are those who dare to mutilate themselves, seeing that they draw down the apostolic curse, and accuse the workmanship of God, and take part with the Manicheans? [*Commentary on Galatians* 5:12 (c. A.D. 395)].

ST. JEROME

You may see a number of women who are widows before they are wives. Others, indeed, will drink sterility and murder a man not yet born, [and some commit abortion] [*Letters* 22:13 (A.D. 384)].

But I wonder why [Jovinianus] set Judah and Tamar before us for an example, unless perhaps even harlots give him pleasure; or Onan, who was slain because he grudged his brother seed [Gn 38:9]. Does he imagine that we approve of any sexual intercourse except for the procreation of children? [*Against Jovinianus* 1:20 (c. A.D. 393)].

ST. AUGUSTINE OF HIPPO

You [Manicheans] make your hearers adulterers of their wives when they take care that the women with whom they copulate do not conceive. They take wives according to the laws of matrimony, by tablets announcing that the marriage is contracted to procreate children; and then, fearing your law [against childbearing] . . . they copulate in a shameful union only to satisfy lust for their wives. They are unwilling to have children, on whose account alone marriages are made. Why, then, that you do not prohibit marriage, as the apostle predicted of you so long ago [1 Tm 4:1–4], when you try to take from marriage what marriage is? When this is taken away, husbands are shameful lovers, wives are harlots, bridal chambers are brothels, fathers-in-law are pimps [*Reply to Faustus the Manichean* 15:7–10 (c. A.D. 400)].

For thus the eternal law, that is, the will of God, Creator of all creatures, taking counsel for the conservation of natural order, permits the delight of mortal flesh to be released from the control of reason in copulation only to propagate progeny, not to serve lust, but to see to the preservation of the race [ibid., 22:30].

For necessary sexual intercourse for begetting [children] is alone worthy of marriage. But what goes beyond this necessity no longer follows reason but lust. And yet it pertains to the character of marriage . . . to yield to the partner unless by fornication the other spouse sins damnably [through adultery]. . . . [T]hey [must] not turn away from them the mercy of God . . . by changing the natural use into what is against nature, which is more damnable when it is done in the case of husband or wife. For, while that natural use, when it pass beyond the compact of marriage, that is, beyond the necessity of begetting [children], is pardonable in the case of a wife, damnable in the case of a harlot; what is against nature is execrable when done in the case of a harlot, but more execrable in the case of a wife. Of so great power is the ordinance of the Creator, and the order of creation, that . . . when the man wishes to use a body part of the wife not allowed for this purpose [orally or anally consummated sex], the wife is more shameful, if she suffer it to take place in her own case, than in the case of another woman [*Good of Marriage* 11–12 (A.D. 401)].

I am supposing, then, although you are not lying [with your wife] for the sake of procreating offspring, you are not for the sake of lust obstructing their procreation by an evil prayer or an evil deed. Those who do this, although they are called husband and wife, are not; nor do they retain any reality of marriage, but with a respectable name cover a shame. Sometimes this lustful cruelty, or cruel lust, comes to this, that they even procure poisons of sterility. . . . Assuredly if both husband and wife are like this, they are not married, and if they were like this from the beginning, they come together [are] not joined in matrimony but in seduction. If both are not like this, either the wife is in a fashion the harlot of her husband or he is an adulterer with his own wife [*Marriage and Concupiscence* 1:15:17 (c. A.D. 419)].

34. Homosexuality

The Christian faith has always rejected homosexual acts as gravely immoral. The Church looks on those who experience same-sex attraction with compassion, just as it looks on all who are tempted to sin (which is to say, everybody). But it cannot pretend that the moral character of homosexual acts is other than it is.

Unfortunately, homosexual activists today often do just that. Some have even argued that Scripture does not condemn such acts, though it clearly does (see, among other passages, Lv 18:22–30; Rom 1:26–27; 1 Cor 6:9; and Jude 7).

The Church Fathers also taught the same, and they are especially harsh against the practice of pederasty, the homosexual corruption of boys by men, as you can see from the biting use of sarcasm by St. Clement of Alexandria.

DIDACHE

You shall not commit murder, you shall not commit adultery [Ex 20:13–14], you shall not commit pederasty, you shall not commit fornication, you shall not steal [Ex 20:15], you shall not practice magic, you shall not practice witchcraft, you shall not murder a child by abortion nor kill what is begotten. You shall not covet the things of your neighbor [Ex 20:17] [*Didache* 2 (c. A.D. 50)].

LETTER OF BARNABAS

You shall not commit fornication; you shall not commit adultery; you shall not be a corrupter of youth [*Letter of Barnabas* 19 (c. A.D. 75)].

You shall not be a corrupter of boys, nor like unto such [ibid.].

ST. JUSTIN MARTYR

[W]e have been taught that to expose newborn children is the part of wicked men; and this we have been taught lest we should do anyone an injury, and lest we should sin against God, first, because we see that almost all so exposed (not only the girls, but also the males) are brought up to prostitution. And as the ancients are said to have reared herds of oxen, or goats, or sheep, or grazing horses, so now we see you rear children only for this shameful use; and for this pollution a multitude of females and hermaphrodites, and those who commit unmentionable iniquities, are found in every nation. And you receive the hire of these, and duty and taxes from them, whom you ought to exterminate from your realm. And anyone who uses such persons, in addition to the godless and infamous and impure intercourse, may possibly be having intercourse with his own child, or relative, or brother. And there are some who prostitute even their own children and wives, and some are openly mutilated for the purpose of sodomy; and they refer these mysteries to the mother of the gods [*First Apology* 27 (c. A.D. 151)].

ST. CLEMENT OF ALEXANDRIA

All honor to that king of the Scythians, whoever Anacharsis was, who shot with an arrow one of his subjects who imitated among the Scythians the mystery of the mother of the gods . . . condemning him as having become effeminate among the Greeks, and a teacher of the disease of effeminacy to the rest of the Scythians [*Exhortation to the Greeks* 2 (c. A.D. 195)].

[According to Greek myth] Baubo [a female native of Eleusis] having received [the goddess] Demeter hospitably, handed to her a refreshing drink; and when she refused it, not having any inclination to drink (for she was very sad), Baubo became annoyed, thought herself slighted, uncovered her shame, and exhibited her nudity to the goddess. Demeter was delighted with the sight—pleased, I repeat, at the spectacle. These are the secret mysteries of the Athenians; these Orpheus records [ibid.].

It is not, then, without reason that the poets call [Hercules] a cruel wretch and a nefarious scoundrel. It was tedious to recount his adulteries of all sorts and debauching of boys. For your gods did not even abstain from boys, one having loved Hylas, another Hyacinthus, another Pelops, another Chrysippus, another Ganymede. Let such gods as these be worshipped by your wives, and let them pray that their husbands be like them—so temperate, that, emulating them in the same practices, they may be like the gods. Such gods let your boys be trained to worship, that they may grow up to be men with the accursed likeness of fornication on them, received from the gods [ibid.].

In accordance with these remarks, conversation about deeds of wickedness is appropriately termed filthy [shameful] speaking, as talk about adultery and pederasty and the like [*Instructor of Children* 2:6 (c. A.D. 197)].

The fate of the Sodomites was judgment to those who had done wrong, instruction to those who hear. The Sodomites, through much luxury, fell into uncleanness, practicing adultery shamelessly and burning with insane love for boys; the all-seeing Word, whose notice those who commit impieties cannot escape, cast his eye on them. The sleepless guard of humanity did not observe their licentiousness in silence; but to dissuade us from imitating them, and training us to his own temperance, falling on some sinners, lest unavenged lust break loose from the restraints of fear, ordered Sodom to be burned, pouring forth a little of the sagacious fire on licentiousness; lest lust, through want of punishment, should throw wide the gates to those who were rushing into voluptuousness. Accordingly, the just punishment of the Sodomites became an image of the salvation that is well calculated for men. For those who have not committed sins like those who were punished, will never receive a like punishment [ibid., 3:8].

TERTULLIAN OF CARTHAGE

[A]ll the other frenzies of passions—impious both toward the bodies and toward the sexes—beyond the laws of nature, we banish not only from the threshold, but from all shelter of the Church, because they are not sins, but monstrosities [*Modesty* 4 (c. A.D. 220)]

ST. CYPRIAN OF CARTHAGE

[T]urn your looks to the abominations of another kind of spectacle to be deplored. . . . Men are emasculated, and all the pride and vigor of their sex is effeminated in the disgrace of their enervated body; and he is more pleasing who has most completely broken down the man into the woman. He grows into praise by virtue of his crime; and the more he is degraded, the more skillful he is considered to be. Such a one is looked upon—oh shame! —and looked upon with pleasure. . . . Nor is authority for the enticing abomination wanting . . . that Jupiter of theirs [is] not more supreme in dominion than in vice, inflamed with earthly love in the midst of his own thunders . . . now breaking forth with the help of birds to violate the purity of boys. And now put the question: Can he who looks upon such things be healthy-minded or modest? Men imitate the gods whom they adore, and to such miserable beings their crimes become their religion [*Letters* 1:8 (c. A.D. 246)].

O, if placed on that lofty watchtower, you could gaze into the secret places—if you could open the closed doors of sleeping chambers and recall their dark recesses to the perception of sight—you would behold things done by immodest persons that no chaste eye could look upon; you would see what even to see is a crime; you would see what people made brutes with the madness of vice deny that they have done, and yet hasten to do—men with frenzied lusts rushing upon men, doing things that afford no gratification even to those who do them [ibid., 9].

NOVATIAN OF ROME

[God forbade the Jews to eat certain foods for symbolic reasons:] For in fishes the roughness of scales is regarded as a sign of their cleanness; rough, and rugged, and unpolished, and substantial, and grave manners are approved in men; while those that are without scales are unclean, because trifling, and fickle, and faithless, and effeminate manners are disapproved. Moreover, what does the law mean when it . . . forbids the swine to be taken for food? It assuredly reproves a life filthy and dirty, and delighting in the garbage of vice. . . . Or when it forbids the hare? It rebukes men deformed into women [*Jewish Foods* 3 (c. A.D. 253)].

EUSEBIUS OF CAESAREA

[H]aving forbidden all unlawful marriage, and all unseemly practice, and the union of women with women and men with men, [God] adds: "Do not defile yourselves with any of these things; for in all these things the nations were defiled, which I will drive out before you. And the land was polluted, and I have recompensed [their] iniquity upon it, and the land is grieved with them that dwell upon it" [Lv 18:24–25] [*Proof of the Gospel* 4:10 (c. A.D. 319)].

ARNOBIUS OF SICCA

[T]he mother of the gods loved [the boy Attis] exceedingly, because he was of most surpassing beauty; and Acdestis [the son of Jupiter], who was his companion, grew up fondling him, and bound to him by wicked compliance with his lust. . . . Afterwards, under the influence of wine, [Attis] admits that he is . . . loved by Acdestis. . . . Then Midas, king of Pessinus, wishing to withdraw the youth from so disgraceful an intimacy, resolves to give him his own daughter in marriage. . . . Acdestis, bursting with rage because of the boy's being torn from him and brought to seek a wife, fills all the guests with frenzied madness; the Phrygians shriek, panic-stricken at the appearance of the gods. . . . [Attis] too, now filled with furious passion, raving frantically and tossed about, throws himself down at last, and under a pine tree mutilates himself, saying, "Take these, Acdestis, for which you have stirred up so great and terribly perilous commotions" [*Against the Heathen* 5:6–7 (c. A.D. 305)].

ST. BASIL OF CAESAREA

He who is guilty of unseemliness with males will be under discipline for the same time as adulterers [*Letters* 217:62 (A.D. 375)].

ST. JOHN CHRYSOSTOM

[Certain men in church] come in gazing about at the beauty of women; others curious about the blooming youth of boys. After this, do you not marvel that [lightning] bolts are not launched [from heaven], and all these things are not plucked up from their foundations? For the things that are done are worthy of thunderbolts and hell; but God, who is long suffering, and of great mercy, forbears his wrath, calling you to repentance and amendment [*Homilies on Matthew* 73:3 (c. A.D. 370)].

[The pagans] were addicted to the love of boys, and one of their wise men made a law that pederasty . . . should not be allowed to slaves, as if it were an honorable thing; and they had houses for this purpose, in which it was openly practiced. And if all that were done among them was related, it would be seen that they openly outraged nature, and no one restrained them. . . . As for their passion for boys, whom they called their *paedica*, it is not fit to be named [*Homilies on Titus* 5:6 (c. A.D. 390)].

All of these affections [in Rom 1:26–27] . . . were vile, but chiefly the mad lust after males; for the soul is more the sufferer in sins, and more dishonored than the body in diseases [*Homilies on Romans* 4 (c. A.D. 391)].

[The men] have done an insult to nature itself. And a more disgraceful thing than these is it when even the women seek after these intercourses, who ought to have more shame than men [ibid.].

And sundry other books of the philosophers are full of this disease. But we do not say that the thing was made lawful, but that they who received this law were pitiable, and objects for many tears. For these are treated in the same way as women that play the whore. Or rather their plight is more miserable. For in the case of the one the intercourse, even if lawless, is according to nature; but this is contrary to law and to nature. For even if there were no hell, and no punishment had been threatened, this would be worse than any punishment [ibid.].

ST. AUGUSTINE OF HIPPO

[T]hose offenses that are contrary to nature are everywhere and at all times to be detested and punished; such were those of the Sodomites, which should all nations commit, they should all be held guilty of the same crime by the divine law, which has not so made men that they should in that way abuse one another [*Confessions* 3:8:15 (c. A.D. 400)].

APOSTOLIC CONSTITUTIONS

[Christians] abhor all unlawful mixtures, and what is practiced by some contrary to nature is wicked and impious [*Apostolic Constitutions* 6:3:11 (c. A.D. 400)].

35. Astrology

The *Catechism of the Catholic Church* states,

> All forms of divination are to be rejected: recourse to Satan or demons, conjuring up the dead or other practices falsely supposed to "unveil" the future. Consulting horoscopes, astrology, palm reading, interpretation of omens and lots, the phenomena of clairvoyance, and recourse to mediums all conceal a desire for power over time, history, and, in the last analysis, other human beings, as well as a wish to conciliate hidden powers. They contradict the honor, respect, and loving fear that we owe to God alone (CCC 2116).

The pagan world was dominated by belief in astrology. Pagans believed that the stars were divinities, or were controlled by divinities. Apollo was the god of the sun, his sister Diana was the goddess of the moon, and the known planets were named after gods—Mercury, Venus, Mars, Jupiter, and Saturn. Because of this common belief, the Old Testament contains repeated injunctions against star worship (Dt 4:19; 17:3; 2 Kgs 17:16; 21:3–5; 23:4; Jer 8:2; 19:12–13; Zep 1:4–6).

In the New Testament age, astrologers taught that all things were in the grip of fate, which could assign one destiny to one man and a different destiny to another. Fate was extremely powerful and sometimes was even said to rule the gods. However, what destiny fate had assigned could be read in the stars.

The Church Fathers imposed strong sanctions against astrology to protect their flocks. In A.D. 120, the mathematician Aquila Ponticus was excommunicated from the church in Rome for astrological heresies. In the quotations below, St. Augustine records that similar sanctions were still used in his day, three centuries later.

TATIAN THE SYRIAN

But men form the material of their apostasy. For, having shown them a plan of the position of the stars, like dice players, they introduced fate, a flagrant injustice. For the judge and the judged are made so by fate [*Address to the Greeks* 8 (c. A.D. 170)].

Such are the demons; these are they who laid down the doctrine of fate. Their fundamental principle was the placing of animals in the heavens. For the creeping things on the earth, and those that swim in the waters, and the quadrupeds on the mountains, with which they lived when expelled from heaven—these they dignified with celestial honor, so that they might themselves be thought to remain in heaven, and, by placing the constellations there, might make the irrational course of life on earth appear rational. Thus the high-spirited and he who is crushed with toil, the temperate and the intemperate, the indigent and the wealthy, are what they are simply because of the controllers of their nativity. For the delineation of the zodiacal circle is the work of gods. And, when the light of one of them predominates, as they express it, it deprives all the rest of their honor; and he who now is conquered at another time gains the predominance. And the seven planets are well pleased with them, as if they were amusing themselves with dice. But we are superior to fate, and instead of wandering demons, we have learned to know one Lord who wanders not [ibid., 9].

TERTULLIAN OF CARTHAGE

We observe among the arts some professions liable to the charge of idolatry. Of astrologers there should be no speaking even; but since one has recently challenged us, defending his profession on his own behalf, I will use a few words. I do not allege that he honors idols, whose names he has inscribed in the heavens, and to whom he has attributed all God's power; but that men, presuming that we are disposed of by the immutable judgment of the stars, think on that account that God is not to be sought after. One proposition I lay down: that those angels, the deserters from God, the lovers of women, were the discoverers of this curious art, and on that account also condemned by God [*Idolatry* 9 (c. A.D. 211)].

ST. HIPPOLYTUS OF ROME

Since, therefore, we have explained the astonishing wisdom of these men, and have not concealed their overwrought art of divination by means of contemplation, neither shall I be silent regarding cases in which those who are deceived act foolishly. For, comparing the forms and dispositions of men with names of stars, how impotent their system is! For we know that those originally conversant with such investigations have called the stars by names in reference to their significance and for facility of future recognition. For what similarity is there of these [heavenly bodies] with the likeness of animals, or what community of nature as regards conduct and energy, that one should allege that a person born in Leo should be irascible, and one born in Virgo moderate, or one born in Cancer wicked [*Refutation of All Heresies* 4:27 (c. A.D. 227)].

It has been easily made evident to all that the heresy of the Peratae is altered in name only from the [art] of the astrologers. And the rest of the books of these [heretics] contain the same method, if it were agreeable to anyone to wade through them all [ibid., 5:10].

LACTANTIUS

[T]he demons are the enemies and harassers of men, and on this account Trismegistus calls them wicked angels, knowing that they were corrupted from heavenly beings, and began to be earthly. These were the inventors of astrology, and soothsaying, and divination, and oracles, and necromancy, and the art of magic, and whatever evil practices besides these men exercise, either openly or in secret [*Divine Institutes* 2:16–17 (c. A.D. 307)].

[Demons] also brought to light astrology, and augury, and divination; and though these things are in themselves false, yet they themselves, the authors of evils, so govern and regulate them that they are believed to be true. . . . By their frauds they have drawn darkness over the human race, that truth might be oppressed, and the name of the supreme and matchless God might be forgotten [*Epitome of the Divine Institutes* 28 (c. A.D. 317)].

CLEMENTINE RECOGNITIONS

Therefore the astrologers, being ignorant of such mysteries, think that these things happen by the courses of the heavenly bodies; hence in their answers to those who go to them to consult them as to future things, they are deceived in very many instances. Nor is it surprising, for they are not prophets; but by long practice the authors of errors find a refuge in those things by which they were deceived, and introduce certain "climacteric periods," that they may pretend a knowledge of uncertain things. For they represent these "climacterics" as times of danger, in which one sometimes is destroyed, sometimes is not destroyed, not knowing that it is not the course of the stars but the operation of demons that regulates these things; and those demons, eager to confirm the error of astrology, deceive men to sin by mathematical calculations, so that when they suffer the punishment of sin, either by the permission of God or by legal sentence, the astrologer may seem to have spoken the truth [*Clementine Recognitions* 9:12 (c. A.D. 320)].

[A]s usually happens when men see unfavorable dreams, and can make nothing certain out of them, when any event occurs, they adapt what they saw in the dream to what has occurred; so also is [the] mathematics [of astrology]. For before anything happens, nothing is declared with certainty; but after something has happened, they gather the causes of the event. And thus often, when the astrologer has been at fault, and the thing happens otherwise, they take the blame to themselves, saying that it was such and such a star that opposed, and that they did not see it; not knowing that their error does not proceed from unskillfulness in their art, but from the inconsistency of the whole system. . . . But we who have learned the reason of this mystery know the cause since, having freedom of will, we sometimes oppose our desires and sometimes yield to them. And therefore the issue of human doings is uncertain, because it depends upon freedom of will. . . . And this is why ignorant astrologers have invented the talk about "climacterics" as their refuge in uncertainties [ibid., 10:12].

COUNCIL OF LAODICEA

They who are of the priesthood, or of the clergy, shall not be magicians, enchanters, mathematicians, or astrologers; nor shall they make what are called amulets, which are chains for their own souls. And those who wear such, we command to be cast out of the Church [Canon 36 (c. A.D. 362)].

ST. ATHANASIUS OF ALEXANDRIA

[Astrologers] have written books of [astrological] tables, in which they show stars, to which they have given the names of saints. And therein they have inflicted on themselves a double reproach, because they have perfected themselves in a lying and contemptible science, and have led the ignorant and simple astray by evil thoughts about the right faith established in truth and upright in the presence of God [*Letters* 39:1 (A.D. 367)].

ST. BASIL OF CAESAREA

But those who overstep the borders, making the words of Scripture their apology for the art of casting nativities, pretend that our lives depend upon the motion of the heavenly bodies, and that thus the Chaldaeans read in the planets what will happen to us. By these very simple words "let them be for signs," they understand neither the variations of the weather, nor the change of seasons; they only see in them, at the will of their imagination, the distribution of human destinies. What do they say in reality? When the planets cross in the signs of the zodiac, certain figures formed by their meeting give birth to certain destinies, and others produce different destinies [*Six Days of Creation* 6:5 (c. A.D. 367)].

ST. JOHN CHRYSOSTOM

[L]et us show forth by our actions all excellencies of conduct, and kindle the fire of virtue abundantly. For "you are lights," says he, "shining in the midst of the world" [Phil 2:15]. And God has given to each of us a greater function than he has to the sun: greater than heaven, and earth, and sea; as much greater, as spiritual things are more excellent than things sensible. When then we look unto the solar orb, and admire its beauty, and body and brightness, let us remember that greater and better is the light in us, as the darkness also is more dreadful unless we take heed, and a deep night oppresses the whole world. This is what we have to dispel and dissolve. It is night not among heretics and among Greeks only, but also in the multitude on our side, in respect to doctrines and to life. For many entirely disbelieve the Resurrection; many fortify themselves with their horoscope; many adhere to superstitious observances, and to omens, and auguries, and presages [*Homilies on First Corinthians* 4:11 (c. A.D. 392)].

ST. AUGUSTINE OF HIPPO

To whom then must we make an answer first—to the heretics or to the astrologers? For both come from the serpent, and desire to corrupt the Church's virginity of heart, which she holds in undefiled faith [*Tractates on John* 8:8 (A.D. 416–417)].

[E]very man twists for himself a rope by his sins. . . . Who makes a long rope? He who adds sin to sin. . . . One has committed a theft. So that he may not be found out, he seeks the astrologer [to prove his innocence]. It was enough to have committed the theft. Why will he add sin to sin? Behold! Two sins [are] committed! When you are forbidden to go to the astrologer, you revile the bishop. Behold! Three sins! When you hear it said of you, "Cast him forth from the Church," you say, "I will go to the party of Donatus." Behold! You add a fourth sin. The rope is growing. Be afraid of the rope. It is good to be corrected here, to be scourged with it, that it may not be said of you at the end, "Bind his hands and feet, and cast him forth into outer darkness" [Mt 22:13]. For "with the cords of his own sins everyone is bound" [Prv 5:22] [ibid., 10:5].

Now I had also repudiated the lying divination and impious absurdities of the astrologers . . . [and] I turned my thoughts to those who are born twins, who generally are born so near one to another that the small distance of time between them (however much force [astrologers] may contend that it has in the nature of things) cannot be noted by human observation or expressed in those [planetary] figures the astrologer examines so that he may pronounce the truth. Nor can they be true; for looking into the same figures he must have foretold the same of Esau and Jacob, but the same did not happen to them. He must therefore speak falsely, or if truly, then, looking into the same figures, he must not speak the same things. Not then by art but by chance would he speak truly [*Confessions* 7:6:8–10 (c. A.D. 400)].

IX. Sacraments and Worship

36. Baptism as a Means of Grace

The New Testament tells us that in baptism we are saved, buried with Christ, incorporated into his body, washed of our sins, regenerated, and cleansed (see Acts 2:38; 22:16; Rom 6:1–4; 1 Cor 6:11; 12:13; Gal 3:26–27; Eph 5:25–27; Col 2:11–12; Ti 3:5; 1 Pt 3:18–22).

Despite this, some claim that baptism is only a symbolic act and that it does not do the things the New Testament describes.

The early Fathers disagreed. They were unanimous in affirming baptism as a means of grace. Protestant early Church historian J. N. D. Kelly writes, "From the beginning baptism was the universally accepted rite of admission to the Church. . . . As regards its significance, it was always held to convey the remission of sins" (*Early Christian Doctrines*, 193–94).

LETTER OF BARNABAS

Concerning [baptism], indeed, it is written that the Israelites should not receive that baptism that leads to the remission of sins, but should procure another for themselves: . . . Notice how he has described at once both the water and the cross. For these words imply, Blessed are they who, placing their trust in the cross, have gone down into the water. . . . This means that we descend into the water full of sins and defilement, but come up bearing fruit in our heart, having the fear [of God] and trust in Jesus in our spirit [*Letter of Barnabas* 11 (c. A.D. 75)].

HERMAS OF ROME

And I said, "I heard, sir, some teachers say that there is no other repentance than what takes place when we descended into the water and received remission of our former sins." He said to me,

"That was sound doctrine you heard; for that is really the case" [*The Shepherd* 2:4:3 (c. A.D. 80)].

SECOND CLEMENT

For if we do the will of Christ, we shall find rest; otherwise, if we disobey his commandments, nothing shall deliver us from eternal punishment. . . . [H]ow can we hope to enter into the royal residence of God unless we keep our baptism holy and undefiled? Or who shall be our advocate, unless we are possessed of works of holiness and righteousness? [*Second Clement* 6 (c. A.D. 80)].

ST. IGNATIUS OF ANTIOCH

Let none of you be found a deserter. Let your baptism endure as your arms; your faith as your helmet; your love as your spear; your patience as a complete panoply [*Letter to St. Polycarp of Smyrna* 6 (c. A.D. 110)].

ST. JUSTIN MARTYR

I will also relate the way in which we dedicated ourselves to God when we were made new through Christ. . . . As many as are persuaded and believe that what we teach and say is true, and undertake to be able to live accordingly, and are instructed to pray and to entreat God with fasting, for the remission of their past sins, we pray and fast with them. Then they are brought by us where there is water, and are regenerated in the same way that we were regenerated. For, in the name of God, the Father and Lord of the universe, and of our Savior Jesus Christ, and of the Holy Spirit, they then receive the washing with water. For Christ also said, "Unless you be born again, you shall not enter into the kingdom of heaven" [*First Apology* 61 (c. A.D. 151)].

ST. THEOPHILUS OF ANTIOCH

Moreover, the things proceeding from the waters were blessed by God, that this also might be a sign of men being destined to receive repentance and remission of sins through the water and washing of regeneration, as many as come to the truth, and are born again, and receive blessing from God [*To Autolycus* 2:16 (c. A.D. 181)].

ST. CLEMENT OF ALEXANDRIA

Being baptized, we are illuminated; illuminated, we become sons; being made sons, we are made perfect; being made perfect, we are made immortal. "I," says he, "have said that you are gods, and all sons of the highest." This work is variously called grace, and illumination, and perfection, and washing: washing, by which we cleanse away our sins; grace, by which the penalties accruing to transgressions are remitted; and illumination, by which that holy light of salvation is beheld—that is, by which we see God clearly [*Instructor of Children* 1:6 (c. A.D. 197)].

TERTULLIAN OF CARTHAGE

Happy is our sacrament of water, in that, by washing away the sins of our early blindness, we are set free and admitted into eternal life. . . . [But] a viper of the Cainite heresy, lately conversant in this quarter, has carried away a great number with her most venomous doctrine, making it her first aim to destroy baptism. This is in accordance with nature; for vipers and asps . . . themselves generally live in arid and waterless places. But we, little fishes after the example of our [great] fish, Jesus Christ, are born in water, have safety in no other way than by permanently abiding in water; so that most monstrous creature, who had no right to teach even sound doctrine, knew full well how to kill the little fishes, by taking them away from the water! [*Baptism* 1 (c. A.D. 203)].

[B]aptism itself is carnal, in that we are plunged in water, but the effect spiritual, in that we are freed from sins [ibid., 7].

ST. HIPPOLYTUS OF ROME

And the bishop shall lay his hand upon [the newly baptized], invoking and saying: "O Lord God, who counted these worthy of the forgiveness of sins through the bath of regeneration, make them worthy to be filled with your Holy Spirit, grant to them your grace [in confirmation], that they may serve you according to your will" [*The Apostolic Tradition* 22 (c. A.D. 215)].

ST. CYPRIAN OF CARTHAGE

While I was still lying in darkness . . . I used to regard it as a difficult matter . . . that a man should be capable of being born again—a truth that divine mercy announced for my salvation—and that a man quickened to a new life in the laver of saving water should be able to put off what he had previously been; and, although retaining his bodily structure, should be changed in heart and soul. . . . But after that, by the help of the water of new birth, the stain of former years was washed away, and a light from above, serene and pure, was infused into my reconciled heart—after that, by the agency of the Spirit breathed from heaven, a second birth had restored me to a new man [*Letters* 1:3–4 (c. A.D. 246)].

ST. APHRAHAT THE PERSIAN SAGE

[F]rom baptism do we receive the Spirit of Christ. For in that hour in which the priests invoke the Spirit, the heavens open and it descends and moves upon the waters [Gn 1:2]. And those that are baptized are clothed in it; for the Spirit stays aloof from those who are born of the flesh, until they come to the new birth by water, and then they receive the Holy Spirit. . . . [I]n the second birth, through baptism, they received the Holy Spirit [*Demonstrations* 6:14 (c. A.D. 340)].

ST. CYRIL OF JERUSALEM

If a man does not receive baptism, he has not salvation; except only martyrs, who even without the water receive the kingdom. For when the Savior, in redeeming the world by his cross, was pierced in the side, he shed blood and water; that men, living in times of peace, might be baptized in water, and, in times of persecution, in their own blood. For martyrdom the Savior is wont to call a baptism, saying, Can you drink the cup that I drink, and be baptized with the baptism that I am baptized with? [Mk

10:38] . . . For you go down into the water, bearing your sins, but the invocation of grace, having sealed your soul, suffers you afterwards not to be swallowed up by the terrible dragon. Having gone down dead in sins, you come up quickened in righteousness [*Catechetical Lectures* 3:10, 12 (c. A.D. 350)].

ST. BASIL OF CAESAREA

For prisoners, baptism is ransom, forgiveness of debts, the death of sin, regeneration of the soul, a resplendent garment, an unbreakable seal, a chariot to heaven, a royal protector, a gift of adoption [*Eulogies on the Martyrs and Sermons on Moral and Practical Subjects* 13:5 (c. A.D. 374)].

COUNCIL OF CONSTANTINOPLE I

We believe . . . in one baptism for the remission of sins [*Nicene Creed* (A.D. 381)].

ST. AUGUSTINE OF HIPPO

The Christians of Carthage have an excellent name for the sacraments, when they say that baptism is "salvation," and the sacrament of the body of Christ is "life." This was derived from that primitive and apostolic Tradition by which the churches of Christ maintain it to be an inherent principle that without baptism and partaking of the supper of the Lord it is impossible for any man to attain the kingdom of God or salvation and everlasting life. So does Scripture testify [*The Merits and the Forgiveness of Sins, and the Baptism of Infants* 1:24:34 (A.D. 412)].

But the sacrament of baptism is undoubtedly the sacrament of regeneration [ibid., 2:27:43].

Baptism, therefore, washes away indeed all sins—absolutely all sins, whether of deeds or words or thoughts, whether original or added, whether committed in ignorance or allowed in knowledge [*Against Two Letters of the Pelagians* 3:5 (c. A.D. 420)].

And this is the meaning of the great sacrament of baptism that is solemnized among us, that all who attain to this grace should

die to sin, as he is said to have died to sin, because he died in
the flesh, which is the likeness of sin; and rising from the font
regenerated, as he arose alive from the grave, should begin a new
life in the Spirit, whatever may be the age of the body. For from
the newborn infant to the old man bent with age, as there is none
shut out from baptism so there is none who does not die to sin in
baptism. But infants die only to original sin; those who are older
also die to all the sins their evil lives have added to the sin they
brought with them [*Handbook on Faith, Hope, and Charity* 42–43
(A.D. 421)].

37. Baptismal Regeneration

One of the major images Scripture uses to describe the saving
action of God in our lives is that of being "born again," "born
from above," "regenerated," given "new life," and made a "new
creation." These are complementary ways of referring to the same
reality.

But when do we receive God's saving action? A key Scripture
passage is John 3:5, in which Jesus tells Nicodemus: "Truly, truly,
I say to you, unless one is born of water and the Spirit, he cannot enter the kingdom of God." The reference to the action of
the Spirit in conjunction with water teaches us that we are born
again, or regenerated, in baptism—a view supported elsewhere in
Scripture (Rom 6:3–4; Col 2:12–13; Ti 3:5).

Some today dispute this and say that we are not regenerated
in baptism, but the early Church Fathers disagreed unanimously.
After a diligent search, I have been unable to find *any* Father who
denied that John 3:5's reference to being born of water and the
Spirit was a reference to baptism.

ST. JUSTIN MARTYR

As many as are persuaded and believe that what we teach and say
is true, and undertake to be able to live accordingly, and are instructed to pray and entreat God with fasting, for the remission of
their past sins, we pray and fast with them. Then they are brought

by us where there is water, and are regenerated in the same way we were ourselves regenerated. For, in the name of God, the Father and Lord of the universe, and of our Savior Jesus Christ, and of the Holy Spirit, they receive the washing with water. For Christ also said, "Unless you be born again, you shall not enter into the kingdom of heaven" [Jn 3:3] [*First Apology* 61 (c. A.D. 151)].

ST. IRENAEUS OF LYONS

And [Naaman] dipped himself . . . seven times in the Jordan [2 Kgs 5:14]. It was not for nothing that Naaman, when suffering from leprosy, was purified upon being baptized, but as an indication to us. For as we are lepers in sin, we are made clean of our old transgressions by means of the sacred water and the invocation of the Lord; we are spiritually regenerated as newborn babes, even as the Lord has declared: "Except a man be born again through water and the Spirit, he shall not enter into the kingdom of heaven" [Jn 3:5] [*Fragments from the Lost Writings of Irenaeus* 34 (c. A.D. 190)].

TERTULLIAN OF CARTHAGE

[T]he prescript is laid down that "without baptism, salvation is attainable by none" (chiefly on the ground of that declaration of the Lord, who says, "Unless one be born of water, he has not life") [*Baptism* 12 (c. A.D. 203)].

ST. HIPPOLYTUS OF ROME

The Father of immortality sent the immortal Son and Word into the world, who came to man in order to wash him with water and the Spirit; and he, begetting us again, breathed into us the breath of life, and imbued us with an incorruptible panoply. If, therefore, man has become immortal, he will also be God. And if he is made God by water and the Holy Spirit after the regeneration of the laver he is also joint heir with Christ after the resurrection from the dead. Which is why I preach: Come, all you kindreds of the nations, to the immortality of the baptism [*Discourse on the Holy Theophany* 8 (c. A.D. 217)].

ST. CYPRIAN OF CARTHAGE

[When] they receive the baptism of the Church . . . then they can finally be fully sanctified and be the sons of God . . . since it is written, "Except a man be born again of water and of the Spirit, he cannot enter into the kingdom of God" [*Letters* 71:1 (c. A.D. 254)].

COUNCIL OF CARTHAGE OF 256

And in the Gospel our Lord Jesus Christ spoke with his divine voice, saying, "Except a man be born again of water and the Spirit, he cannot enter the kingdom of God" [Jn 3:5]. . . . Thus, unless they receive saving baptism in the Catholic Church, which is one, they cannot be saved, but will be condemned with the carnal in the judgment of the Lord Christ [Council of Carthage (A.D. 256)].

CLEMENTINE RECOGNITIONS

But you will perhaps say, "What does the baptism of water contribute to the worship of God?" In the first place, because it pleases. In the second place, because when you are regenerated and born again of water and of God, the frailty of your former birth through men, is cut off, and . . . you shall be able to attain salvation; but otherwise it is impossible. For thus has the true prophet testified to us with an oath: "Verily, I say to you, that unless a man is born again of water . . . he shall not enter into the kingdom of heaven" [*Clementine Recognitions* 6:9 (c. A.D. 320)].

ST. CYRIL OF JERUSALEM

When going down into the water, think not only of the element, but look for salvation by the power of the Holy Spirit: for without both you cannot possibly be made perfect. It is not I that say this, but the Lord Jesus Christ, who has the power in this matter: for he says, Except a man be born anew (and he adds the words) of water and of the Spirit, he cannot enter into the kingdom of God [Jn 3:3]. Neither does he who is baptized with water, but not found worthy of the Spirit, receive the grace in perfection; nor if a man be virtuous in his deeds, but receive not the seal by water, shall he enter into the kingdom of heaven. A bold saying, but not mine, for it is Jesus who has declared it: and here is the proof of the statement from Holy Scripture. Cornelius was a just man, who was honored with a vision of angels, and had set up his prayers and almsgiving as a good memorial before God in heaven [*Catechetical Lectures* 3:4 (c. A.D. 350)].

ST. ATHANASIUS OF ALEXANDRIA

[A]s we are all from earth and die in Adam, so being regenerated from above of water and Spirit, in the Christ we are all quickened [*Four Discourses Against the Arians* 3:26:33 (c. A.D. 360)].

ST. BASIL OF CAESAREA

This then is what it is to be born again of water and of the Spirit, the being made dead being effected in the water, while our life is wrought in us through the Spirit. In three immersions and with three invocations the great mystery of baptism is performed, so that the type of death may be fully figured, and that by the Tradition of the divine knowledge the baptized may have their souls enlightened. It follows that if there is any grace in the water, it is not of the nature of the water, but of the presence of the Spirit [*The Holy Spirit* 15:35 (A.D. 375)].

ST. AMBROSE OF MILAN

There are, however, many who think that because we are baptized with water and the Spirit, there is no difference in the offices of water and the Spirit, and that they do not differ in nature. They do not observe that we are buried in the element of water that we may rise again renewed by the Spirit. For in the water is the representation of death, in the Spirit is the pledge of life, that the body of sin may die through the water, which encloses the body as it were in a tomb, that by the power of the Spirit we may be renewed from the death of sin, being born again in God [*The Holy Spirit* 1:6:75–76 (A.D. 381)].

The Church was redeemed at the price of Christ's blood. Jew or Greek, it makes no difference; but if he believes, he must circumcise himself from his sins [in baptism, Col 2:11–12] so that he can be saved . . . for no one ascends into the kingdom of heaven except through the sacrament of baptism. . . . "Unless a man be born again of water and the Holy Spirit, he cannot enter the kingdom of God" [*Abraham* 2:11:79–84 (A.D. 387)].

Therefore read that the three witnesses in baptism, the water, the blood, and the Spirit [1 Jn 5:7], are one, for if you take away one of these, the sacrament of baptism does not exist. For what is water without the cross of Christ? A common element, without any sacramental effect. Nor, again, is there the sacrament of regeneration without water: "For except a man be born again of water and of the Spirit, he cannot enter into the kingdom of God" [Jn 3:5]. Now, even the catechumen believes in the cross of the Lord Jesus, with which he is signed; but unless he be baptized in the name of the Father, and of the Son, and of the Holy Spirit, he cannot receive remission of sins or the gift of spiritual grace [*The Mysteries* 4:20 (c. A.D. 390)].

ST. GREGORY OF NAZIANZ

Such is the grace and power of baptism; not an overwhelming of the world as of old, but a purification of the sins of each individual, and a complete cleansing of all the bruises and stains of sin. And since we are made of body and soul, and the one part is visible, the other invisible, so the cleansing is twofold, by water and the spirit; the one received visibly in the body, the other invisibly and apart from the body; the one typical, the other real and cleansing the depths [*Orations* 40:7–8 (A.D. 381)].

ST. GREGORY OF NYSSA

[In] the birth by water and the Spirit, [Jesus] himself led the way in this birth, drawing down upon the water, by his own baptism, the Holy Spirit; so that he became the firstborn of those who are spiritually born again, and gave the name of brethren to those who partook in a birth like his own by water and the Spirit [*Against Eunomius* 2:8 (c. A.D. 382)].

ST. JOHN CHRYSOSTOM

[N]o one can enter into the kingdom of heaven except he be regenerated through water and the Spirit, and he who does not eat the flesh of the Lord and drink his blood is excluded from eternal life, and if all these things are accomplished only by means of the holy hands of the priest, how will anyone, without them, be able to escape the fire of hell, or attain those crowns reserved for the victorious? These [priests] truly are entrusted with the pangs of spiritual travail and the birth that comes through baptism: by their means we put on Christ, and are buried with the Son of God, and become members of that blessed head [the Mystical Body of Christ] [*The Priesthood* 3:5–6 (c. A.D. 388)].

APOSTOLIC CONSTITUTIONS

Be contented with one baptism alone, that which is into the death of the Lord [Rom 6:3; Col 2:12–13]. . . . [H]e that will not be baptized out of contempt will be condemned as an unbeliever, and reproached as ungrateful and foolish. For the Lord says: "Except a man be baptized of water and of the Spirit, he shall by no means enter into the kingdom of heaven" [Jn 3:5]. And again: "He that believes and is baptized shall be saved; but he that believes not shall be damned" [Mk 16:16] [*Apostolic Constitutions* 6:3:15 (c. A.D. 400)].

ST. AUGUSTINE OF HIPPO

But the possibility of regeneration through the office of the will of another, when the child is presented to receive the sacred rite, is the work exclusively of the Spirit by whom the child presented is regenerated. For it is not written, "Except a man be born again by the will of his parents, or by the faith of those presenting the child, or of those administering the ordinance," but, "Except a man be born again of water and of the Spirit" [Jn 3:5]. By the water, therefore, which holds the sacrament of grace in its outward form, and by the Spirit who bestows the benefit of grace in its inward power, canceling the bond of guilt, and restoring natural goodness, the man deriving his first birth originally from Adam [*Letters* 98:2 (A.D. 408)].

If unbaptized persons die confessing Christ, this confession remits sins as if they were washed in the sacred font of baptism. For he who said, "Except a man be born of water and of the Spirit, he cannot enter into the kingdom of God" [Jn 3:5] also made an exception in their favor, in that other sentence in which he clearly said, "Whosoever shall confess me before men, him will I confess also before my Father which is in heaven" [*City of God* 13:7 (c. A.D. 419)].

38. The Necessity of Baptism

According to 1 Peter 3:21: "Baptism . . . now saves you, not as a removal of dirt from the body, but as an appeal to God for a clear conscience, through the Resurrection of Jesus Christ."

In keeping with this language, the *Nicene Creed* states, "I confess one baptism for the forgiveness of sins."

And the *Catechism of the Catholic Church* states: "The Lord himself affirms that baptism is necessary for salvation [Jn 3:5]. . . . Baptism is necessary for salvation for those to whom the Gospel has been proclaimed and who have had the possibility of asking for this sacrament [Mk 16:16]" (CCC 1257).

The necessity of baptism for salvation is broadly recognized among Christians, including non-Catholic ones. For example, Martin Luther wrote: "Baptism is no human plaything but is instituted by God himself. Moreover, it is solemnly and strictly commanded that we must be baptized or we shall not be saved. We are not to regard it as an indifferent matter, then, like putting on a new red coat. It is of the greatest importance that we regard baptism as excellent, glorious, and exalted" (*Large Catechism* 4:6).

But God has not made baptism necessary in an absolute sense, so that anyone who fails to receive it is lost. Down through history Christians have recognized that there are exceptions, and that it is possible to be saved through "baptism of blood" (martyrdom for Christ) or "baptism of desire" (a desire for baptism that has not yet been received). Even those who do not understand the importance of baptism can be said to have an unconscious desire for it if they would be willing to do what God wants them to do for their salvation.

Thus the *Catechism of the Catholic Church* states: "Those who die for the faith, those who are catechumens, and all those who, without knowing of the Church but acting under the inspiration of grace, seek God sincerely and strive to fulfill his will, are saved even if they have not been baptized" (CCC 1281; the salvation of unbaptized infants is also possible; see CCC 1260–61, 1283).

As the following passages from the Church Fathers illustrate, Christians in the first ages recognized the ordinary necessity of water baptism as well as the legitimacy of baptism by desire or blood.

HERMAS OF ROME

And I said, "I heard, sir, some teachers say that there is no other repentance than what takes place when we descended into the water and received remission of our former sins." He said to me, "That was sound doctrine you heard; for that is really the case" [*The Shepherd* 2:4:3 (c. A.D. 80)].

ST. JUSTIN MARTYR

As many as are persuaded and believe that what we teach and say is true, and undertake to be able to live accordingly, and are instructed to pray and entreat God with fasting, for the remission of their past sins . . . are brought by us where there is water, and are regenerated in the same way we were ourselves regenerated. For, in the name of God, the Father and Lord of the universe, and of our Savior Jesus Christ, and of the Holy Spirit, they receive the washing with water. For Christ also said, "Unless you be born again, you shall not enter into the kingdom of heaven" [Jn 3:3] [*First Apology* 61 (c. A.D. 151)].

TERTULLIAN OF CARTHAGE

Happy is our sacrament of water, in that, by washing away the sins of our early blindness, we are set free and admitted into eternal life. . . . [But] a viper of the Cainite heresy, lately conversant in this quarter, has carried away a great number with her most venomous doctrine, making it her aim to destroy baptism. This is in accordance with nature; for vipers and asps . . . themselves generally live in arid and waterless places. But we, little fishes after the example of our [great] fish, Jesus Christ, are born in water, and find safety by permanently abiding in water; so that most monstrous creature, who had no right to teach even sound doctrine, knew full well how to kill the little fishes, by taking them away from the water! [*Baptism* 1 (c. A.D. 203)].

Without baptism, salvation is attainable by none [ibid., 12].

We have a second font (itself one with the former) of blood, about which the Lord said, "I have to be baptized with a baptism," when he had been baptized already. For he had come "by means of water and blood" [1 Jn 5:6], just as John has written; that he might be baptized by the water, glorified by the blood—to make us, in like manner, called by water, chosen by blood. These two baptisms he sent out from the wound in his pierced side, in order that they who believed in his blood might be bathed with the water; they who had been bathed in the water might drink the blood. This baptism stands in lieu of being bathed in the font when that has not been received, and restores it when lost [ibid., 16].

CLEMENTINE HOMILIES

[P]erhaps some one will say, "What does it contribute to piety to be baptized with water?" In the first place, because you do what is pleasing to God; and in the second place, being born again to God by water, by reason of fear you change your first generation, which is of lust, and thus may obtain salvation. But otherwise it is impossible. For the prophet has sworn to us, saying, "Truly I say to you, unless you are regenerated by living water in the name of Father, Son, and Holy Spirit, you shall not enter the kingdom of heaven." Therefore come. For there is something here that is merciful from the beginning, borne upon the water, and rescues those who are baptized this way from future punishment, offering as gifts to God the good deeds of the baptized whenever they are done after baptism. Flee to the waters, for baptism alone can quench the violence of fires. He who will not still bears the spirit of strife, because of which he will not approach the living water for his own salvation. [*Clementine Homilies* 11:26 (c. A.D. 217)].

ORIGEN OF ALEXANDRIA

It is not possible to receive forgiveness of sins without baptism [*Exhortation to Martyrdom* 30 (A.D. 235)].

ST. CYPRIAN OF CARTHAGE

Not even the baptism of a public confession and blood can profit a heretic to salvation, because there is no salvation out of the Church [*Letters* 72:21 (c. A.D. 255)].

Let men of this kind, who are aiders and favorers of heretics, know first, that those catechumens hold the sound faith and truth of the Church, and advance from the divine camp to do battle with the devil, with a full and sincere acknowledgment of God the Father, and of Christ, and of the Holy Spirit; then, that they are not deprived of the sacrament of baptism who are baptized with the most glorious and greatest baptism of blood, about which the Lord said that he had "another baptism to be baptized with" [ibid., 72:22].

ST. CYRIL OF JERUSALEM

If a man does not receive baptism, he has not salvation; except only martyrs, who even without the water receive the kingdom. For when the Savior, in redeeming the world by his cross, was pierced in the side, he shed blood and water; that men, living in times of peace, might be baptized in water, and, in times of persecution, in their own blood. For martyrdom the Savior is wont to call a baptism, saying, Can you drink the cup that I drink, and be baptized with the baptism that I am baptized with? [Mk 10:38] . . . For you go down into the water, bearing your sins, but the invocation of grace, having sealed your soul, suffers you not afterwards to be swallowed up by the terrible dragon. Having gone down dead in sins, you come up quickened in righteousness [*Catechetical Lectures* 3:10, 12 (c. A.D. 350)].

ST. GREGORY OF NAZIANZ

I know also a fourth baptism—that by martyrdom and blood, which Christ himself underwent—and this one is far more august than all the others, as it cannot be defiled by after-stains [*Orations* 39:17 (A.D. 381)].

ST. AMBROSE OF MILAN

But I hear you lamenting because [the Emperor Valentinian] had not received the sacrament of baptism. Tell me, what else could we have, except the will to it, the asking for it? He too now had this desire, and after he came into Italy it was begun, and a short time ago he signified that he wished to be baptized by me. Did he not have the grace he desired? Did he not have what he eagerly sought? Certainly, because he sought it, he received it. What else does it mean: "Whatever just man shall be overtaken by death, his soul shall be at rest" [Wis 4:7]? [*Sympathy at the Death of Valentinian* (A.D. 392)].

ST. AUGUSTINE OF HIPPO

In three ways are sins remitted in the Church; by baptism, by prayer, by the greater humility of penance; yet God does not remit sins except to the baptized. The very sins that he remits first, he remits only to the baptized [*Sermon to Catechumens on the Creed* 16 (c. A.D. 395)].

I do not hesitate for a moment to place the Catholic catechumen, who is burning with love for God, before the baptized heretic; nor do we dishonor the sacrament of baptism that the latter has already received, the former not as yet; nor do we consider that the sacrament of the catechumen is preferable to the sacrament of baptism, even when we acknowledge that some catechumens are better and more faithful than some baptized persons. . . . For Cornelius, even before his baptism, was filled with the Holy Spirit [Acts 10:44]; Simon, even after baptism, was puffed up with an unclean spirit [*On Baptism, Against the Donatists* 4:21 (A.D. 400)].

That the place of baptism is sometimes supplied by martyrdom is supported by an argument that the blessed Cyprian adduces from the thief, to whom, though he was not baptized, it was yet said, "Today shall you be with me in Paradise" [Lk 23:43]. On considering this again and again, I find that not only martyrdom for the sake of Christ may supply what was wanting of baptism, but also faith and conversion of heart, if recourse may not be had to the celebration of the mystery of baptism for want of time [ibid., 4:22:30].

When we speak of within and without in relation to the Church, it is the position of the heart that we must consider, not of the body. . . . All who are within [the Church] in heart are saved in the unity of the ark [by baptism of desire] [ibid., 5:28:39].

[According to] apostolic Tradition . . . the churches of Christ maintain it to be an inherent principle that without baptism and partaking of the supper of the Lord it is impossible for any man to attain the kingdom of God or salvation and everlasting life. So does Scripture testify [*The Merits and the Forgiveness of Sins, and the Baptism of Infants* 1:24:34 (A.D. 412)].

If unbaptized persons die confessing Christ, this confession is of the same efficacy for the remission of sins as if they were washed in the sacred font of baptism. For he who said, "Except a man be born of water and of the Spirit, he cannot enter into the kingdom of God" [Jn 3:5] also made an exception in their favor, in that other sentence in which he clearly said, "Whosoever shall confess me before men, him will I confess also before my Father which is in heaven" [*City of God* 13:7 (c. A.D. 419)].

POPE ST. LEO I

And because through the transgression of the first man the whole stock of the human race was tainted, no one can be set free from the state of the old Adam save through Christ's sacrament of baptism, in which there are no distinctions between the reborn, as says the apostle: "For as many of you as were baptized in Christ did put on Christ: there is neither Jew nor Greek" [Gal 3:27–28] [*Letters* 15:10(11) (A.D. 445)].

39. Trinitarian Baptism

For a sacrament to be valid, three things have to be present: the correct form, the correct matter, and the correct intention. With baptism, the correct form is baptizing "in the name of the Father and of the Son and of the Holy Spirit" (Mt 28:19), the correct matter is water, and the correct intention is to do what the Church does.

Unfortunately, not all religious organizations use this form. In fact, Jehovah's Witnesses use no formula at all in their baptisms, and an even larger group, the "Jesus Only" Pentecostals, baptize "in the name of Jesus." As a result, the baptisms of these groups are invalid.

Both groups also reject the Trinity. Jehovah's Witnesses claim that Jesus is not God but a created, supernatural being, a heresy known as Arianism, and the "Jesus Only" or "Oneness" Pentecostals claim that there is only a single person—Jesus—in the Godhead, a heresy known as Sabellianism.

Oneness Pentecostals note that Jesus told the apostles to baptize in "the name" (singular) of the Father, the Son, and the Spirit, but they make the mistake of assuming that the name is Jesus.

Jesus may not intend us to understand the baptismal formula in terms of a single, literal name. Saying to do something "in the name of" the Father, the Son, and the Holy Spirit may be analogous to telling a soldier that he should fight "in the name of" his country, his family, and the cause of liberty. This doesn't mean that the soldier's country, family, and the cause of liberty all share one literal name.

On the other hand, if there is a single name that Jesus has in mind in this passage, it likely isn't "Jesus" but "Yahweh." This name is applied to both the Father and the Son in the New Testament. In Acts 2:34–36, Peter quotes Psalm 110:1, applying the term "Lord" to the Father, but in the Old Testament original, the term corresponding to "Lord" is actually *Yahweh*. In Philippians 2:10–11, Paul quotes Isaiah 45:19–24, applying a prophecy about the Lord to the Son. And again in the Old Testament original, the term corresponding to "Lord" in this passage is actually *Yahweh*. And if the name Yahweh applies to the Father and the Son, it can be applied to the Spirit.

Oneness Pentecostals also argue that the New Testament talks about people being baptized "in the name of Jesus," but there are only four such passages (Acts 2:38; 8:16; 10:48; 19:5), and these passages do not use consistent language (some say "Lord Jesus," other say "Jesus Christ").

It may be that those particular passages are not attempting to provide the formula used in baptism, but rather are trying to distinguish Christian baptism from other forms of baptism that were current in the day. It would be cumbersome to repeat "baptized in the name of the Father and of the Son and of the Holy Spirit" every time you refer to Christian baptism, and may have been natural to look for shorter ways to say it.

Thus the phrase "baptized in the name of Jesus" may simply be Luke's way to distinguish Christian baptism from other baptisms, such as John's baptism (which he mentions in Acts 1:5, 22; 10:37; 11:16; 13:24; 18:25; 19:4), Jewish proselyte baptism, and the baptisms of pagan cults (such as Mithraism). The phrase also indicates the person into whose Mystical Body baptism incorporates us (Rom 6:3).

None of the passages that Oneness Pentecostals point to should undo the foundational text in which Jesus Christ instructed his Church to "make disciples of all nations, baptizing them in the name of the Father and of the Son and of the Holy Spirit" (Mt 28:19).

That is how Jesus said to do baptism, and that is how the Church Fathers baptized, as the following passages show.

DIDACHE

[Y]ou baptize this way: Having first said all these things, baptize in the name of the Father, and of the Son, and of the Holy Spirit, in living water. But if you don't have living water, baptize in other water; and if you cannot baptize in cold, then baptize in warm. But if you have not either, pour water three times on the head in the name of Father and Son and Holy Spirit. But before the baptism let the baptizer fast, and the baptized, and whoever else can; but you shall order the baptized to fast one or two days before [Didache 7 (c. A.D. 50)].

TATIAN THE SYRIAN

Then said Jesus unto them, "I have been given all authority in heaven and earth; and as my Father has sent me, so I also send you. Go now into all the world, and preach my gospel in all the creation; and teach all the peoples, and baptize them in the name of the Father and the Son and the Holy Spirit; and teach them to keep all whatsoever I commanded you: and lo, I am with you all the days, unto the end of the world" [Mt 28:18–20] [Diatesseron 55 (c. A.D. 170)].

ST. HIPPOLYTUS OF ROME

When the one being baptized goes down into the water, the one baptizing him shall put his hand on him and ask, "Do you believe in God, the Father Almighty?" And he that is being baptized shall answer, "I believe." Then, with his hand on the head of the one to be baptized, he shall baptize him once, then he shall ask, "Do you believe in Christ Jesus . . . ?" And when he says, "I believe," he is baptized again. Again shall he ask, "Do you believe in the Holy Spirit and the holy Church and the resurrection of the flesh?" The one being baptized then answers, "I believe." And so he is baptized a third time [*Apostolic Tradition* 21 (c. A.D. 215)].

TERTULLIAN OF CARTHAGE

After his Resurrection he promises in a pledge to his disciples that he will send them the promise of his Father [Lk 24:49]; and lastly, he commands them to baptize into the Father and the Son and the Holy Spirit, not into a uni-personal God. And indeed it is not once but three times that we are immersed into the three Persons, at each mention of their names [*Against Praxeas* 26 (c. A.D. 218)].

ORIGEN OF ALEXANDRIA

Why, when the Lord himself told his disciples that they should baptize all peoples in the name of the Father and of the Son and of the Holy Spirit, does this apostle [Paul] employ the name of Christ alone in baptism, saying, "We who have been baptized into Christ"; for indeed, legitimate baptism is had only in the name of the Trinity [*Commentary on Romans* 5:8 (c. A.D. 248)].

ACTS OF XANTHIPPE AND POLYXENA

Then Probus . . . leapt into the water, saying, "Jesus Christ, Son of God, and everlasting God, let all my sins be taken away by this water." And Paul said, "We baptize thee in the name of the Father and Son and Holy Spirit." After this he made him to receive the Eucharist of Christ [*Acts of Xanthippe and Polyxena* 21 (c. A.D. 250)].

ST. CYPRIAN OF CARTHAGE

Finally, when, after the Resurrection, the apostles are sent by the Lord to the heathens, they are bidden to baptize the Gentiles in the name of the Father, and of the Son, and of the Holy Spirit. How, then, do some say that a Gentile baptized without, outside the Church, and in opposition to the Church, so that it be only in the name of Jesus Christ, can obtain remission of sin, when

Christ himself commands the heathen to be baptized in the full and united Trinity? [*Letters* 72:18 (c. A.D. 255)].

EUSEBIUS OF CAESAREA

We believe . . . each of these to be and to exist: the Father, truly Father, and the Son, truly Son, and the Holy Spirit, truly Holy Spirit, as our Lord, sending forth his disciples to preach, said, "Go teach all nations, baptizing them in the name of the Father and of the Son, and of the Holy Spirit," about whom we confidently affirm that so we hold, and so we think, and so we have always held, and we maintain this faith until death, anathematizing every godless heresy [*Letter on the Council of Nicaea* 3 (A.D. 325)].

ST. CYRIL OF JERUSALEM

You were led by the hand to the holy pool of divine baptism, as Christ was carried from the cross to this sepulcher before us [the tomb of Jesus at Jerusalem]. And each of you was asked if he believed in the name of the Father, and of the Son, and of the Holy Spirit. And you spoke that saving confession, and descended into the water three times, and again ascended, and in this the three days of Christ's burial was suggested as a symbol [*Catechetical Lectures* 20:4 (c. A.D. 350)].

ST. ATHANASIUS OF ALEXANDRIA

And the whole faith is summed up and secured in this, that a Trinity should ever be preserved, as we read in the Gospel, "Go and baptize all the nations in the name of the Father and of the Son and of the Holy Spirit" [Mt 28:19]. And entire and perfect is the number of the Trinity [*On the Councils of Arminium and Seleucia* 1:2:28 (c. A.D. 361)].

ST. BASIL OF CAESAREA

The Holy Spirit, too, is numbered with the Father and the Son, because he is above creation, and is ranked as we are taught by the words of the Lord in the Gospel, "Go and baptize in the name of the Father and of the Son and of the Holy Spirit" [Mt 28:19]. He who places the Spirit before the Son, or says he is older than the Father, resists the ordinance of God, and is a stranger to the sound faith, since he fails to preserve the form of doxology that he has received, but adopts some newfangled device in order to be pleasing to men [*Letters* 52:4 (c. A.D. 370)].

ST. AMBROSE OF MILAN

Moreover, Christ himself says: "I and the Father are One" [Jn 10:30]. "One," said he, that there be no separation of power and nature; but again, "We are," that you may recognize Father and Son, for as much as the perfect Father is believed to have begotten the perfect Son, and the Father and the Son are One, not by confusion of Person, but by unity of nature. We say, then, that there is one God, not two or three Gods [*Faith* 1:1:9–10 (c. A.D. 379)].

ST. GREGORY OF NAZIANZ

[N]ot yet perhaps is there upon your soul any writing good or bad; and you want to be written upon today, and formed by us unto perfection. Let us go within the cloud. Give me the tables of your heart; I will be your Moses, though this be a bold thing to say; I will write on them with the finger of God a new Decalogue [Ex 38:28]. I will write on them a shorter method of salvation. And if there be any heretical or unreasoning beast, let him remain below, or he will run the risk of being stoned by the Word of truth. I will baptize you and make you a disciple in the name of the Father and of the Son and of the Holy Spirit; and these Three have one common name, the Godhead. And you shall know by appearances [Mt 28:19] and by words that you reject all ungodliness, and are united to all the Godhead [*Oration* 40:45 (A.D. 381)].

ST. JEROME

For seeing that a man baptized in the name of the Father and the Son and the Holy Spirit becomes a temple of the Lord, and that while the old abode is destroyed a new shrine is built for the Trinity, how can you say that sins can be remitted among the Arians without the coming of the Holy Spirit? How is a soul purged from its former stains that does not have the Holy Spirit? [*Dialogue Against the Luciferians* 6 (c. A.D. 382)].

ST. GREGORY OF NYSSA

And we, in receiving baptism . . . conceal ourselves in [the water] as the Savior did in the earth: and by doing this three times we represent for ourselves that grace of the Resurrection, which was wrought in three days. And this we do, not receiving the sacrament in silence, but while the names of the three sacred Persons in whom we believe are spoken over us, in whom we also hope, and from whom comes to us our present and our future existence [*The Baptism of Christ* (c. A.D. 383)].

ST. AUGUSTINE OF HIPPO

Baptism in the name of the Father and of the Son and of the Holy Spirit has Christ for its authority, not any man, whoever he may be; and Christ is the truth, not any man [*Answer to the Letters of Petilian the Donatist* 4:24:57 (A.D. 402)].

O Lord our God, we believe in you, the Father and the Son and the Holy Spirit. For the truth would not say, "Go, baptize all nations in the name of the Father and of the Son and of the Holy Spirit," . . . unless you were a Trinity [*The Trinity* 15:28:51 (c. A.D. 408)].

THEODORET OF CYR

[W]hat need is there of many words, when it is possible to refute falsehood in few? We provide that those who year by year come up for holy baptism should carefully learn the faith set forth at Nicaea by the holy and blessed Fathers; and initiating them as we have been bidden, we baptize them in the name of the Father and of the Son and of the Holy Spirit, pronouncing each name singly [*Letters* 145 (A.D. 450)].

40. Infant Baptism

The great majority of Christians recognize the practice of infant baptism, though some groups do not. These groups argue that baptism should only be bestowed on people who have attained a certain age and are capable of asking for it. Nowhere in the New Testament, they point out, do we read of infants being baptized.

That is true. But it is also true that nowhere do we read of children being raised in Christian families to a certain age and then being baptized. The accounts of baptism in the New Testament deal with converts from Judaism or paganism, not the children of those who are already believers. Concerning them, there is no explicit mention of baptism, whether in infancy or later.

As with the mode of baptism (see chapter 2), Scripture simply never tells us whether the proper recipients of baptism include infants or not, but there are passages that are consistent with and even suggestive of infant baptism.

Luke 18:15–16 tells us that "they were bringing even infants" to Jesus; and he himself related this to the kingdom of God: "Let the children come to me . . . for to such belongs the kingdom of God." This passage does not deal with baptism, but it does establish a principle that is relevant. If "even infants" are fit subjects for "the kingdom of God," why should they be denied baptism and membership in Christ's mystical body?

There is a passage in Acts in which baptism is under discussion. Peter declares, "Repent, and be baptized, every one of you, in the name of Jesus Christ for the forgiveness of your sins; and you shall receive the gift of the Holy Spirit. For the promise is to you *and to your children*" (Acts 2:38–39). Even more noteworthy are the passages that describe whole households being baptized (Acts 16:33; 1 Cor 1:16). These may well have included infants and small children.

Baptism is the Christian rite of initiation, the equivalent of circumcision for Jews. In fact, St. Paul calls it "the circumcision of Christ," telling us: "In him you were also circumcised with

... the circumcision of Christ, having been buried with him in baptism and raised with him through your faith in the power of God, who raised him from the dead" (Col 2:11–12).

Circumcision could be applied not only to converts to Judaism, who already possessed faith in God, but also to the sons in Jewish families, who would be raised in the faith. Baptism, as the Christian equivalent, can also be applied to converts who already have faith and children who will be raised in the faith.

This is something the Church Fathers recognized. Although in some centuries it was common to delay baptism—including until late in life for fear of sinning or falling away after baptism—the validity of baptizing infants was not challenged, and doing so was seen as an urgent priority if it appeared that a child would die.

In fact, in the 200s there was a controversy regarding whether baptism should be delayed until the eighth day after birth, like circumcision (see quotation from Cyprian, below; cf. Lv 12:2–3).

Consider, too, that Church Fathers raised in Christian homes would hardly have upheld infant baptism as apostolic if their own baptisms had been deferred until the age of reason.

An instructive case is that of St. Irenaeus of Lyons, who affirms that we are born again in baptism and that infants can be born again. He may well have been baptized as an infant himself when he was born in Smyrna around the year 140. If so, he might have been baptized by the then-bishop of Smyrna—St. Polycarp, who was a personal disciple of St. John.

ST. IRENAEUS OF LYONS

For he came to save all through himself—all, I say, who through him are born again to God—infants, and children, and boys, and youths, and old men [*Against Heresies* 2:22:4 (c. A.D. 189)].

And [Naaman] dipped himself . . . seven times in the Jordan [2 Kgs 5:14]. It was not for nothing that Naaman, when suffering from leprosy, was purified upon being baptized, but as an indication to us. For as we are lepers in sin, we are made clean of our old transgressions by means of the sacred water and the invocation of the Lord; we are spiritually regenerated as newborn babes, even as the Lord has declared: "Except a man be born again through water and the Spirit, he shall not enter into the kingdom of heaven" [Jn 3:5] [*Fragments from the Lost Writings of Irenaeus* 34 (c. A.D. 190)].

ST. HIPPOLYTUS OF ROME

The children shall be baptized first. All the children who can answer for themselves, let them answer. If there are any children who cannot answer for themselves, let their parents answer for them, or someone else from their family [*Apostolic Tradition* 21 (c. A.D. 215)].

ORIGEN OF ALEXANDRIA

Every soul that is born into flesh is soiled by the filth of wickedness and sin. . . . In the Church, baptism is given for the remission of sins, and, according to the usage of the Church, baptism is given even to infants. If there was nothing in infants that required the remission of sins and nothing in them pertinent to forgiveness, the grace of baptism would seem superfluous [*Homilies on Leviticus* 8:3 (c. A.D. 249)].

EARLY CHRISTIAN INSCRIPTION

Sweet Tyche lived one year, ten months, and twenty-five days. Received [the grace of baptism] on the eighth day before the Kalends [the first day of the month]. Gave up her soul on the same day [*Christian Inscriptions*, no. 27 (c. A.D. 250)].

EARLY CHRISTIAN INSCRIPTION

Florentius erected this monument to his well-deserving son Appronianus, who lived one year, nine months, and five days. Since he was dearly loved by his grandmother, and she saw that he was going to die, she asked of the Church that he should depart from the world a believer [*Christian Inscriptions*, no. 40 (c. A.D. 250)].

ST. CYPRIAN OF CARTHAGE

But in respect of the case of the infants, which you [Fidus] say ought not to be baptized within the second or third day after their birth, and that the law of ancient circumcision should be followed, so that one who is just born should not be baptized and sanctified within the eighth day, we all thought very differently in our council. For no one agreed with the course you thought should be taken; rather we all judge that the mercy and grace of God is not to be refused to anyone born of man [*Letters* 58:2 (c. A.D. 253)].

But when even to the greatest sinners, and to those who had sinned much against God, when they subsequently believed, remission of sins is granted—and nobody is hindered from baptism and from grace—how much ought we to shrink from hindering an infant, who, being newly born, has not sinned, except that being born after the flesh according to Adam, he has contracted the contagion of the ancient death at its earliest birth, he approaches more easily on this account the reception of the forgiveness of sins—that to him are remitted not his own sins, but the sins of another [ibid., 58:5].

ST. GREGORY OF NAZIANZ

Have you an infant child? Do not let sin get any opportunity, but let him be sanctified from his childhood; from his very tenderest age let him be consecrated by the Spirit. Fearest thou the seal on account of the weakness of nature? O what a small-souled mother, and of how little faith! [*Orations* 40:17 (A.D. 381)].

Be it so, some will say, in the case of those who ask for baptism; what have you to say about those who are still children, and conscious neither of the loss nor of the grace? Are we to baptize them too? Certainly, if any danger presses. For it is better that they should be unconsciously sanctified than that they should depart unsealed and uninitiated [ibid., 40:28].

ST. JOHN CHRYSOSTOM

You see the many benefits of baptism, and some think its heavenly grace consists only in the remission of sins, but we have enumerated ten honors [it bestows]! For this reason we baptize even infants, though they are not defiled by [personal] sin; so that there may be given to them holiness, righteousness, adoption, inheritance, brotherhood with Christ, and that they may be [Christ's] members [*Baptismal Catecheses* in St. Augustine, *Against Julian* 1:6:21 (c. A.D. 388)].

ST. AUGUSTINE OF HIPPO

And if anyone seek for divine authority in this matter, though what is held by the whole Church, and not instituted by councils but as a matter of invariable custom, is rightly held to have been handed down by apostolic authority. . . . Therefore, when others take the vows for them, that the celebration of the sacrament may be complete in their behalf, it unquestionably avails for their dedication to God, because they cannot answer for themselves [*On Baptism, Against the Donatists* 4:24:32 (A.D. 400)].

The custom of Mother Church in baptizing infants is certainly not to be scorned, nor is it to be regarded in any way as superfluous, nor is it to be believed that its Tradition is anything but apostolic [*Literal Interpretation of Genesis* 10:23 (c. A.D. 408)].

COUNCIL OF CARTHAGE OF 401

It seemed good that whenever there were not found reliable witnesses who could testify that without any doubt they were baptized, and when the children themselves were not, on account of their tender age, able to answer concerning the giving of the sacraments to them, all such children should be baptized without scruple, lest hesitation deprive them of the cleansing of the sacraments. This was urged by the Moorish legates, our brethren, since they redeem many such from the barbarians [September session of council, Canon 7 (A.D. 401)].

ST. AUGUSTINE OF HIPPO

The blessed Cyprian, indeed, said, in order to correct those who thought that an infant should not be baptized before the eighth day, that it was not the body but the soul that needed to be saved from perdition—in which statement he was not inventing any new doctrine, but preserving the firmly established faith of the Church; and he, along with some of his colleagues in the episcopal office, held that a child may be properly baptized immediately after its birth [*Letters* 166:8:23 (A.D. 415)].

By this grace baptized infants too are ingrafted into [Christ's] body, infants who certainly are not yet able to imitate anyone. Christ, in whom all are made alive . . . gives the most hidden grace of his Spirit to believers, grace that he secretly infuses even into infants. . . . It is an excellent thing that the Punic [North Africans descended from the Phoenicians] Christians call baptism, salvation, and the sacrament of Christ's body nothing else than life. Whence does this derive, except from an ancient and, as I suppose, apostolic Tradition, by which the churches of Christ hold inherently that without baptism and participation at the table of the Lord it is impossible for any man to attain the kingdom of God or salvation and life eternal? This is the witness of Scripture, too. . . . If anyone wonders why children born of the baptized should themselves be baptized, let him attend briefly to this. . . . The sacrament of baptism is most assuredly the sacrament of regeneration [*The Merits and the Forgiveness of Sins, and the Baptism of Infants* 1:10; 1:24:34; 2:27:43 (A.D. 412)].

41. Confirmation

The sacrament of confirmation is referenced in biblical passages, including Acts 8:14–17, 9:17, 19:6, and Hebrews 6:2, which speak of a laying on of hands for the purpose of bestowing the Holy Spirit.

Hebrews 6:2 is especially important because it is not a narrative account of how confirmation was given and, thus, cannot be dismissed as something unique to the Apostolic Age. In fact, the passage refers to confirmation as an "elementary teaching," since confirmation, like baptism, is a sacrament of initiation into the Christian life.

We read: "Therefore let us leave the elementary teachings of Christ and go on to maturity, not laying again the foundation of repentance from acts that lead to death, and of faith in God, instruction about baptisms, the laying on of hands, the resurrection of the dead, and eternal judgment" (Heb 6:1–2). This passage encapsulates the Christian's journey toward heaven—repentance, faith, baptism, confirmation, resurrection, and judgment.

The "laying on of hands" mentioned in the passage is confirmation. The other kinds of the imposition of hands—for ordination and for healing—are not done to every Christian and would not be part of the basic teachings for the ordinary Christian's journey.

As the following passages show, the Church Fathers recognized confirmation, sometimes speaking of the imposition of hands, and sometimes of the anointing with oil that is part of the rite.

ST. THEOPHILUS OF ANTIOCH

[A]re you unwilling to be anointed with the oil of God? We are called Christians on this account, because we are anointed with the oil of God [*To Autolycus* 1:12 (c. A.D. 181)].

TERTULLIAN OF CARTHAGE

After this, when we have issued from the font, we are thoroughly anointed with a blessed unction—[a practice derived] from the old discipline, in which on entering the priesthood, men were anointed with oil from a horn, ever since Aaron was anointed by Moses. Thus Aaron is called "Christ," from the "chrism," which is "the unction"; which, when made spiritual, furnished an appropriate name for the Lord, because he was "anointed" with the

Spirit by God the Father; as written in the Acts: "For truly they were gathered together in this city against your holy Son whom you have anointed." Thus, too, in our case, the unction runs carnally, but profits spiritually; in the same way as the act of baptism is carnal, in that we are plunged in water, but the effect spiritual, in that we are freed from sins [Baptism 7 (c. A.D. 203)].

It would suffice to say, indeed, that there is not a soul that can at all procure salvation, except it believe while it is in the flesh, so true is it that the flesh is the very condition on which salvation hinges. . . . The flesh, indeed, is washed, that the soul may be cleansed; the flesh is anointed, that the soul may be consecrated; the flesh is signed (with the cross), that the soul may be fortified; the flesh is shadowed with the imposition of hands, that the soul may be illuminated by the Spirit; the flesh feeds on the body and blood of Christ, that the soul may fatten on its God. They cannot then be separated in their recompense when they are united in their service [Resurrection of the Flesh 8 (c. A.D. 210)].

ST. HIPPOLYTUS OF ROME

The bishop will then lay his hand upon them, invoking, "Lord God, you who have made these worthy of the removal of sins through the bath of regeneration, make them worthy to be filled with your Holy Spirit, grant to them your grace, that they might serve you according to your will, for to you is the glory, Father and Son with the Holy Spirit, in the holy Church, now and throughout the ages of the ages. Amen." After this he pours the oil into his hand, and laying his hand on each of their heads, says, "I anoint you with holy oil in God the Father Almighty, and Christ Jesus, and the Holy Spirit." Then, after sealing each of them on the forehead, he shall give them the kiss of peace and say, "The Lord be with you." And the one who has been baptized shall say, "And with your spirit." So shall he do to each one [Apostolic Tradition 21–22 (c. A.D. 215)].

ST. CYPRIAN OF CARTHAGE

[I]n the name of the same Christ, are not hands laid upon the baptized persons among them, for the reception of the Holy Spirit? [*Letters* 73:5 (A.D. 253)].

[O]ne is not born by the imposition of hands when he receives the Holy Spirit, but in baptism, that being already born, he may receive the Holy Spirit, even as it happened in the first man Adam. For first God formed him, and then breathed into his nostrils the breath of life. For the Spirit cannot be received, unless he who receives first has an existence. But . . . the birth of Christians is in baptism [ibid.].

It is also necessary that he who is baptized should be anointed; so that, having received the chrism, the anointing, he may be anointed of God, and have in him the grace of Christ [ibid., 69:2 (A.D. 255)].

But in respect of the assertion of some concerning those who had been baptized in Samaria, that when the apostles Peter and John came, only hands were imposed on them, that they might receive the Holy Spirit, yet that they were not re-baptized; we see that that place does not, dearest brother, touch the present case. For they who had believed in Samaria had believed with a true faith; and, in the Church that is one, and which alone can bestow the grace of baptism and remit sins, had been baptized by Philip the deacon, whom the same apostles had sent. And because they had obtained a legitimate and ecclesiastical baptism, there was no need that they should be baptized anymore, but that what was needed was performed by Peter and John; that prayer being made for them, and hands being imposed, the Holy Spirit should be invoked and poured out upon them, which now is done among us, so that they who are baptized in the Church are brought to the prelates of the Church, and by our prayers and by the imposition of hands obtain the Holy Spirit, and are perfected with the Lord's seal [ibid., 72:9 (c. A.D. 255)].

COUNCIL OF CARTHAGE OF 256

And in the Gospel our Lord Jesus Christ spoke with his divine voice, saying, "Except a man be born again of water and the Spirit, he cannot enter the kingdom of God" [Jn 3:5]. This is the Spirit that from the beginning was borne over the waters; for neither can the Spirit operate without the water, nor the water without the Spirit. Certain people interpret for themselves incorrectly when they say that by imposition of the hand they receive the Holy Spirit, and are thus received, when it is manifest that they ought to be born again in the Catholic Church by both sacraments [Council of Carthage (A.D. 256)].

TREATISE ON RE-BAPTISM

[I]t has been asked among the brethren what course ought specially to be adopted towards the persons of those who . . . baptized in heresy . . . and subsequently departing from their heresy, and fleeing as supplicants to the Church of God, should repent with their whole hearts, and only now perceiving the condemnation of their error, implore from the Church the help of salvation. . . . [A]ccording to the most ancient custom and ecclesiastical tradition, it would suffice, after that baptism that they have received outside the Church . . . that only hands should be laid upon them by the bishop for their reception of the Holy Spirit, and this imposition of hands would afford them the renewed and perfected seal of faith [*Treatise on Re-Baptism* 1 (c. A.D. 257)].

[B]y imposition of the bishop's hands the Holy Spirit is given to everyone who believes, as in the case of the Samaritans, after Philip's baptism, the apostles did to them by laying on of hands [Acts 8:14–17]; in this same way they conferred on them the Holy Spirit [ibid., 3].

ST. CYRIL OF JERUSALEM

[A]fter you had come up from the pool of the sacred streams, there was given an unction, the anti-type of that with which Christ was anointed; and this is the Holy Spirit. . . . But beware of supposing this to be plain ointment. For as the bread of the Eucharist, after the invocation of the Holy Spirit, is mere bread no longer, but the body of Christ, so also this holy ointment is no longer simple or common ointment after invocation, but it is Christ's gift of grace, and, by the advent of the Holy Spirit, is made fit to impart his divine nature. It is symbolically applied to your forehead and your other senses; and while your body is anointed with the visible ointment, your soul is sanctified by the Holy and life-giving Spirit. . . . For as Christ after his baptism, and the visitation of the Holy Spirit, went forth and vanquished the adversary, so you, after holy baptism and the mystical chrism, having put on the whole armor of the Holy Spirit, are to stand against the power of the adversary, and vanquish it, saying, I can do all things through Christ who strengthens me [Phil 4:13] [*Catechetical Lectures* 21:1, 3–4 (c. A.D. 350)]

[David says,] you have anointed my head with oil. With oil he anointed your head upon your forehead, for the seal that you have of God; that you may be made the engraving of the signet, holiness unto God [ibid., 22:7].

ST. SERAPION OF THMUIS

[Prayer for blessing the holy chrism:] "God of powers, aid of every soul that turns to you and comes under your powerful hand in your only-begotten. We beseech you, that through your divine and invisible power of our Lord and Savior Jesus Christ, you may effect in this chrism a divine and heavenly operation, so that those baptized and anointed in the tracing with it of the sign of the saving cross of the only-begotten . . . as if reborn and renewed through the bath of regeneration, may be made participants in the gift of the Holy Spirit and, confirmed by this seal, may remain firm and immovable, unharmed and inviolate" [*Sacramentary of Serapion* 25:1 (c. A.D. 350)].

COUNCIL OF LAODICEA

They who are baptized must after baptism be anointed with the heavenly chrism, and be partakers of the kingdom of Christ [Canon 48 (c. A.D. 362)].

ST. PACIAN OF BARCELONA

If, then, the power of both baptism and confirmation, greater by far than charisms, is passed on to the bishops, so too is the right of binding and loosing [*Three Letters to the Novatianist Sympronian* 1:6 (c. A.D. 383)].

APOSTOLIC CONSTITUTIONS

[H]ow dare any man speak against his bishop, by whom the Lord gave the Holy Spirit among you upon the laying on of his hands, by whom you have learned the sacred doctrines, and have known God, and have believed in Christ, by whom you were known of God, by whom you were sealed with the oil of gladness and the ointment of understanding, by whom you were declared to be the children of light, by whom the Lord in your illumination testified by the imposition of the bishop's hands [*Apostolic Constitutions* 2:4:32 (c. A.D. 400)].

AFRICAN CODE

Since in the former council it was decreed, as your unanimity remembers as well as I do, that those who as children were baptized by the Donatists, and not yet being able to know the pernicious character of their error, and afterward when they had come to the use of reason, had received the knowledge of the truth, abhorred their former error, and were received (in accordance with the ancient order) by the imposition of the hand into the Catholic Church of God spread throughout the world [Canon 57(61) (A.D. 419)].

42. The Real Presence

The doctrine of the Real Presence asserts that in the Holy Eucharist, Jesus is present—body and blood, soul and divinity—under the appearances of bread and wine. This teaching is based on a variety of Scriptural passages (see 1 Cor 10:16–17; 11:23–29; and, especially, Jn 6:32–71).

The early Church Fathers interpreted these passages literally. In summarizing their teaching on Christ's Real Presence, Protestant historian of the early Church J. N. D. Kelly writes: "Eucharistic teaching, it should be understood at the outset, was in general unquestioningly realist, i.e., the consecrated bread and wine were taken to be, and were treated and designated as, the Savior's body and blood" (*Early Christian Doctrines*, 440).

Kelly also writes:

> Ignatius roundly declares that . . . the bread is the flesh of Jesus, the cup his blood. Clearly he intends this realism to be taken strictly, for he makes it the basis of his argument against the Docetists' denial of the reality of Christ's body. . . . Irenaeus teaches that the bread and wine are really the Lord's body and blood. His witness is, indeed, all the more impressive because he produces it quite incidentally while refuting the Gnostic and Docetic rejection of the Lord's real humanity (197–98).

He continues:

> Hippolytus speaks of "the body and the blood" through which the Church is saved, and Tertullian regularly describes the bread as "the Lord's body." The converted pagan, he remarks, "feeds on the richness of the Lord's body, that is, on the Eucharist." The realism of his theology comes to light in the argument, based on the intimate relation of body and soul, that just as in baptism the body is washed with water so that the soul may be cleansed, so in the Eucharist "the flesh feeds upon Christ's body and blood so that the soul may be filled with God." Clearly his assumption is that the Savior's body and blood are as real as the baptismal water.

Cyprian's attitude is similar. Lapsed Christians who claim communion without doing penance, he declares, "do violence to his body and blood, a sin more heinous against the Lord with their hands and mouths than when they denied him." Later he expatiates on the terrifying consequences of profaning the sacrament, and the stories he tells confirm that he took the Real Presence literally (211–12).

ST. IGNATIUS OF ANTIOCH

I have no taste for corruptible food nor for the pleasures of this life. I desire the bread of God, which is the flesh of Jesus Christ, who was of the seed of David; and for drink I desire his blood, which is love incorruptible [*Letter to the Romans* 7 (c. A.D. 110)].

Take note of those who hold heterodox opinions on the grace of Jesus Christ, which have come to us, and see how contrary their opinions are to the mind of God. . . . They abstain from the Eucharist and from prayer because they do not confess that the Eucharist is the flesh of our Savior Jesus Christ, flesh that suffered for our sins and that the Father, in his goodness, raised up again. They who deny the gift of God are perishing in their disputes [*Letter to the Smyrnaeans* 6–7 (c. A.D. 110)].

ST. JUSTIN MARTYR

We call this food Eucharist, and no one else is permitted to partake of it, except one who believes our teaching to be true and who has been washed in the washing that is for the remission of sins and for regeneration [i.e., has received baptism] and is thereby living as Christ enjoined. For not as common bread nor common drink do we receive these; but since Jesus Christ our Savior was made incarnate by the word of God and had both flesh and blood for our salvation, so too, as we have been taught, the food that has been made into the Eucharist by the eucharistic prayer set down by him, and by the change of which our blood and flesh is nurtured, is both the flesh and the blood of that incarnated Jesus [*First Apology* 66 (c. A.D. 151)].

ST. IRENAEUS OF LYONS

If the Lord were from other than the Father, how could he rightly take bread, which is of the same creation as our own, and confess it to be his body and affirm that the mixture in the cup is his blood? [*Against Heresies* 4:33:2 (c. A.D. 189)].

He has declared the cup, a part of creation, to be his own blood, from which he causes our blood to flow; and the bread, a part of creation, he has established as his own body, from which he gives increase to our bodies. When the mixed cup [wine and water] and the baked bread receive the Word of God and become the Eucharist, the body of Christ, and from these the substance of our flesh is increased and supported, how can they say that the flesh is not capable of receiving the gift of God, which is eternal life—flesh that is nourished by the body and blood of the Lord, and is in fact a member of him? [ibid., 5:2:2–3].

ST. CLEMENT OF ALEXANDRIA

"Eat my flesh," [Jesus] says, "and drink my blood." The Lord supplies us with these intimate nutrients, he delivers over his flesh and pours out his blood, and nothing is lacking for the growth of his children [*Instructor of Children* 1:6 (c. A.D. 197)].

TERTULLIAN OF CARTHAGE

[T]here is not a soul that can at all procure salvation, except it believe while it is in the flesh, so true is it that the flesh is the very condition on which salvation hinges. And since the soul is, in consequence of its salvation, chosen to the service of God, it is the flesh that actually renders it capable of such service. The flesh, indeed, is washed [in baptism], that the soul may be cleansed. . . . The flesh is shadowed with the imposition of hands [in confirmation], that the soul may be illuminated by the Spirit; the flesh feeds [in the Eucharist] on the body and blood of Christ, that the soul may fatten on its God [*Resurrection of the Flesh* 8 (c. A.D. 210)].

ST. HIPPOLYTUS OF ROME

"And she has furnished her table": That denotes the promised knowledge of the Holy Trinity; it also refers to his honored and undefiled body and blood, which day by day are administered and offered sacrificially at the spiritual divine table, as a memorial of that first and ever-memorable table of the spiritual divine supper" [fragment from *On Proverbs* (c. A.D. 217)].

ORIGEN OF ALEXANDRIA

Formerly there was baptism in an obscure way. . . . Now, however, in full view, there is regeneration in water and in the Holy Spirit. Formerly, in an obscure way, there was manna for food; now, however, in full view, there is the true food, the flesh of the Word of God, as he himself says: "My flesh is true food, and my blood is true drink" [Jn 6:56] [*Homilies on Numbers* 7:2 (c. A.D. 249)].

ST. CYPRIAN OF CARTHAGE

[Paul] threatens, moreover, the stubborn and forward, and denounces them, saying, "Whosoever eats the bread or drinks the cup of the Lord unworthily, is guilty of the body and blood of the Lord" [1 Cor 11:27]. All these warnings being scorned and despised, [lapsed Christians will often take Communion] before their sin is expiated, before confession has been made of their crime, before their conscience has been purged by sacrifice and by the hand of the priest, before the offense of an angry and threatening Lord has been appeased, [and so] violence is done to his body and blood; and they sin against their Lord more with their hand and mouth than when they denied their Lord [*The Lapsed* (Treatise 3) 15–16 (A.D. 251)].

COUNCIL OF NICAEA I

It has come to the knowledge of the holy and great synod that, in some districts and cities, the deacons administer the Eucharist to the presbyters [i.e., priests], though neither canon nor custom permits that they who have no right to offer [the Eucharistic sacrifice] should give the body of Christ to them that do offer [it] [Canon 18 (A.D. 325)].

ST. APHRAHAT THE PERSIAN SAGE

After having spoken thus [at the Last Supper], the Lord rose up from the place where he had made the Passover and had given his body as food and his blood as drink, and he went with his disciples to the place where he was to be arrested. But he ate of his own body and drank of his own blood, while he was pondering on the dead. With his own hands the Lord presented his own body to be eaten, and before he was crucified he gave his blood as drink [*Demonstrations* 12:6 (c. A.D. 340)].

ST. CYRIL OF JERUSALEM

[A]s the bread and wine of the Eucharist before the invocation of the Trinity, which is holy and worthy of adoration, were simple bread and wine, after the invocation the bread becomes the body of Christ, and the wine the blood of Christ [*Catechetical Lectures* 19:7 (c. A.D. 350)].

Consider therefore the bread and the wine not as bare elements, for they are, according to the Lord's declaration, the body and blood of Christ; for even though sense suggests this to you, let faith establish you. Judge not the matter from the taste, but from faith be fully assured without misgiving, that the body and blood of Christ have been vouchsafed to you. . . . Having learned these things, and been fully assured that the seeming bread is not bread, though sensible to taste, but the body of Christ; and that the seeming wine is not wine, though the taste will have it so, but the blood of Christ; and that of this David sung of old, saying, "And bread strengthens man's heart, to make his face to shine with oil, strengthen your heart," by partaking of it as spiritual, and "make the face of your soul to shine" [ibid., 22:6, 9].

ST. AMBROSE OF MILAN

Perhaps you may be saying, "I see something else; how can you assure me that I am receiving the body of Christ?" It only remains for us to prove it. And how many are the examples we might use! . . . Christ is in that sacrament, because it is the body of Christ [*The Mysteries* 9:50, 58 (c. A.D. 390)].

THEODORE OF MOPSUESTIA

When [Christ] gave the bread he did not say, "This is the symbol of my body," but, "This is my body." In the same way, when he gave the cup of his blood he did not say, "This is the symbol of my blood," but, "This is my blood." For he wanted us to look upon the [eucharistic elements] after their reception of grace and the coming of the Holy Spirit not according to their nature, but to receive them as they are, the body and blood of our Lord. We ought . . . not to see [the elements] merely as bread and cup, but as the body and blood of the Lord, into which they were transformed by the descent of the Holy Spirit [*Catechetical Homilies* 5:1 (c. A.D. 410)].

ST. AUGUSTINE OF HIPPO

Christ was carried in his own hands when, referring to his own body, he said, "This is my body" [Mt 26:26]. For he carried that body in his hands [*Explanations of the Psalms* 33:1 (c. A.D. 405)].

I promised you [new Christians], who have now been baptized, a sermon in which I would explain the sacrament of the Lord's table. . . . The bread you see on the altar, having been sanctified by the word of God, is the body of Christ. The chalice, or rather, what is in the chalice, having been sanctified by the word of God, is the blood of Christ [*Sermons* 227 (c. A.D. 411)].

What you see is the bread and the chalice; that is what your own eyes report to you. But your faith obliges you to accept that the bread is the body of Christ and the chalice is the blood of Christ.

This has been said very briefly, which may perhaps be sufficient for faith; yet faith does not desire instruction [ibid., 272].

We will necessarily add this also. Proclaiming the death, according to the flesh, of the only-begotten Son of God, that is Jesus Christ, confessing his Resurrection from the dead, and his Ascension into heaven, we offer the unbloody sacrifice in the churches, and so go on to the mystical thanksgivings, and are sanctified, having received his holy flesh and the precious blood of Christ the Savior of us all. And not as common flesh do we receive it; God forbid: nor as of a man sanctified and associated with the Word according to the unity of worth, or as having a divine indwelling, but as truly the life-giving and very flesh of the Word himself. For he is the life according to his nature as God, and when he became united to his flesh, he made it also to be life-giving [Session 1, *Letter of Cyril to Nestorius* (A.D. 431)].

43. *The Sacrifice of the Mass*

The Eucharist is not only a commemorative meal but a sacrifice. The *Catechism of the Catholic Church* explains:

> Because it is the memorial of Christ's Passover, the Eucharist is also a sacrifice. The sacrificial character of the Eucharist is manifested in the very words of institution: "This is my body which is given for you" and "This cup which is poured out for you is the New Covenant in my blood." In the Eucharist Christ gives us the very body which he gave up for us on the cross, the very blood which he "poured out for many for the forgiveness of sins."
>
> The Eucharist is thus a sacrifice because it re-presents (makes present) the sacrifice of the cross, because it is its memorial and because it applies its fruit: [Christ], our Lord and God, was once and for all to offer himself to God the Father by his death on the altar of the cross, to accomplish there an everlasting redemption.

But because his priesthood was not to end with his death, at the Last Supper "on the night when he was betrayed," [he wanted] to leave to his beloved spouse the Church a visible sacrifice (as the nature of man demands) by which the bloody sacrifice which he was to accomplish once for all on the cross would be re-presented, its memory perpetuated until the end of the world, and its salutary power be applied to the forgiveness of the sins we daily commit.

The sacrifice of Christ and the sacrifice of the Eucharist are *one single sacrifice*: "The victim is one and the same: the same now offers through the ministry of priests, who then offered himself on the cross; only the manner of offering is different." "And since in this divine sacrifice which is celebrated in the Mass, the same Christ who offered himself once in a bloody manner on the altar of the cross is contained and is offered in an unbloody manner. . ." (CCC 1365–67).

The Church Fathers shared this faith in the sacrificial character of the Eucharist. Protestant early Church historian J. N. D. Kelly writes that in the early Church

> the Eucharist was regarded as the distinctively Christian sacri-fice. . . . Malachi's prediction (1:10–11) that the Lord would reject Jewish sacrifices and instead would have "a pure offering" made to him by the Gentiles in every place was seized upon by Christians as a prophecy of the Eucharist. *Didache* indeed actually applies the term *thusia*, or sacrifice, to the Eucharist. . . .
>
> It was natural for early Christians to think of the Eucharist as a sacrifice. The fulfillment of prophecy demanded a solemn Chris-tian offering, and the rite itself was wrapped in the sacrificial atmo-sphere with which our Lord invested the Last Supper. The words of institution, "Do this" (*touto poieite*), must have been charged with sacrificial overtones for second-century ears; Justin at any rate understood them to mean, "Offer this." . . . The bread and wine, moreover, are offered "for a memorial (*eis anamnasin*) of the pas-sion," a phrase which in view of his identification of them with the Lord's body and blood implies much more than an act of purely spiritual recollection (*Early Christian Doctrines*, 196–97).

DIDACHE

Assemble on the Lord's day, and break bread and offer the Eucharist; but first make confession of your faults, so that your sacrifice may be pure. Anyone who has a difference with his fellow is not to take part until he has been reconciled, so as to avoid profaning your sacrifice [Mt 5:23–24]. For this is the offering of which the Lord said, "Everywhere and always bring me a sacrifice that is undefiled, for I am a great king, says the Lord, and my name is the wonder of nations" [Mal 1:11, 14] [*Didache* 14 (c. A.D. 50)].

POPE ST. CLEMENT I

Our sin will not be small if we eject from the episcopate those who blamelessly and holily have offered its sacrifices. Blessed are those presbyters who have already finished their course, and who have obtained a fruitful and perfect release [*Letter to the Corinthians* 44:4–5 (A.D. 70)].

ST. IGNATIUS OF ANTIOCH

Take heed, then, to have but one Eucharist. For there is one flesh of our Lord Jesus Christ, and one cup to [show forth] the unity of his blood; one altar; as there is one bishop, along with the presbytery and deacons, my fellow servants: that so, whatsoever you do, you may do it according to [the will of] God [*Letter to the Philadelphians* 4 (c. A.D. 110)].

ST. JUSTIN MARTYR

Hence God speaks by the mouth of Malachi, one of the twelve [prophets], as I said before, about the sacrifices at that time presented by you: "I have no pleasure in you, says the Lord; and I will not accept your sacrifices at your hands: for, from the rising of the sun unto the going down of the same, my name has been glorified among the Gentiles, and in every place incense is offered to my name, and a pure offering: for my name is great among the Gentiles, says the Lord: but you profane it" [Mal 1:10–12]. [So] he then speaks of those Gentiles, namely us, who in every place offer sacrifices to him, that is, the bread of the Eucharist, and also the cup of the Eucharist [*Dialogue with Trypho* 41 (c. A.D. 155)].

ST. IRENAEUS OF LYONS

He took from among creation bread, and gave thanks, saying, "This is my body." The cup likewise, which is from among the creation to which we belong, he confessed to be his blood. He taught the new sacrifice of the new covenant, of which Malachi, one of the twelve [minor] prophets, had signified beforehand: "You do not do my will, says the Lord Almighty, and I will not accept a sacrifice at your hands. For from the rising of the sun to its setting my name is glorified among the Gentiles, and in every place incense is offered to my name, and a pure sacrifice; for great is my name among the Gentiles, says the Lord Almighty" [Mal 1:10–11]. By these words he makes it plain that the former people will cease to make offerings to God; but that in every place sacrifice will be offered to him, and indeed, a pure one, for his name is glorified among the Gentiles [*Against Heresies* 4:17:5 (c. A.D. 189)].

ST. CYPRIAN OF CARTHAGE

For if Jesus Christ, our Lord and God, is himself the chief priest of God the Father, and has first offered himself a sacrifice to the Father, and has commanded this to be done in commemoration of himself, certainly that priest truly discharges the office of Christ, who imitates what Christ did; and he then offers a true and full sacrifice in the Church to God the Father, when he proceeds to offer it according to what he sees Christ himself to have offered [*Letters* 62:14 (A.D. 253)].

ST. SERAPION OF THMUIS

Accept therewith our hallowing too, as we say, "Holy, holy, holy Lord Sabaoth, heaven and earth are full of your glory." Heaven is full, and full is the earth, with your magnificent glory, Lord of virtues. Full also is this sacrifice, with your strength and your communion; for to you we offer this living sacrifice, this unbloody oblation [*Sacramentary of Serapion* 13:3 (c. A.D. 350)].

ST. CYRIL OF JERUSALEM

Then having sanctified ourselves by these spiritual hymns, we beseech the merciful God to send forth his Holy Spirit upon the gifts lying before him; that he may make the bread the body of Christ, and the wine the blood of Christ; for whatever the Holy Spirit has touched is surely sanctified and changed. Then, after the spiritual sacrifice, the bloodless service, is completed, over that sacrifice of propitiation we entreat God for the common peace of the Churches, for the welfare of the world; for kings; for soldiers and allies; for the sick; for the afflicted; and, in a word, for all who stand in need of succor we all pray and offer this sacrifice [*Catechetical Lectures* 23:7–8 (c. A.D. 350)].

ST. GREGORY OF NAZIANZ

[C]ease not both to pray and to plead for me when you draw down the Word by your word, when with a bloodless cutting you sever the body and blood of the Lord, using your voice for the sword [*Letter to Amphilochius* 171 (c. A.D. 383)].

ST. AMBROSE OF MILAN

We saw the prince of priests coming to us, we saw and heard him offering his blood for us. We follow, because we are able, being priests, and we offer the sacrifice on behalf of the people. Even if we are of but little merit, still, in the sacrifice, we are honorable. Even if Christ is not now seen as the one who offers the sacrifice, nevertheless it is he himself who is offered in sacrifice here on earth when the body of Christ is offered. Indeed, to offer himself he is made visible in us, he whose word makes holy the sacrifice that is offered [*Commentaries on Twelve Psalms of David* 38:25 (c. A.D. 389)].

ST. JOHN CHRYSOSTOM

For when you see the Lord sacrificed, and laid upon the altar,
and the priest standing and praying over the victim, and all the
worshippers empurpled with that precious blood, can you then
think that you are still among men, and standing upon the earth?
Are you not, on the contrary, immediately translated to heaven?
[*The Priesthood* 3:4 (c. A.D. 388)].

Reverence now, oh reverence, this table of which we all are partakers! [1 Cor 10:16–18.] Christ, who was slain for us, the victim
who is placed thereon! [*Homilies on Romans* 8 (c. A.D. 391)].

"The cup of blessing that we bless, is it not a communion of
the blood of Christ?" Very persuasively spoke he, and awfully.
For what he says is this: "This that is in the cup is what flowed
from his side, and of that do we partake." But he called it a cup
of blessing, because holding it in our hands, we so exalt him in
our hymn, wondering, astonished at his unspeakable gift, blessing him, among other things, for the pouring out of this self-same
draught that we might not abide in error: and not only for the
pouring it out, but also for imparting it to us all. "Wherefore if
you desire blood," says he, "redden not the altar of idols with
the slaughter of brute beasts, but my altar with my blood." Tell
me, what can be more tremendous than this? [*Homilies on First
Corinthians* 24:3 (c. A.D. 392)].

And in the old covenant, because they were in an imperfect state,
the blood they used to offer to idols he himself submitted to receive, that he might separate them from those idols; which was
a proof of his unspeakable affection: but here he transferred the
service to what is far more awful and glorious, changing the very
sacrifice itself, and instead of the slaughter of irrational creatures,
commanding to offer up himself [ibid.].

What then? Do not we offer every day? We offer indeed, but making a remembrance of his death, and this [remembrance] is one

and not many. How is it one and not many? Because that [sacrifice] was once for all offered, [and] carried into the holy of holies. This is a figure of that [sacrifice] and a remembrance. For we always offer the same, not one sheep now and tomorrow another, but always the same thing: so that the sacrifice is one. And yet by this reasoning, since the offering is made in many places, are there many Christs? But Christ is one everywhere, being complete here and complete there also, one body. Even while offered in many places, he is one body and not many bodies; so also [he is] one sacrifice [*Homilies on Hebrews* 17:6 (c. A.D. 403)].

ST. AUGUSTINE OF HIPPO

Was not Christ once for all offered up in his own person as a sacrifice? And yet, is he not likewise offered up in the sacrament as a sacrifice, not only in the special solemnities of Easter, but also daily among our congregations; so that the man who, being questioned, answers that he is offered as a sacrifice in that ordinance, declares what is strictly true? [*Letters* 98:9 (A.D. 408)].

For when he says in another book, which is called Ecclesiastes, "There is no good for a man except that he should eat and drink" [Qo 2:24], what can he be more credibly understood to say [prophetically] than what belongs to the participation of this table, which the mediator of the New Testament himself, the priest after the order of Melchizedek, furnishes with his own body and blood? For that sacrifice has succeeded all the sacrifices of the Old Testament, which were slain as a shadow of what was to come. . . . Because, instead of all these sacrifices and oblations, his body is offered and is served up to the partakers of it [*City of God* 17:20 (c. A.D. 419)].

ST. SECHNALL OF IRELAND

[St. Patrick] proclaims boldly to the [Irish] tribes the name of the Lord, to whom he gives the eternal grace of the washing of salvation; for their offenses he prays daily unto God; for them also he offers up to God worthy sacrifices [*Hymn in Praise of St. Patrick* 13 (c. A.D. 444)].

44. Confession

Are all our sins—past, present, and future—forgiven once and for all when we become Christians? Not according to the Bible, or the early Church Fathers. Scripture nowhere states that our future sins are forgiven; instead, it teaches us to pray for ongoing forgiveness: "And forgive us our debts, as we also have forgiven our debtors" (Mt 6:12).

The means by which God forgives sins after baptism is confession: "If we confess our sins, he is faithful and just, and will forgive our sins and cleanse us from all unrighteousness" (1 Jn 1:9). Minor or venial sins can be confessed directly to God, but for grave or mortal sins (see chapter 31), which destroy the spiritual life of the soul, God has instituted a different means for obtaining forgiveness: the sacrament known as confession, penance, or reconciliation. Since it is not possible to confess all our many daily faults, sacramental reconciliation is required only for mortal sins—but it is required (at least for those who are able to go to confession), or Christ would not have commanded it.

This sacrament is rooted in the mission God gave to Christ in his capacity as the Son of man to forgive sins (see Mt 9:6). Thus, the crowds who witnessed this new power "glorified God, who had given such authority *to men*" (Mt 9:8; note the plural "men"). After his Resurrection, Jesus passed on his mission to forgive sins to his ministers, telling them, "As the Father has sent me, even so I send you. . . . Receive the Holy Spirit. If you forgive the sins of any, they are forgiven; if you retain the sins of any, they are retained" (Jn 20:21–23).

Over time, the forms in which the sacrament has been administered have changed. In the early Church, publicly known sins (such as apostasy) were often confessed openly in church, though private confession to a priest was an option for privately committed sins. Still, confession was not just something done in silence to God alone, but something done "in church," as *Didache* (c. A.D. 50) indicates.

Penances also tended to be performed before rather than after absolution, and they were much more strict than those of today (ten years' penance for abortion, for example, was common in the early Church).

But the principles of the sacrament have always been the same, as the following quotations reveal. Of special significance is the recognition that confession and absolution must be received by a sinner before receiving Holy Communion, for "whoever . . . eats the bread or drinks the cup of the Lord in an unworthy manner will be guilty of profaning the body and blood of the Lord" (1 Cor 11:27).

DIDACHE

In the church you shall acknowledge your transgressions, and you shall not come near for your prayer with an evil conscience. This is the way of life. . . . But every Lord's day gather yourselves together and break bread and give thanksgiving after having confessed your transgressions, that your sacrifice may be pure [Didache 4, 14 (c. A.D. 50)].

LETTER OF BARNABAS

You shall judge righteously. You shall not make a schism, but you shall pacify those that contend by bringing them together. You shall confess your sins. You shall not go to prayer with an evil conscience. This is the way of light [Letter of Barnabas 19 (c. A.D. 75)].

ST. IGNATIUS OF ANTIOCH

And as many as shall return into the unity of the Church in the exercise of repentance, these, too, shall belong to God, that they may live according to Jesus Christ [Letter to the Philadelphians 3 (c. A.D. 110)].

For where there is division and wrath, God does not dwell. To all those who repent, the Lord grants forgiveness, if they turn in penitence to the unity of God, and to communion with the bishop [ibid., 8].

ST. IRENAEUS OF LYONS

[The Gnostic disciples of Marcus] have deluded many women, who have their consciences seared as with a hot iron [2 Tm 3:6]. Some of them, indeed, make a public confession of their sins; but others are ashamed to do this, and in a tacit kind of way, despairing of [attaining to] the life of God, have, some of them, apostatized altogether; while others hesitate between the two courses [*Against Heresies* 1:13:7 (c. A.D. 189)].

TERTULLIAN OF CARTHAGE

Yet most men either shun this work, as a public exposure of themselves, or else defer it from day to day. I presume [they are] more mindful of modesty than salvation; just like men who, having contracted some malady in the more private parts of the body, avoid the probing of physicians, and so perish of their own bashfulness. [*Repentance* 10 (c. A.D. 203)].

ST. HIPPOLYTUS OF ROME

After this, one of the bishops present, at the request of all, laying his hand on him who is ordained bishop, shall pray this way: O God and Father of our Lord Jesus Christ . . . pour forth the power that is from you, of "the princely Spirit" that you delivered to your beloved Child, Jesus Christ, and that he bestowed on your holy apostles, who established the Church that hallows you everywhere, for the endless glory and praise of your name. Father, "who knows the hearts [of all]" grant this servant, who you have chosen for the episcopate, to feed your holy flock and serve as your high priest blamelessly night and day, and unceasingly turn away wrath from your face and offer to you the gifts of the holy Church. And that by the high priestly Spirit he may have authority "to forgive sins" according to your command [*Apostolic Tradition* 2–3 (c. A.D. 215)].

ORIGEN OF ALEXANDRIA

In addition to these there is also a seventh [remission of sins], but it is hard and laborious: the remission of sins through penance, when the sinner washes his pillow in tears [Ps 6:7], when his tears are his nourishment day and night [Ps 41:4], and when he does not shrink from declaring his sin to a priest of the Lord and from seeking medicine [*Homilies on Leviticus* 2:4 (c. A.D. 249)].

ST. CYPRIAN OF CARTHAGE

Sinners may do penance for a set time, and according to the rules of discipline come to public confession, and by imposition of the hand of the bishop and clergy receive the right of Communion. [But now some] with their time [of penance] still unfulfilled . . . they are admitted to Communion, and their name is presented; and while the penitence is not yet performed, confession is not yet made, the hands of the bishop and clergy are not yet laid upon them, the Eucharist is given to them; although it is written, "Whosoever shall eat the bread and drink the cup of the Lord unworthily, shall be guilty of the body and blood of the Lord" [1 Cor 11:27] [*Letters* 9:2 (A.D. 250)].

Moreover, how much are they both greater in faith and better in their fear, who . . . with grief and simplicity confess this very thing to God's priests, and make the conscientious avowal, put off from them the load of their minds . . . I entreat you, beloved brethren, that each one should confess his own sin, while he who has sinned is still in this world, while his confession may be received, while the satisfaction and remission made by the priests are pleasing to the Lord [ibid., 28–29].

And do not think, dearest brother, that either the courage of the brethren will be lessened, or that martyrdoms will fail for this cause, that repentance is relaxed to the lapsed, and that the hope of peace is offered to the penitent. . . . For to adulterers even a time of repentance is granted by us, and peace is given [ibid., 51:20 (A.D. 252)].

But I wonder that some are so obstinate as to think that repentance is not to be granted to the lapsed, or to suppose that pardon is to be denied to the penitent, when it is written, "Remember whence you are fallen, and repent, and do the first works" [Rv 2:5], which certainly is said to him who has fallen, and whom the Lord exhorts to rise up again by his deeds [of penance], because it is written, "Alms deliver from death" [Tb 12:9] (ibid., 51:22).

Also, the apostle testifies, and says, "You cannot drink the cup of the Lord and the cup of devils; you cannot be partakers of the Lord's table and of the table of devils." He threatens, moreover, the stubborn and disobedient, and denounces them, saying, "Whosoever eateth the bread or drinketh the cup of the Lord unworthily, is guilty of the body and blood of the Lord." All these warnings being scorned and contemned, before their sin is expiated, before confession has been made of their crime, before their conscience has been purged by sacrifice and by the hand of the priest, before the offense of an angry and threatening Lord has been appeased, violence is done to his body and blood; and they sin now against their Lord more with their hand and mouth than when they denied their Lord [*The Lapsed* 15–16 (A.D. 251)].

ST. APHRAHAT THE PERSIAN SAGE

And to you [priests] also, disciples of our illustrious physician, it is fitting that you should not withhold healing from him who needs healing. Whoever shows his wound to you, give him the medicine of penitence; and whoever is ashamed to show his disease, you shall exhort him not to conceal from you, and when he has revealed to you do not publish it, lest by means of it the innocent should be considered as debtors by enemies and those who hate them [*Demonstrations* 7:4 (c. A.D. 340)].

ST. BASIL OF CAESAREA

It is necessary to confess our sins to those to whom the dispensation of God's mysteries has been entrusted. Those doing penance of old are found to have done it before the saints. It is written in the Gospel that they confessed their sins to John the Baptist; but in Acts they confessed to the apostles, by whom also all were baptized [*Rules Briefly Treated* 288 (c. A.D. 375)].

ST. JOHN CHRYSOSTOM

For they who inhabit the earth and make their abode are entrusted with the administration of things that are in heaven, and have received an authority that God has not given to angels or archangels. For it has not been said to them, "Whatsoever you shall bind on earth shall be bound in heaven, and whatsoever you shall loose on earth shall be loosed in heaven" [Mt 18:18]. They who rule on earth have authority to bind, but only the body: whereas this binding lays hold of the soul and penetrates the heavens; and what priests do here below God ratifies above, and the master confirms the sentence of his servants. For indeed what is it but all manner of heavenly authority has he given them when he says, "Whose sins you remit they are remitted, and whose sins you retain they are retained?" [Jn 20:23]. What authority could be greater than this? "The Father has committed all judgment to the Son?" [Jn 5:22]. But I see it all put into the hands of these men by the Son. For they have been conducted to this dignity as if they were already translated to heaven [*The Priesthood* 3:5 (c. A.D. 388)].

ST. AMBROSE OF MILAN

For the Lord willed that the power of binding and loosing should be alike, and each sanctioned by a similar condition. So he who has not the power to loose has not the power to bind. For as, according to the Lord's word, he who has the power to bind also has the power to loose, their teaching destroys itself, because they who deny that they have the power of loosing ought also to deny that of binding. For how can the one be allowed and the other disallowed? It is plain and evident that either each is allowed or each is disallowed in the case of those to whom each has been given. Each is allowed to the Church, neither to heresy, for this power has been entrusted to priests alone [*Penance* 1:2:7 (c. A.D. 388)].

ST. JEROME

If the serpent, the devil, bites someone secretly, he infects that person with the venom of sin. And if the one who has been bit-

ten keeps silence and does not do penance, and does not want
to confess his wound . . . then his brother and his master, who
have the word [of absolution] that will cure him, cannot very well
assist him [*Commentary on Ecclesiastes* 10:11 (c. A.D. 388)].

ST. AUGUSTINE OF HIPPO

When you have been baptized, hold fast to a good life in the commandments of God, that you may guard your baptism even to the
end. I do not tell you that you will live here without sin; but they
are venial, without which this life is not. For the sake of all sins
was baptism provided; for the sake of light sins, without which we
cannot be, was prayer provided. What has the prayer? "Forgive us
our debts, as we also forgive our debtors." Once for all we have
washing in baptism, every day we have washing in prayer. Only,
do not commit those things for which you must be separated from
Christ's body: which be far from you! For those whom you have
seen doing penance, who have committed heinous things, either
adulteries or some enormous crimes: for these they do penance.
Because if theirs had been light sins, daily prayer would suffice
to blot these out. . . . In three ways then are sins remitted in the
Church; by baptism, by prayer, by the greater humility of penance
[*Sermon to Catechumens on the Creed* 15, 16 (c. A.D. 395)].

45. Bishop, Priest, and Deacon

The sacrament of holy orders is conferred in three ranks of clergy:
bishops, priests, and deacons.

Bishops (*episcopoi*) could have the care of multiple congregations—all those in a given city or region—and appoint, ordain,
and discipline priests and deacons. They were sometimes called
"evangelists" in the New Testament. Examples of first-century
bishops include Timothy and Titus (1 Tm 5:19–22; 2 Tm 4:5; Ti
1:5).

Priests (*presbuteroi*) are also known as "presbyters" or "elders."
In fact, the English term "priest" is simply a contraction of the

Greek word *presbuteros*. They have the responsibility of teaching, governing, and providing the sacraments in particular congregations (1 Tm 5:17; Jas 5:14–15).

Deacons (*diakonoi*) assist the bishops and are responsible for teaching and administering certain Church tasks, such as the distribution of food (Acts 6:1–6).

In the Apostolic Age, the terms for these offices were still somewhat fluid. Sometimes a term would be used in a technical sense as the title of an office, sometimes not, and this informal use of terms exists even today, as when a Protestant pastor who is actually an elder is called a "minister" (Greek, *diakonos*), though he is not a member of his congregation's deacon board.

In the Apostolic Age Paul sometimes described himself as a *diakonos* ("servant" or "minister"; see also 2 Cor 3:6, 6:4, 11:23; Eph 3:7), though he was an apostle and thus held an office much higher than that of deacon. On another occasion Peter described himself as a "fellow elder" (1 Pt 5:1), though being an apostle, he also had a much higher office than that of an ordinary elder.

The term for bishop, *episcopos* ("overseer"), was as fluid. Sometimes it seems to designate the overseer of a congregation (the priest), sometimes the person who was the overseer of all the congregations in a city or area (the bishop or evangelist), and sometimes the highest-ranking clergyman in the local church— who could be an apostle, if one were staying there at the time.

By the beginning of the second century the terms had achieved the fixed form in which they are used today to designate the three offices.

As the following quotations illustrate, the early Church Fathers recognized all three offices and regarded them as essential to the Church's structure. Especially significant are the letters of Ignatius, bishop of Antioch, who traveled from his home city to Rome, where he was executed around A.D. 110. On the way he wrote letters to the churches he passed. Each of them possessed the same threefold ministry. Without it, Ignatius said, a group could not be called a church.

ST. IGNATIUS OF ANTIOCH

Since, then, I have had the privilege of seeing you, through Damas your most worthy bishop, and through your worthy presbyters Bassus and Apollonius, and through my fellow-servant the deacon Sotio, whose friendship may I ever enjoy, because he is subject to the bishop as to the grace of God, and to the presbytery as to the law of Jesus Christ [*Letter to the Magnesians* 2 (c. A.D. 110)].

Since therefore I have, in the persons before mentioned, beheld the whole multitude of you in faith and love, I exhort you to try to do all things with a divine harmony, while your bishop presides in the place of God, and your presbyters in the place of the assembly of the apostles, along with your deacons, who are most dear to me, and are entrusted with the ministry of Jesus Christ, who was with the Father before the beginning of time, and in the end was revealed. Do all then, imitating the same divine conduct, respect one another, and let no one look upon his neighbor after the flesh, but continually love each other in Jesus Christ. Let nothing exist among you that may divide you; but be united with your bishop, and those that preside over you, as a type and evidence of your immortality [ibid., 6].

Study, therefore, to be established in the doctrines of the Lord and the apostles, so that all things, whatever you do, may prosper in the flesh and spirit; in faith and love; in the Son, and in the Father, and in the Spirit; in the beginning and in the end; with your most admirable bishop, and the well-compacted spiritual crown of your presbytery, and the deacons who are according to God. Be subject to the bishop, and to one another, as Jesus Christ to the Father, according to the flesh, and the apostles to Christ, and to the Father, and to the Spirit; that so there may be a union both fleshly and spiritual [ibid., 13].

For, since you are subject to the bishop as to Jesus Christ, you appear to me to live not after the manner of men, but according to Jesus Christ, who died for us, so that by believing in his death

you may escape from death. It is therefore necessary that, as you
indeed do, without the bishop you should do nothing, but should
also be subject to the presbytery, as to the apostle of Jesus Christ,
who is our hope, in whom, if we live, we shall [at last] be found.
It is fitting also that the deacons, as [the ministers] of the mysteries of Jesus Christ, should in every respect be pleasing to all.
For they are not ministers of meat and drink, but servants of the
Church of God. They are bound, therefore, to avoid all grounds
of accusation [against them], as they would do fire [*Letter to the
Trallians* 2 (c. A.D. 110)].

In like manner, let all reverence the deacons as an appointment of
Jesus Christ, and the bishop as Jesus Christ, who is the Son of the
Father, and the presbyters as the sanhedrin of God, and assembly
of the apostles. Apart from these, there is no Church. Concerning
all this, I am persuaded that you are of the same opinion. For I have
received the manifestation of your love, and still have it with me,
in your bishop, whose very appearance is highly instructive, and
his meekness in itself a power; whom I imagine even the ungodly
must reverence, seeing they are also pleased that I do not spare
myself. But shall I, when permitted to write on this point, reach
such a height of self-esteem, that though being a condemned man,
I should issue commands to you as if I were an apostle? [ibid., 3].

He that is within the altar is pure, but he that is without is not
pure; that is, he who does anything apart from the bishop, and
presbytery, and deacons, such a man is not pure in his conscience
[ibid., 7].

For though some would have deceived me according to the flesh,
yet the Spirit, as being from God, is not deceived. For it knows
both from where it comes and where it goes [Jn 3:8], and detects
the secrets [of the heart]. For, when I was among you, I cried, I
spoke with a loud voice: Give heed to the bishop, and to the presbytery and deacons. Now, some suspected me of having spoken
thus, as knowing beforehand the division caused among you by

some. But he is my witness, for whose sake I am in bonds, that I got no intelligence from any man. But the Spirit proclaimed these words: Do nothing without the bishop; keep your bodies as the temples of God; love unity; avoid divisions; be the followers of Jesus Christ, even as he is of his Father [*Letter to the Philadelphians* 7 (c. A.D. 110)].

ST. CLEMENT OF ALEXANDRIA

Innumerable commands such as these are written in the holy Bible pertaining to chosen persons, some to presbyters, some to bishops, some to deacons, others to widows, of whom we shall have another opportunity of speaking. Many things spoken in enigmas, many in parables, may benefit those who fall in with them. But it is not my province, says the instructor, to teach these any longer. But we need a teacher of the exposition of those sacred words, to whom we must direct our steps [*Instructor of Children* 3:12 (c. A.D. 197)].

[T]he grades here in the Church, of bishops, presbyters, deacons, are imitations of the angelic glory, and of the economy that, the Scriptures say, awaits those who, following the footsteps of the apostles, have lived in perfection of righteousness according to the gospel [*Miscellanies* 6:13 (c. A.D. 207)].

ST. HIPPOLYTUS OF ROME

When a deacon is to be ordained he is chosen after the fashion of those things said above, the bishop alone in like manner imposing his hands upon him as we have prescribed. In the ordaining of a deacon, this is the reason why the bishop alone is to impose his hands upon him: he is not ordained to the priesthood, but to serve the bishop and to fulfill the bishop's command. He has no part in the council of the clergy, but is to attend to his own duties and is to acquaint the bishop with such matter as are needful. He does not receive that Spirit which the presbytery possesses and in which the presbyters share. He receives only what is entrusted to him under the bishop.

For this reason, then, the bishop shall ordain a deacon. On a presbyter, however, let the presbyters impose their hands because of the common and like Spirit of the clergy. Even so, the presbyter has only the power to receive, and has not the power to give. That is why a presbyter does not ordain the clergy; for at the ordaining of a presbyter, he but seals while the bishop ordains.

Over a deacon, then, let the bishop speak thus:

"O God, you who have created all and put it in order by your Word; Father of our Lord Jesus Christ, whom you sent to minister to your will and to make clear to us your desires, give the Holy Spirit of grace and earnestness and diligence to this your servant, whom you have chosen to serve your Church and to offer in your holy places the gifts which are offered to you offered by your chosen high priests, so that he may serve with a pure heart and without blame, and that, ever giving praise to you, he may be accounted by your good will as worthy of this high office: through your Son Jesus Christ our Lord, through whom be glory and honor to you, the Father and the Son with the Holy Spirit, both now and through the ages. Amen" [*Apostolic Tradition* 9 (c. A.D. 215)].

ORIGEN OF ALEXANDRIA

Not fornication only, but even marriages make us unfit for ecclesiastical honors; for neither a bishop, nor a presbyter, nor a deacon, nor a widow is able to be twice married [*Homilies on Luke* 17 (c. A.D. 235)].

COUNCIL OF ELVIRA

Bishops, presbyters, and deacons may not leave their own places for the sake of commerce, nor are they to be traveling about the provinces, frequenting the markets for their own profit. Certainly for the procuring of their own necessities they can send a freedman or a hireling or a friend or whomever: but if they wish to engage in business, let them do so within the province [Canon 19 (c. A.D. 300)].

COUNCIL OF NICAEA I

It has come to the knowledge of the holy and great synod that, in some districts and cities, the deacons administer the Eucharist to the presbyters, though neither canon nor custom permits that they who have no right to offer should give the body of Christ to them that do offer. And this has also been made known, that certain deacons now touch the Eucharist even before the bishops. Let all such practices be utterly done away with, and let the deacons remain within their own bounds, knowing that they are the ministers of the bishop and the inferiors of the presbyters. Let them receive the Eucharist according to their order, after the presbyters, and let either the bishop or the presbyter administer to them [Canon 18 (A.D. 325)].

ST. JOHN CHRYSOSTOM

[In Philippians 1:1 Paul says] "Paul and Timothy, servants of Christ Jesus, to all the saints in Christ Jesus who are at Philippi, fellow bishops and deacons: Grace to you, and peace, from God our Father, and the Lord Jesus Christ." Here, as writing to those of equal honor, he does not set down his rank of teacher, but another, and that a great one. And what is that? He calls himself a "servant," and not an apostle. For great truly is this rank too, and the sum of all good things, to be a servant of Christ, and not merely to be called so. "The servant of Christ" is truly a free man in respect to sin, and being a genuine servant, he is not a servant to any other, since then he would not be Christ's servant, but by halves. And in again writing to the Romans also, he says, "Paul, a servant of Jesus Christ" [Rom 1:1]. But writing to the Corinthians and to Timothy he calls himself an "apostle." Why is this? Not because they were superior to Timothy. Far from it. But rather he honors them, and shows them attention, beyond all others to whom he wrote. For he also bears witness to great virtue in them. For besides, there indeed he was about to order many things, and therefore assumed his rank as an apostle. But here he gives them no injunctions but such as they could perceive of themselves.

"To the saints in Christ Jesus who are at Philippi." Since it was likely that the Jews too would call themselves "saints" from the first oracle, when they were called a "holy people, a people for God's own possession" [Ex 19:6; Dt 7:6, etc.]; for this reason he added, "to the saints in Christ Jesus." For these alone are holy, and those henceforward profane. "To the fellow bishops and deacons." What is this? Were there several bishops of one city? Certainly not; but he called the presbyters so. For then they still interchanged the titles, and the bishop was called a deacon. For this reason in writing to Timothy, he said, "Fulfill your ministry," when he was a bishop. For that he was a bishop appears by his saying to him, "Lay hands hastily on no man" [1 Tm 5:22]. And again, "Which was given you with the laying on of the hands of the presbytery" [1 Tm 4:14]. Yet presbyters would not have laid hands on a bishop [*Homilies on Philippians* 1 (c. A.D. 402)].

ST. PATRICK

I, Patrick, the sinner, am the most rustic and the least of all the faithful . . . had for my father Calpornius, a deacon, a son of Potitus, a priest, who belonged to the village of Bannavem Taberniae. . . . At that time I was barely sixteen years of age . . . and I was led into captivity in Ireland with many thousands of persons, in accordance with our desserts, for we turned away from God, and kept not his commandments, and were not obedient to our priests, who were wont to admonish us for our salvation [*Confession of St. Patrick* 1 (c. A.D. 452)].

I, Patrick, the sinner, unlearned as everybody knows, avow that I have been established a bishop in Ireland. Most assuredly I believe that I have received from God what I am. And so I dwell in the midst of barbarous heaths, a stranger and an exile for the love of God [*Letter to the Soldiers of Coroticus* 1 (c. A.D. 452)].

46. Women Priests?

Can women be ordained to the priesthood? This question has been much debated in the modern world, and the Church has always answered in the negative. The basis for this is in the New Testament and in the writings of the Church Fathers.

In the first century women could publicly pray and prophesy in church (1 Cor 11:1–16), but they could not be clergy. This was not simply a matter of cultural conditioning. There were priestesses all over the Roman world, and if Jesus had intended the Church to confer this office on women, he would have ordained women. He showed himself unconstrained by other cultural expectations —indeed, he challenged and overturned numerous ideas and institutions, at times shocking people.

Christ's choice not to ordain women, not even his sinless Mother, has thus been taken by the Church to be definitive.

The quotations from the Church Fathers indicate that women played an active role in the Church in the age of the Fathers— when there were orders of virgins, widows, and deaconesses— and they reveal that they were not ordained.

In 1994 Pope John Paul II declared that the Church does not have the power to ordain women, stating,

> Although the teaching that priestly ordination is to be reserved to men alone has been preserved by the constant and universal tradition of the Church and firmly taught by the magisterium in its more recent documents, at the present time in some places it is nonetheless considered still open to debate, or the Church's judgment that women are not to be admitted to ordination is considered to have a merely disciplinary force. Wherefore, in order that all doubt may be removed regarding a matter of great importance, a matter which pertains to the Church's divine constitution itself, in virtue of my ministry of confirming the brethren (see Lk 22:32) I declare that the Church has no authority whatsoever to confer priestly ordination on women and that this judgment is to be definitively held by all the Church's faithful (*Ordinatio Sacerdotalis* 4).

The following year the Congregation for the Doctrine of the Faith added that this teaching "requires definitive assent, since, founded on the written Word of God, and from the beginning constantly preserved and applied in the tradition of the Church, it has been set forth infallibly by the ordinary and universal magisterium" (*Responsum ad dubium* of October 25, 1995).

The following quotations from the Fathers constitute part of the Tradition on which this infallible teaching rests. The role of women was different in society and in the Church in the age of the Fathers than it is now, but the following quotations illustrate the Fathers' rejection of the idea that women should fulfill the roles of ordained clergy.

ST. IRENAEUS OF LYONS

[The heretic Marcus], handing mixed cups to the women, bids them to consecrate these in his presence. When this has been done, he produces another cup of much larger size than the one the deluded woman has consecrated, and pouring from the smaller one consecrated by the woman into the one brought forward by himself, he at the same time pronounces these words, "May that Charis who is before all things, and who transcends all knowledge and speech, fill your inner man, and multiply in you her own knowledge, by sowing the grain of mustard seed in you as in good soil." Repeating certain other similar words, and thus goading on the wretched woman [to madness], he then appears a worker of wonders when the large cup is seen to have been filled out of the small one, so as even to overflow by what has been obtained from it. By accomplishing several other similar things, he has completely deceived many, and drawn them away after him [*Against Heresies* 1:13:2 (c. A.D. 189)].

TERTULLIAN OF CARTHAGE

[I]t matters not to them, however different their treatment of subjects, provided that they can conspire together to storm the citadel of the one truth. All are puffed up, all offer you knowledge. Their catechumens are perfect before they are fully taught. The very women of these heretics, how wanton they are! For they are bold enough to teach, to dispute, to enact exorcisms, to undertake cures [*Prescription Against Heretics* 41 (c. A.D. 200)].

[A female heretic], lately conversant in this quarter, has carried away a great number with her most venomous doctrine, making it her aim to destroy baptism. This is in accordance with nature; for vipers and asps . . . themselves generally live in arid and waterless places. But we, little fishes after the example of our [great] fish, Jesus Christ, are born in water, and find safety in no other way than by permanently abiding in water; so that most monstrous creature, who had no right to teach even sound doctrine, knew full well how to kill the little fishes, by taking them away from the water! [*Baptism* 1 (c. A.D. 203)].

It is not permitted for a woman to speak in the church [1 Cor 14:34–35], but neither [is it permitted her] . . . to offer, nor to claim to herself a lot in any manly function, not to say sacerdotal office [*Veiling of Virgins* 9 (c. A.D. 209)].

ST. HIPPOLYTUS OF ROME

When a widow is appointed, she is not ordained, but is chosen by name. But if she lost her husband a long time previously, appoint her. But if she recently lost her husband, do not trust her. And even if she is old let her be tested for a while, for often the passions [even] grow old within someone who gives place for them in herself. Let the widow be instituted by word only and [then] let her be reckoned among the [enrolled] widows. But she shall not be ordained, because she does not offer the oblation nor has she a [liturgical] ministry. But ordination is for the clergy on account of their [liturgical] ministry. But the widow is appointed for prayer, and this is [a function] of all [*Apostolic Tradition* 11 (c. A.D. 215)].

DIDASCALIA

It is neither right nor necessary therefore that women should be teachers, and especially about the name of Christ and the redemption of his Passion. For you have not been appointed to this, O women, and especially widows, that you should teach, but that you should pray and entreat the Lord God. For he the Lord God, Jesus Christ our teacher, sent us the Twelve to instruct the people and the Gentiles; and there were with us women disciples, Mary Magdalene and Mary the daughter of James, and the other Mary; but he did not send them to instruct the people with us [*Didascalia* 3:6:1–2 (c. A.D. 225)].

FIRMILIAN OF CAESAREA

[T]here suddenly arose among us a certain woman, who in a state of ecstasy announced herself as a prophetess and acted as if filled with the Holy Spirit. . . . Through the deceptions and illusions of the demon, this woman had previously set about deluding believers in a variety of ways. Among the means by which she had deluded many was daring to pretend that, through proper invocation, she consecrated bread and performed the Eucharist. She offered up the sacrifice to the Lord in a liturgical act that corresponds to the usual rites, and she baptized many, all the while misusing the customary and legitimate wording of the [baptismal] question. She carried all these things out in such a manner that nothing seemed to deviate from the norms of the Church [quoted in Cyprian's *Letters* 74:10 (c. A.D. 255)].

COUNCIL OF NICAEA I

Similarly, in regard to the deaconesses, as with all who are enrolled in the register, the same procedure is to be observed. We have made mention of the deaconesses, who have been enrolled in this position, although, not having been in any way ordained, they are certainly to be numbered among the laity [Canon 19 (A.D. 325)].

COUNCIL OF LAODICEA

[T]he so-called "presbyteresses" or "presidentesses" are not to be ordained in the Church [Canon 11 (c. A.D. 362)].

ST. JOHN CHRYSOSTOM

[W]hen one is required to preside over the Church and to be entrusted with the care of so many souls, the whole female sex must retire before the magnitude of the task, and the majority of men also, and we must bring forward those who to a large extent surpass all others and soar as much above them in excellence of spirit as Saul overtopped the whole Hebrew nation in bodily stature [*Priesthood* 2:2 (c. A.D. 388)].

APOSTOLIC CONSTITUTIONS

[T]he "man is the head of the woman" [1 Cor 11:3], and he is originally ordained for the priesthood; it is not just to abrogate the order of the creation and leave the first to come to the last part of the body. For the woman is the body of the man, taken from his side and subject to him, from whom she was separated for the procreation of children. For he says, "He shall rule over you" [Gn 3:16]. For the first part of the woman is the man, as being her head. But if in the foregoing constitutions we have not permitted [women] to teach, how will anyone allow them, contrary to nature, to perform the office of the priest? For this is one of the ignorant practices of Gentile atheism, to ordain women priests to the female deities, not one of the constitutions of Christ [*Apostolic Constitutions* 3:1:9 (c. A.D. 400)].

Appoint, [O bishop], a deaconess, faithful and holy, for the ministering of women. For sometimes it is not possible to send a deacon into certain houses of women, because of unbelievers. Send a deaconess, because of the thoughts of the petty. A deaconess is of use to us also in many other situations. First of all, in the baptizing of women, a deacon will touch only their forehead with the holy oil, and afterwards the female deacon herself anoints them [ibid., 3:16:1].

A virgin is not ordained, for we have no such command from the Lord [1 Cor 7:25]; for this is a state of voluntary trial, not for the reproach of marriage, but on account of leisure for piety [ibid., 8:3:24].

A widow is not ordained; yet if she has lost her husband a great while and has lived soberly and blamelessly and has taken extraordinary care of her family, as Judith and Anna—those women of great reputation—let her be chosen into the order of widows [ibid., 8:3:25].

A deaconess does not bless, but neither does she perform anything else that is done by presbyters and deacons, but she guards the doors and greatly assists the presbyters, for the sake of decorum, when they are baptizing women [ibid., 8:3:28].

47. The Permanence of Marriage

Jesus taught: "Everyone who divorces his wife and marries another commits adultery, and he who marries a woman divorced from her husband commits adultery" (Lk 16:18; see also Mk 10:11–12).

St. Paul was equally firm: "Thus a married woman is bound by law to her husband as long as he lives. . . . Accordingly, she will be called an adulteress if she lives with another man while her husband is alive" (Rom 7:2–3).

These were difficult sayings to hear, particularly in Greco-Roman culture, which allowed for easy divorce and remarriage. Nevertheless, the early Church Fathers proclaimed Christ's teaching on the indissolubility of marriage.

Today the Catholic Church does the same in our modern, secular, easy-divorce culture (see CCC 1614–15).

The Church acknowledges that there are situations in which spouses can no longer live together, but separation or civil divorce does not mean that they are no longer married in the eyes of God.

This is particularly so among people who are baptized, for between two baptized persons matrimony has the status of a sacrament, and once the sacrament of matrimony has been consummated, it cannot be dissolved by anything but death.

However, if a couple did not have a valid marriage in the first place, then they are not bound to each other and would be free to marry again. To deal with this kind of situation, the Church has established the annulment process to investigate the validity of marriages. (For more information on this process, see booklet *Annulments: What You Need to Know*, published by Catholic Answers).

If, however, a couple has a valid, consummated, sacramental marriage, then, even though in some cases there may be good reasons for them to live apart and even to obtain a legal separation or civil divorce, in God's eyes they are not free to remarry (CCC 1649).

This is not a commandment of men, but one that comes directly from Jesus Christ. As Paul said, "To the married I give charge, not I but the Lord, that the wife should not separate from her husband (but if she does, let her remain single or else be reconciled to her husband)—and that the husband should not divorce his wife" (1 Cor 7:10).

Fortunately, God will ensure that the sacramentally married have the grace necessary to live out their marriage vows and either stay married or live continently. Whenever we face a trial, God makes sure that we will have the grace we need to overcome it. As Paul says, "No temptation has overtaken you that is not common to man. God is faithful, and he will not let you be tempted beyond your strength, but with the temptation will also provide the way of escape, that you may be able to endure it" (1 Cor 10:13).

As the following quotations from the early Church Fathers

illustrate, they recognized the seriousness of Christ's teaching regarding the indissolubility of marriage.

HERMAS OF ROME

What then shall the husband do, if the wife continue in this disposition [adultery]? Let him divorce her, and let the husband remain single. But if he divorce his wife and marry another, he too commits adultery [*The Shepherd* 2:4:1 (c. A.D. 80)].

ST. JUSTIN MARTYR

Concerning chastity, [Jesus] uttered such sentiments as these: "Whosoever looks upon a woman to lust after her, has committed adultery with her already in his heart before God." And, "If your right eye offend you, cut it out; for it is better for you to enter into the kingdom of heaven with one eye, than, having two eyes, to be cast into everlasting fire." And, "Whosoever shall marry her that is divorced from another husband commits adultery." And, "There are some who have been made eunuchs of men, and some who were born eunuchs, and some who have made themselves eunuchs for the kingdom of heaven's sake; but all cannot receive this saying" [Mt 19:12]. So that all who, by human law, are twice married, and those who look upon a woman to lust after her, are in the eye of our master sinners. For not only he who in act commits adultery is rejected by him, but also he who desires to commit adultery: since not only our works, but also our thoughts, are open before God [*First Apology* 15 (c. A.D. 151)].

ST. CLEMENT OF ALEXANDRIA

That the Scripture counsels marriage, and allows no release from the union, is expressly contained in the Law, "You shall not put away your wife, except for the cause of fornication"; and it regards as fornication the marriage of those separated while the other is alive. Not to deck and adorn herself beyond what is becoming renders a wife free of calumnious suspicion, while she devotes herself assiduously to prayers and supplications; avoiding frequent departures from the house, and shutting herself up as far as possible from the view of all not related to her, and deeming housekeeping of more consequence than impertinent trifling. "He that takes a woman that has been put away," it is said, "commits adultery; and if one puts away his wife, he makes her an adulteress," that is, compels her to commit adultery. And not only is he who puts her away guilty of this, but he who takes her, by giving to the woman the opportunity of sinning; for if he did not take her, she would return to her husband [*Miscellanies* 2:23 (c. A.D. 207)].

ORIGEN OF ALEXANDRIA

And even he who withholds himself from his wife often makes her an adulteress when he does not satisfy her desires, even though he does so under the appearance of greater gravity and self-control. And perhaps this man is more culpable who, so far as it rests with him, makes her an adulteress when he does not satisfy her desires than he who, for other reason than fornication, has sent her away —for poisoning or murder or any of the most grievous sins. But as a woman is an adulteress, even though she seems to be married to a man, while the former husband is still living so also the man who seems to marry her who has been put away, does not so much marry her as commit adultery with her according to the declaration of our Savior [*Commentaries on Matthew* 14:24 (c. A.D. 249)].

COUNCIL OF ELVIRA

Likewise, let the faithful woman, who has left an adulterous husband and attracts another faithful one, be forbidden to marry; if she should marry, let her not receive Communion unless he whom she has left has previously departed this world; unless by chance the exigency of illness should compel the giving [of Communion as Viaticum] [Canon 9 (c. A.D. 300)].

ST. BASIL OF CAESAREA

That he who, having another man's wife or spouse taken away from him, marries another is guilty of adultery with the first, not with the second [*Letters* 199:37 (A.D. 375)].

ST. AMBROSE OF MILAN

You dismiss your wife as if by right and without being charged with wrongdoing; and you suppose it is proper for you to do so because no human law forbids it; but divine law forbids it. Anyone who obeys men ought to stand in awe of God. Hear the law of the Lord, which even they who propose our laws must obey: "What God has joined together let no man put asunder" [*Commentary on Luke* 8:5 (c. A.D. 389)].

ST. JEROME

Do not tell me about the violence of the ravisher, about the persuasiveness of a mother, about the authority of a father, about the influence of relatives, about the intrigues and insolence of servants, or about household [financial] losses. So long as a husband lives, be he adulterer, be he sodomite, be he addicted to every kind of vice, if she left him on account of his crimes, he is her husband still and she may not take another [*Letters* 55:3 (c. A.D. 393)].

Wherever there is fornication and a suspicion of fornication, a wife is freely dismissed. Because it is always possible that someone may calumniate the innocent and, for the sake of a second joining in marriage, act in criminal fashion against the first, it is commanded that when the first wife is dismissed, a second may not be taken while the first lives [*Commentaries on Matthew* 3:19:9 (A.D. 398)].

ST. AUGUSTINE OF HIPPO

Neither can it rightly be held that a husband who dismisses his wife because of fornication and marries another does not commit adultery. For there is also adultery on the part of those who, after the repudiation of their former wives because of fornication, marry others. This adultery, nevertheless, is certainly less serious than that of men who dismiss their wives for reasons other than fornication and take other wives. Therefore, when we say: "Whoever marries a woman dismissed by her husband for reason other than fornication commits adultery," we speak the truth. But we do not thereby acquit of this crime the man who marries a woman who was dismissed because of fornication. We do not doubt that both are adulterers. We pronounce him an adulterer who dismissed his wife for cause other than fornication and marries another, nor do we thereby defend from the taint of this sin the man who dismissed his wife because of fornication and marries another. We recognize that both are adulterers, though the sin of one is more grave than that of the other. No one is so unreasonable to say that a man who marries a woman whose husband has dismissed her because of fornication is not an adulterer, while maintaining that a man who marries a woman dismissed without the ground of fornication is an adulterer. Both of these men are guilty of adultery [*Adulterous Marriages* 1:9:9 (c. A.D. 419)].

A woman begins to be the wife of no later husband unless she has ceased to be the wife of a former one. She will cease to be the wife of a former one, however, if that husband should die, not if he commit fornication. A spouse, therefore, is lawfully dismissed for cause of fornication; but the bond of chastity remains. That is why a man is guilty of adultery if he marries a woman who has been dismissed even for this very reason of fornication [ibid., 2:4:4].

It is certainly not fecundity only, the fruit of which is offspring, nor chastity only, whose bond is fidelity, but also a certain sacramental bond in marriage that is recommended to believers in wedlock. Accordingly it is enjoined by the apostle: "Husbands, love your wives, even as Christ also loved the Church" [Eph 5:25]. Of this bond the substance is this, that the man and the woman who are joined together in matrimony should remain inseparable as long as they live; and that it should be unlawful for one consort to be parted from the other, except for the cause of fornication [Mt 5:32]. For this is preserved in the case of Christ and the Church; so that, as a living one with a living one, there is no divorce, no separation for ever [*Marriage and Concupiscence* 1:10:11 (c. A.D. 419)].

In matrimony, however, let these nuptial blessings be the objects of our love—offspring, fidelity, the sacramental bond. Offspring, not that it be born only, but born again; for it is born to punishment unless it be born again to life. Fidelity, not such as even unbelievers observe one towards the other, in their ardent love of the flesh. For what husband, however impious himself, likes an adulterous wife? Or what wife, however impious she be, likes an adulterous husband? This is indeed a natural good in marriage, though a carnal one. But a member of Christ ought to be afraid of adultery, not on account of himself, but of his spouse; and ought to hope to receive from Christ the reward of that fidelity that he shows to his spouse. The sacramental bond, again, which is lost neither by divorce nor by adultery, should be guarded by husband and wife with concord and chastity [ibid., 1:17:19].

48. Sabbath or Sunday?

Some religious organizations (Seventh-day Adventists, Seventh Day Baptists, and certain others) claim that Christians should not worship on Sunday but on Saturday, the Jewish Sabbath. They assert that, at some point after the Apostolic Age, the Church "changed" the day of worship from Saturday to Sunday.

However, passages from Scripture such as Acts 20:7, 1 Corinthians 16:2, Colossians 2:16–17, and Revelation 1:10 indicate that, even during New Testament times, the Sabbath was no longer binding and that Christians worship on the Lord's Day, Sunday, instead.

Some of the early Church Fathers compared the observance of the Sabbath to the observance of the rite of circumcision, and from that maintained that if circumcision was abolished (Gal 5:1–6), so also the observance of the Sabbath must have been abolished. The following quotations show that the first Christians understood this principle and that they gathered for worship on Sunday.

DIDACHE

Assemble on the Lord's Day, and break bread and offer the Eucharist; but first make confession of your faults, so that your sacrifice may be pure. Anyone who has a difference with his fellow is not to take part until he has been reconciled, so as to avoid profaning your sacrifice [Mt 5:23–24]. For this is the offering of which the Lord said, "Everywhere and always bring me a sacrifice that is undefiled, for I am a great king, says the Lord, and my name is the wonder of nations" [Mal 1:11, 14] [*Didache* 14 (c. A.D. 50)].

LETTER OF BARNABAS

Wherefore, also, we keep the eighth day [Sunday] with joyfulness, the day also on which Jesus rose again from the dead [*Letter of Barnabas* 15 (c. A.D. 75)].

ST. IGNATIUS OF ANTIOCH

[T]herefore, those who were brought up in the ancient order of things have come to the possession of a new hope, no longer observing the Sabbath, but living in the observance of the Lord's Day, on which our life has sprung up again by him and by his death [*Letter to the Magnesians* 9 (c. A.D. 110)].

ST. JUSTIN MARTYR

But Sunday is the day on which we all hold our common assembly, because it is the first day on which God, having wrought a change in the darkness and matter, made the world; and Jesus Christ our Savior on the same day rose from the dead [*First Apology* 67 (c. A.D. 151)].

[W]e too would observe the fleshly circumcision, and the Sabbaths, and in short all the feasts, if we did not know for what reason they were enjoined [on] you—namely, on account of your transgressions and the hardness of your heart. . . . [H]ow is it, Trypho, that we would not observe those rites that do not harm us—I speak of fleshly circumcision and Sabbaths and feasts? . . . God enjoined you to keep the Sabbath, and imposed on you other precepts for a sign, as I have already said, on account of your unrighteousness and that of your fathers [*Dialogue with Trypho* 18, 21 (c. A.D. 155)].

TERTULLIAN OF CARTHAGE

[L]et him who contends that the Sabbath is still to be observed as a balm of salvation, and circumcision on the eighth day . . . teach us that, for the time past, righteous men kept the Sabbath or practiced circumcision, and were thus rendered "friends of God." For if circumcision purges a man, since God made Adam uncircumcised, why did he not circumcise him, even after his sinning, if circumcision purges? . . . Therefore, since God originated Adam uncircumcised and unobservant of the Sabbath, consequently his offspring, Abel, offering him sacrifices, uncircumcised and unobservant of the Sabbath, was by him [God] commended [Gn 4:1–7; Heb 11:4]. . . . Noah also, uncircumcised—yes, and unobservant of the Sabbath—God freed from the deluge. For Enoch too, most righteous man, uncircumcised and unobservant of the Sabbath, he translated from this world, who did not first taste death in order that, being a candidate for eternal life, he might show us that we also may, without the burden of the Law of Moses, please God [*Answer to the Jews* 2 (c. A.D. 203)].

ORIGEN OF ALEXANDRIA

Hence it is not possible that the [day of] rest after the Sabbath should have come into existence from the seventh [day] of our God. On the contrary, it is our Savior who, after the pattern of his own rest, caused us to be made in the likeness of his death, and hence also of his Resurrection [*Commentary on John* 2:27 (c. A.D. 229)].

ST. VICTORINUS OF PETTAU

This sixth day [Friday] is called parasceve, that is to say, the preparation of the kingdom. For he perfected Adam, whom he made after his image and likeness. But for this reason he completed his works before he created angels and fashioned man, lest they should falsely assert that they had been his helpers. On this day also, on account of the Passion of the Lord Jesus Christ, we make either a station to God, or a fast. On the seventh day he rested from all his works, and blessed it, and sanctified it. On the former day we are accustomed to fast rigorously, that on the Lord's Day we may go forth to our bread with thanksgiving. And let the parasceve become a rigorous fast, lest we should appear to observe any Sabbath with the Jews, which Christ himself, the Lord of the Sabbath, says by his prophets that "his soul hates" [Is 1:13–14]; which Sabbath he in his body abolished [*Creation of the World* (A.D. 270)].

EUSEBIUS OF CAESAREA

[The early saints of the Old Testament] did not care about circumcision of the body; neither do we [Christians]. They did not care about observing Sabbaths, nor do we. They did not avoid certain kinds of food, neither did they regard the other distinctions that Moses first delivered to their posterity to be observed as symbols; nor do Christians of the present day do such things [*Church History* 1:4:8 (c. A.D. 312)].

ST. CYRIL OF JERUSALEM

Fall away neither into the sect of the Samaritans, nor into Judaism: for Jesus Christ has ransomed you. Stand aloof from all observance of Sabbaths, and from calling any indifferent meats common or unclean [*Catechetical Lectures* 4:37 (c. A.D. 350)].

COUNCIL OF LAODICEA

Christians must not Judaize by resting on the Sabbath, but must work on that day, rather honoring the Lord's day; and, if they can, resting then as Christians. But if any shall be found to be Judaizers, let them be anathema from Christ [Canon 29 (c. A.D. 362)].

ST. JOHN CHRYSOSTOM

And that you may learn that we know this from the first, the lawgiver, when he afterwards gave laws, and said, "You shall not kill" [Ex 20:13], did not add, "since murder is an evil thing," but simply said, "You shall not kill"; for he merely prohibited the sin, without teaching. How was it then when he said, "You shall not kill," that he did not add, "because murder is a wicked thing." The reason was that conscience had taught this beforehand; and he speaks thus to those who know and understand the point. This is why when he speaks to us of another commandment, not known to us by the dictates of conscience, he not only prohibits, but adds the reason. When, for instance, he gave the commandment respecting the Sabbath, "On the seventh day you shall do no work"; he gave the reason for this cessation. "Because on the seventh day God rested from all his works which he had begun to make" [Ex 20:10]. And again; "Because thou were a servant in the land of Egypt" [Dt 21:18]. For what purpose, then, did he add a reason respecting the Sabbath, but did no such thing in regard to murder? Because this commandment was not one of the leading ones. It was not one of those that were accurately defined by our conscience, but a kind of partial and temporary one; and for this reason it was abolished afterwards. But those that are necessary and uphold our life are the following: "You shall not kill. You shall not commit adultery. You shall not steal." On this account he adds no reason in this case, nor enters into any instruction on the matter, but is content with the bare prohibition [*Homilies on the Statues* 12:9 (A.D. 387)].

You have put on Christ, you have become a member of the Lord, and been enrolled in the heavenly city, and you still grovel in the Law? How is it possible for you to obtain the kingdom? Listen to Paul's words, that the observance of the Law overthrows the gospel, and learn, if you will, how this comes to pass, and tremble, and shun this pitfall. Wherefore do you keep the Sabbath, and fast with the Jews? [*Commentary on Galatians* 2:17 (c. A.D. 395)].

The rite of circumcision was venerable in the Jews' account, because the Law itself gave way to it, and the Sabbath was less esteemed than circumcision. The Sabbath was broken so that circumcision might be performed; but so the Sabbath might be kept, circumcision was never broken; and mark, I pray, the dispensation of God. This is found to be even more solemn than the Sabbath, as not being omitted at certain times. When it is done away, much more is the Sabbath [*Homilies on Philippians* 10 (c. A.D. 402)].

APOSTOLIC CONSTITUTIONS

And on the day of our Lord's Resurrection, which is the Lord's Day, meet more diligently, sending praise to God who made the universe by Jesus, and sent him to us, and condescended to let him suffer, and raised him from the dead. Otherwise what apology will he make to God who does not assemble on that day to hear the saving word concerning the Resurrection, on which we pray three times standing in memory of him who arose in three days, in which is performed the reading of the prophets, the preaching of the gospel, the oblation of the sacrifice, the gift of the holy food? [*Apostolic Constitutions* 2:7:60 (c. A.D. 400)].

ST. AUGUSTINE OF HIPPO

Well, now, I should like to be told what is in these Ten Commandments, except the observance of the Sabbath, that ought not to be kept by a Christian—whether it prohibit the making and worshipping of idols and of any other gods than the one true God, or the taking of God's name in vain; or prescribe honor to parents; or give warning against fornication, murder, theft, false witness, adultery, or coveting other men's property? Which of these commandments would anyone say that the Christian ought not to

keep? Is it possible to contend that it is not the law that was written on those two tablets that the apostle describes as "the letter
that kills," but the law of circumcision and the other sacred rites
that are now abolished? [*The Spirit and the Letter* 23 (A.D. 412)].

X. Mary, the Saints, the Miraculous

49. Mary, Full of Grace

The Fathers of the Church taught that Mary received a number of distinctive blessings in order to make her a more fitting mother for Christ. These included her role as the New Eve (corresponding to Christ's role as the New Adam), her Immaculate Conception, her spiritual motherhood of all Christians, and her Assumption into heaven. These gifts were given to her by God's grace. She did not earn them, but she possessed them nonetheless.

The key to understanding these graces is Mary's role as the New Eve, on which the Fathers were quite clear. Because she is the New Eve, she—like the New Adam—was born immaculate, just as the first Adam and Eve were created immaculate. As the New Eve, she is mother of the New Humanity (Christians), just as the first Eve was the mother of humanity. And, as the New Eve, she shares the fate of the New Adam. Whereas the first Adam and Eve died and went to dust, the New Adam and Eve were lifted up bodily to heaven.

Of particular interest in the following quotations from the Fathers are those that speak of Mary's immaculate nature. We will all one day be rendered immaculate (sinless), but Mary, as the prototypical Christian—the first to say "yes" to Jesus—received this grace early. God granted her freedom from sin to make her a fitting mother for his Son.

Even before the terms "original sin" and "immaculate conception" had been developed, early passages imply the concepts. Many works mention that Mary gave birth to Jesus without pain. Pain in childbearing is part of the penalty of original sin (Gn 3:16), thus, Mary could not have been under that penalty. By God's grace, she was made immaculate in anticipation of her Son's redemptive death on the cross. The Church therefore describes Mary as "the most excellent fruit of redemption" (CCC 508).

ASCENSION OF ISAIAH

And the story regarding the infant was spread abroad in Bethlehem. Some said: "The Virgin Mary has borne a child, before she was married two months." And many said, "She has not borne a child, nor has a midwife gone up (to her), nor have we heard the cries of (labor) pains" [*Ascension of Isaiah* 11:12–14 (c. A.D. 90)].

ODES OF SOLOMON

So the Virgin became a Mother with great mercies. And she labored and bore the Son, but without pain, because it did not occur without purpose. And she did not seek a midwife, because he caused her to give life [*Odes of Solomon* 19:7–9 (c. A.D. 125)].

ST. JUSTIN MARTYR

[Jesus] became man by the Virgin so that the course that was taken by disobedience in the beginning through the agency of the serpent might also be the course by which it would be put down. Eve, a virgin and undefiled, conceived the word of the serpent and bore disobedience and death. But the Virgin Mary received faith and joy when the angel Gabriel announced to her the glad tidings that the Spirit of the Lord would come upon her and the power of the most high would overshadow her, for which reason the holy one being born of her is the Son of God. And she replied, "Be it done unto me according to your word" [Lk 1:38] [*Dialogue with Trypho* 100 (c. A.D. 155)].

ST. IRENAEUS OF LYONS

In accordance with this design, Mary the Virgin is found obedient, saying, "Behold the handmaid of the Lord; be it unto me according to your word" [Lk 1:38]. But Eve was disobedient; for she did not obey when she was a virgin. And even as she, having a husband, Adam, but being nevertheless as yet a virgin (for in paradise "they were both naked, and were not ashamed" [Gn 2:25], since they, having been created a short time previously, had no understanding of the procreation of children: for it was necessary that they should first come to adult age, and then multiply from that time onward), having become disobedient, was made the cause of death, both to herself and to the entire human race; so also did Mary, having a man betrothed [to her], and being nevertheless a virgin, by yielding obedience, become the cause of salvation, both to herself and the whole human race. And on this account does the law term a woman betrothed to a man, the wife of him who had betrothed her, although she was as yet a virgin; thus indicating the reference back from Mary to Eve, because what is joined together could not otherwise be put asunder than by inversion of the process by which these bonds of union had arisen; so that the former ties be canceled by the latter, that the latter may set the former again at liberty. And it has, in fact, happened that the first compact looses from the second tie, but that the second tie takes the position of the first, which has been canceled. For this reason did the Lord declare that the first should in truth be last, and the last first [Mt 19:30; 20:16]. And the prophet, too, indicates the same, saying, "instead of fathers, children have been born unto you." For the Lord, having been born "the first-begotten of the dead [Rv 1:5]," and receiving into his bosom the ancient fathers, has regenerated them into the life of God, he having been made the beginning of those who live, as Adam became the beginning of those who die [1 Cor 15:20–22]. Therefore Luke, commencing the genealogy with the Lord, carried it back to Adam, indicating that it was he who regenerated them into the gospel of life, and not they him. And thus also it was that the knot of Eve's disobedience was loosed by the obedience of Mary. For what the virgin Eve had bound fast through unbelief, this did the Virgin Mary set free through faith [*Against Heresies* 3:22:4 (c. A.D. 189)].

That the Lord then was manifestly coming to his own things, and was sustaining them by means of that creation that is supported by himself, and was making a recapitulation of that disobedience that had occurred in connection with a tree, through the obedience that was [exhibited by himself when he hung] upon a tree, [the effects] also of that deception being done away with, by that virgin Eve, who was already espoused to a man, was unhappily misled— was happily announced, through means of the truth [spoken] by the angel to the Virgin Mary, who was [also espoused] to a man. For just as the former was led astray by the word of an angel, so that she fled from God when she had transgressed his word; so did the latter, by an angelic communication, receive the glad tidings that she should sustain God, being obedient to his word. And if the former did disobey God, yet the latter was persuaded to be obedient to God, in order that the Virgin Mary might become the patroness of the virgin Eve. And thus, as the human race fell into bondage to death by means of a virgin, so is it rescued by a Virgin; virginal disobedience having been balanced in the opposite scale by virginal obedience. For in the same way the sin of the first created man receives amendment by the correction of the first-begotten [ibid., 5:19:1].

TERTULLIAN OF CARTHAGE

But that I may lose no opportunity of supporting my argument from the name of Adam, why is Christ called Adam by the apostle, unless it be that, as man, he was of that earthly origin? And even reason maintains the same conclusion, because it was by just the contrary operation that God recovered his own image and likeness, of which he had been robbed by the devil. For it was while Eve was yet a virgin that the ensnaring word crept into her ear, which was to build the edifice of death. Into a virgin's soul, in like manner, must be introduced that Word of God, which was to raise the fabric of life; so that what had been reduced to ruin by this sex might by the selfsame sex be recovered to salvation. As Eve had believed the serpent, so Mary believed the angel. The delinquency that the one occasioned by believing, the other by believing effaced [*The Flesh of Christ* 17 (c. A.D. 210)].

ST. EPHRAIM THE SYRIAN

You alone and your Mother are more beautiful than any others, for there is no blemish in you nor any stains upon your Mother. Who of my children can compare in beauty to these? [*Nisibene Hymns* 27:8 (c. A.D. 370)].

ST. AMBROSE OF MILAN

Let, then, the life of Mary be as it were virginity itself, set forth in a likeness, from which, as from a mirror, the appearance of chastity and the form of virtue is reflected. From this you may take your pattern of life, showing, as an example, the clear rules of virtue: what you have to correct, to effect, and to hold fast [*Virgins* 2:2:6 (A.D. 377)].

The first thing that kindles ardor in learning is the greatness of the teacher. What is greater [to teach by example] than the Mother of God? What more glorious than she whom glory itself chose? What more chaste than she who bore a body without contact with another body? For why should I speak of her other virtues? She was a virgin not only in body but also in mind, who stained the sincerity of its disposition by no guile, who was humble in heart, grave in speech, prudent in mind, sparing of words, studious in reading, resting her hope not on uncertain riches, but on the prayer of the poor, intent on work, modest in discourse; wont to seek not man but God as the judge of her thoughts, to injure no one, to have goodwill towards all, to rise up before her elders, not to envy her equals, to avoid boastfulness, to follow reason, to love virtue. When did she pain her parents even by a look? When did she disagree with her neighbors? When did she despise the lowly? When did she avoid the needy? [ibid., 2:2:7].

Come, then, and search out your sheep, not through your servants or hired men, but do it yourself. Lift me up bodily and in the flesh, which is fallen in Adam. Lift me up not from Sarah but from Mary, a virgin not only undefiled, but a virgin whom grace had made inviolate, free of every stain of sin [*Commentary on Psalm 118* 22:30 (c. A.D. 387)].

ST. AUGUSTINE OF HIPPO

[T]hat one female, not only in the Spirit, but also in the flesh, is both a Mother and a virgin. And a Mother indeed in the Spirit, not of our head, which is the Savior himself, of whom rather she was born after the Spirit: for as much as all who have believed in him, among whom is herself also, are rightly called "children of the bridegroom," but clearly the Mother of his members, which are we: in that she wrought together by charity, that faithful ones should be born in the Church, who are members of that head: but in the flesh, the Mother of the head himself [*Holy Virginity* 6 (A.D. 401)].

We must except the holy Virgin Mary, concerning whom I wish to raise no question when it touches the subject of sins, out of honor to the Lord; for from him we know what abundance of grace for overcoming sin in every particular was conferred upon her who had the merit to conceive and bear him who undoubtedly had no sin [1 Jn 3:5]. Well, then, if, with this exception of the Virgin, we could only assemble together all the forementioned holy men and women, and ask them whether they lived without sin while they were in this life, what can we suppose would be their answer? [*Nature and Grace* 36:42 (A.D. 415)].

PSEUDO-MELITO

If therefore it might come to pass by the power of your grace, it has appeared right to us your servants that, as you, having overcome death, do reign in glory, so you should raise up the body of your Mother and take her with you, rejoicing, into heaven. Then said the Savior: "Be it done according to your will" [*Passing of the Virgin* 16:2–17:1 (c. A.D. 475)].

TIMOTHY OF JERUSALEM

Therefore the Virgin is immortal to this day, seeing that he who had dwelt in her transported her to the regions of her Assumption [*Homily on Simeon and Anna* (c. A.D. 500)].

PSEUDO-JOHN

[T]he Lord said to his Mother, "Let your heart rejoice and be glad, for every favor and every gift has been given to you from my Father in heaven and from me and from the Holy Spirit. Every soul that calls upon your name shall not be ashamed, but shall find mercy and comfort and support and confidence, both in the world that now is and in what is to come, in the presence of my Father in the heavens" [*Falling Asleep of Mary* (c. A.D. 550)].

And from that time forth all knew that the spotless and precious body had been transferred to paradise [ibid.].

ST. GREGORY OF TOURS

The course of this life having been completed by blessed Mary, when now she would be called from the world, all the apostles came together from their various regions to her house. And when they had heard that she was about to be taken from the world, they kept watch together with her. And behold, the Lord Jesus came with his angels, and, taking her soul, he gave it over to the angel Michael and withdrew. At daybreak, however, the apostles took up her body on a bier and placed it in a tomb, and they guarded it, expecting the Lord to come. And behold, again the Lord stood by them; the holy body having been received, he commanded that it be taken in a cloud into paradise, where now, rejoined to the soul, [Mary's body] rejoices with the Lord's chosen ones and is in the enjoyment of the good of an eternity that will never end [*Eight Books of Miracles* 1:4 (c. A.D. 590)].

50. Mary, Mother of God

Periodically in history the description of Mary as the Mother of God has been controversial, but the title is well founded.

Mothers provide genetic material for their children and carry their children in their wombs. Mary did both of these things with Jesus. She was his mother. Jesus, in turn, was God, as we have seen (chapter 17). But if Mary is the Mother of Jesus and Jesus is God, then Mary is the Mother of God.

She is not his mother in the sense that she is older than God or the source of her Son's divinity, for she is neither. Rather, we say that she is the Mother of God in the sense that she carried in her womb a divine Person—Jesus Christ, God "in the flesh" (2 Jn 7; see also Jn 1:14)—and contributed genetic matter to his human form.

To avoid this conclusion, some have asserted that Mary did not carry God in her womb but only Christ's human nature. This is a philosophical mistake, though. Mothers do not carry "natures" in their wombs. They carry persons in their wombs, and the Person that was in Mary's womb was God.

The first time this controversy appeared in Church history was in the 400s, when the patriarch of Constantinople, Nestorius, objected to describing Mary as *Theotokos* (Greek, "God-bearer" or "one who bore God" in her womb). He preferred to say that she was *Christotokos*, the bearer of Christ, but he articulated himself in a way that suggested to others that he thought Jesus was actually two people—one human, one divine. This misunderstanding of Christ's nature was rejected at the Council of Ephesus in 431, which also affirmed that Mary can legitimately be called *Theotokos*.

Though today it is often Protestants who question this language, thoughtful Protestant theologians—including the original reformers—recognized its legitimacy. Both Martin Luther and John Calvin insisted on Mary's divine maternity.

In fact, it appears that even Nestorius himself may not have believed the heresy named after him. After the Council of Ephesus he went to a monastery, where he continued to profess his orthodoxy and where he died in communion with the Church.

The following passages from the Church Fathers, both before and after the Council of Ephesus, show their recognition of Mary as the Mother of God.

ST. IRENAEUS OF LYONS

The Virgin Mary, being obedient to his word, received from an angel the glad tidings that she would bear God [*Against Heresies*, 5:19:1 (c. A.D. 189)].

ST. GREGORY THAUMATURGUS

For Luke, in the inspired Gospel narratives, delivers a testimony not to Joseph only, but also to Mary the Mother of God, and gives this account with reference to the very family and house of David [*Four Homilies* 1 (c. A.D. 256)].

It is our duty to present to God, like sacrifices, all the festivals and hymnal celebrations; and first of all, the Annunciation to the holy Mother of God, that is, the salutation made to her by the angel, "Hail, thou that art highly favored!" [ibid., 2].

ST. METHODIUS OF PHILIPPI

While [Simeon] was thus exultant, and rejoicing with exceeding great and holy joy, what had before been spoken of in a figure by the prophet Isaiah, the holy Mother of God now manifestly fulfilled [*Oration on Simeon and Anna* 7 (c. A.D. 300)].

Hail to you forever, you Virgin Mother of God, our unceasing joy, for unto you do I again return. . . . Hail, you fount of the Son's love for man. . . . Therefore we pray you, the most excellent among women, who boast in the confidence of your maternal honors, unceasingly to keep us in remembrance. O holy Mother of God, remember us, I say, who make our boast in you, and who in august hymns celebrate your memory, which will ever live, and never fade away [ibid., 14].

ST. PETER OF ALEXANDRIA

[T]hey came to the church of the most blessed Mother of God, and Ever-Virgin Mary, which, as we began to say, he had constructed in the western quarter, in a suburb, for a cemetery of the martyrs [*The Genuine Acts of Peter of Alexandria* (A.D. 305)].

ST. CYRIL OF JERUSALEM

The Father bears witness from heaven to his Son. The Holy Spirit bears witness, coming down in the form of a dove. The archangel Gabriel bears witness, bringing the good tidings to Mary. The Virgin Mother of God bears witness [*Catechetical Lectures* 10:19 (c. A.D. 350)].

ST. ATHANASIUS OF ALEXANDRIA

The Word begotten of the Father from on high, inexpressibly, inexplicably, incomprehensibly, and eternally, is he that is born in time here below of the Virgin Mary, the Mother of God [*Incarnation of the Word* 8 (c. A.D. 365)].

ST. AMBROSE OF MILAN

The first thing that kindles ardor in learning is the greatness of the teacher. What is greater than the Mother of God? What more glorious than she whom glory itself chose? [*Virgins* 2:2:6 (A.D. 377)].

ST. GREGORY OF NAZIANZ

If anyone does not agree that holy Mary is Mother of God, he is at odds with the Godhead [*Letter to Cledonius the Priest* 101 (A.D. 382)].

ST. JEROME

As to how a virgin became the Mother of God, [Rufinus of Aquileia] has full knowledge; as to how he himself was born, he knows nothing [*Apology Against Rufinus* 2:10 (A.D. 401)].

Do not marvel at the novelty of the thing, if a Virgin gives birth to God [*Commentaries on Isaiah* 3:7:15 (c. A.D. 409)].

THEODORE OF MOPSUESTIA

When, therefore, they ask, "Is Mary mother of man or Mother of God?" we answer, "Both!" The one by the very nature of what was done and the other by relation. Mother of man because it was a man who was in the womb of Mary and who came forth from there, and the Mother of God because God was in the man who was born [*The Incarnation* 15 (c. A.D. 410)].

ST. CYRIL OF ALEXANDRIA

I have been amazed that some are utterly in doubt as to whether or not the holy Virgin is able to be called the Mother of God. For if our Lord Jesus Christ is God, how should the holy Virgin who bore him not be the Mother of God? [*Letter to the Monks of Egypt* 1 (c. A.D. 427)].

ST. JOHN CASSIAN

And so you say, O heretic, whoever you may be, who deny that God was born of the Virgin, that Mary the Mother of our Lord Jesus Christ ought not to be called *Theotokos*, that is, Mother of God, but *Christotokos*, that is, only the Mother of Christ, not of God. For no one, you say, brings forth what is anterior in time. And of this utterly foolish argument by which you think that the birth of God can be understood by carnal minds, and fancy that the mystery of his majesty can be accounted for by human reasoning, we will, if God permits, say something later on. In the meanwhile we will now prove by divine testimonies that Christ is God, and that Mary is the Mother of God. Hear then how the angel of God speaks to the shepherds of the birth of God [*The Incarnation* 2:2 (c. A.D. 429)].

You cannot then help admitting that the grace comes from God. It is God then who has given it. But it has been given by our Lord Jesus Christ. Therefore the Lord Jesus Christ is God. But if he be, as he certainly is, God, then she who bore God is *Theotokos*, that is, the Mother of God [ibid., 2:5].

ST. VINCENT OF LERINS

Nestorius, whose disease is of an opposite kind, while pretending that he holds two distinct substances in Christ, brings in of a sudden two Persons, and with unheard of wickedness would have two sons of God, two Christs—one God, the other man, one begotten of his Father, the other, born of his Mother. For which reason he maintains that St. Mary ought to be called not *Theotokos* [the Mother of God], but *Christotokos* [the Mother of Christ], seeing that she gave birth not to the Christ who is God, but to the Christ who is man [*Notebooks* 12:35 (c. A.D. 434)].

51. Mary, Ever Virgin

Today most Protestants claim that Mary bore children other than Jesus. They point to the biblical passages that refer to the "brethren of the Lord." But none of these passages state that they were children of Mary.

According to some theories, the "brethren" of the Lord were actually his cousins. There was no distinct term for "cousin" in Aramaic, and the term "brother" has a broader usage in that language. This theory was popularized in later times, but the earliest explanation of who the brethren of the Lord were is found in a document known as the *Protoevangelium of James*, which was written around A.D. 150 and affirms Mary's perpetual virginity. In fact, according to patristics scholar Johannes Quasten: "The principal aim of the whole writing is to prove the perpetual and inviolate virginity of Mary before, in, and after the birth of Christ" (*Patrology*, 1:120-21).

This document, like all the writings of the patristic age, is neither canonical nor infallible, but it is early, and it may contain accurate historical traditions.

The *Protoevangelium* records that when Mary's birth was foretold, her mother, St. Anne, vowed that she would devote the child to the service of the Lord, as in the Old Testament the prophet Samuel had been vowed by his mother to the Lord's service (1 Sm 1:11). According to St. Anne's vow, Mary would serve the Lord at the temple, as women had for centuries (1 Sm 2:22).

According to this document, Mary thus was a consecrated virgin from her infancy. However, owing to considerations of ceremonial cleanliness, it was eventually necessary for Mary, a "virgin of the Lord," to have a guardian or protector who would respect her vow of virginity. Thus the *Protoevangelium* states that Joseph, an elderly widower who already had children, was chosen to be her spouse.

This would also explain why Joseph appears to have died by the time of Jesus' adult ministry, since he does not appear during it in the Gospels and since Mary is entrusted to John, rather than to her husband, Joseph, at the crucifixion.

According to the *Protoevangelium*, Joseph was required to regard Mary's vow of virginity with the utmost respect. The gravity of his responsibility as the guardian of a virgin was indicated by the fact that, when she was discovered to be with child, he had to answer to the temple authorities, who thought him guilty of defiling a virgin of the Lord. Mary was also accused of having forsaken the Lord by breaking her vow.

The *Protoevangelium* thus understands that the brethren of the Lord were Jesus' stepbrothers (children of Joseph) rather than half-brothers (children of Mary). This was the most common view until the time of St. Jerome in the fourth century. It was he who popularized the idea that the brethren of the Lord were his cousins.

Interestingly, the Protestant Reformers themselves—Martin

Luther, John Calvin, and Ulrich Zwingli—honored the perpetual virginity of Mary and saw it as fully compatible with Scripture, as when—at the Annunciation—Mary asks how she will bear a Son since she "know[s] not man" (Lk 1:34)—a statement that would otherwise be difficult to explain if, as Joseph's betrothed, she was planning an ordinary conjugal union.

PROTOEVANGELIUM OF JAMES

And, behold, an angel of the Lord stood by, saying: "Anna, Anna, the Lord has heard your prayer, and you shall conceive, and shall bring forth; and your seed shall be spoken of in all the world." And Anna said: "As the Lord my God lives, if I beget either male or female, I will bring it as a gift to the Lord my God; and it shall minister to him in holy things all the days of its life." . . . And [from the time she was three] Mary was in the temple of the Lord as if she were a dove that dwelt there [*Protoevangelium of James* 4, 8 (c. A.D. 150)].

And when she was twelve years old a council of the priests was held, which said: "Behold, Mary has reached the age of twelve years in the temple of the Lord. What shall we do with her, lest she defile the sanctuary of the Lord?" And they said to the high priest: "You stand by the altar of the Lord; go in, and pray concerning her; and whatever the Lord shall manifest unto you, that will we do." And the high priest went in, taking the robe with the twelve bells into the holy of holies; and he prayed about her. And behold an angel of the Lord stood by him, and said to him: "Zacharias, Zacharias, go out and assemble the widowers of the people, and let them bring each his rod; and to whomever the Lord shall show a sign, his wife shall she be." . . . And Joseph [was chosen]. . . . And the priest said to Joseph, "You have been chosen by lot to take into your keeping the Virgin of the Lord." But Joseph refused, saying, "I have children, and I am an old man, and she is a young girl" [ibid., 8–9].

And Annas the scribe came to [Joseph] . . . and saw that Mary was with child. And he ran away to the priest and said to him, "Joseph, whom you vouched for, has committed a grievous crime." And the priest said, "How so?" And he said, "He has defiled the virgin he received out of the temple of the Lord and has married her by stealth" [ibid., 15].

And the priest said, "Mary, why have you done this? Why have you brought your soul low and forgotten the Lord your God?" . . . And she wept bitterly and said, "As the Lord my God lives, I am pure before him, and know not a man" [ibid.].

ORIGEN OF ALEXANDRIA

But some say, basing it on a tradition in the Gospel according to Peter, as it is called, or "The Book [*Protoevangelium*] of James," that the brothers of Jesus were sons of Joseph by a former wife, whom he married before Mary. Now those who say so wish to preserve the honor of Mary in virginity to the end, so that her body, which was appointed to minister to the Word, which said, "The Holy Spirit shall come upon you, and the power of the Most High shall overshadow you" [Lk 1:35], might not know intercourse with a man after the Holy Spirit came into her and the power from on high overshadowed her. And I think it reasonable that Jesus was the first fruit among men of the purity that consists in chastity, and Mary among women; for it is not pious to ascribe to any other than her the first fruit of virginity [*Commentary on Matthew* 10:17 (c. A.D. 249)].

ST. ATHANASIUS OF ALEXANDRIA

Therefore let those who deny that the Son is from the Father by nature and proper to his essence deny also that he took true human flesh of Mary Ever-Virgin [*Four Discourses Against the Arians* 2:70 (c. A.D. 360)].

ST. JEROME

Now that I have cleared the rocks and shoals I must spread sail and make all speed to reach his epilogue. Feeling himself to be a smatterer, he there produces Tertullian as a witness and quotes the words of Victorinus, bishop of Petavium. Of Tertullian I say no more than that he did not belong to the Church. But as regards Victorinus, I assert what has already been proved from the Gospel —that he spoke of the brothers of the Lord not as being sons of Mary, but brethren in the sense I have explained, that is to say, in point of kinship, not by nature. We are, however, spending our strength on trifles, and, leaving the fountain of truth, are following tiny streams of opinion. Might I not array against you the whole series of ancient writers? Ignatius, Polycarp, Irenaeus, St. Justin Martyr, and many other apostolic and eloquent men, who against Ebion, Theodotus of Byzantium, and Valentinus, held these same views, and wrote volumes full of wisdom. If you read what they wrote, you would be a wiser man. But I think it better to reply briefly to each point than to linger any longer and extend my book to an undue length [*Perpetual Virginity of Blessed Mary* 19 (A.D. 383)].

We believe that God was born of the Virgin, because we read it. That Mary was married after she brought forth, we do not believe, because we do not read it. Nor do we say this to condemn marriage, for virginity itself is the fruit of marriage; but because when we are dealing with saints we must not judge rashly. If we adopt possibility as the standard of judgment, we might maintain that Joseph had several wives because Abraham had, and so had Jacob, and that the Lord's brothers were the issue of those wives, an invention that some hold with a rashness that springs from audacity, not piety. You say that Mary did not continue a virgin: I claim still more that Joseph himself, on account of Mary, was a virgin, so that from a virgin wedlock a virgin son was born [ibid., 21].

POPE ST. SIRICIUS I

Surely, we cannot deny that regarding the sons of Mary the statement is justly censured, and your holiness rightly abhors it, that from the same virginal womb from which Christ was born, another offspring was brought forth. For neither would the Lord Jesus have chosen to be born of a Virgin if he had judged she would be so incontinent, that with the seed of human copulation she would pollute the generative chamber of the Lord's body, the palace of the eternal king [*Letter to Bishop Anysius* (A.D. 392)].

ST. AMBROSE OF MILAN

Imitate [Mary], holy mothers, who in her only dearly beloved Son set forth so great an example of maternal virtue; for neither have you sweeter children, nor did the Virgin seek the consolation of being able to bear another son [*Letters* 63:111 (A.D. 396)].

ST. AUGUSTINE OF HIPPO

Thus Christ by being born of a Virgin who, before she knew who was to be born of her, had determined to continue a Virgin, chose to approve, rather than to command, holy virginity. And thus, even in the female herself, in whom he took the form of a servant, he willed that virginity should be free [*Holy Virginity* 4:4 (A.D. 401)].

LEPORIUS

We confess, therefore, that our Lord and God, Jesus Christ, the only Son of God, born of the Father before the ages, and in times most recent, made man of the Holy Spirit and the Ever-Virgin Mary [*Document of Amendment* 3 (A.D. 426)].

POPE ST. LEO I

The origin is different but the nature alike: not by intercourse with man but by the power of God was it brought about: for a Virgin conceived, a Virgin bore, and a Virgin she remained [*Sermons* 22:2 (A.D. 450)].

COUNCIL OF CONSTANTINOPLE II

If anyone will not confess that the Word of God . . . came down from the heavens and was made flesh of holy and glorious Mary, Mother of God and Ever Virgin, and was born from her, let him be anathema [*Capitula of the Council* 2 (A.D. 553)].

52. Intercession of the Saints

Fundamentalists sometimes challenge the Catholic practice of asking saints and angels to pray on our behalf. Although this practice is not prominent in Scripture, there are places where the Bible directs us to invoke those in heaven and ask them to pray with us.

Thus, in Psalm 103 we pray, "Bless the Lord, O you his angels, you mighty ones who do his word, hearkening to the voice of his word! Bless the Lord, all his hosts, his ministers that do his will!" (Ps 103:20-21). And in the opening verses of Psalm 148 we pray, "Praise the Lord! Praise the Lord from the heavens, praise him in the heights! Praise him, all his angels, praise him, all his host!"

Not only do those in heaven pray with us, they also pray for us. In the book of Revelation, John sees that "the twenty-four elders [the leaders of the people of God in heaven] fell down before the Lamb, each holding a harp, and with golden bowls full of incense, which are the prayers of the saints" (Rv 5:8). Thus the saints in heaven offer to God the prayers of the saints on earth.

Angels do the same thing: "[An] angel came and stood at the altar [in heaven] with a golden censer; and he was given much incense to mingle with the prayers of all the saints upon the golden altar before the throne; and the smoke of the incense rose with the prayers of the saints from the hand of the angel before God" (Rv 8:3-4).

Jesus warned us not to look down on children, because their guardian angels have assured access to the Father to intercede for their charges: "See that you do not despise one of these little ones; for I tell you that in heaven their angels always see the face of my Father who is in heaven" (Mt 18:10).

Because he is the only person who is both God and man, and because he is the mediator of the New Covenant, Jesus Christ is the unique mediator between man and God (1 Tm 2:5), but this does not mean that we cannot or should not ask our fellow Christians to pray with us and for us (1 Tm 2:1-4). In fact, it would make sense to ask the intercession of those Christians in heaven, who have already had their sanctification completed, for "[t]he prayer of a righteous man has great power in its effects" (Jas 5:16).

As the following passages show, the early Church Fathers recognized that those in heaven can and do intercede for us, and applied this teaching in their own prayer lives.

HERMAS OF ROME

[The Shepherd said:] "But those who are weak and slothful in prayer hesitate to ask anything from the Lord; but the Lord is full of compassion, and gives without fail to all who ask him. But you, [Hermas,] having been strengthened by the holy angel [you saw], and having obtained from him such intercession, and not being slothful, why do you not ask understanding of the Lord, and receive it from him?" [*The Shepherd* 3:5:4 (A.D. 80)].

ST. CLEMENT OF ALEXANDRIA

In this way is [the true Christian] always pure for prayer. He also prays in the society of angels, as being already of angelic rank, and he is never out of their holy keeping; and though he pray alone, he has the choir of the saints standing with him [in prayer] [*Miscellanies* 7:12 (c. A.D. 207)].

EARLY CHRISTIAN INSCRIPTION

Blessed Sozon gave back [his spirit] aged nine years; may the true Christ [receive] your spirit in peace, and pray for us [*Christian Inscriptions*, no. 25 (c. A.D. 250)].

EARLY CHRISTIAN INSCRIPTION

Gentianus, a believer, in peace, who lived twenty-one years, eight months, and sixteen days, and in your prayers ask for us, because we know that you are in Christ [*Christian Inscriptions*, no. 29 (c. A.D. 250)].

EARLY CHRISTIAN INSCRIPTION

Pray for your parents, Matronata Matrona. She lived one year, fifty-two days [*Christian Inscriptions*, no. 36 (c. A.D. 250)].

ST. CYPRIAN OF CARTHAGE

Let us remember one another in concord and unanimity. Let us on both sides always pray for one another. Let us relieve burdens and afflictions by mutual love, that if any one of us, by the swiftness of divine condescension, shall go from here first, our love may continue in the presence of the Lord, and our prayers for our brothers and sisters not cease in the presence of the Father's mercy [*Letters* 56:5 (A.D. 252)].

RYLANDS PAPYRUS 470

Mother of God, [listen to] my petitions; do not disregard us in adversity, but rescue us from danger [*Rylands Papyrus 470* (c. A.D. 300)].

ST. METHODIUS OF PHILIPPI

Hail to you forever, you Virgin Mother of God, our unceasing joy, for to you do I again return. You are the beginning of our feast; you are its middle and end; the pearl of great price that belongs to the kingdom; the fat of every victim, the living altar of the bread of life. Hail, you treasure of the love of God. Hail, you fount of the Son's love for man. . . . You gleamed with the insupportable fires of a most fervent charity, bringing forth in the end what was conceived of you . . . making manifest the mystery hidden and unspeakable, the invisible Son of the Father—the Prince of Peace, who in a marvelous manner showed himself as less than all littleness [*Oration on Simeon and Anna* 14 (c. A.D. 300)].

[W]e pray you, the most excellent among women, who boastest in the confidence of your maternal honors that you would unceasingly keep us in remembrance. O holy Mother of God, remember us, I say, who make our boast in you, and who in august hymns celebrate the memory, which will ever live, and never fade away [ibid.].

And also, O honored and venerable Simeon, you earliest host of our holy religion and teacher of the Resurrection of the faithful, be our patron and advocate with the Savior God, whom you were deemed worthy to receive into your arms. We, together with you, sing our praises to Christ, who has the power of life and death, saying, "You are the true light, proceeding from the true light; the true God, begotten of the true God" [ibid.].

ST. CYRIL OF JERUSALEM

[During the Eucharistic Prayer] we commemorate those who have already fallen asleep: first, the patriarchs, prophets, apostles, and martyrs, that in their prayers and supplications God would receive our petition [*Catechetical Lectures* 23:9 (c. A.D. 350)].

EARLY CHRISTIAN INSCRIPTION

Atticus, sleep in peace, secure in your safety, and pray anxiously for our sins [*Christian Inscriptions*, no. 37 (c. A.D. 350)].

ST. GREGORY OF NAZIANZ

Yes, I am well assured that [my father's] intercession is of more avail now than was his instruction in former days, since he is closer to God, now that he has shaken off his bodily fetters, and freed his mind from the clay that obscured it, and holds conversation naked with the nakedness of the prime and purest mind [*Orations* 18:4 (A.D. 374)].

PECTORIUS OF AUTUN

Aschandius, my father, beloved of my heart, with my sweet mother and my brothers, be mindful of your Pectorius abiding in the peace of the Fish [Christ] [*Christian Inscriptions* no. 42 (Epitaph of Pectorius) (c. A.D. 375)].

ST. JOHN CHRYSOSTOM

For he who wears the purple himself goes to embrace those tombs, and, laying aside his pride, stands begging the saints to be his advocates with God, and he that wears the crown implores the tentmaker and the fisherman, though dead, to be his patrons [*Homilies on Second Corinthians* 26:2:5 (c. A.D. 392)].

ST. JEROME

You say, in your pamphlet, that as long as we are alive we can pray for one another; but once we die, the prayer of no person for another can be heard, and all the more because the martyrs, though they [Rv 6:10] cry for the avenging of their blood, have never been able to obtain their request. If apostles and martyrs while still in the body can pray for others, when they ought still to be anxious for themselves, how much more must they do so when once they have won their crowns, overcome, and triumphed? [*Against Vigilantius* 6 (A.D. 406)].

ST. AUGUSTINE OF HIPPO

It is true that Christians pay religious honor to the memory of the martyrs, both to excite us to imitate them, and to obtain a share in their merits and the assistance of their prayers [*Reply to Faustus the Manichean* 20:21 (c. A.D. 400)].

This it was that the blessed martyrs did in their burning love; and if we celebrate their memories not in an empty form, and, in the banquet at which they were filled to the full, approach the table of the Lord, we must, as they did, also be making similar preparations. For on these very grounds we do not commemorate them at that table in the same way, as we do others who now rest in peace, by praying for them, but rather that they should pray for us, that we may walk in their footsteps [*Tractates on John* 84:1 (A.D. 416–17)].

For the souls of the pious dead are not separated from the Church, which even now is the kingdom of Christ; otherwise there would

be no remembrance made of them at the altar of God in the partaking of the body of Christ, nor would it do any good in danger
to run to baptism, that we might not pass from this life without it;
nor to reconciliation, if by penitence or a bad conscience anyone
may be severed from his body [*City of God* 20:9 (c. A.D. 419)].

53. Ongoing Miracles

Does God still do miracles? Virtually all Christians would answer
yes, he does. Otherwise there would be no point in praying to
him for help in this life. But God can work subtly or dramatically,
and there is a difference between, for example, how God might
help you find a spouse and the parting of the Red Sea. One type
of divine intervention does not obviously override the way nature
normally operates; the other does.

As a result, some Christians have questioned whether God still
does the kind of miracle that is overtly supernatural in origin—
something that nature does not do on its own—and some have
argued that the "age of miracles" of this kind is over, though Scripture neither claims nor predicts this.

In fact, overtly supernatural miracles have been reported down
through history. Historian Ramsay MacMullen notes that contemporary miracles played a central role in Christian apologetics
in the early centuries:

> When careful assessment is made of passages in the ancient written
> evidence that clearly indicate motive . . . leading a person to con-
> version, they show (so far as I can discover): first, the operation of
> a desire for blessings . . . second, and much more attested, a fear
> of physical pain . . . third, and most frequent, credence in miracles
> (*Christianizing the Roman Empire*, 108).

> Christian writers themselves . . . portray the learned and sophis-
> ticated as having been won over by sheer force of logic, and the
> unlearned, by a sort of stupefaction or terror before the greatness
> of God's power (ibid., 109).

The Church Fathers, for their part, certainly recognized the ongoing, miraculous operation of God in the world.

MARTYRDOM OF POLYCARP

When he had pronounced this amen, and finished his prayer, those who were appointed for the purpose kindled the fire. And as the flame blazed forth in great fury, we who witnessed it beheld a great miracle, and have been preserved so that we might report to others what took place. For the fire, shaping itself into the form of an arch, like the sail of a ship when filled with the wind, encompassed as by a circle the body of the martyr. And he appeared within not like flesh that is burned, but like bread that is baked, or like gold and silver glowing in a furnace. Moreover, we perceived a sweet odor, as if frankincense or some precious spices had been smoking there. At length, when those wicked men perceived that his body could not be consumed by the fire, they commanded an executioner to go near and pierce him with a dagger. On his doing this, there came forth a dove, and a great quantity of blood, so that the fire was extinguished; and everyone wondered that there should be such a difference between the unbelievers and the elect [*The Martyrdom of Polycarp* 15–16 (c. A.D. 156)].

ST. IRENAEUS OF LYONS

[Heretics are] so far . . . from being able to raise the dead, as the Lord raised them and the apostles did by means of prayer, and as has been frequently done in the [Catholic] brotherhood on account of some necessity. The entire church in that particular locality entreating with much fasting and prayer, the spirit of the dead man has returned, and he has been given in answer to the prayers of the saints [*Against Heresies* 2:31:2 (c. A.D. 189)].

TERTULLIAN OF CARTHAGE

We have faith for a defense, if we are not smitten with distrust, in immediately making the sign [of the cross] and commanding and smearing the heel with the beast. Finally, we often aid even the heathen in this way, who see that we have been endowed by God with that power that the apostle [Paul] first used when he despised the viper's bite [Acts 28:3] [*Antidote for the Scorpion's Sting* I (c. A.D. 211)].

EUSEBIUS OF CAESAREA

The citizens of that parish mention many other miracles of Narcissus, in the tradition of the brethren who succeeded him; among which they relate the following wonder he performed. They say that the oil once failed while the deacons were watching through the night at the great paschal vigil. They were dismayed, so Narcissus directed those who attended to the lights to draw water and bring it to him. This being done, he prayed over the water, and with firm faith in the Lord, commanded them to pour it into the lamps. And when they did it, contrary to all expectation, by a wonderful and divine power the water was changed into oil. A small portion of it has been preserved even to this day by many of the brethren there as a memento of the wonder [*Church History* 6:9:1–3 (c. A.D. 312)].

ST. ATHANASIUS OF ALEXANDRIA

So take these as an example, beloved Dracontius, and do not say, or believe those who say, that the bishop's office is an occasion of sin, or that it gives rise to temptations to sin. For it is possible for a bishop to hunger and thirst [Phil 4:12], as Paul did. You can drink no wine, like Timothy [1 Tm 5:23], and fast constantly too, like Paul [2 Cor 11:27], in order that after their example you may feed others with your words, and while thirsting for lack of drink, water others by teaching. Let not your advisers, then, allege these things. For we know bishops who fast, and monks who eat. We know bishops who drink no wine, and monks who do. We know bishops who work wonders, and monks who do not [*Festal Letters* 49:9 (c. A.D. 354)].

ST. JOHN CHRYSOSTOM

For even in our generation, in the instance of Julian, who surpassed all in ungodliness, many strange things happened. When the Jews were attempting to raise up the temple at Jerusalem, fire burst out from the foundations and utterly hindered them; and when both his treasurer, and his uncle and namesake, made the sacred vessels the subject of insolence, the one was "eaten with worms, and gave up the ghost," the other "burst asunder." Moreover, the fountains failed when sacrifices were made there, and the entrance of famine in the cities where the emperor went was a very great sign. For it is usual with God to do such things when evils are multiplied [*Homilies on Matthew* 4:2 (c. A.D. 370)].

ST. BASIL OF CAESAREA

But where shall I rank the great Gregory, and the words uttered by him? Should we not place among apostles and prophets a man who walked by the same Spirit as they [2 Cor 12:18]; who never through all his days diverged from the footprints of the saints; who maintained, as long as he lived, the exact principles of evangelical citizenship? I am sure that we shall do the truth a wrong if we refuse to number that soul with the people of God, shining as it did like a beacon in the Church of God; for by the working of the Spirit the power he had over demons was tremendous, and so gifted was he with the grace of the word "for obedience to the faith among . . . the nations" [Rom 1:5], that, although only seventeen Christians were handed over to him, he brought all the people in town and country to God. In Christ's mighty name, he commanded rivers to change their course, and caused a lake, which was a ground of quarrel to some covetous brethren, to dry up. Moreover, his predictions of things to come did not fall short of those of the great prophets [*The Holy Spirit* 29:74 (A.D. 375)].

ST. AMBROSE OF MILAN

As I do not wish anything that takes place here in your absence to escape the knowledge of your holiness, you must know that we have found some bodies of holy martyrs. For after I dedicated the basilica, many said to me: "Consecrate this as you did the Roman basilica." And I answered: "Certainly I will if I find any relics of martyrs." And at once a kind of prophetic ardor entered my heart. Why should I use many words? God favored us, and even the clergy who were bidden to clear away the earth from the spot before the chancel screen of Ss. Felix and Nabor were afraid. I found the fitting signs, and on bringing in some on whom hands were to be laid, the power of the holy martyrs became so manifest that even while I was silent, one was seized and thrown prostrate at the holy burial place. We found two men of marvelous stature, such as those of ancient days. All the bones were perfect, and there was much blood. During those two days there was an enormous concourse of people. Quickly we arranged the whole in order, and as evening was now coming on transferred them to the basilica of Fausta, where watch was kept during the night, and some received the laying on of hands. On the following day we moved the relics to the basilica called Ambrosian. During the removal a blind man was healed [*Letters* 22:1–2 (c. A.D. 386)].

ST. JEROME

[S]he set out accompanied by her handmaids and eunuchs, and was hardly persuaded by her husband to take an ass to ride upon. On reaching the saint she said, "I pray you by Jesus our most merciful God, I beseech you by his cross and blood, to restore to me my three sons, so that the name of our Lord and Savior may be glorified in the city of the Gentiles. Then his servants shall enter Gaza and the idol Marnas fall to the ground." At first he refused and said that he never left his cell and was not accustomed to enter a house, much less the city; but she threw herself upon the ground and cried repeatedly, "Hilarion, servant of Christ, give me back my children: Antony kept them safe in Egypt, you save them in Syria." All present were weeping, and the saint himself wept as he denied her. But the woman did not leave him until he promised that he would enter Gaza after sunset. On coming there he made the sign of the cross over the bed and fevered limbs of each, and called upon the name of Jesus. Marvelous efficacy of the name! As if from three fountains the sweat burst forth at the same time. In that very hour they took food, recognized their mourning mother, and, with thanks to God, warmly kissed the saint's hands [*Life of St. Hilarion* 14 (A.D. 390)].

ST. AUGUSTINE OF HIPPO

In the same city of Carthage lived Innocentia, a very devout woman of the highest rank in the state. She had cancer in one of her breasts, a disease that physicians say is incurable. Ordinarily, therefore, they either amputate, and so separate from the body the diseased member, or, to prolong the patient's life, though death is inevitable even if delayed, they abandon all remedies, following the advice of Hippocrates. This lady had been advised by a skillful physician who was intimate with her family; and she gave herself to God alone in prayer. When Easter approached, she was instructed in a dream to wait for the first woman to came out from the baptistry after being baptized, and ask her to make the sign of Christ upon her sore. She did so, and was immediately cured [*City of God* 22:8 (c. A.D. 419)].

For even now miracles are wrought in the name of Christ, whether by his sacraments or by the prayers or relics of his saints. . . . But who but a very small number are aware of the cure that was wrought upon Innocentius . . . at Carthage, in my presence, and under my own eyes? . . . For he and all his household were devoutly pious. He was being treated by medical men for fistulae, of which he had a large number. . . . He had already undergone an operation but needed another. . . . [H]e cast himself down . . . and began to pray; but in what a manner, with what earnestness and emotion, with what a flood of tears, with what groans and sobs that shook his whole body and almost prevented him speaking. . . . [And when the] surgeons arrived, everything was ready; the frightful instruments were produced; all looked on in wonder and suspense. . . . [But the surgeon] found a perfectly firm scar! No words of mine can describe the joy, and praise, and thanksgiving to the merciful and almighty God that were poured from the lips of all with tears of gladness. Let the scene [of rejoicing] be imagined rather than described! [ibid.].

A gouty doctor of the same city, when he had given his name for baptism and had been forbidden the day before his baptism from being baptized that year by black woolly-haired boys who appeared to him in his dreams (and whom he understood to be devils), and when . . . he refused to obey them but overcame them and would not defer being washed in the washing of regeneration, was relieved in the very act of baptism, not only of the extraordinary pain he was tortured with, but also of the disease itself [ibid.].

What am I to do? I am so pressed by the promise of finishing this work that I cannot record all the miracles I know, and doubtless several of our adherents, when they read what I have narrated, will regret that I have omitted many that they, as well as I, certainly know. Even now I beg these persons to excuse me and to consider how long it would take me to relate all those miracles, which the necessity of finishing the work I have undertaken forces me to omit. . . . Even now, therefore, many miracles are wrought, the same God who wrought those we read of [in the Bible is] still performing them, by whom he will and as he will [ibid.].

54. Private Revelation

Catholic theology commonly distinguishes between what is known as public revelation and private revelation. Public revelation— which is the kind of revelation we find in Scripture—is binding on all Christians in all ages. By contrast, private revelation is binding only on those to whom it is given.

The Catholic Church teaches that public revelation is closed until the Second Coming. The *Catechism of the Catholic Church* states: "The Christian economy, therefore, since it is the new and definitive Covenant, will never pass away; and no new public revelation is to be expected before the glorious manifestation of our Lord Jesus Christ" (CCC 66).

Private revelation, however, is ongoing:

> Throughout the ages, there have been so-called 'private' revelations, some of which have been recognized by the authority of the Church. They do not belong, however, to the deposit of faith. It is not their role to improve or complete Christ's definitive revelation, but to help live more fully by it in a certain period of history. Guided by the magisterium of the Church, the *sensus fidelium* [i.e., collective sense of the faithful] knows how to discern and welcome in these revelations whatever constitutes an authentic call of Christ or his saints to the Church. Christian faith cannot accept "revelations" that claim to surpass or correct the revelation of which Christ is the fulfillment, as is the case in certain non-Christian religions and also in certain recent sects which base themselves on such "revelations" (CCC 67).

But just as some in non-Catholic circles have claimed that the age of miracles is over, so some have claimed that the age of revelation—even private revelation—is over. Yet this is something that Scripture never says. None of the New Testament authors say that God is going to stop using visions and related phenomena prior to the Second Coming. St. Paul expresses the proper Christian attitude toward these phenomena this way: "Do not quench the Spirit. Do not despise prophetic utterances. Test everything; retain what is good" (1 Thes 5:19–21).

As the following passages from the early Church Fathers illustrate, they shared this attitude and recognized the ongoing presence of private revelations in the Church.

HERMAS OF ROME

The vision I saw, my brethren, was of the following nature. . . . [An] old woman approached, accompanied by six young men. . . . [And] she said to me . . . "Lo! Do you not see opposite to you a great tower, built upon the waters, of splendid square stones?" For the tower was built square by the six young men who had come with her. But myriads of men were carrying stones to it, some dragging them from the depths, others removing them from the land, and they handed them to these six young men. . . . [And the woman said:] "The tower that you see being built is myself, the Church. . . . It is built upon the waters . . . because your life has been and will be 'saved through water' [1 Pt 3:20–21]. . . . The six young men . . . are the holy angels of God. . . . The other persons who are engaged in carrying the stones . . . are also holy angels of the Lord . . . [And] when the tower is finished and built, then comes the end" [*The Shepherd* 1:3:1–8 (c. A.D. 80)].

ST. JUSTIN MARTYR

For the prophetical gifts remain with us [Christians], even to the present time. And hence you [Jews] ought to understand that [the gifts] formerly among your nation have been transferred to us [*Dialogue with Trypho* 82 (c. A.D. 155)].

MARTYRDOM OF POLYCARP

And while he was praying, a vision presented itself to him three days before he was taken; and, behold, the pillow under his head seemed to be on fire. Turning to those who were with him, he said to them prophetically, "I must be burned alive." . . . Speaking thus, they cried out, and asked Philip the Asiarch to let loose a lion upon Polycarp. But Philip answered that it was not lawful for him to do so, seeing the shows of wild beasts were already finished. Then it seemed good to them to cry out together that Polycarp should be burned alive [*Martyrdom of Polycarp* 5, 12 (c. A.D. 156)].

Polycarp was . . . bishop of the Catholic Church at Smyrna, and a teacher in our own day who combined apostle and prophet in his own person. For indeed, every word that fell from his lips either has had or will have its fulfillment [ibid., 16].

ST. IRENAEUS OF LYONS

Likewise we hear of many brethren in the Church who possess prophetic gifts and who through the Spirit speak all kinds of languages and who bring to light for the general benefit the hidden things of men, and declare the mysteries of God [*Against Heresies* 5:6:1 (c. A.D. 189)].

ST. PIONIUS OF SMYRNA

I again, Pionius, wrote them from the previously written copy, having carefully searched into them, and the blessed Polycarp having manifested them to me through a revelation, even as I shall show in what follows. I have collected these things, when they had almost faded away through the passing of time, that the Lord Jesus Christ may gather me along with his elect into his heavenly kingdom, to whom, with the Father and the Holy Spirit, be glory forever and ever. Amen [*Martyrdom of Polycarp*, copyist note 2 (c. A.D. 250)].

EUSEBIUS OF CAESAREA

And while [the Emperor Constantine] was praying with fervent entreaty, a most marvelous sign appeared to him from heaven, which might have been hard to believe had it been related by anyone else. But since the victorious emperor himself long afterwards declared it to the writer of this history [Eusebius], when he was honored with his acquaintance and society, and confirmed his statement by an oath, who could fail to credit the story, especially since the testimony of subsequent time has established its truth? He said that at about noon, when the day was already beginning to decline, he saw a trophy of a cross of light in the heavens, above the sun, and bearing the inscription, "Conquer by This." He was struck with amazement, and his whole army also, which had followed him on this expedition and witnessed the miracle. He said [to me], moreover, that he did not know the meaning of this apparition. And while he continued to ponder and reason on it, night suddenly came on; then in his sleep the Christ of God appeared to him with the same sign he had seen in the heavens, and commanded him to make a likeness of that sign and to use it as a safeguard in all engagements with his enemies. . . . [B]eing struck with amazement at the extraordinary vision, and resolving to worship no other God save him who had appeared to him, he sent for those who were acquainted with the mysteries of [God's] doctrines and inquired who that God was and what was intended by the sign of the vision he had seen [*Life of Constantine* 1:28–32 (c. A.D. 337)].

ST. ANTHONY OF EGYPT

[Anthony told his monks:] When, therefore, [demons] come by night to you and wish to tell the future, or say "We are the angels," give no heed, for they lie. . . . But if they shamelessly stand their ground, capering, and change their forms of appearance, fear them not, nor shrink, nor heed them as though they were good spirits. For the presence of good or evil can easily be distinguished with the help of God. The vision of the holy ones is not fraught with distraction, "For they will not strive, nor cry, nor shall anyone hear their voice" [Mt 12:19; see also Is 42:2]. But they come quietly and gently so that an immediate joy, gladness, and courage arise in the soul. For the Lord who is our joy is with them, and the power of God the Father [Athanasius, *Life of St. Anthony* 35 (c. A.D. 359)].

ST. AUGUSTINE OF HIPPO

For even now miracles are wrought in the name of Christ, whether by his sacraments or by the prayers or relics of his saints. . . . The miracle that was wrought at Milan when I was there . . . [and when people] had gathered to the bodies of the martyrs Protasius and Gervasius, which had long lain concealed and unknown but were now made known to the bishop Ambrose in a dream and discovered by him [*City of God* 22:8 (c. A.D. 419)].

A certain man by [the] name Curma [was in a coma]. . . . Yet he saw many things as in a dream; when at last after a great many days he woke up, he told what he had seen. . . . [He also saw] Hippo, where he was baptized by me. . . . After much else, he narrated how he had, moreover, been led into paradise and how it was said to him there, when he was dismissed to return to his own family, "Go, be baptized if you want to be in this place of the blessed." He said it was already done. He who was talking with him replied, "Go, be truly baptized, for you only saw that in a vision." After this he recovered, went his way to Hippo . . . was baptized [and] at the close of the holy days [of Easter] returned to his own place. . . . Why should we not believe these to be angelic operations through the dispensation of the providence of God? [*Care to Be Had for the Dead* 15–16 (A.D. 421)].

[T]he martyrs, by the very benefits that are given to them that pray, indicate that they take an interest in the affairs of men. . . . For not only by effects of benefits, but in the very beholding of men, it is certain that the confessor Felix . . . appeared when the barbarians were attacking Nola, as we have heard not by uncertain rumors but by sure witness [ibid., 19].

SOZOMEN OF CONSTANTINOPLE

Gregory of Nazianzen presided over those who maintain the "consubstantiality" of the Holy Trinity, and assembled them together in a little dwelling, which had been altered into a house of prayer by those who held the same opinions and had a like form of worship. It subsequently became one of the most conspicuous in the city, and is so now, not only for the beauty and number of its structures, but also for the advantages accruing to it from the visible manifestations of God. For the power of God was manifested there, and was helpful both in waking visions and in dreams, often for the relief of many diseases and for those afflicted by some sudden change in their affairs. The power was accredited to Mary, the Mother of God, the holy Virgin, for she does manifest herself in this way [*Church History* 7:5 (c. A.D. 444)].

ST. PATRICK

[In Ireland] one night I heard in my sleep a voice saying to me, "You fast well; soon you will go to your fatherland." And again, after a very short time, I heard the heavenly voice saying to me,

"Lo, your ship is ready." And it was not near at hand, but was distant, perhaps two hundred miles. And I had never been there, nor did I know any person living there. And then I shortly took flight and left the man with whom I had been for six years. And I came in the strength of God, who prospered my way for good; and I met with nothing to alarm me until I reached that ship [*Confession of St. Patrick* 17 (c. A.D. 452)].

And once more, after a few years, I was in Britain with my family. . . . And there I saw in a vision in the night of a man whose name was Victoricus coming from Ireland with countless letters. He gave me one of them, and I read the beginning of the letter, which was entitled "The Voice of the Irish." And while I was reading it aloud, I thought I heard the voices of those who dwelled beside the Wood of Foclut [in Ireland], which is near the Western Sea. And they cried, as with one mouth, "We beseech you, holy youth, to come and walk once more among us!" [ibid., 23].

Let those who will, laugh and mock. I will not be silent or conceal the signs and wonders that were shown to me by the Lord many years before they came to pass, since he knows all things even before the world's beginnings [ibid., 45].

XI. The Last Things

55. Salvation Outside the Church

The *Catechism of the Catholic Church* refers to Christ's Church as "the universal sacrament of salvation" (CCC 774–76). It states: "The Church in this world is the sacrament of salvation, the sign and the instrument of the communion of God and men" (CCC 780).

Many misunderstand the nature of this teaching. At one extreme, some think that it makes no difference what church or even what religion one belongs to, and that salvation can be attained equally through any of them. At the other extreme, some claim that anyone who is not a full-fledged member of the Catholic Church will be damned.

The following quotations from the Church Fathers avoid both extremes. They show that the early Church recognized that it is normatively necessary to be a Catholic to be saved (see CCC 846; Vatican II, *Lumen Gentium* 14), but there are exceptions; it is possible for people to be saved who through no fault of their own are not in full communion with the Catholic Church (CCC 847).

Notice that the same Fathers who declare the normative necessity of being Catholic also declare the possibility of salvation for some who are not Catholics, who can be saved by what later came to be known as "baptism of blood" or "baptism of desire" (see chapter 38). The Fathers likewise affirm the possibility of salvation for those who lived before Christ and who were not part of Israel, the Old Testament church.

Although salvation is possible for those not in full communion with the Church, to refuse to enter it knowingly and deliberately or to separate from it through heresy or schism remains a mortal sin.

ST. IGNATIUS OF ANTIOCH

Do not err, my brethren. If any man follows him that makes a schism in the Church, he shall not inherit the kingdom of God. If anyone walks according to a strange opinion, he does not agree with the Passion [of Christ]. Take heed, then, to have but one Eucharist. For there is one flesh of our Lord Jesus Christ, and one cup to [show forth] the unity of his blood; one altar; as there is one bishop, along with the presbytery and deacons, my fellow servants: that so, whatever you do, you do it according to [the will of] God [*Letter to the Philadelphians* 3–4 (c. A.D. 110)].

ST. JUSTIN MARTYR

We have been taught that Christ is the firstborn of God, and we have declared that he is the Word of whom every race of men are partakers; and those who live reasonably are Christians, even though they have been thought atheists; as, among the Greeks, Socrates and Heraclitus, and men like them; and among the barbarians, Abraham, and Ananias, and Azarias, and Misael, and Elias, and many others whose actions and names we now decline to recount, because we know it would be tedious. So that even those who lived before Christ, and lived without reason, were wicked and hostile to Christ, and slew those who lived reasonably. But he who, through the power of the Word, according to the will of God the Father and Lord of all, was born of a Virgin as a man, and was named Jesus, and was crucified, and died, and rose again, and ascended into heaven, an intelligent man will be able to comprehend from what has been said [*First Apology* 46 (c. A.D. 151)].

ST. IRENAEUS OF LYONS

In the Church God has placed apostles, prophets, teachers, and every other working of the Spirit, of whom none are sharers who do not conform to the Church, but who defraud themselves of life by an evil mind and an even worse way of acting. Where the

Church is, there is the Spirit of God; where the Spirit of God is, there is the Church and all grace [*Against Heresies* 3:24:1 (c. A.D. 189)].

[The spiritual man] shall also judge those who give rise to schisms, who are destitute of the love of God, and who look to their own special advantage rather than to the unity of the Church; and who for trifling reasons, or any kind of reason that occurs to them, cut in pieces and divide the great and glorious body of Christ, and so far as they are able, destroy it—men who talk of peace while they give rise to war, and who in truth strain out a gnat but swallow a camel. For they can bring about no "reformation" of enough importance to compensate for the evil arising from their schism. . . . True knowledge consists in the doctrine of the apostles, and the ancient constitution of the Church throughout all the world, and the distinctive manifestation of the body of Christ according to the successions of the bishops, by which they have handed down that Church that exists in every place [i.e., the Catholic Church] [ibid., 4:33:7–8].

ST. CLEMENT OF ALEXANDRIA

Accordingly, before the advent of the Lord, philosophy was necessary to the Greeks for righteousness. And now it is conducive to piety, as a kind of preparatory training to those who attain faith through demonstration. "For your foot," it is said, "will not stumble, if you refer what is good, whether belonging to the Greeks or to us, to Providence" [Prv 3:23]. For God is the cause of all good things; but of some primarily, as of the Old and the New Testament; and of others by consequence, as philosophy. Perhaps philosophy was given to the Greeks directly and primarily, until the Lord should call them [*Miscellanies* 1:5 (c. A.D. 207)].

ORIGEN OF ALEXANDRIA

[T]here was never a time when God did not wish to make men live righteous lives; but he continually showed his care for the improvement of the rational animal by affording him occasions for the exercise of virtue. For in every generation the wisdom of God, passing into those souls it ascertains to be holy, converts them into friends and prophets of God [*Against Celsus* 4:7 (c. A.D. 248)].

If someone of that people wishes to be saved, let him come into this house, so that he may be able to obtain his salvation. . . . Let no one, then, be persuaded otherwise, nor let anyone deceive himself; outside this house, that is, outside the Church, no one is saved. For if anyone go outside, he shall be guilty of his own death [*Homilies on Joshua* 3:5 (c. A.D. 250)].

ST. CYPRIAN OF CARTHAGE

Nor let them think that the way of life or of salvation is still open to them, if they have refused to obey the bishops and priests, since in Deuteronomy the Lord God says, "And the man that will do presumptuously, and will not listen to the priest or judge, whoever he shall be in those days, that man shall die, and all the people shall hear and fear, and do no more presumptuously" [Dt 17:12]. God commanded those who did not obey his priests to be slain, and those who did not listen to his judges who were appointed at that time. And indeed they were slain with the sword, when the circumcision of the flesh was yet in force; but now that circumcision has begun to be of the spirit among God's faithful servants, the proud and stubborn are slain with the sword of the Spirit, in that they are cast out of the Church. For they cannot live out of it, since the house of God is one, and there can be no salvation to any except in the Church [*Letters* 61:4 (c. A.D. 249)].

Whoever is separated from the Church and is joined to an adulteress [a schismatic church] is separated from the promises of the Church; nor can anyone who forsakes the Church of Christ attain the rewards of Christ. He is a stranger; he is profane; he is an enemy. He can no longer have God for his Father, who does not have the Church for his mother [*Unity of the Catholic Church* 6, first edition (Treatise 1) (A.D. 251)].

When we say, "Do you believe in eternal life and the remission of sins through the holy Church?" we mean that remission of sins is not granted except in the Church [*Letters* 69:2 (A.D. 255)].

Not even the baptism of a public confession and blood can profit a heretic to salvation, because there is no salvation out of the Church [ibid., 72:21 (c. A.D. 255)].

Peter himself, showing and vindicating the unity, has commanded and warned us that we cannot be saved except by the one baptism of the one Church. He says, "In the ark of Noah a few, that is, eight souls, were saved by water. Similarly, baptism will in like manner save you" [1 Pt 3:20–21]. In how short and spiritual a summary has he set forth the sacrament of unity! In that baptism of the world in which its ancient wickedness was washed away, he who was not in the ark of Noah could not be saved by water. Likewise, neither can he be saved by baptism who has not been baptized in the Church, which is established in the unity of the Lord according to the sacrament of the one ark [ibid., 73:11 (c. A.D. 253)].

TREATISE ON RE-BAPTISM

[O]utside the Church there is no Holy Spirit. Sound faith moreover cannot exist, not only among heretics, but even among those who are established in schism [*Treatise on Re-Baptism* 10 (c. A.D. 257)].

LACTANTIUS

[I]t is the Catholic Church alone that retains true worship. This is the fountain of truth, this is the abode of the faith, this is the temple of God; if anyone shall not enter, or if anyone shall leave, he is estranged from the hope of life and eternal salvation. No one should flatter himself with persevering strife. For the contest is about life and salvation, which, unless it is carefully and diligently kept in view, will be lost and extinguished. But, however, because all the separate assemblies of heretics call themselves Christians in preference to others, and think that theirs is the Catholic Church, it must be known that the true Catholic Church is that in which there is confession and repentance, which treats in a wholesome manner the sins and wounds to which the weakness of the flesh is liable [*Divine Institutes* 4:30 (c. A.D. 307)].

ST. JEROME

Heretics bring sentence upon themselves since by their own choice they withdraw from the Church, a withdrawal that, since they are aware of it, constitutes damnation. Between heresy and schism there is this difference: heresy involves perverse doctrine, while schism separates one from the Church on account of disagreement with the bishop. Nevertheless, there is no schism that does not trump up a heresy to justify its departure from the Church [*Commentaries on Titus* 3:10–11 (c. A.D. 386)].

ST. AUGUSTINE OF HIPPO

[W]e believe also in the holy Church, [intending thereby] assuredly the Catholic. For both heretics and schismatics style their congregations churches. But heretics, in holding false opinions regarding God, do injury to the faith itself; while schismatics, on the other hand, in wicked separations break off from brotherly charity, although they may believe just what we believe. As a result neither do the heretics belong to the Catholic Church, which loves God; nor do the schismatics form a part of the same, inasmuch as it loves the neighbor, and consequently readily forgives the neighbor's sins, because it prays that forgiveness may be extended to itself by him who has reconciled us to himself, doing away with all past things, and calling us to a new life And until we reach the perfection of this new life, we cannot be without sins. Nevertheless it is a matter of consequence of what sort those sins may be [*Faith and the Creed* 10:21 (A.D. 393)].

The apostle Paul has said, "Reject a man that is a heretic after the first and second admonition, knowing that such a man is subverted and sins, and condemns himself" [Ti 3:10–11]. But though the doctrine men hold may be false and perverse, if they do not maintain it with passionate obstinacy, especially when they have not devised it by the rashness of their own presumption, but have accepted it from parents who had been misguided and fallen into error, and if they are with anxiety seeking the truth, and are prepared to be set right when they have found it, such men are not to be counted heretics [*Letters* 43:1 (A.D. 397)].

[J]ust as baptism is of no profit to the man who renounces the world in words and not in deeds, so it is of no profit to him who is baptized in heresy or schism; but each of them, when he amends his ways, begins to profit from what was not profitable before, but was already in him [*On Baptism, Against the Donatists* 4:4:6 (A.D. 400)].

I do not hesitate for a moment to place the Catholic catechumen, who is burning with love for God, before the baptized heretic; nor do we dishonor the sacrament of baptism that the latter has already received, the former not as yet; nor do we consider that the sacrament of the catechumen is preferable to the sacrament of baptism, even when we acknowledge that some catechumens are better and more faithful than some baptized persons. . . . For Cornelius, even before his baptism, was filled with the Holy Spirit [Acts 10:44]; Simon, even after baptism, was puffed up with an unclean spirit [*On Baptism, Against the Donatists* 4:21:29 (A.D. 400)].

ST. FULGENCE OF RUSPE

Anyone who receives the sacrament of baptism, whether in the Catholic Church or in a heretical or schismatic one, receives the whole sacrament; but salvation, which is the strength of the sacrament, he will not have, if he has had the sacrament outside the Catholic Church. He must return to the Church, not so that he might receive the sacrament of baptism again, which no one dare repeat in any baptized person, but so that he may receive eternal life in Catholic society, which no one who remains estranged from the Catholic Church may obtain, even with the sacrament of baptism [*Rule of Faith* 43 (c. A.D. 524)].

56. Reward and Merit

St. Paul tells us that God "will reward every man according to his works: to those who by perseverance in working good seek for glory and honor and immortality, he will give eternal life. There will be . . . glory and honor and peace for every one who does good, the Jew first and also the Greek. For God shows no partiality" (Rom 2:6–11; see also Gal 6:6–10).

In the second century, the Latin word *meritum* ("merit") was introduced as a translation for the Greek word for "reward," and so entered the theological vocabulary. The doctrine of merit and the doctrine of reward are two ways of expressing the same concept.

Some misunderstand Catholic teaching on merit, thinking that Catholics believe that one must do good works to come to God and be saved. This is the opposite of what the Church teaches. The Council of Trent stressed that "none of those things which precede justification, whether faith or works, merit the grace of justification; for if it is by grace, it is not now by works; otherwise, as the apostle [Paul] says, grace is no more grace" (*Decree on Justification* 8, citing Rom 11:6).

The Catholic Church teaches that only Christ can merit in the strict sense; mere man cannot. The *Catechism of the Catholic Church* states: "With regard to God, there is no strict right to any merit on the part of man. Between God and us there is an immeasurable inequality, for we have received everything from him, our Creator" (CCC 2007).

At most, humans can have a kind of merit when, under the impetus of God's grace, they perform acts that please him and that he has promised to reward (Rom 2:6–11; Gal 6:6–10). Thus God's grace and his promise form the foundation for all human merit (see CCC 2008).

Though the Protestant community typically does not like the term "merit," it recognizes that, under the impetus of grace, Christians do perform acts that are pleasing to God and that he has promised to reward. They thus admit the substance of the doctrine, even if they express it differently.

The following passages illustrate what the Church Fathers had to say on the relationship between merit and grace.

ST. IGNATIUS OF ANTIOCH

Give heed to the bishop, that God may give heed to you. My soul is for theirs that are submissive to the bishop, to the presbyters, and to the deacons, and may my portion be with them in God! Labor together with one another; strive in company together; run together; suffer together; sleep together; and awake together, as the stewards, and associates, and servants of God. Please him under whom you fight, and from whom you receive your wages. Let none of you be found a deserter. Let your baptism endure as your arms; your faith as your helmet; your love as your spear; your patience as complete armor. Let your works be the charge assigned to you, that you may receive a worthy recompense. Be long-suffering with one another, in meekness, as God is towards you. May I have joy of you for ever! [*Letter to Polycarp and Smyrna* 6 (c. A.D. 110)].

ST. JUSTIN MARTYR

We have learned from the prophets, and we believe it is true, that punishments, and chastisements, and good rewards, are rendered according to the merit of each man's actions. If it is not so, then all things happen by fate, and nothing is in our own power. If it is fated that this man be good, and this other evil, the former is not meritorious nor the latter blameworthy [*First Apology* 43 (c. A.D. 151)].

TATIAN THE SYRIAN

The bad man may be justly punished, having become depraved through his own fault, but the just man may be deservedly praised for his virtuous deeds, since in the exercise of his free choice he refrained from transgressing the will of God [*Address to the Greeks* 7 (c. A.D. 170)].

ATHENAGORAS OF ATHENS

And we shall make no mistake in saying that the final cause of an intelligent life and rational judgment is to be occupied uninterruptedly with those objects to which the natural reason is chiefly adapted, and to delight unceasingly in the contemplation of him who is, and of his decrees, notwithstanding that the majority of men, because they are affected too passionately and too violently by things below, pass through life without attaining this object. For the large number of those who fail to reach the end that belongs to them does not make void the common lot, since the examination relates to individuals, and the reward or punishment of lives ill or well spent is proportionate to the merit of each [*Resurrection of the Dead* 25 (c. A.D. 178)].

ST. THEOPHILUS OF ANTIOCH

For he who gave the mouth for speech, and formed the ear to hear, and made the eye to see, will examine all things, and will judge righteous judgment, rendering merited awards to each. To those who by patient continuance in well-doing [Rom 2:7] seek immortality, he will give life everlasting, joy, peace, rest, and abundance of good things, which neither has eye seen, nor ear heard, nor has it entered into the heart of man to conceive [1 Cor 2:9]. But to the unbelieving and despisers, who obey not the truth, but are obedient to unrighteousness, when they have been filled with adulteries and fornications, and filthiness, and covetousness, and unlawful idolatries, there shall be anger and wrath, tribulation and anguish [Rom 2:8–9], and at the last everlasting fire shall possess such men [*To Autolycus* 1:14 (c. A.D. 181)].

ST. IRENAEUS OF LYONS

This able wrestler [Paul], exhorts us to the struggle for immortality, that we may be crowned, and may deem the crown precious, namely, what is acquired by our struggle, but which does not encircle us of its own accord. And the harder we strive, the more valuable it is; the more valuable it is, so much the more should we esteem it. And indeed things that come spontaneously are not esteemed as highly, as those that are reached by much anxious care [*Against Heresies* 4:37:7 (c. A.D. 189)].

TERTULLIAN OF CARTHAGE

Again, we [Christians] affirm that a judgment has been ordained by God according to the merits of every man [*To the Nations* 19 (A.D. 197)].

In former times the Jews enjoyed much of God's favor, when the fathers of their race were noted for their righteousness and faith. So it was that as a people they flourished greatly, and their kingdom attained a lofty eminence; and so highly blessed were they, that for their instruction God spoke to them in special revelations, pointing out to them beforehand how they should merit his favor and avoid his displeasure [*Apology* 21 (A.D. 197)].

For God, never giving his sanction to the condemnation of good deeds, because they are his own (of which, being the author, he must necessarily be the defender too), is in like manner the acceptor of them, and if the acceptor, likewise the rewarder [*Repentance* 2 (c. A.D. 203)].

ST. HIPPOLYTUS OF ROME

And being present at his judicial decision, all men and angels and demons shall utter one voice, saying, "Righteous is your judgment," in which voice the justification will be seen in the awarding to each what is just; since those who have done well shall righteously be assigned eternal bliss, and the lovers of iniquity shall be given eternal punishment. And the fire that is unquenchable and without end awaits these latter, and a certain fiery worm that does not die, and that does not waste the body, but continues bursting forth from the body with unending pain. No sleep will give them rest; no night will soothe them; no death will deliver them from punishment; no voice of interceding friends will profit them [*Against Plato, On the Cause of the Universe* 3 (c. A.D. 220)].

ST. CYPRIAN OF CARTHAGE

The Lord denounces [Christian evildoers], and says, "Many shall say to me in that day, 'Lord, Lord, have we not prophesied in your name, and in your name have cast out devils, and in your name done many wonderful works?' And then I will say to them, 'I never knew you: depart from me, you who work iniquity' " [Mt 7:21–23]. There is need of righteousness, that one may deserve well from God the judge; we must obey his precepts and warnings, that our merits may receive their reward [*Unity of the Catholic Church*, first edition (Treatise 1) 15 (A.D. 251)].

And you who are a wealthy and rich matron in Christ's Church, anoint your eyes, not with the ointment of the devil, but with Christ's salve, that you may be able to attain to see God, by deserving well of God, both by good works and character [*Works and Alms* (Treatise 8) 14 (A.D. 253)].

LACTANTIUS

Let every one train himself to justice, mold himself to self-restraint, prepare himself for the contest, equip himself for virtue, that if by any chance an adversary shall wage war, he may be driven from what is upright and good by no force, no terror, and no tortures, and may not give himself up to senseless fictions, but in his uprightness acknowledge the true and only God, cast away pleasures, by whose attractions the lofty soul is depressed to the earth, may hold fast innocence, may be of service to as many as possible, may gain for himself incorruptible treasures by good works, that he may be able, with God for his judge, to gain for the merits of his virtue either the crown of faith, or the reward of immortality [*Epitome of the Divine Institutes* 73 (c. A.D. 317)].

ST. CYRIL OF JERUSALEM

The root of all good works is the hope of the Resurrection; for the expectation of the recompense steels the soul to do good works.

For every laborer is ready to endure the toils, if he sees its reward [*Catechetical Lectures* 18:1 (c. A.D. 350)].

ST. JEROME

Now our work is, according to our different virtues, to prepare for ourselves a different future. . . . If we are all to be equal in heaven, in vain do we humble ourselves here that we may be greater there. . . . Why do virgins persevere? Widows toil? Why do married women practice continence? Let us all sin, and when once we have repented, we shall be on the same footing as the apostles [*Against Jovinianus* 2:32–34 (c. A.D. 393)].

ST. AUGUSTINE OF HIPPO

We are commanded to live righteously, and the reward is set before us of our meriting happiness in eternal life. But who is able to live righteously and do good works unless he has been justified by faith? [*Various Questions to Simplician* 1:2:21 (c. A.D. 396)].

He bestowed forgiveness; the crown he will pay out. Of forgiveness he is the donor; of the crown, he is the debtor. Why debtor? Did he receive something? . . . The Lord made himself a debtor not by receiving something but by promising something. One does not say to him, "Pay for what you received," but "Pay what you promised" [*Explanations of the Psalms* 83:16 (c. A.D. 405)].

What merits of his own has the saved to boast of when, if he were dealt with according to his merits, he would be damned? Have the just then no merits at all? Of course they do, for they are the just. But they had no merits by which they were made just [*Letters* 194:3:6 (A.D. 418)].

What merit, then, does a man have by which he might receive grace, when our every good merit is produced in us only by grace and when God, crowning our merits, crowns nothing else but his own gifts to us? [ibid., 194:5:19].

ST. PROSPER OF AQUITAINE

Indeed, a man who has been justified, who from impious has been made pious, receives a gift, since he had no antecedent good merit, by which gift he may acquire merit. Thus, what was begun in him by Christ's grace can also be augmented by the industry of his free choice, but never in the absence of God's help, without which no one is able to progress or to continue in doing good [*Responses on Behalf of Augustine* 6 (c. A.D. 431)].

ST. SECHNALL OF IRELAND

Hear, all you who love God, the holy merits of Patrick the bishop, a man blessed in Christ; how, for his good deeds, he is likened to the angels, and, for his perfect life, he is like the apostles [*Hymn in Praise of St. Patrick* 1 (c. A.D. 444)].

57. Purgatory

All Christians agree that we will not sin in heaven. Sin and final glorification are incompatible. Therefore, between the sinfulness of this life and the glory of heaven, we must be made pure. Between death and glory there must be a purification.

The *Catechism of the Catholic Church* states:

All who die in God's grace and friendship, but still imperfectly purified, are indeed assured of their eternal salvation; but after death they undergo purification, so as to achieve the holiness necessary to enter the joy of heaven. The Church gives the name purgatory to this final purification of the elect, which is entirely different from the punishment of the damned (CCC 1030–31).

The concept of an after-death purification from sin and its consequences is also indicated in New Testament passages such as 1 Corinthians 3:11–15 and Matthew 5:25–26.

The fact that we can assist the dead who are in need of purification has been part of the Judeo-Christian tradition since before the time of Christ, as revealed in the Old Testament (2 Mc 12:41–45) as well as in other pre-Christian Jewish works, including one that states that Adam will be in mourning "until the day of dispensing punishment in the last years, when I will turn his sorrow into joy" (*The Life of Adam and Eve* 46–47). Orthodox Jews to this day believe in the final purification, and for a period of time after the death of a loved one, they recite a prayer known as the Mourner's Kaddish for the repose of their loved one's soul.

Jews, Catholics, and the Eastern Orthodox proclaim the reality of the final purification, even if it is articulated in different ways in the different communities.

Other ideas—that purgatory is a particular "place" in the afterlife or that it takes time to accomplish purification there—are speculations rather than doctrines. For its part, the Catholic Church leaves the specific nature of the purification—including whether it takes time or is accomplished instantly—as a matter of theological speculation. For example, in his encyclical *Spe Salvi*, Pope Benedict XVI noted the theory of some theologians that purgatory consists in a transforming encounter with the love of Christ, that burns away all remaining impurities in the saved (see sections 45–47 in the encyclical).

However the final purification is conceived, the following quotations from the early Church Fathers show that it has been part of the Christian faith from the beginning—and that the prayers of the living can help those experiencing it.

EARLY CHRISTIAN INSCRIPTION

My mother is Eucharis and my father is Pius.[1] I pray you, O brethren, to pray when you come here, and to ask in your common prayers the Father and the Son. May it be in your minds to

---

[1] This inscription may be using code to ask the reader for prayers. The terms *Eucharis* (Greek, "Eucharist," "Thanksgiving"), *Pius* (Latin, "Pious"), and *Agape* (Greek, "Love," "Charity") may deliberately mask the identity of the deceased Christian asking for prayers and serve as a way of signaling the Christian community that it is their prayers the deceased desires.

remember dear Agape that the omnipotent God may keep Agape safe forever [*Christian Inscriptions* 34 (c. A.D. 150)].

ACTS OF PAUL AND THECLA

And after the exhibition, Tryphaena again receives her. For her daughter Falconilla had died, and said to her in a dream: Mother, you shall have this stranger Thecla in my place, so that she may pray for me, and that I may be transferred to the place of the just [*Acts of Paul and Thecla* (c. A.D. 160)].

ST. ABERCIUS OF HIERAPOLIS

I, the citizen of a chosen city, erected this in my lifetime that I may have in time to come a place in which to lay my body. My name is Abercius, the disciple of the holy Shepherd, who feeds the flocks of his sheep on the hills and plains, and who has great eyes that look into every place. . . . These things I, Abercius, commanded to be written when I was on earth; and truly I was seventy-two years old. Let him who understands this, and everyone who agrees with it, pray for Abercius [*Christian Inscriptions*, no. 43 (Epitaph of Abercius) (c. A.D. 190)].

MARTYRDOM OF PERPETUA AND FELICITY

[T]hat very night, this was shown to me in a vision: I [Perpetua] saw Dinocrates going out from a gloomy place, where there were several others, and he was very thirsty, with a filthy countenance and pallid color, and the wound on his face that he had when he died. Dinocrates, who had been my brother after the flesh, seven years of age, died miserably with disease. . . . For him I had made my prayer, and between him and me there was a large interval, so that neither of us could approach the other . . . and [I] knew that my brother was in suffering. But I trusted that my prayer would bring help to his suffering; and I prayed for him every day until we passed over into the prison of the camp, for we were to fight in the camp's [wild beast] show. Then . . . I made my prayer for my brother day and night, groaning and weeping that he might be granted to me. Then, on the day on which we remained in fetters, this was shown to me: I saw that the place that I had formerly observed to be in gloom was now bright; and Dinocrates, with a clean body well clad, was finding refreshment. . . . [And] he went away from the water to play joyously, as children do, and I awoke. Then I understood that he had been removed from the place of punishment [*Martyrdom of Perpetua and Felicity* 2:3–4 (c. A.D. 203)].

TERTULLIAN OF CARTHAGE

[T]hat allegory of the Lord [Mt 5:25–26] . . . is extremely clear and simple in its meaning: . . . [Beware unless, as] a transgressor of your agreement, before God the judge . . . he deliver you over to the angel who is to execute the sentence, and he commit you to the prison of hades, out of which there will be no dismissal until the smallest even of your delinquencies be paid off in the period before the resurrection. What can be a more fitting meaning than this? What a truer interpretation? [*Treatise on the Soul* 35 (c. A.D. 210)].

We offer sacrifices for the dead on their birthday anniversaries [the date of death, their birth into eternal life] [*Chaplet* 3 (A.D. 211)].

A woman, after the death of her husband . . . prays for his soul and asks that he may, while waiting, find rest; and that he may share in the first Resurrection. And each year, on the anniversary of his death, she offers the sacrifice [*Monogamy* 10 (c. A.D. 218)].

ST. CYPRIAN OF CARTHAGE

The strength of the true believer remains unshaken; and with those who fear and love God with their whole heart, their integrity continues steady and strong. For to adulterers even a time of repentance is granted by us, and peace is given. Yet virginity is not thus deficient in the Church, nor does the glorious design of continence languish through the sins of others. The Church, crowned with so many virgins, flourishes; and chastity and modesty preserve the tenor of their glory. Nor is the vigor of continence broken down because repentance and pardon are given to the adulterer. It is one thing to stand for pardon, another thing to attain glory. It is one thing, when cast into prison, not to go out from there until one has paid the uttermost farthing; another thing at once to receive the wages of faith and courage. It is one thing, tortured by long suffering for sins, to be cleansed and long purged by fire; another to have purged all sins by suffering. It is one thing to be in suspense until the sentence of God at the day of judgment; another to be at once crowned by the Lord [*Letters* 51:20 (A.D. 252)].

LACTANTIUS

But when he shall have judged the righteous, he will also try them with fire. Then they whose sins shall exceed either in weight or in number shall be scorched by the fire and burned. But they whom full justice and maturity of virtue has imbued will not see that fire; for they have something of God in themselves that repels and rejects the violence of the flame. So great is the force of innocence that the flame shrinks from it without doing harm; it has received this power from God, that it burns the wicked, and is under the command of the righteous [*Divine Institutes* 7:21 (c. A.D. 307)].

ST. CYRIL OF JERUSALEM

Then we commemorate also those who have fallen asleep before us, first patriarchs, prophets, apostles, martyrs, that at their prayers and intercessions God will receive our petition. Then on behalf of the holy fathers and bishops who have fallen asleep before us, and in a word all who in past years have fallen asleep among us, believing that it will be a very great benefit to the souls for whom the supplication is put up, while that holy and most awful sacrifice is set forth [*Catechetical Lectures* 23:9 (c. A.D. 350)].

ST. GREGORY OF NYSSA

If a man distinguishes in himself what is peculiarly human from what is irrational, and if he be on the watch for a life of greater urbanity for himself, in this present life he will purify himself of any evil contracted, and overcome the irrational by reason. If he has inclined to the irrational pressure of the passions . . . he may afterward, in a very different manner, be very much interested in what is better, when, after his departure out of the body, he gains knowledge of the difference between virtue and vice and finds that he is not able to partake of divinity until he has been purged of the filthy contagion in his soul by the purifying fire [*Sermon on the Dead* (c. A.D. 382)].

ST. JOHN CHRYSOSTOM

Let us then give them aid and perform commemoration for them. For if the children of Job were purged by the sacrifice of their father, why do you doubt that when we too offer for the departed, some consolation arises to them, since God is wont to grant the petitions of those who ask for others? [*Homilies on First Corinthians* 41:8 (c. A.D. 392)].

Mourn for those who have died in wealth, and did not from their wealth think of any solace for their soul, those who had power to wash away their sins and would not. Let us all weep for these in private and in public, but with propriety, with gravity, not so as to make exhibitions of ourselves; let us weep for these, not one day, or two, but all our life. Such tears spring not from senseless passion, but from true affection. The other sort are of senseless passion. For this reason they are quickly quenched, but if they spring from the fear of God, they always abide with us. Let us weep for these; let us assist them according to our power; let us think of some assistance for them, small though it be, yet still let us assist them. In what way? By praying and entreating others to make prayers for them, by continually giving to the poor on their behalf [*Homilies on Philippians* 3 (c. A.D. 402)].

ST. AUGUSTINE OF HIPPO

There is an ecclesiastical discipline, as the faithful know, in which the names of the martyrs are read aloud in that place at the altar of God where prayer is not offered for them. Prayer, however, is offered for other dead who are remembered. It is wrong to pray for a martyr, to whose prayers we ought ourselves be commended [*Sermons* 159:1 (C. A.D. 411)].

[T]emporary punishments are suffered by some in this life only, by others after death, by others both now and then; but all of them before that last and strictest judgment. But of those who suffer temporary punishments after death, all are not doomed to those everlasting pains that are to follow that judgment; for to some, as we have already said, what is not remitted in this world is remitted in the next, that is, they are not punished with the eternal punishment of the world to come [*City of God* 21:13 (c. A.D. 419)].

It is a matter that may be inquired into, and either ascertained or left doubtful, whether some believers shall pass through a kind of purgatorial fire,[2] and in proportion to whether they loved with more or less devotion the goods that perish, be less or more quickly delivered from it. This cannot, however, be the case for those of whom it is said that they shall not inherit the kingdom of God, unless after suitable repentance their sins be forgiven them [*Handbook on Faith, Hope, and Charity* 69 (A.D. 421)].

During the time, moreover, that intervenes between a man's death and the final resurrection, the soul dwells in a hidden retreat, where it enjoys rest or suffers affliction in proportion to the merit it earned by the life it led on earth. Nor can it be denied that the souls of the dead are benefited by the piety of their living friends, who offer the sacrifice of the Mediator, or give alms in the church on their behalf. But these services are of advantage only to those who during their lives have earned such merit that services of this kind can help them. For there is a manner of life that is neither so good as not to require these services after death, nor so bad that such services are of no avail after death [ibid., 109–10].

---

[2] What Augustine is treating as speculative here is whether the purification will take place by fire; in other passages he has already asserted that it will take place—the question is by what means.

THE LAST THINGS

58. Hell

The doctrine of hell is so frightening that many sects end up deny-ing it. Unitarian-Universalists, Seventh-day Adventists, Jehovah's Witnesses, Christadelphians, Christian Scientists, New Agers, and Mormons have all rejected or modified the doctrine of hell so rad-ically that in their view it is no longer an eternal threat to the soul.

But the eternal nature of hell is stressed in the New Testament. In Mark 9:47–48, Jesus warns us, "[I]t is better for you to en-ter the kingdom of God with one eye than with two eyes to be thrown into hell, where the worm does not die, and the fire is not quenched." And in Revelation 14:11, we read: "And the smoke of their torment goes up for ever and ever; and they have no rest, day or night, these worshippers of the beast and its image, and whoever receives the mark of its name."

And hell is not just a theoretical possibility. Jesus warns us that people go there, telling us, "Enter by the narrow gate; for the gate is wide and the way is easy, that leads to destruction, and those who enter by it are many. For the gate is narrow and the way is hard, that leads to life, and those who find it are few" (Mt 7:13–14).

The *Catechism of the Catholic Church* states: "The teaching of the Church affirms the existence of hell and its eternity. Imme-diately after death the souls of those who die in a state of mortal sin descend into hell, where they suffer the punishments of hell, 'eternal fire.' The chief punishment of hell is eternal separation from God, in whom alone man can possess the life and happiness for which he was created and for which he longs" (CCC 1035).

In his 1994 book *Crossing the Threshold of Hope*, Pope John Paul II lamented that too often "preachers, catechists, teachers . . . no longer have the courage to preach the threat of hell" (p. 183).

Concerning the reality of hell, the pope wrote: "In point of fact, the ancient councils rejected the theory . . . according to which the world would be regenerated after destruction, and ev-ery creature would be saved; a theory which abolished hell. . . . [T]he words of Christ are unequivocal. In Matthew's Gospel he speaks clearly of those who will go to eternal punishment (see also Mt 25:46). [But] who will these be? The Church has never made any pronouncement in this regard" (pp. 185–86).

As the following quotations from the early Church Fathers show, they were firm about the reality of an eternal hell.

SECOND CLEMENT

By what course of conduct, then, shall we attain these things, but by leading a holy and righteous life, and by deeming these worldly things as not belonging to us, and not fixing our desires upon them? For if we desire to possess them, we fall away from the path of righteousness [*Second Clement* 5 (c. A.D. 80)].

It is of the great day of judgment he speaks, when they shall see those among us who were guilty of ungodliness and erred in their estimate of the commands of Jesus Christ. The righteous, having succeeded in enduring the trials and hating the indulgences of the soul, whenever they witness how those who have swerved and denied Jesus by words or deeds are punished with grievous torments in fire unquenchable, will give glory to their God and say, "There will be hope for him who has served God with his whole heart" [ibid., 17].

ST. IGNATIUS OF ANTIOCH

Those that corrupt families shall not inherit the kingdom of God [1 Cor 6:9–10]. If, then, those who do this as respects the flesh have suffered death, how much more shall this be true of anyone who corrupts by wicked doctrine the faith of God, for which Jesus Christ was crucified! Anyone becoming defiled [in this way], shall go away into everlasting fire, and so shall everyone who listens unto him [*Letter to the Ephesians* 16 (c. A.D. 110)].

ST. JUSTIN MARTYR

And more than all other men are we your helpers and allies in promoting peace, seeing that we hold this view, that it is impossible for the wicked, the covetous, the conspirator, and for the virtuous to escape the notice of God, and that each man goes to everlasting punishment or salvation according to the value of his actions. For if all men knew this, no one would choose wickedness even for a little, knowing that he goes to the everlasting punishment of fire; but would by all means restrain himself, and adorn himself with virtue, that he might obtain the good gifts of God, and escape the punishments [*First Apology* 12 (c. A.D. 151)].

But, as we said above, wicked devils perpetrated these things. And we have learned that only those are deified who have lived near God in holiness and virtue; and we believe that those who live wickedly and do not repent are punished in everlasting fire (ibid., 21).

[Jesus] shall come from heaven with glory, accompanied by his angelic host, when he shall raise the bodies of all men who have lived, and shall clothe the worthy with immortality, and shall send the wicked, endued with eternal sensibility, into everlasting fire with the wicked devils [ibid., 52].

MARTYRDOM OF POLYCARP

[The martyrs] despised all the torments of this world, redeeming themselves from eternal punishment by [the suffering of] a single hour. For this reason the fire of their savage executioners appeared cool to them. For they kept before their view the escape from that fire that is eternal and shall never be quenched [*Martyrdom of Polycarp* 2 (c. A.D. 156)].

TO DIOGNETUS

Then you will see, while still on earth, that God in the heavens rules over [the universe]; then you will begin to speak the mysteries of God; then will you love and admire those who suffer punishment because they will not deny God; then will you condemn the deceit and error of the world when you will know what it is to live truly in heaven, when you will despise what is here esteemed to be death, when you will fear what is truly death, which is reserved for those who shall be condemned to the eternal fire,

which will afflict those even to the end who are committed to it.
Then will you admire those who for righteousness's sake endure
the fire that is but for a moment, and will count them happy when
you will know [the nature of] that fire [*To Diognetus* 10 (c. A.D.
160)].

ATHENAGORAS OF ATHENS

For if we believed that we should live only the present life, then
we might be suspected of sinning, through being enslaved to flesh
and blood, or overmastered by gain or carnal desire; but since we
know that God is witness to what we think and what we say by
night and by day, and that he, himself being light, sees all things
in our heart, we are persuaded that when we are removed from
the present life we shall live another life, better than the present
one, and heavenly, not earthly (since we shall abide near God,
and with God, free from all change or suffering in the soul, not
as flesh, even though we shall have flesh, but as heavenly spirit),
or, falling with the rest, a worse one and in fire; for God has not
made us as sheep or beasts of burden, that we should perish and
be annihilated. On these grounds it is not likely that we should
wish to do evil, or deliver ourselves over to the great judge to be
punished [*Plea for the Christians* 31 (c. A.D. 177)].

ST. THEOPHILUS OF ANTIOCH

But do you also, if you please, give reverential attention to the
prophetic Scriptures, and they will make your way plainer for es-
caping the eternal punishments, and obtaining the eternal prizes
of God. For he who gave the mouth for speech, and formed the
ear to hear, and made the eye to see, will examine all things, and
will judge righteous judgment, rendering merited awards to each.
To those who by patient continuance in well-doing [Rom 2:7]
seek immortality, he will give life everlasting, joy, peace, rest, and
abundance of good things, which neither has eye seen, nor ear
heard, nor has it entered into the heart of man to conceive [1 Cor
2:9]. But to the unbelieving and despisers, who obey not the truth,
but are obedient to unrighteousness, when they have been filled

with adulteries and fornications, and filthiness, and covetousness, and unlawful idolatries, there shall be anger and wrath, tribulation and anguish [Rom 2:8–9], and at the last everlasting fire shall possess such men [*To Autolycus* 1:14 (c. A.D. 181)].

ST. IRENAEUS OF LYONS

[T]hat he may send "spiritual wickednesses" [Eph 6:12], and the angels who transgressed and became apostates, together with the ungodly, and unrighteous, and wicked, and profane among men, into everlasting fire [*Against Heresies* 1:10:1 (c. A.D. 189)].

Thus also the punishment of those who do not believe the Word of God, and despise his advent, and are turned away backwards, is increased; being not merely temporal, but eternal. For to whomever the Lord shall say, "Depart from me, you cursed, into everlasting fire" [Mt 25:41], these will be damned forever [ibid., 4:28:2].

TERTULLIAN OF CARTHAGE

[T]hese have further set before us the proof he has given of his majesty in his judgments by floods and fires, the rules appointed by him for securing his favor, as well as the retribution in store for ignoring, forsaking, and keeping them, as being there at the end of all to judge his worshippers to everlasting life, and the wicked to the doom of fire without end and without break [*Apology* 18 (A.D. 197)].

[T]hen the whole human race shall be raised again, to have its dues meted out according to what it merited in the period of good or evil, and then to have these paid out through the immeasurable ages of eternity. After this there is neither death nor repeated resurrections, but we shall be the same that we are now, and still unchanged—the servants of God, ever with God, clothed with the proper substance of eternity; but the profane, and all who are not true worshippers of God, shall be consigned to the punishment of everlasting fire—that fire that, from its very nature, directly ministers to their incorruptibility [ibid., 48].

ST. HIPPOLYTUS OF ROME

And being present at his judicial decision, all men and angels and demons, shall utter one voice, saying, "Righteous is your judgment," in which voice the justification will be seen in the awarding to each what is just; since those who have done well shall righteously be assigned eternal bliss, and the lovers of iniquity shall be given eternal punishment. And the fire that is unquenchable and without end awaits these latter, and a certain fiery worm that does not die, and that does not waste the body, but continues bursting forth from the body with unending pain. No sleep will give them rest; no night will soothe them; no death will deliver them from punishment; no voice of interceding friends will profit them [*Against Plato, On the Cause of the Universe* 3 (c. A.D. 220)].

MINUCIUS FELIX

And I am not ignorant that many, conscious of what they deserve, desire rather than believe that they shall be nothing after death; for they would prefer to be altogether extinguished than to be restored for the purpose of punishment. . . . There is no measure or termination to these torments. The intelligent fire burns the limbs and restores them, feeds on them and nourishes them, as the fires of the thunderbolts strike the bodies, and do not consume them [*Octavius* 34–35 (c. A.D. 226)].

ST. CYPRIAN OF CARTHAGE

An ever-burning Gehenna and the punishment of being devoured by living flames will consume the condemned; nor will there be any way the tormented can ever have respite or be at an end. Souls along with their bodies will be preserved for suffering in unlimited agonies. . . . The grief at punishment will then be without the fruit of repentance; weeping will be useless, and prayer ineffectual. Too late will they believe in eternal punishment, who would not believe in eternal life [*To Demetrian* 24 (A.D. 252)].

LACTANTIUS

[T]he sacred writings inform us in what way the wicked are to undergo punishment. For because they have committed sins in their bodies, they will again be clothed with flesh, that they may make atonement in their bodies; and yet it will not be the flesh with which God clothed man, like our earthly body, but indestructible, and abiding forever, that it may be able to hold out against tortures and everlasting fire, which is different from this fire of ours, which we use for the necessary purposes of life, and which is extinguished unless it be sustained by fuel. But that divine fire always lives by itself, and flourishes without any nourishment. . . . Thus, without any wasting of bodies, which regain their substance, it will only burn and affect them with a sense of pain. But when [God] shall have judged the righteous, he will also try them with fire [*Divine Institutes* 7:21 (c. A.D. 307)].

ST. CYRIL OF JERUSALEM

We shall be raised therefore, all with our bodies eternal, but not all with bodies alike: for if a man is righteous, he will receive a heavenly body, that he may be able worthily to converse with angels; but if a man is a sinner, he shall receive an eternal body, fitted to endure the penalties of sins, that he may burn eternally in fire, nor ever be consumed. And righteously will God assign this portion to either company; for we do nothing without the body. We blaspheme with the mouth, and with the mouth we pray. With the body we commit fornication, and with the body we keep chastity. With the hand we rob, and by the hand we bestow alms; and the rest in like manner. Since the body has been our minister in all things, it shall also share with us in the future the fruits of the past [*Catechetical Lectures* 18:19 (c. A.D. 350)].

59. Reincarnation?

Adherents of the New Age movement often claim that early Christians believed in reincarnation. Shirley MacLaine, for example, recalls being taught as a New Ager: "The theory of reincarnation is recorded in the Bible. But the proper interpretations were struck from it during an ecumenical council meeting of the Catholic Church in Constantinople sometime around A.D. 553, called the First Council of Nicaea" (*Out on a Limb*, 234–35).

There is no historical basis for this claim. There was no Council of Nicaea in A.D. 553. There were two ecumenical councils held at Nicaea, in A.D. 325 and 787, and there was a council held at Constantinople in A.D. 553, but none of these councils addressed the subject of reincarnation.

The closest the Second Council of Constantinople came to addressing reincarnation was to condemn Origen, who believed souls exist in heaven before birth. But the idea of the preexistence of the soul is not the same thing as reincarnation, as Origen's own writings show. In actuality, among the Church Fathers he was one of the most vocal critics of reincarnation!

The idea that Origen taught reincarnation appears to have originated in the book *Reincarnation in Christianity* by Geddes MacGregor (Wheaton, Ill.: Theosophical Publishing House, 1978). The author admits that he has no evidence, but nevertheless asserts: "I am convinced he taught reincarnation in some form" (p. 58). You may judge from the passages below—including those from Origen's own pen—whether this is likely.

ST. IRENAEUS OF LYONS

We may subvert their doctrine of transmigration from body to body by this fact, that souls remember nothing of the events that took place in their previous states of existence. For if they were sent forth with this object, that they should have experience of every kind of action, they must of necessity retain a remembrance of those things that have been previously accomplished, that they might fill up those in which they are still deficient, and not hover, without intermission, round the same pursuits, spend their labor wretchedly in vain (for the mere union of a body [with a soul] could not altogether extinguish the memory and contemplation of those things that had formerly been experienced), and especially as they came [into the world] for this very purpose. . . .

With reference to these objections, Plato, that ancient Athenian, who was the first to introduce this opinion, when he could not set them aside, invented the [notion of] a cup of oblivion, imagining that in this way he would escape this difficulty. He attempted no proof, but simply replied dogmatically that when souls enter into this life, they are caused to drink of oblivion by that demon who watches them, before they enter into the bodies [assigned them]. It escaped him that [by speaking thus] he fell into a greater perplexity. For if the cup of oblivion can obliterate the memory of all the deeds that have been done, how, O Plato, do you obtain knowledge of this? [*Against Heresies* 2:33:1–2 (c. A.D. 189)].

TERTULLIAN OF CARTHAGE

Come now, if some philosopher affirms, as Laberius holds, following an opinion of Pythagoras, that a man may have his origin from a mule, a serpent from a woman, and with skill of speech twists every argument to prove his view, will he not gain acceptance for it [among the pagans], and work in some conviction that, on account of this, they should abstain from eating animal food? May anyone be persuaded that he should abstain, lest by chance in his beef he eats an ancestor of his? But if a Christian promises the return of a man from a man, and the actual Gaius [resurrected] from Gaius . . . they will not . . . grant him a hearing. If there is any ground for the moving to and fro of human souls into different bodies, why may they not return to the very one they have left? [*Apology* 48 (A.D. 197)].

ORIGEN OF ALEXANDRIA

And [Jn 1:21] they asked him, "What then? Are you Elijah?" And he said, "I am not." No one can fail to remember in this connection what Jesus says of John [Mt 11:14], "If you will receive it, this is Elijah which is to come." Why, then, does John say to those who ask him, "Are you Elijah?" "I am not." And how can it be also true that John is Elijah who is to come, according to the words of Malachi [Mal 4:5–6], "And behold I send unto you Elijah the Tishbite, before the great and notable day of the Lord come, who shall restore the heart of the father to the son, and the heart of a man to his neighbor, lest I come, and utterly smite the earth." The words of the angel of the Lord, too, who appeared to Zacharias, as he stood at the right hand of the altar of incense, are similar to the prophecy of Malachi: "And [Lk 1:13] your wife Elizabeth shall bear you a son, and you shall call his name John." And a little further on: "And he shall go before his face in the spirit and power of Elijah to turn the hearts of the fathers to the children, and the disobedient to the wisdom of the just, to make ready for the Lord a people prepared for him." [Lk 1:17] As for the first point, one might say that John did not know that he was Elijah. This will be the explanation chosen by those who find in our passage support for their doctrine of transcorporation, as if the soul clothed itself in a fresh body and did not remember its former lives. These thinkers will also point out that some of the Jews assented to this doctrine when they spoke about the Savior as if he were one of the old prophets, and had risen not from the tomb but from his birth. His mother Mary was well known, and Joseph the carpenter was supposed to be his father, and it could readily be supposed that he was one of the old prophets risen from the dead. The same person will offer the text in Genesis, "I will destroy the whole resurrection," and will thereby reduce those who find in Scripture solutions of false probabilities a great difficulty in respect of this doctrine. Another, however, a churchman, who repudiates the doctrine of transcorporation as a false one, and does not admit that the soul of John ever was Elijah, may appeal to the words of the angel, and point out that it is not the soul of Elijah that is spoken of at John's birth, but the spirit and power of Elijah [*Commentary on John* 6:7 (c. A.D. 229)].

As for the spirits of the prophets, these are given to them by God and are spoken of as being in a way their property, as "The spirits of the prophets are subject to the prophets" [1 Cor 14:32] and "The spirit of Elijah rested upon Elisha" [2 Kgs 2:15]. Thus, it is said, there is nothing absurd in supposing that John, "in the spirit and power of Elijah," turned the hearts of the fathers to the children and that it was on account of this spirit that he was called "Elijah who is to come" [ibid.].

If the doctrine [of reincarnation] was widely current, ought not John to have hesitated to pronounce upon it, lest his soul had actually been in Elijah? And here our churchman will appeal to history, and will bid his antagonists [to] ask experts of the secret doctrines of the Hebrews if they really entertain such a belief. For if it should appear that they do not, then the argument based on that supposition is shown to be baseless [ibid.].

Someone might say, however, that Herod and some of those of the people held the false dogma of the transmigration of souls into bodies, so that they thought that the former John had appeared again by a fresh birth, and had come from the dead into life as Jesus. But the time between the birth of John and the birth of Jesus, which was not more than six months, does not permit this false opinion to be believed. And perhaps some idea like this was in the mind of Herod, that the powers that worked in John had passed over to Jesus, in consequence of which he was thought by the people to be John the Baptist. And one might use the following argument: Just as because of the spirit and the power of Elijah, and not because of his soul, it is said about John, "This is Elijah who is to come" [Mt 11:14] . . . so Herod thought that the powers in John's case caused in him works of baptism and teaching—for John did not do one miracle [Jn 10:41]—but in

Jesus [they caused] miraculous portents [*Commentary on Matthew* 10:20 (c. A.D. 249)].

Now the Canaanite woman, having come, worshipped Jesus as God, saying, "Lord, help me," but he answered and said, "It is not possible to take the children's bread and cast it to the little dogs." . . . [O]thers, then, who are strangers to the doctrine of the Church, assume that souls pass from the bodies of men into the bodies of dogs, according to their varying degree of wickedness; but we . . . do not find this at all in the divine Scripture [ibid., 11:17].

In this place [when Jesus said Elijah had come and referred to John the Baptist] it does not appear to me that by Elijah the soul is spoken of, lest I fall into the doctrine of transmigration, which is foreign to the Church of God, and not handed down by the apostles, nor anywhere set forth in the Scriptures [ibid., 13:1].

But if . . . the Greeks, who introduce the doctrine of transmigration, laying down things in harmony with it, do not acknowledge that the world is coming to corruption, it is fitting that when they have looked the Scriptures straight in the face, which plainly declare that the world will perish, they should either disbelieve them or invent a series of arguments about the interpretation of things concerning the consummation, which even if they wish they will not be able to do [ibid.].

ARNOBIUS OF SICCA

[M]an's real death [is] when souls that do not know God shall be consumed in long-protracted torment with raging fire, into which certain fiercely cruel beings shall cast them. . . . [T]here is no reason that [one] should mislead us, should hold our vain hopes to us, and carried away by an extravagant opinion of themselves, and say that souls are immortal, next in point of rank to the God and ruler of the world, descended from that parent and sire. . . . [And] while we are moving swiftly down toward our mortal bodies, causes pursue us from the world's circles, through the working of which we become bad—aye, most wicked . . . [and] that the souls of wicked men, on leaving their human bodies, pass into cattle and other creatures [*Against the Heathen* 2:14–15 (c. A.D. 305)].

LACTANTIUS

What of Pythagoras, who was first called a philosopher, who judged that souls were indeed immortal, but that they passed into other bodies, either of cattle, or of birds, or of beasts? Would it not have been better that they should be destroyed, together with their bodies, than thus to be condemned to pass into the bodies of other animals? Would it not be better not to exist at all, than, after having had the form of a man, to live as a swine or a dog? And the foolish man, to gain credit for his saying, said that he himself had been Euphorbus in the Trojan War, and that, when he was slain, he passed into other figures of animals, and at last became Pythagoras. O happy man! to whom alone so great a memory was given; or rather unhappy, who, when changed into a sheep, was not permitted to be ignorant of what he was! And would to heaven that he alone had been thus senseless! [*Epitome of the Divine Institutes* 36 (c. A.D. 317)].

ST. BASIL OF CAESAREA

[A]void the nonsense of those arrogant philosophers who do not blush to liken their soul to that of a dog, who say that they have themselves formerly been women, shrubs, or fish. Have they ever been fish? I do not know, but I say that in their writings they show less sense than fish [*Six Days of Creation* 8:2 (c. A.D. 367)].

ST. AMBROSE OF MILAN

It is a cause for wonder that though they [the heathen] . . . say that souls pass and migrate into other bodies. . . . But let those who have not been taught doubt [the resurrection]. For us who have read the law, the prophets, the apostles, and the gospel, it is not lawful to doubt [*On the Death of Satyrus* 2:65–66 (A.D. 378)].

But is their opinion preferable who say that our souls, when they have passed out of these bodies, migrate into the bodies of beasts or of various other living creatures? . . . For what is so like a marvel as to believe that men could have been changed into the forms of beasts? How much greater a marvel would it be that the soul that rules man should take on the nature of a beast so opposed to that of man, and being capable of reason should be able to pass over to an irrational animal, than that the form of the body should have been changed? [ibid., 2:127].

ST. GREGORY OF NYSSA

[I]f one should search carefully, he will find that their doctrine is of necessity brought down to this. They tell us that one of their sages said that he was born a man, and afterwards assumed the form of a woman, and flew about with the birds, and grew as a bush, and obtained the life of an aquatic creature; and he who said these things about himself did not, as far as I can judge, go far from the truth: for doctrines like this, that say that one soul passed through so many changes, are really fitting for the chatter of frogs or jackdaws, or the stupidity of fishes, or the insensibility of trees [*Making of Man* 28:3 (A.D. 379)].

ST. JOHN CHRYSOSTOM

As for doctrines on the soul, there is nothing very shameful that [the disciples of Plato and Pythagoras] have left unsaid, asserting that the souls of men become flies and gnats and bushes and that God himself is a [similar] soul, with similar indecencies. . . . At one time he says that the soul is of the substance of God; at another, after having exalted it thus, immoderately and impiously, he exceeds again in a different way, and treats it with insult, making it pass into swine and asses and other animals of less esteem than these [*Homilies on John* 2:3, 6 (c. A.D. 391)].

60. *The Resurrection of the Body*

The Bible tells us that when Jesus returns, he will raise all who have died, giving them back their bodies. These will be the same ones they had in earthly life—but they will now be undying and, for the righteous, they will be transformed into a glorified state, freed from suffering and pain (1 Cor 15:35–44; 1 Jn 3:2).

The resurrection of the body is an essential Christian doctrine, as St. Paul declares: "If the dead are not raised then Christ has not been raised. If Christ has not been raised, your faith is futile and you are still in your sins. Then those also who have fallen asleep in Christ have perished" (1 Cor 15:16–18).

The *Catechism of the Catholic Church* reiterated this long-defined teaching, stating, " 'We believe in the true resurrection of this flesh that we now possess' (Council of Lyons II). We sow a corruptible body in the tomb, but he raises up an incorruptible body, a 'spiritual body' (see 1 Cor 15:42–44)" (CCC 1017).

As the following quotations from the Church Fathers show, this has been the teaching of the Christian faith since the very beginning.

POPE ST. CLEMENT I

Let us consider, beloved, how the Lord continually proves to us that there shall be a future resurrection, of which he has rendered the Lord Jesus Christ the first fruits by raising him from the dead. Let us contemplate, beloved, the resurrection that is at all times taking place. Day and night declare to us a resurrection. The night sinks to sleep, and the day arises; the day departs, and the night comes on. Let us behold the fruits [of the earth], how the sowing of grain takes place. The sower goes forth, and casts it into the ground; and the seed being thus scattered, though dry and naked when it fell upon the earth, is gradually dissolved. Then out of its dissolution the mighty power of the providence of the Lord raises it up again, and from one seed many arise and bring forth fruit [*Letter to the Corinthians* 24:1–5 (A.D. 70)].

SECOND CLEMENT

And let no one of you say that this very flesh shall not be judged, nor rise again. Consider in what [state] you were saved, in what you received sight, if not while you were in this flesh. We must preserve the flesh as the temple of God. For as you were called in the flesh, so shall you [be judged] in the flesh. As Christ the Lord who saved us, though he was first a Spirit became flesh, and thus called us, so shall we also receive the reward in this flesh. Let us therefore love one another, that we may all attain to the kingdom of God [*Second Clement* 9 (c. A.D. 80)].

ST. POLYCARP OF SMYRNA

[W]hoever perverts the sayings of the Lord for his own desires, and says that there is neither resurrection nor judgment, is the firstborn of Satan. Let us leave the foolishness and the false teaching of the crowd and turn back to the word that was delivered to us in the beginning [*Letter to the Philippians* 7 (c. A.D. 135)].

ST. ARISTIDES OF ATHENS

[Christians] have the commandments of the Lord Jesus Christ impressed upon their hearts, and they observe them, awaiting the resurrection of the dead and the life of the world to come [*Apology* 15 (c. A.D. 140)].

ST. JUSTIN MARTYR

For the prophets have proclaimed two advents of his: the one, which is already past, when he came as a dishonored and suffering man; but the second, when, according to prophecy, he shall come from heaven in glory, accompanied by his angelic host, when he shall raise the bodies of all men who have lived, and shall clothe the worthy with immortality, and shall send those of the wicked, endued with eternal sensibility, into everlasting fire with the wicked devils [*First Apology* 52 (c. A.D. 151)].

But, in truth, he has even called the flesh to the resurrection, and promises to it everlasting life. For where he promises to save man, there he gives the promise to the flesh. For what is man but the reasonable animal composed of body and soul? Is the soul by itself man? No, but the soul of man. Would the body be called man? No, but it is called the body of man. If, then, neither of these is by itself man, then the two together are called man, and God has called man to life and resurrection, he has called not a part, but the whole, which is the soul and the body [*The Resurrection* 8 (c. A.D. 153)].

TATIAN THE SYRIAN

We believe that there will be a resurrection of bodies after the consummation of all things [*Address to the Greeks* 6 (c. A.D. 170)].

ST. THEOPHILUS OF ANTIOCH

For God will raise your flesh immortal with your soul; and then, having become immortal, you will see the immortal, if now you believe in him; and then you will know that you have spoken unjustly against him. But you do not believe that the dead are raised. When the resurrection takes place, then you will believe, whether you want to or not; and your faith shall be reckoned for unbelief, unless you believe now [*To Autolycus* 1:7–8 (c. A.D. 181)].

ST. IRENAEUS OF LYONS

For the Church, although dispersed throughout the whole world even to the ends of the earth, has received from the apostles and from their disciples the faith in . . . the raising up again of the flesh of all humanity, in order that to Jesus Christ our Lord and God and Savior and King, with the approval of the invisible Father, every knee shall bend of those in heaven and on earth and under the earth, and every tongue shall confess him, and he may make just judgment of them all [*Against Heresies* 1:10:1 (c. A.D. 189)].

TERTULLIAN OF CARTHAGE

As being there at the end of all to judge his worshippers to everlasting life, and the wicked to the doom of fire without end and without break, raising up again all the dead from the beginning, reforming and renewing them with the object of awarding either recompense [*Apology* 18 (A.D. 197)].

Touching the resurrection of the dead [1 Cor 15:12], let us first inquire how some persons then denied it. No doubt in the same way in which it is even now denied, since the resurrection of the flesh always has men to deny it. But many wise men claim a divine nature for the soul, and are confident of its undying destiny, and even the multitude worship the dead in the presumption they boldly entertain that their souls survive. As for our bodies, however, it is clear that they perish either at once by fire or the wild beasts, or even when most carefully kept by the passage of time. When, therefore, the apostle refutes those who deny the resurrection of the flesh, he defends, in opposition to them, the precise matter of their denial, that is, the resurrection of the body. You have the whole answer wrapped up in this. All the rest is superfluous. Now on this very point, the resurrection of the dead, it is necessary that the proper force of the words should be accurately maintained. The word *dead* expresses simply that which has lost the vital principle, by means of which it used to live. Now the body is what loses life, and as the result of losing it becomes dead. To the body, therefore, the term *dead* is only suitable. Moreover, as resurrection accrues to what is dead, and *dead* is a term applicable only to a body, only the body alone has a resurrection incidental to it. So the word *resurrection*, or rising again, embraces only what has fallen down. "To rise," indeed, can be said of what has never fallen down, but had been lying down. But "to rise again" can be said only of what has fallen down; because it is by rising again, in consequence of its having fallen down, that it is said to have re-risen. For the syllable "re" always implies repetition. We say, therefore, that the body falls to the ground by death, as facts show, in accordance with the law of God. For to the body it was said, "Dust you are, and unto dust shall you return" [*Against Marcion* 5:9 (c. A.D. 209)].

And so the flesh shall rise again, wholly in every man, in its own identity, in its absolute integrity. Wherever it may be, it is in safe keeping in God's presence, through that most faithful "mediator between God and man, (the man) Jesus Christ" [1 Tm 2:5], who shall reconcile God to man, and man to God; the spirit to the flesh, and the flesh to the spirit [*Resurrection of the Flesh* 63 (c. A.D. 210)].

MINUCIUS FELIX

See, therefore, how for our consolation all nature suggests a future resurrection. The sun sinks down and arises, the stars pass away and return, the flowers die and revive again, after their wintry decay the shrubs resume their leaves, and seeds do not flourish unless they are rotted. Thus the body in the sepulchre is like the trees that in winter hide their verdure with a deceptive dryness. Why are you in haste for it to revive and return, while the winter is still raw? We must wait also for the springtime of the body. And I know that many, conscious of what they deserve, desire rather than believe that they shall be nothing after death; for they would prefer to be altogether extinguished, rather than to be restored for the purpose of punishment [*Octavius* 34 (c. A.D. 226)].

ST. APHRAHAT THE PERSIAN SAGE

Therefore, O fool, be instructed by this, that each of the seeds is clothed in its own body. Never do you sow wheat yet reap barley, and never do you plant a vine and it produced figs; but everything grows according to its nature. Thus also the body that was laid in the earth is what shall rise again [*Demonstration* 8:3 (c. A.D. 340)].

ST. CYRIL OF JERUSALEM

For this body shall be raised not remaining weak as now; but raised the very same body, though by putting on incorruption it shall be fashioned anew—as iron blending with fire becomes fire, or rather as he knows how, the Lord who raises us. This body therefore shall be raised, but it shall abide not as it now is, but an eternal body; no longer needing for its life nourishment as now, nor stairs for its ascent, for it shall be made spiritual, a marvelous thing, such as we cannot worthily speak of [*Catechetical Lectures* 18:18 (c. A.D. 350)].

COUNCIL OF CONSTANTINOPLE I

We confess one baptism for the forgiveness of sins; we look for a resurrection of the dead and life in the age to come. Amen [*Nicene Creed* (A.D. 381)].

ST. AUGUSTINE OF HIPPO

Far be it from us to fear that the omnipotence of the Creator cannot, for the resuscitation and reanimation of our bodies, recall all the portions that have been consumed by beasts or fire, or have been dissolved into dust or ashes, or have decomposed into water, or evaporated into the air [*City of God* 22:20:1 (c. A.D. 419)].

God, the wonderful and inexpressible artisan, will, with a wonderful and inexpressible speed, restore our flesh from the whole of the material of which it was made, and it will make no difference to its reconstruction whether hairs go back to hairs and nails go back to nails, or whatever of these had perished be changed to flesh and be assigned to other parts of the body, while the providence of the artisan will take care that nothing unseemly result [*Handbook on Faith, Hope, and Charity* 89 (A.D. 421)].

ATHANASIAN CREED

[Jesus Christ] sits at the right hand of God the Father almighty; thence he shall come to judge the living and the dead; at his coming all men have to rise again with their bodies and will render an account of their own deeds; and those who have done good will go into life everlasting, but those who have done evil into eternal fire [Rom 2:6–11]. This is the Catholic faith; unless everyone believes this faithfully and firmly, he cannot be saved [*Athanasian Creed* (c. A.D. 425)].

61. The Antichrist

Sometimes anti-Catholics make the assertion that the pope is the Antichrist. This was part of anti-Catholic rhetoric at the time of the Reformation. Thus the Lutheran *Book of Concord* states that "the pope is the real Antichrist who has raised himself over and set himself against Christ. . . . Accordingly, just as we cannot adore the devil himself as our lord or God, so we cannot suffer his apostle, the pope or Antichrist, to govern us as our head or lord" (*Smalcald Articles* 2:4:10, 14).

Similarly, the Presbyterian and Anglican *Westminster Confession* states, "There is no other head of the church but the Lord Jesus Christ; nor can the pope of Rome in any sense be the head thereof; but is that Antichrist, that man of sin, and that son of perdition, that exalteth himself in the church against Christ, and all that is called God" (25:6).

While such claims may have helped justify the break with Rome at the time of the Reformation, they are not plausible on scriptural grounds and—thanks be to God—many Protestants today recognize this and reject the papal Antichrist theory.

For their part, the Fathers of the Church certainly did not identify the pope as the Antichrist, but they entertained a variety of ideas about the Antichrist. They saw him as a government official—a king coming to power in the ruins of the Roman Empire. Some argued that he would probably be Jewish, possibly from the tribe of Dn But rather than claiming to be the vicar or emissary of Jesus Christ, as the pope does, the Antichrist would claim that Jesus was not the Christ but that he—the Antichrist—was instead. He would then seduce many of the Jewish people by attempting to fulfill the political aspirations they held for the Messiah.

There are many possible views one can hold regarding the Antichrist, but the various views of the Church Fathers show how foreign the papal Antichrist theory was to the early Christians.

DIDACHE

[T]he whole time of your faith will not profit you unless you are made complete in the last time. For in the last days false prophets and corrupters shall be multiplied, and sheep shall be turned into wolves . . . and then shall appear the world-deceiver as the Son of

God, and do signs and wonders, and the earth shall be delivered into his hands [*Didache* 16 (c. A.D. 50)].

ST. POLYCARP OF SMYRNA

For whoever does not confess that Jesus Christ has come in the flesh is Antichrist [1 Jn 4:3], and whoever does not confess the testimony of the cross is of the devil; and whosoever perverts the oracles of the Lord to his own lusts, and says that there is neither a resurrection nor a judgment, he is the firstborn of Satan [*Letter to the Philippians* 7 (c. A.D. 135)].

ST. IRENAEUS OF LYONS

[B]y means of the events that shall occur in the time of Antichrist it is shown that he, being an apostate and a robber, is anxious to be adored as God; and that, although a mere slave, he wishes himself to be proclaimed as a king. For he [Antichrist] being imbued with the power of the devil, shall come, not as a righteous king, nor as a legitimate king, in subjection to God, but an impious, unjust, and lawless one . . . setting aside idols to persuade [men] that he is God, raising himself up as the only idol. . . . Moreover, [Paul] has also pointed out this that I have shown in many ways, that the temple in Jerusalem was made by the direction of the true God. For the apostle, speaking in his own person, distinctly called it the temple of God . . . in which the enemy shall sit, endeavoring to show himself as Christ [*Against Heresies* 5:25:1–2 (c. A.D. 189)].

Moreover, another danger, by no means trifling, shall overtake those who falsely presume that they know the name of Antichrist. For if these men assume one name, when this [Antichrist] shall come having another name, they will be easily led away by him, as supposing him not to be the expected one. . . . It is therefore more certain, and less hazardous, to await the fulfillment of the prophecy, than to make surmises and cast about for any names that may present themselves, since many names can be found possessing the number mentioned; and the same question will, after all, remain unsolved [ibid., 5:30:2–3].

But when this Antichrist shall have devastated all things in this world, he will reign for three years and six months, and sit in the temple at Jerusalem; and then the Lord will come from heaven in the clouds, in the glory of the Father, sending this man and those who follow him into the lake of fire [ibid., 5:30:4].

ST. HIPPOLYTUS OF ROME

Now, as our Lord Jesus Christ, who is also God, was prophesied of in the form of a lion, on account of his royalty and glory, in the same way have the Scriptures spoken of Antichrist as a lion, on account of his tyranny and violence. For the deceiver seeks to liken himself in all things to the Son of God. Christ is a lion, so Antichrist is a lion; Christ is a king [Jn 18:37], so Antichrist is a king. The Savior was manifested as a lamb [Jn 1:29], so he too will appear as a lamb, though within he is a wolf. The Savior came into the world in the circumcision, and he will come in the same way. . . . The Savior raised up and showed his holy flesh like a temple [Jn 2:19], and he will raise a temple of stone in Jerusalem [*Antichrist* 6 (c. A.D. 200)].

[W]e find it written about Antichrist . . . "Dan is a lion's cub, and he shall leap from Bashan" [Dt 33:22]. But that no one may err by supposing that this is said of the Savior, let him listen carefully. "Dan," he says, "is a lion's cub"; and in naming the tribe of Dan, he declared the tribe from which Antichrist is destined to spring. For as Christ springs from the tribe of Judah, so Antichrist is to spring from the tribe of Dn And that the case stands thus, we also see in the words of Jacob: "Let Dan be a serpent, lying upon the ground, biting the horse's heel" [Gn 49:17]. What, then, is meant by the serpent but Antichrist, the deceiver who is mentioned in Genesis [Gn 3:1], who deceived Eve and supplanted Adam? . . . [I]t is out of the tribe of Dan, then, that that tyrant and king, that dread judge, that son of the devil, is destined to arise [ibid., 14].

TERTULLIAN OF CARTHAGE

[T]he man of sin, the son of perdition, who must first be revealed before the Lord comes, "who opposes and exalts himself above all that is called God, or that is worshipped; who is to sit in the temple of God, and boast himself as being God?" [2 Thes 2:3–4]. According to our view, he is Antichrist; as it is taught us in both the ancient and the new prophecies, and especially by the apostle John, who says that "already many false prophets are gone out into the world," the forerunners of Antichrist, who deny that Christ is come in the flesh [1 Jn 4:1–3], and do not acknowledge Jesus [to be the Christ], meaning in God the Creator [*Against Marcion* 5:16 (c. A.D. 209)].

ST. CYPRIAN OF CARTHAGE

If [the heretics] desire peace, let them lay aside their arms. If they make atonement, why do they threaten? Or if they threaten, let them know that they are not feared by God's priests. For even Antichrist, when he comes, will not enter into the Church [even though] he threatens; neither shall we yield to his arms and violence, [though] he declares that he will destroy us if we resist [*Letters* 54:19 (A.D. 253)].

[B]oth baptism is one and the Holy Spirit is one and the Church, founded by Christ the Lord upon Peter, by a source and principle of unity, is also one. Hence it results that with [heretics and schismatics] all things are futile and false, nothing that they have done ought to be approved by us. . . . And the blessed apostle John, keeping the commandments and precepts of the Lord, has laid it down in his letter and said, "You have heard that Antichrist shall come; even now there are many antichrists, whereby we know that it is the last time . . ." [1 Jn 2:18]. Wherefore we who are with the Lord and maintain the unity of the Lord, and according to his condescension administer his priesthood in the Church, should repudiate and reject and regard as profane whatever his adversaries and the Antichrists do; and to those who, coming out of error and wickedness, acknowledge the true faith of the one Church, we should give the truth of unity and faith, by means of all the sacraments of divine grace [ibid., 69:3].

[B]ecause there can be nothing common to falsehood and truth, to darkness and light, to death and immortality, to Antichrist and

Christ, we ought by all means to maintain the unity of the Catholic Church, and not give way to the enemies of faith and truth in any respect. Neither must we prescribe this from custom, but overcome opposite custom by reason. For neither did Peter, whom first the Lord chose, and upon whom he built his Church, when Paul disputed with him about circumcision, claim anything to himself insolently, nor arrogantly assume anything; so as to say that he held the primacy, and that he ought to be obeyed by novices and those lately come. Nor did he despise Paul because he had previously been a persecutor of the Church, but admitted the counsel of truth, and easily yielded to the lawful reason Paul asserted, furnishing thus an illustration to us of concord and patience [ibid., 70:2–3].

ON THE END OF THE WORLD

[The Antichrist] will build the temple in Jerusalem, and will restore it again speedily, and give it over to the Jews [*On the End of the World* 23–25 (c. A.D. 267)].

LACTANTIUS

[A] king shall arise out of Syria, born from an evil spirit, the overthrower and destroyer of the human race, who shall destroy what is left by the former evil, together with himself. . . . But that king will be most disgraceful in himself, and a prophet of lies; and he will call himself God, and will order himself to be worshipped as the Son of God; and power will be given him to do signs and wonders, the sight of which he may entice men to adore him. He will command fire to come down from heaven, and the sun to stand and leave its course, and an image to speak; and these things shall be done at his word. . . . Then he will attempt to destroy the temple of God, and persecute the righteous people [*Divine Institutes* 7:17 (c. A.D. 307)].

ST. CYRIL OF JERUSALEM

But this aforesaid Antichrist is to come when the times of the Roman Empire shall have been fulfilled, and the end of the world is drawing near. There shall rise up together ten kings of the Romans, reigning in different parts perhaps, but all about the same time; and after these an eleventh, the Antichrist, who by his magical craft shall seize upon the Roman power; and of the kings who reigned before him, he will humble three, and the remaining seven he will keep in subjection to himself. At first he will put on a show of mildness (as though he were a learned and discreet person), and soberness and benevolence [*Catechetical Lectures* 15:12 (c. A.D. 350)].

And again he says, Who opposes and exalts himself against all that is called God, or that is worshipped (against every God; Antichrist will abhor the idols), so that he seats himself in the temple of God [2 Thes 2:4]. What temple then? He means the temple of the Jews, which has been destroyed. For God forbid that it should be the one in which we are! Why do we say this? That we may not be supposed to favor ourselves. For if he comes to the Jews as Christ, and desires to be worshipped by the Jews, he will make great account of the temple, that he may beguile them; making it seem that he is the man of the race of David who shall build up the temple that was erected by Solomon. And Antichrist will come at the time when there shall not one stone in the temple of the Jews that is left upon another, according to the doom pronounced by our Savior; for when either decay of time, or demolition ensuing on the pretense of new buildings, or from any other causes, shall have overthrown all the stones, I mean not merely of the outer circuit, but of the inner shrine also, where the cherubim were, then shall he come with all signs and lying wonders, exalting himself against all idols; at first making a pretense of benevolence, but afterwards displaying his relentless temper, and that chiefly against the saints of God. For he says, I beheld, and the same horn made war with the saints; and elsewhere, there shall be a time of trouble, such as never was since there was a nation upon earth, even to that time. Dreadful is that beast, a mighty dragon, unconquerable by man, ready to devour; concerning whom we have more to speak of out of the divine Scriptures, yet we will content ourselves at present with thus much, in order to keep within compass [ibid., 15:15].

ST. AUGUSTINE OF HIPPO

Daniel prophesies of the last judgment in such a way as to indicate that Antichrist shall first come, and to carry on his description to the eternal reign of the saints. For when in prophetic vision he had seen four beasts, signifying four kingdoms, and the fourth conquered by a certain king, who is recognized as Antichrist, and after this the eternal kingdom of the Son of Man, that is to say, of Christ [*City of God* 20:23 (c. A.D. 419)].

Translations Used

The writings quoted in this book were composed in a variety of languages, including Hebrew, Aramaic, Greek, Latin, and others. The translations presented here were drawn from the following sources:

The Ante-Nicene Fathers: The Writings of the Fathers down to A.D. 325 (ten volumes), edited by Alexander Roberts and James Donaldson.

The Nicene and Post-Nicene Fathers: Series I (fourteen volumes),

The Nicene and Post-Nicene Fathers: Series II (fourteen volumes), edited by Philip Schaff and Henry Wace

This set, commonly referred to as "the thirty-eight volume set," was published between 1867 and 1900 for T. & T. Clark of Edinburgh, Scotland. It is the standard translation that is used throughout this work except for those passages noted below. It is commonly available online.

The additional translations used were:

The Apostolic Tradition of St. Hippolytus of Rome, edited by Gregory Dix and Henry Chadwick (Ridgefield, Conn.: Morehouse Publishing, 1992).

This work furnished the quotations from the quotation from St. Hippolytus's *Apostolic Tradition* in chapter 36 and in chapter 46.

The Ascension of Isaiah, R. H. Charles (London: Adam and Charles Black, 1900).

This work furnished the quotation from *The Ascension of Isaiah*.

The Apocryphal New Testament, by M. R. James (Berkeley, Calif.: Apocryphile Press, 2004).

This work furnished the quotation from Pseudo-Melito's *The Passing of the Virgin*.

The Canon of the New Testament, Bruce M. Metzger (Oxford: Clarendon Press, 1987).

This work furnished the translation of the Muratorian Fragment.

Christian Inscriptions, H. P. V. Nunn, M.A., (New York: The Macmillan Company, 1920).

This work furnished the quotations labeled "Early Christian Inscription" and for the epitaph of St. Abercius of Hierapolis and the epitaph of Pectorius of Autun. The numbering system for these is that used in the book.

Contraception: A History of Its Treatment by the Catholic Theologians and Canonists, John T. Noonan, Jr. (Cambridge, Mass.: Belknap Press of Harvard University Press, 1986).

This work furnished the second quotation from Lactantius in chapter 33.

Didascalia Apostolorum, R. Hugh Connolly (Oxford: Clarendon Press, 1929).

This translation furnished the quotation from the *Didascalia* in chapter 46.

The Earliest Christian Hymnbook: The Odes of Solomon, James H. Charlesworth (Eugene, Oregon: Cascade Books, 2009).

This work furnished the quotation from *The Odes of Solomon*.

The Faith of the Early Fathers, 3 volumes edited by William Jurgens (Collegeville, Minn.: The Liturgical Press, 1970–1979).

This translation furnished the quotations from Didymus the Blind,
St. Hilary of Poitiers, Evagrius of Pontus, and St. Cyril of Alexan-
dria in chapter 14; St. Athanasius of Alexander and St. Fulgence of
Ruspe in chapter 16; St. Melito of Sardis in chapter 17; Didymus
the Blind, St. Epiphanius of Salamis, St. Cyril of Alexandria, and
St. Fulgence of Ruspe in chapter 19; St. Epiphanius of Salamis in
chapter 23; St. Ephraim the Syrian in chapter 27; *Poem Against the
Marcionites* and Pope St. Damasus I in chapter 28; St. Optatus of
Milevis, Pope St. Innocent I, Pope St. Celestine I, and St. Peter
Chrysologus in chapter 30; St. Pacian of Barcelona and St. Caesar-
ius of Arles in chapter 31; St. Basil of Caesarea in chapter 36. St.
Ambrose of Milan in chapters 37 and 38; Origen of Alexandria
and St. John Chrysostom in chapter 40; St. Serapion of Thmuis in
chapter 41; Origen of Alexandra, St. Aphrahat the Persian Sage,
Theodore of Mopsuestia, and St. Augustine of Hippo in chapter
42; St. Serapion of Thmuis and St. Ambrose of Milan in chapter 43; Origen of Alexandria and St. Jerome in chapter 44; St.
Hippolytus, Origen of Alexandria, and the Council of Elvira in
chapter 45; St. Ambrose and St. Jerome of Milan in chapter 47;
St. Ephraim the Syrian and St. Gregory of Tours in chapter 49;
St. Cyril of Alexandria, St. Athanasius of Alexandra, St. Gregory
of Nazianz, and Theodore of Mopsuestia in chapter 50; Leporius
in chapter 51; Origen of Alexandra, St. Jerome, and St. Fulgence
of Ruspe in chapter 55; St. Augustine of Hippo and St. Prosper of
Aquitaine in chapter 56; St. Gregory of Nyssa and St. Augustine
of Hippo in chapter 57; and St. Cyprian of Carthage in chapter 58.

The Fathers of the Church: A New Translation (Washington, D.C.:
   Catholic University of America Press, 1947).

This translation furnished the quotation from St. Ambrose of Milan in chapter 21.

*Fathers of the Church (vol. 71): Origen, Homilies on Genesis and Exo-
   dus*, translated by Ronald E. Heine (Washington, D.C.: Catholic
   University of America Press, 1982).

This work furnished the quotation from Origen's *Homilies on Genesis* in chapter 21.

The Greek and Latin Traditions regarding the Procession of the Holy Spirit, Pontifical Council for Promoting Christian Unity (Rome: Libreria Editrice Vaticana, 1995).

This work furnished the quotation from St. John of Damascus's work *Dialogue against the Manicheans.*

The Legacy of Saint Patrick: As Found in his Own Writings, Martin P. Harney, S.J. (Boston: St. Paul Editions, 1979).

This work furnished all quotations from St. Patrick and St. Sechnall.

On Genesis, St. Augustine, John E. Rotelle, ed. (Hyde Park, N.Y.: New City Press, 2002).

This work furnished the quotations from St. Augustine's work *Literal Interpretation of Genesis* in chapter 21.

The Proof of the Gospel: Being the Demonstratio Evangelica of Eusebius of Caesarea, W.J. Farrar (London: Society for Promoting Christian Knowledge, 1920).

This work furnished the quotation from Eusebius of Caesarea in chapter 34.

The Sources of Catholic Dogma, translated by Roy J. Defarrari, based on the 30th edition of Denzinger's *Enchiridion Symbolorum*, (Powers Lake, N.D.: Marian House, n.d.).

This work furnished all quotations from the *Athanasian Creed* in chapter 19; the Council of Rome, the Council of Carthage of 397, and Pope St. Innocent I in chapter 22; the quotation from the Council of Elvira in chapter 47; and from Pope St. Siricius in chapter 51.

The Teachings of the Church Fathers, edited by John R. Willis, S.J. (San Francisco: Ignatius Press, 2002).

This work furnished the quotation from St. Fulgence of Ruspe in chapter 13.

Theotokos: A Theological Encyclopedia of the Blessed Virgin Mary, Michael O'Carroll (Wilmington, Del.: Michael Glazier, Inc., 1988).

This work furnished the quotation from Timothy of Jerusalem.

Documents Used

The following is a list of the specific documents used in this book from the age of the Fathers. They are organized alphabetically by author. Numbers in [square brackets] indicate the date of the document. *Italic* numbers indicate the chapter in which a particular passage of a document is quoted. Material in (parentheses) indicate alternate titles for a particular work.

Consider the following entry:

EUSEBIUS OF CAESAREA
Church History [c. A.D. 312]
  (*Ecclesiastical History, History
  of the Church*)

1:4:8	*48*
3:4:9–10	*29*
4:21	*23*
5:23:1–24:11	*30*
5:28:3	*28, 29*
6:9:1–3	*53*

Letter on the Council of Nicaea
  [A.D. 325] (*Letter to the People
  of His Diocese*), *39*
Proof of the Gospel [c. A.D. 319]
  4:10   *34*

This tells us that three works of Eusebius of Caesarea are quoted in this book. The first we refer to as *Church History*, though other works call it *Ecclesiastical History* and *History of the Church*. It was written around (Latin, *circa*, abbreviated "c.") the year 312. Passage 1:4:8 (Book 1, Chapter 4, Section 8) of *Church History* is quoted in our chapter 48. The entry then lists other passages from *Church History* that are quoted, as well as passages from two more of Eusebius's works: *Letter on the Council of Nicaea* (sometimes called the *Letter to the People of His Diocese*) and *Proof of the Gospel*.

Alternate designations for the documents are provided to make it easier for the reader to identify them in other works, but the number of alternate designations for patristic documents is so great that we cannot be exhaustive.

For example, in Latin many of the titles of these documents begin with *de*, a Latin preposition that means "on," "concerning," or "about." This preposition appears so frequently in Latin titles that many translators drop it as an unnecessary and repetitive word. Thus a document titled *De Fide* in Latin might be translated into English as either *On Faith* or just *Faith*. To make matters worse, Latin has no articles—that is, no equivalents for the words "a," "an," and "the." This means that the translator has to decide whether to add any of them. *De Fide* could thus be translated *Faith, A Faith, The Faith, On Faith, On a Faith, On the Faith, About Faith, About the Faith, Concerning Faith*, and so on. To keep matters simple, we have generally omitted translations of *de*, as well as articles, at the front of document titles, though in a few cases we have included them.

The difference between Latin and Greek can also cause variant titles. In some editions a work will be listed by its Latin title (e.g., *De Principiis*) and in others by its Greek title (e.g., *Peri Archon*). Some editions may not translate a title from the original language. With only a few exceptions (*Didache, Didascalia*), we have translated all document titles into English.

Alternate document titles also can be caused by a tendency of translators to use old fashioned words (e.g., "epistle" instead of "letter," "enchiridion" instead of "handbook") or by a tendency to add unnecessary words (e.g., *Commentary on the Gospel of St. John the Divine* instead of *Commentary on John*). In this book we have sought to use modern terms and to omit unnecessary words in document titles.

In a few cases there are document entries with no section numbers listed. For example:

St. Gregory Thaumaturgus
Declaration of Faith [c. A.D. 265], *13, 15, 17, 18, 19*

This lists several chapters that St. Gregory Thaumaturgus's *Declaration of Faith* is quoted in, but it does not list numbered sections *within* the document that are quoted in these chapters. This is because the *Declaration of Faith* is a very short document and subdivisions of it are not necessary. Numbered subsections also might be omitted in the cases of longer documents that do not subdivide easily or that are not subdivided in the thirty-eight-volume set from which most of these quotations are taken.

~

Scripture Index

18:10	354	1:21	401
18:18	310	1:29	414
19:12	326	2:19	414
19:30	339	3:3	261–63, 265, 268
20:16	230	3:5	261–63, 265, 267,
22:13	255		273, 289, 342
23:6	161	3:8	314
23:9	23	4:24	103–104
24	36, 226	5:18	122
24:42	226	5:22	310
25:41	396	6:32–71	292
25:46	393	6:56	295
26:26	297	6:64	140
28:18–20	275	6:67–69	177–191
28:19–20	10	8:58	108, 122
28:19	10, 108, 273, 275,	8:59	108
	277, 278	10:30	111, 122, 278
Mark		10:41	402
7:8	22	14:1–2	108
9:47–48	392	14:12, 28	116
10:11–12	324	14:16–17, 26	116
10:38	259, 260, 271	15:26	116, 136
16:16	266, 267	16:10	116
Luke		16:13	24, 116
1:13	401	16:13–15	116
1:17	401	17	116
1:34	350	17:3	97
1:35	351	18:37	414
1:38	338	20:21–23	305
16:18	324	20:22	141
18:15–16	280	20:23	310
22:32	224, 319	20:28	122–23
23:43	272	21:17	191, 196, 208,
24:37–43	85		216, 224
24:39	103	*Acts*	
24:49	276	1:5, 22	274
John		1:8	35
1:1, 14	130	2:10–11	42
1:14	85, 344	2:32–33	116
		2:33	136